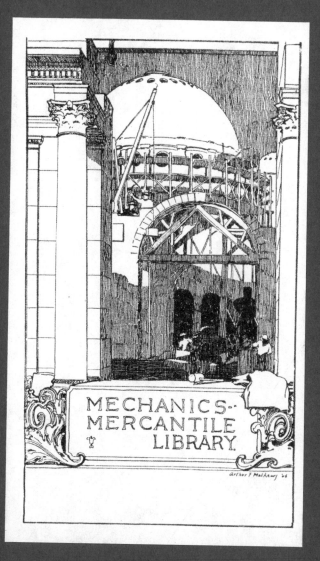

MECHANICS-
MERCANTILE
LIBRARY.

Arthur F. Mathews '06

What Soldiers Do

WHAT SOLDIERS DO

Sex and the
American GI
in World War II
France

Mary Louise Roberts

THE UNIVERSITY OF CHICAGO PRESS
CHICAGO AND LONDON

Mary Louise Roberts is professor of history at the University of
Wisconsin–Madison and the author of *Disruptive Acts: The New Woman in
Fin-de-Siècle France* and *Civilization without Sexes: Reconstructing Gender in
Postwar France, 1917–1927*.

The University of Chicago Press, Chicago 60637
The University of Chicago Press, Ltd., London
© 2013 by The University of Chicago
All rights reserved. Published 2013.
Printed in the United States of America

22 21 20 19 18 17 16 15 14 13   1 2 3 4 5

ISBN-13: 978-0-226-92309-3 (cloth)
ISBN-13: 978-0-226-92312-3 (e-book)

Library of Congress Cataloging-in-Publication Data

Roberts, Mary Louise.
   What soldiers do : sex and the American GI in World War II France /
Mary Louise Roberts.
       pages. cm
   Includes bibliographical references and index.
   ISBN 978-0-226-92309-3 (cloth: alkaline paper) — ISBN 978-0-226-92312-3
(e-book)   1. United States. Army—Officers—Sexual behavior—France—
History—20th century.   2. Soldiers—Sexual behavior—Political
aspects—United States.   3. Sex—Military aspects—France—History—
20th century.   4. World War, 1939–1945—France—History.   5. World
War, 1939–1945—United States—History.   6. Soldiers—United States—
Attitudes.   7. Sex—France.   8. United States—Foreign relations—
France—History—20th century.   9. France—Foreign relations—United
States—History—20th century.   I. Title.
   D769.8.S6R63 2013
   940.53'1—dc23
                                                          2012033963

♾ This paper meets the requirements of ANSI / NISO Z39.48-1992
(Permanence of Paper).

Dedicated in loving memory to my parents

EMMIE ROBERTS AND JAMES H. ROBERTS

Contents

ix   Acknowledgments

I   Introduction

PART ONE: ROMANCE

15   **1** Soldier, Liberator, Tourist

57   **2** The Myth of the Manly GI

85   **3** Masters in Their House

PART TWO: PROSTITUTION

113   **4** Amerilots and Harlots

133   **5** The Silver Foxhole

159   **6** Dangerous Indiscretions

PART THREE: RAPE

195   **7** The Innocent Suffer

239   **8** Black Terror on the *Bocage*

255   Conclusion: Two Victory Days

263   Notes

341   Index

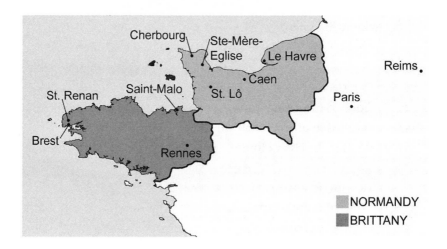

Map of Normandy and Brittany

Acknowledgments

IT GIVES ME GREAT PLEASURE to thank the many sources of funding I received to research and write this book. I am grateful to the John Simon Guggenheim Memorial Foundation for making possible a research leave during the academic year 2007–8. The Institute for Research in the Humanities at the University of Wisconsin provided extremely valuable time to write, both in the spring of 2005 as a visiting fellow and in the last two years as a senior fellow. I am most in debt to the truly extraordinary resources at the Graduate School of the University of Wisconsin–Madison, which provided me with a Vilas Associate Fellowship in 2005, a sabbatical in the spring of 2010, and generous summer grants throughout the research process. The support of the Graduate School has deeply enriched my life as a scholar and significantly broadened my research horizons. I am indebted to Judith Kornblatt and Susan Cook, in particular, for their support. In addition to these sources, the Center for European Studies at the University of Wisconsin provided travel funds at a key moment in my research, and the Women's Studies Research Center provided crucial time away from teaching in the spring of 2009. Finally, a grant from the University of Wisconsin System Institute on Race and Ethnicity made it possible for me to obtain the very costly court-martial transcripts from the US Army Judiciary.

One of the pleasures of writing *What Soldiers Do* has been the discovery of the French departmental and municipal archives. For their extremely courteous, warm, and professional guidance, I would like to thank Sylvie Barot at Les Archives Municipales de la Ville du Havre; Manonmani Restif at Les Archives Départementales de la Marne; Bruno Corre and Fabrice Michelet at Les Archives Départmentales du Finistère, Patrick Héliès at Les Archives Départmentales du Morbihan, and Louis Le Roc'h Morgère at Les Archives Départmentales du Calvados. I am particularly indebted to Alain Talon at Les Archives Départementales et du Patrimoine de la Manche for his generosity with time and resources. Also in Normandy, Stéphane Simonnet, Directeur Scientifique at Le Mémorial de Caen, could not have been more welcoming and helpful. In Paris, Françoise Gicquel and Grégory Auda at Les Archives de la Préfecture de la Police and Anne-Marie Pathé at the Institut d'Histoire du Temps Présent gave me excellent guidance. In the United States, I received superb help from Kenneth Schlessinger at the National Archives, David Keough at the US Army Military History Institute, and Steven Fullwood at The Schomburg Center for Research in Black Culture.

What Soldiers Do sometimes took me far away from my own field of France and gender, and much of the book could not have been written without the help of the American historians at the University of Wisconsin–Madison. I would like to thank John Cooper, Nan Enstad, John Hall, Susan Johnson, and Will Jones for their vital guidance and criticism. Stan Kutler provided me with contacts at the National Archives, as well as much-appreciated early enthusiasm for the project. In doing so, he gave me the confidence to venture into something completely new. For their critical readings and support, I would also like to thank Suzanne Desan, Fran Hirsch, Florencia Mallon, David McDonald, David Sorkin, Steve Stern, and John Tortorice. Stan Payne read a draft of the whole book and gave me the benefit of his vast knowledge of the Second World War. Laird Boswell also read the entire manuscript with the utmost care and precision; I am so lucky and grateful to be his colleague and friend.

Beyond Madison, I want to thank the anonymous readers for the University of Chicago Press and Oxford University Press. Their incisive suggestions made *What Soldiers Do* a much better book. Once again Susan Bielstein has been an extraordinary editor, providing general wisdom and detailed criticism in equal measure. I so appreciate her belief in this book. It has also been a great pleasure to work with Mark Reschke and the efficient, quick-witted Anthony Burton. Despite illness, Dor Hesselgrave shared his memories of Paris with me in the last months of his life; I am so thankful to him and to Gwenyth Claughton for putting us in touch. André Lambelet, Adriane Lentz-Smith, Bronson Long, Rebecca Pulju, and Tyler Stovall all provided invaluable research leads and critical readings. Ellen Amster, Holly Grout, Jeffrey Merrick, and Dan Sherman of the Wisconsin French History group offered extremely helpful comments on a draft of chapter 5, as did the anonymous readers for *French Historical Studies*. An earlier version of chapter 6 was published in the *American Historical Review*; I am very grateful for the incisive and meticulous criticism I received from the anonymous reviewers at this journal. This book also gained enormously from the audiences in France and the United States who read drafts or listened to talks and offered suggestions, comments, and questions. I would like to thank the hosts who made such encounters possible: Andrew Aisenberg, Marie Chessel, J. P. Daughton, Laura Lee Downs, R. Douglas Hurt, Hilary Miller, Malachi Haim Hacohen, Lloyd S. Kramer, Patricia Lorcin, Sarah Maza, Rachel Nuñez, Stephen Schloesser, Jennifer Sessions, Judith Surkis, Timothy Snyder, Don Reid, and Whitney Walton. I am also deeply appreciative of the French scholars who offered warm collegiality: Patrice Arnaud, Bruno Cabanes, Guillaume Piketty, Jean Quellien, Fabrice Virgili, and particularly Laura Lee Downs and Patrick Fridenson. Andy Myszewski, Jeff Hobbs, and Kelly Jakes provided excellent research assistance. Without a doubt the graduate students at the UW are the center of my intellectual world. I am so fortunate to have them in my life. Finally and most importantly, I want to thank Joan Scott, Bonnie Smith, Christine Stansell, and William Reddy for being so supportive of my career as a scholar. Without them, this book would not have been possible.

While writing *What Soldiers Do* was mostly a solitary journey, I was greatly helped along the way—body, mind, and soul—by Jeff Liggon,

Katy Nelson, and the inspiring women at Zucca Pilates. May Fraydas is a reason to get up on Sunday morning, and every other day, for that matter. My three older sisters, Elizabeth Baer, Pamela Bonina, and Katherine Gaudet, are more precious to me than they could ever know. Susan Zaeske has given me days of her life researching in the National Archives, and countless hours editing every chapter of *What Soldiers Do*. Her skills as a historian and an editor are formidable, and her contribution to the book is beyond measure. Her belief in me has made all the difference in my life.

What Soldiers Do is dedicated to the memory of my parents, Emmie and Jim Roberts. I wrote it while grieving their deaths in 2006 and 2007. The years I explore in this book were pivotal for my parents. In 1944, the two met and fell in love while my father served in the navy. The next year they married, and in March 1946, they welcomed their first child into the world. Although my father had his doubts about a book on "what went wrong in Normandy," he knew me well enough not to question my patriotism. In writing *What Soldiers Do*, I have tried to live up to the standards of honesty and integrity he and my mother modeled throughout their lives. Following my father's gift for seeing humor in all things, I have also tried to make the book not only serious but fun.

Introduction

IN THE SUMMER OF 1945, thousands of American GIs overran Le Havre, a port city in Normandy. With the war over, the soldiers were waiting for a boat home. A year earlier the Allies had freed the region from German control. The people of Le Havre were not ungrateful, but they now found their city virtually occupied by their liberators. Le Havre was in a state of siege, bemoaned the mayor Pierre Voisin in a letter to Colonel Weed, the American regional commander. The good citizens of his city were unable to take a walk in the park or visit the grave of a loved one without coming across a GI engaged in sex with a prostitute. At night, drunken soldiers roamed the street looking for sex, and as a result "respectable" women could not walk alone. Not only were "scenes contrary to decency" taking place day and night, complained Voisin, but "the fact that youthful eyes are exposed to such public spectacles is not only scandalous but intolerable."

Voisin had already dispatched policemen to patrol the parks, but the GIs ignored them. He had tried putting the prostitutes on trains to Paris, but flush with cash, the women got off at the first stop and took taxis back. So the mayor was writing Weed yet again. Could the Americans construct a regulated brothel north of town? Voisin suggested they set up special tents in a location convenient to their camps. The brothel would be overseen by US military police and medical personnel to make sure sexual activity was medically safe as well as discrete.

Prostitutes would be treated, and venereal disease rates would drop. The city could be allowed to get on with life.

But Voisin was wasting his time. In a return letter, Weed washed his hands of the crisis. Prostitution was Voisin's problem, not his, Weed replied. If the prostitutes were sick, the GIs could not be held accountable. Regulation of sex by the US military was out of the question. High command would not allow it, mostly because they feared that journalists would report on any such operation and news of GI promiscuity would make its way back home. Weed also shrugged off the growing problem of venereal disease. Although he made some vague promises about providing medical personnel, nothing materialized. Voisin was soon writing another letter, this time to his own superiors to ask for money. Public funds were running dry; the venereal wards were overwhelmed; the sick women had nowhere to go. What was the mayor to do?[1]

Weed was not the only American commander to dismiss the French on matters of sex. Like many officers, he probably thought they would not even notice the sight of sex in public. Wasn't sex a French specialty? Why then would public sex bother them? Indeed, the GIs had grown up hearing stories of sexual adventure from fathers who fought in France in 1917–18. Such stories led a generation of men to believe that France was a land of wine, women, and song. Bill Mauldin's 1944 cartoon of a soldier proclaiming "This is th'town my pappy told me about" played on this image of an eroticized France. (See figure Intr.1.) In the months before and after the landings, military propaganda gave such preconceptions new life for a second generation of soldiers.[2] As a result the general opinion along the line was that, in *Life* journalist Joe Weston's words, "France was a tremendous brothel inhabited by 40,000,000 hedonists who spent all their time eating, drinking [and] making love."[3]

This sexual fantasy, in turn, had an important political effect, which was to complicate the postwar French bid for political autonomy. At all levels of military command, officials shared the prejudice that the French were morally degraded and therefore perhaps not able to govern themselves. By so flagrantly disregarding sexual and social norms

"This is th' town my pappy told me about."

FIGURE INTRO. 1. Bill Mauldin cartoon. "This is th' town my pappy told me about." From *Stars and Stripes*, 6 September 1944. Used with permission from Stars and Stripes. © 1944, 2012 Stars and Stripes.

in Le Havre, the GIs also expressed their moral condescension, relaying the message that it was hardly necessary to behave in a civil manner toward the French. If GIs were having sex wherever they pleased, that was because the inhabitants of Le Havre—as respectable members of a community, as citizens of a sovereign nation—had become invisible to them. Weed's response to Voisin also registered growing confidence on the part of the US military that it could have the world its way. That confidence dictated that American soldiers needed an outlet for their sexual energies, so French women should provide one. It valued the health of the American soldier more than that of the French prostitute. Finally, US military policy protected American families from the spectacle of GI promiscuity while leaving French families unable to escape it.

Sexual relations gained political significance during the years of the American presence in France because the period was transitional for both nations. The United States was crossing the golden threshold of global power. By contrast, France was waking up to its many losses. The defeat of 1940 had been a catastrophe, the German occupation a humiliation. Now the presence of American soldiers on French soil meant liberation, yes, but also evidence of international decline. That disparity in war fortunes meant the two nations had many matters to work out between them. First was the issue of French sovereignty: Would the army impose a military government like the one already established in Italy? Or would the French be allowed to govern themselves? Also vital was the role of the United States in Europe. Its military victory on the Continent was absolute, and it had established bases throughout France and Germany. How much would this triumphant new power come to dominate a broken Europe?

Much can be learned about these questions, this book argues, by looking at how the US military managed GI sexual intimacy in France. There is no question that the United States took advantage of its military presence in France to influence a great deal of economic and political life there. Managing sex between GIs and French women was a key component of this control. The US government harbored no imperial ambitions *within* Europe, but it did seek to control a European balance of power for several reasons: to create a frontier against the Soviet Union, to "protect" Europe from communism, and to delineate a sphere of influence that would enhance its global power.[4] While the landings were a noble mission, they also opened a pivotal phase in the rise of American political dominance. As the historian Irvin Wall has put it, by the end of the war, "the Americans had tried to, and discovered that they could not, make and break French regimes. But they had also become accustomed to the exercise of an unprecedented degree of meddling in internal French affairs."[5]

The question of French autonomy had not yet been decided at the time of the Allied invasion. The US military seemed determined to wrest sovereignty from its only credible bidder, Gen. Charles de Gaulle. Neither Franklin D. Roosevelt nor Winston Churchill formally recognized de Gaulle as a sovereign leader, despite his control over much of the Resistance and the Committee of National Liberation (CFLN), which operated at both local and national levels. The Anglo-American military alliance was not committed to a free France, and planned to install a military government called AMGOT, modeled after the Allied one established in Sicily in 1943.[6] When the Allies finally decided on a date for the landings, de Gaulle was told only at the last minute, and given no assurance of sovereignty. In Roosevelt's opinion, since the French people could not vote, there was no way of knowing if they wanted de Gaulle as their sovereign leader.[7] Furthermore, without consulting the general, the Allies also printed a new currency for soldiers about to embark for Normandy.

Despite such obstacles weighing against de Gaulle and the CFLN, they strongly resisted the AMGOT plan.[8] As soon as the Americans began liberating French towns, de Gaulle installed his regional *commissaires* in them, winning control over the country in an illegal manner. Shortly after D-day de Gaulle arrived in Normandy and was acclaimed by crowds in Bayeux and throughout the region. The Allies continued to dismiss him, however, and refused to formally recognize his government until late October 1944, almost five months after the invasion.[9] This Allied reluctance became reason enough for de Gaulle, his struggling CFLN, and the Resistance generally to deeply suspect American intentions in France. Although the Allies eventually abandoned AMGOT, it persisted in the form of rumors, fueling the belief that the Americans were there to dominate rather than liberate.[10]

Interactions between US military officers and French authorities at the local level during the summer of 1944 discredit such rumors. Re-

ports filed by de Gaulle's *commissaires* in Normandy demonstrate that
Franco-Allied relations varied widely over the region and lacked any
pattern of aggression. The experience of François Coulet, de Gaulle's
commissaire in Normandy, is a case in point.[11] On the one hand, Coulet
wrote reports to Paris complaining that US officers in Normandy refused to recognize his authority and were attempting to make arrests
and force local elections.[12] On the other hand, Coulet's correspondence also includes assurances to the French Army that the Allies had
not made any laws or appointments without the consent of authorities like himself.[13] Where tensions between the GIs and the French
government existed, they appeared to be local skirmishes rather than
the result of any strategic plan.

In fact, no firm principle concerning sovereignty guided US military officials in their dealings with the local population. Partly this
plan was strategic: the two nations would form a military association,
uncomplicated by political commitments, until the war was won.[14] In
addition, a fundamental ambiguity confused power relations between
the two nations: unlike Germany, Japan, or even Italy, France was *both*
a US ally *and* a conquered state. On the one hand, the massive force of
the American military and its status as liberator of the French people
left little doubt who was in control. On the other hand, Charles de
Gaulle struggled successfully to establish some degree of political
autonomy. Muddled lines of authority also vexed Civil Affairs (CA),
the branch of the US military that assumed primary responsibility
for restoring order in liberated territories. Civil Affairs was to further
the war effort by controlling population flows and establishing basic
services in towns and cities. According to French journalist Jacques
Kayser, CA officers tried to avoid questions of politics and collaborate
peacefully with *commissaires* such as Coulet.[15] In cases where property
disputes were to be settled or Nazi collaborators removed from office,
local authorities often stepped in to do the job.[16] But in some areas,
CA officers also set up elections, detained criminals, and closed busi-
nesses, provoking vigorous protest.

Ambiguity in the lines of authority conferred greater importance
to sexual relations and how they might be managed. Struggles be-

tween American and French officials over sex—which brothels would be declared off-limits, how to police streetwalkers, how to contain venereal disease, how to prosecute accusations of rape, how to keep the streets safe at night—rekindled the unresolved question of who exactly was in charge. In the absence of a clear directive, such clashes, which took place at all levels of US military command and French state bureaucracy, became a means to work out the issue of French national sovereignty. In this way sexual relations anchored a struggle for power between France and the United States.

This book, then, explores how sex was used to negotiate authority between the two nations. While it addresses larger issues of international relations, its evidentiary approach is close to the ground, specifically, the Norman *bocage* where the GIs and French civilians got to know each other during the summer of 1944. Because this book engages the question of how the human body, in particular the sexual body, is historically implicated in relations of power, it attends to the sights, sounds, tastes, and smells of the American invasion—in other words, its visceral impact on the French senses. It then goes on to focus on three kinds of sex between GIs and French women during the US military presence: romance, prostitution, and rape. Sex took place between individual persons, sometimes in public but more often in homes and bedrooms. Despite their private nature, however, sexual relations came to possess larger political meanings and provided crucial models of dominance and submission. Paying female civilians to have sex taught millions of GIs to expect subservience from the French. Similarly, watching women sell their bodies—or worse still, hearing their stories of rape—forced French men to recognize their own diminished position in the world. In these cases, the French female body realigned power relations between the two nations.

Because the US military equated France with libidinal satisfaction, sex became integral to how it construed the Normandy campaign. With very few exceptions the GIs had no emotional attachment to the French people or the cause of their freedom.[17] How, then, to motivate the soldiers to fight? In other theaters of war, military propagandists had used pinups—images of gorgeous all-American girls like

Rita Hayworth—to conceive the nation in a way they believed would inspire the soldiers. Similarly, they billed the Normandy campaign as an erotic adventure. In particular, a photograph featuring a happy GI embraced by ecstatic French girls presented the American mission as a sexual romance. (See figure Intr. 2.) Disseminated in the military press, this photo portrayed the invasion in mythic terms as a mission to save French women from the evils of Nazism. Victory was defined as putting a smile on the face of *la française* who would duly reward the soldier with a kiss. In this way, propagandists played not only on

FIGURE INTRO. 2. The manly GI. Photo © RDA/Getty Images.

sexual fantasies, but also the GI's desire to be a manly soldier—to rescue and protect as well as destroy and kill.

Propagandists had no idea that such a myth of the Normandy mission would eventually lead to something like the situation in Le Havre. Once aroused, the GI libido proved difficult to contain. In fact the myth sprang from two wells of uneasiness on the part of the US military. First, it shored up a weary manhood. American soldiers in Italy had been sorely tested by loss, grief, and death. The acts of rescue, protection, and sexual dominance all restored a GI's sense of manliness crucial for the successful prosecution of the war.

Second, the myth seemed to address military fears that the GIs were not ready for a new, more global American role. Political stewardship was new to the United States, a nation that in one generation had shifted from being an isolationist country to a world power. In a much-discussed editorial appearing at the time in *Le figaro*, the well-known French political scientist André Siegfried characterized the United States as quite suddenly attaining stature as a "giant." Some years before, Siegfried's very popular book *America Comes of Age* (1927) had declared the United States to be a new and formidable European rival.[18] Now, Siegfried noted, Americans seemed to have embarked on a voyage for global engagement without having chosen it. Despite their indisputable military might, Americans still clung to isolationism economically, and were afraid of being "had" by Europeans in political matters.[19] Siegfried got it right when he argued that the Americans were caught between what they had become to others and how they saw themselves. The GIs landing on French soil had to learn their new position as "giants." Conceiving the war as a valiant rescue mission provided an accessible and appealing way for the GIs to understand that role. If global leadership entailed sexual romance with French women, what was not to like?

Nothing indeed and that became the problem: the myth of the manly GI turned out to be *too* successful. Sexual fantasies about France did indeed motivate the GI to get off the boat and fight. But such fantasies also unleashed a veritable tsunami of male lust. The GIs were known for their promiscuity in all theaters, whether European, Mediterranean, or Pacific. Still the case of Le Havre appears exceptionally bad, with the GIs having sex anywhere and everywhere in broad daylight in full public view. Brothels, parks, bombed-out buildings, cemeteries, railway tracks—all became landscapes for sex in French cities. Paris, in particular, became a celestial city of total erotic satisfaction, though not without ill effects among the soldiers, who suffered soaring rates of venereal disease.

In struggling to control the unruly effects of the fantasies they had created, military authorities learned to become Siegfried's "giants." The military management of sexual behavior served to delineate and consolidate US authority in northern France. As it did in other theaters of war, the military downplayed the role of GIs in spreading venereal infection. Shifting to women the primary responsibility for sexually transmitted disease had the tonic effect of avoiding accountability for both its expense and suffering. Blaming the French also justified regulation of the mobility and health of civilian populations. The army felt justified in declaring all French women objects of American control, thus depriving the French government of its prerogative to manage its own population. As in Le Havre, the army everywhere insisted on keeping French sexual labor invisible to the US public back home. Social disruption and venereal disease were the results.

Rape posed an even greater threat to the myth of the American mission as sexual romance. In the summer of 1944, Norman women launched a wave of rape accusations against American soldiers, threatening to destroy the erotic fantasy at the heart of the operation. The specter of rape transformed the GI from rescuer-warrior to violent intruder. Forced to confront the sexual excesses incited by its own propaganda, the army responded not by admitting the full range of the problem, but by scapegoating African American soldiers as the primary perpetrators of the rapes. Within the year, twenty-five black soldiers had been summarily tried and executed on French soil, hanged by rope. Cooperation between the US military and French civilians account for the proliferation of rape convictions against black soldiers. Both sides shared a deadly set of racist attitudes and a fear that they were losing power. For the US military, the raped woman undermined its control over its mission in Europe. For civilians, she symbolized the loss of control over their own country.

Sex was fundamental to how the US military framed, fought, and won the war in Europe. Far from being a marginal release from the pressures of combat, sexual behavior stood at the center of the story in the form of myth, symbol, and model of power. By contending that sex mattered, this book presents GI sexual conduct as neither innocent of power nor unimportant in effect. Too often in the past, such promiscuity has been dismissed as "boys-will-be-boys" behavior, a mere sideshow of the war fueled by the extraordinary needs of men in battle. Military historians have largely ignored the sexual habits of American soldiers, considering it a historically inconsequential matter. The historian Stephen Ambrose, for example, makes only passing reference to "girls" in his popular histories.[20] By contrast, this book brings sex to the center of the story and demonstrates its profoundly political character at this moment. Historians have amply demonstrated that sexual contact between GIs and women shaped American foreign policy and the "Americanization" of defeated Japan and Germany.[21] This book builds on such work by demonstrating that postwar transnational relations, far from being confined to diplomatic or political circles, were shaped at every level of society, and often emerged through specific cultures of gender and sexuality. Weed's refusal to deal with prostitution in Le Havre says a lot about his sense of privilege at that particular moment. As for Voisin, he had no response for Weed. That kind of American arrogance—and the French humiliation it produced—profoundly shaped relations between the two nations.

PART ONE

Romance

1

Soldier, Liberator, Tourist

IN THE WEE HOURS of 6 June 1944, Angèle Levrault, a sixty-year-old schoolmistress from Sainte-Mère-Église, awoke with a start. She rose from her bed and exited the back door to use her outhouse. She heard odd fluttering sounds. What she found in her backyard was stranger still: a man with a face streaked in war paint had landed in her garden and was trying to cut himself free from a parachute. Madame Levrault stood frozen in her nightgown. The man's eyes met hers. He raised his finger to his lips, signaling her to be silent, and then slipped away into the night. Although she did not know it at the time, Madame Levrault had just met Private Robert M. Murphy of the Eighty-Second Airborne Division, one of the first Americans to land in France on D-day.[1] A few hours after their encounter in the garden, thousands of Murphy's countrymen would take their first step onto French land at Omaha and Utah Beach. Thousands of others would take their last step on that sand, if they took a step at all. Before the end of that day, 2,499 Americans would perish on the beaches of Normandy.[2] They would reach the shores of France but die before they met even a single French person. Still others, of course, survived the beaches and fought their way across the north of France. Those soldiers are the subject of this book.

For good reason, the Normandy landings have become a sacred event in the American imagination. Historians, politicians, and filmmakers have celebrated the campaign as a great moment in the his-

tory of the Second World War. There is no doubt they are right. But
the story, at least as it has been told by American historians, suffers
by focusing too narrowly on military strategy. As the new military
history has demonstrated, wars cannot be separated from the values
and preoccupations of those peoples fighting them.[3] It is also crucial,
then, to widen our analytic lens in order to consider the encounter between the American soldier and the French civilian. That relationship
began at dawn on the sixth of June in places like Angèle Levrault's
garden; it ended in Le Havre some two years later when the last GI
got on a boat home.

Because historical narratives focus almost exclusively on the day-
to-day heroics of the American GI, they slight the French and leave
half the story untold. French civilians appear only at the peripheries
of the scene, their roles reduced to inert bystanders or joyous celebrants of liberation. In short, they form nothing more than a landscape against which the Allies fight for freedom. Stephen Ambrose's
very popular histories of the Normandy campaign typify this marginalization of the French. In *Citizen Soldiers*, a history of the army
from Normandy to the Battle of the Bulge, Ambrose mentions the
Normans only once, implying that they were collaborationists: "[The
landings] came as a shock to the Normans, who had quite accommodated themselves to the German occupation."[4] In Ambrose's three
histories of the campaign, he recounts only one incident in which the
Normans help the Allies, and several in which they betray the GIs.[5]
Otherwise, they appear to be children eager to kiss the Americans'
hands, delighted at their liberation, but largely passive and mute.[6] In
sum, Ambrose reproduces what he sees as the general GI view of
French civilians—as "ungrateful, sullen, lazy and dirty."[7]

One aim of this chapter is to amend that view by revisiting the
Normandy campaign as it was seen through French eyes. What was
D-day like for the Normans? How did they respond to having their
homes, their fields, and their farms turned into a theater of war? Norman accounts of the invasion, recorded in diaries, letters, and memoirs, give us an extraordinarily fresh, vivid account of the months
prior to and after the invasion. If Normans appeared to be "ungrate-

ful" and "sullen" to the GIs, as Ambrose believed, they had good reason to be. For them, D-day did not begin on the sixth of June. Rather it started in the fall of 1943, when the Allies initiated preinvasion bombing on northern France. The Normans watched their railways, bridges, workplaces, and homes burn to the ground. For this reason, they dreaded as much as awaited the landings. The war came as a distant thunder, then crashed like an angry storm. As it broke, it produced horrific sights and smells—the rot of animal and human flesh, the stench of death. Normans recounted their encounter with death in a terrible grammar of sounds, sights, smells, and tastes. An estimated 19,890 civilians lost their lives in the Battle of Normandy. During the first two days of the campaign alone, about three thousand were killed—roughly the same number of Allied soldiers killed in that period.[8]

Nevertheless the Normans also felt profound gratitude to the Allies for restoring their freedom. However horrible the squall of war, it eventually delivered Americans, with their funny-looking jeeps, their spectacular boots, and their honey-smelling cigarettes. Every Norman remembers the moment when they saw their first American. "We simply did not believe our eyes," recalled Jacques Perret. "After so many years of occupation, deprivation, alerts, bombings, there were our liberators, 'our Americans.'"[9] Jacques-Alain de Sédouy, a boy of eight in 1944, remembered his first GI in this way: "He could have been a Martian who had fallen out of the sky and we would not have examined him with more curiosity. I could not take my eyes off this man who had come from his distant land in order to liberate France."[10]

Revisiting the campaign from the French side not only gives us a novel, more comprehensive view of the campaign, but also corrects Ambrose's portrayal of French civilians in three crucial ways. First, far from being traitors or passive by-standers, ordinary Normans readily joined the Allies in their struggle against the Germans. Besides taking up arms, civilians provided crucial intelligence about the terrain and the enemy. They also risked their lives to hide fallen parachutists, harbor stranded infantrymen, and care for the wounded. With very few exceptions, they were comrades and fighters. Second, while there is no question that French civilians welcomed their liberators with wonder and gratitude, it is too simple to portray them as happy celebrants of their own liberation. Although Normans felt enormous relief when the Germans at last departed, they were also forced to endure the war in their own backyard. A fundamental contradiction characterized the Allied mission: the GIs were to both conquer and liberate, demolish and reconstruct. As one journalist said of the civilians in Caen, "their liberators are also destroyers."[11] In this part of France, anger, fear, and loss stripped the moment of its bliss. Liberation was a harrowing experience in which happiness had to share the heart with sorrow. Putting Franco-American relations at the center of the story revises our understanding of the costs paid in the Norman campaign. The Americans did not have a monopoly on suffering, nor did they fight alone.

Lastly, a transatlantic approach alters our view of the American experience in Europe. By focusing on encounters between GIs and civilians, we can appreciate the full extent of the soldiers' precarious position in the ETO (European theater of operations). Not only were they warriors fighting for their lives, but also strangers in a strange land. An incident recounted by infantryman John Baxter evokes this sense of alienation. One morning, Baxter's unit drove by convoy through a small village. A French peasant stood and watched them pass through. "We stopped briefly at an intersection and one of our Arkansas soldiers, a man named Mathis, leaned out of the truck and addressed the old man. 'Hey, Mister!,' he barked, 'How far are we from Okalona, Arkansas?' It broke up the convoy."[12] Mathis's joke rested not only on the French man's ignorance of Okalona but also on the idea of the GI as a tourist. It presented the American soldier as a lost traveler trying to find his way home. Unlike tourists to France, the Allies did not expect a warm greeting on Omaha Beach. A good thing, too, as the Germans decidedly did not give them one. But like travelers, they were deposited in an alien landscape, forced to navigate unknown streets, witness unfamiliar customs, and converse with people in a language they did not understand.

The full complexity of the American mission in Europe emerges only when we see the campaign in this way: as an encounter between two allies as well as two enemies. While France was a battlefield, it was also an unknown place, and as such, experienced by GIs in terms not unlike those of a tourist. Such cultural encounters have been overlooked by military historians reluctant to take their eyes off the battlefield. But for millions of GIs, the discovery that a very different world *indeed* lay beyond the Jersey shore—or San Francisco Bay, for that matter—was central to their war experience. For the GIs, the recognition of cultural difference was unavoidable, astonishing, and often life changing. "From the moment we hit the beaches," wrote infantryman Aramais Hovsepian to his brothers, "you could tell it was a different country. The air even smelled different!"[13] "England was a little like home but France is really a foreign country," recorded Jan Giles in his diary.[14] GI Orval Faubus titled his memoir of France *A Faraway Land*. With the awareness of difference came the excitement of being in a strange, distant place. Minutes after Charles E. Frohman's company arrived in Normandy, someone pointed out a French street sign. "Everything else was forgotten in a series of awed Oh's and Ah's," remembered Frohman, who was from Columbus, Ohio. "It was the first distinctly French thing we had ever seen. It looked like something out of a fairy tale book. It just didn't look real."[15] Like many visitors to France, the GIs peered over maps, babbled in high school French, wondered why the second floor was called the first floor, and stared in utter bewilderment at bidets.[16]

The recognition of cultural difference, with its lessons of tolerance and humility, became a legacy of the war for a generation of American men, and thus merits closer historical attention. Thinking about the GI as a tourist can also help to explain the arrogance he often felt toward the French. As soldiers, the Americans bore weapons and wielded enormous power. But as tourists, they were dependent on civilians for local knowledge of geography, language, and customs. In this way, they tacked back and forth between authority and dependence, command and vulnerability. Like many tourists, the GIs dealt with their helplessness by making large (and largely unfounded) generalizations about the French. When in their discomfort Americans succumbed to this reflex to categorize, they made sex the defining element of French civilization.

Countless GIs arrived in Normandy with the notion that France was a playground of easy women and loose morals. Once there, they gave candy to children, shook the hands of young men, learned about the woods from peasants, and saved the lives of old women. In other words, they interacted with civilians in complex, very different ways. At the same time, when confronted with a strange culture, the GIs clung to prejudices they already held about the French. In particular, they focused on French behaviors concerning the body, including public nudity, kissing, and love making. By the end of the summer, the French had become—as an entire people—primitive and oversexed. This view of the Gallic race as uncivilized echoed American imperial thinking in the past. Here it would degrade French efforts to restore an autonomous government, as well as justify US military management in matters of health, sanitation, and transportation.

A Surrealist Mixed Spectacle of Deliverance and Death

While everyone in Europe awaited the invasion, what it meant for an individual depended on where he or she happened to be in the summer of 1944. Anne Frank was in hiding in Amsterdam. For her and her family, the "long-awaited liberation" meant hope. "It fills us with fresh courage and makes us strong again," she wrote in her diary on the sixth of June.[17] Anguish was what Françoise Seligman was feeling in Paris that morning. "A kind of inner panic paralyzed me," the French woman remembered. "If they fail, if they leave, the proof will have been made that France has become an impregnable bastion of Nazi power, and we will never ever be liberated."[18] For the civilians in Normandy, where the battle claimed both homes and human lives, the landings took on yet another meaning. A woman named Yvonne living near Mortain called her day of liberation a "surrealist mixed spectacle of deliverance and death."[19]

The burden of loss was not new on D-day. The invasion had created a reason for the French to endure the weary days of scarcity,
humiliation, and deprivation. At the same time, for months before
the landings, Allied bombardment had wreaked havoc with Norman
lives. Military planners had launched a bombing campaign the previous fall to prevent the Nazis from moving troops and supplies to
the front in the opening weeks of the Normandy campaign.[20] So as
not to betray the location of the Allied landings, bombing occurred
over all of France, with the targeting of bridges, roads, and railways
as well as oil depots and other German installations. In the year 1944
alone, 503,000 tons of bombs fell on France, and 35,317 civilians were
killed.[21] The populations of Nantes, Cambrai, Saint-Étienne, Caen,
and Rouen all suffered heavy casualties, with hundreds or thousands
reported dead or wounded.[22] A bombardment of B-17s on a train in
which resistance member Jean Collet was traveling appeared to him
as a "strange ballet of death: you saw the bombs unleashed from the
plane and falling in your direction. Then they disappeared from view
due to their rapidity of speed. Then one instant after a terrifying whistle they would explode in a dreadful crash. Meanwhile we were flat-
tened against the ground to avoid the explosions."[23] Civilians suffered
the devastation of homes, workplaces, and farms. As a result, many
felt more fear than hope about the coming invasion. "The landings
are both yearned and dreaded," wrote a Caen prefect in early 1944,
"one hopes for a decisive victory while also making a selfish wish that
it won't happen where one lives."[24]

It was only human to want the Allies to come—only somewhere
else. But specific circumstances also aggravated fear and resentment.
For one, the Nazis chose to use bombardment like a hammer to nail
in anti-Allied feeling. In widely disseminated handbills and other
forms of propaganda, the Germans claimed that the United States
had a "Machiavellian plan," which was to take over the French Empire, destroy France, and colonize Europe itself.[25] (See figure 1.1.) Because they could kindle anti-Allied feeling with the destruction caused
by the bombing, the Nazis provided neither a warning system nor a
temporary shelter for the Normans. To counter such propaganda, the

Les Américains aiment les Français

FIGURE I.I. "The Americans Love the French." Courtesy of Bibliothèque Historique de la ville de Paris.

Allies air-dropped leaflets reassuring civilians. "We know that these bombardments add to the suffering of certain among you. We do not pretend to ignore that," conceded one brochure. "Move away as much as possible from ironworks, railway stations, junctions, train depots, repair shops."[26] The warnings were considered to be earnest but pointless as civilians had no choice but to work and live around strategic targets.

A second major issue was imprecision in bombing. The "flying fortress" B-17 bomber—the pride of the American air force—provoked a clenched French fist for missing its target so often. The Normans considered the British to be superior to the Americans in precision bombing.[27] As early as October 1943, the Gaullist resistance organ CFLN (Comité français de la libération nationale) reported that the French were sick "of accumulating ruins and deaths without results."[28] While some civilians found comfort in the French adage that to make an omelet, you have to break eggs, others wondered, "why was it necessary to break so many?"[29] Nor did civilians perceive any rational plan, according to the CFLN. Bridges were destroyed several times over in a period of days, then left alone for months, so that the Germans could rebuild them.[30] The bombings were "barbarian," and they should be stopped.[31] In their reports on public opinion, the CFLN claimed civilians believed Nazi warnings concerning American imperial ambitions. Besides economic greed, the Americans were guilty of harshness in the Versailles treaty, indifference to German rearmament in the 1930s, slowness in entering the war, and collaboration with Vichy official Admiral Darlan in North Africa. Even the delay in the invasion became a kind of "treason."[32]

Because the CFLN, following de Gaulle, distrusted the Allies, it no doubt exaggerated the anti-Americanism rippling through the French population.[33] But you didn't have to be in the Gaullist resistance to be fed up with Allied bombing.[34] French refugees interviewed by the BBC after their arrival in England also complained of the "appalling" effects of bombing throughout the nation. In Nantes, they related, "there was such violent irritation" that when an American pilot, shot down on French soil, offered a civilian a cigarette, he spat on it. Another refugee complained of Modane, near Grenoble, where the Allies dropped their bombs four kilometers away from the railway station despite having been given detailed maps.[35] The deep-down, gnawing fear was that the bombs would keep coming while the invasion would not. France would be destroyed but not liberated. "It would be possible to annihilate Europe without annihilating the war," wrote Alfred Fabre-Luce in his journal just before the invasion.[36]

The prelanding destruction of the French countryside eroded faith in the Allies. For months, civilians' feelings toward them had been a muddle of admiration and rage. Allied victories in North Africa had given the French their first reason to believe that the Nazi war machine could be beaten.[37] American success in bringing clothes, cigarettes, and food to civilians in Tunisia and Algeria raised hopes everywhere on the continent.[38] But anger still warped the joy of liberation. "Having stood by impotent, enraged and revolted by the savage destruction" of his hometown, Augustin Maresquier was determined to suppress his happiness upon seeing his first American. But his joy, he realized, was stronger than his own resolution not to feel it.[39] Fourteen-year-old Claude Bourdon had the same "strange surprise" when she was liberated: despite her fury concerning the destruction of her home, "my heart began to beat violently; I was ready to burst into sobs of joy."[40]

The damage—and resentment—would only increase after the landings. Neither the destruction nor the anger stopped. The Battle of Normandy was long, discouraging, and costly. In contrast to the battle-weary residents of northern and eastern France, Normans had not experienced a war firsthand for many generations.[41] Strategic coastal towns such as Cherbourg and Saint-Malo were heavily bombed. Le Havre was nearly destroyed, as were Caen and Saint-Lô. The wreckage was psychological as well as physical. "Nothing could be more painful," wrote George Duhamel in the fall of 1944, "than to be wounded by one's own friends."[42] Once again, superfluous bombing sparked outrage. Civil Affairs reported on 28 July that the French were furious about "what is considered to be unnecessary bombing and shelling of towns."[43] While the Allied objective was to destroy German installations and troops, in many cases, such as Caen, bombing continued even though the Germans had supposedly left.[44] In Le Havre, French officials angrily pointed out that some three thousand civilians had been killed while fewer than ten German bodies had been found.[45] As late as mid-October, Civil Affairs was still reporting that "resentment is more widespread and does not appear to be lessening" in Le Havre.[46]

The results of the bombing were personally devastating. "Our faces were lit by flame light," remembered Antoine Anne, "you could see the fear, emotion, and horror inscribed upon them. Facing the inferno, we became all too aware of those buried under the flames. A crushing silence fell upon us." He had lost his entire family except the child he held in his arms.[47] Countless other children witnessed death for the first time. Twelve-year-old Robert Simon, for example, watched a close friend die, then greeted the Americans with "an inner wound and a heavy heart."[48] As thousands of Normans found themselves homeless, they took to the road, seeking out family and shelter in distant villages. The constant walking was hard on the legs and feet, particularly those of the elderly and children. When some weeks later they returned, everything was gone. "My house, my childhood, NOTHING. There was NOTHING left," remembered Madame Dold-Lomet about her homecoming in Saint-Malo.[49] Of Saint-Lô, Jacques Petit wrote in his journal: "my town no longer exists. How many weeks of madness were necessary to wipe all traces of my childhood? How can I possibly find them again?"[50]

Saint-Lô, in particular, became a "martyred village," its churches "murdered" and "amputated."[51] Civil Affairs reported "embittered" complaints from refugees declaring the bombing "excessive."[52] "All was macabre desolation," remembered one Civil Affairs officer of Saint-Lô. He wondered, "how could a city so shattered ever survive?"[53] "The city looked as though it had been pulled up by its roots, put through a giant mixmaster then dumped back out again," remembered Frank Freese.[54] "The desperate despair of destruction" was how Chester Hansen, aid to Omar Bradley, described it.[55] "Mounting ruins on a cracked, punctured, blistered terrain"—this is what one young Norman saw when he emerged from a shelter.[56] Refugees going through on their way home described the city as wrapped in "a silence of death."[57] "We go through Saint-Lô in a deathly silence," wrote one Norman in his diary. "The town is nothing but an enormous field of ruins, without a soul."[58] American radio operator Sim Copans had the same response: "There was absolutely nobody in the streets, and the atmosphere was eerie. . . . It was really a horrifying sight."[59] When résistante Lucie Aubrac returned to France after the Liberation, she also traveled through the town. "I had no fear at any moment," she later remembered, "except perhaps at Saint-Lô. The town had been terribly bombed by the Allies. The houses collapsed like paper cartons! It was spectacular and frightening."[60]

Even in towns less damaged, the war left its mark. "Think of taking a drive on a maze of narrow country roads," urged reporter Andy Rooney, "where every farmhouse is an armed fortress, every church steeple a sniper's observation post, every stone wall conceals infantry with rifles and machine guns, and where, at every curve in a road, there may be a tank with an 88mm gun trained on the curve you're coming around. That's the way it was in Normandy in June and July of 1944."[61] Overnight Normandy had become a war zone. Booby traps transformed the famous hedgerows into deadly weapons. Fine wires lay across roads to trigger explosions. Apple orchards harbored German mortar stations. Barns hid German artillery.[62] Knowing that the GIs were souvenir hunters, the Nazis also left behind military paraphernalia rigged with explosives. When Raymond Avignon picked up a German helmet, an American soldier saved his life by making him put it down, showing him an iron thread that would trigger an explosion, then removing it with "meticulous" care.[63]

The effect of this transformation was to deliver up the uncanny—to render the known unknown. "Familiar places appeared unrecognizable," noted Charles Lemeland, then twelve. "It seemed there was now something horrible and monstrous hiding there. The endless road, bordered by houses and farms, was absolutely deserted except for dead animals—a German shepherd and a pig side by side—and a few dead men." After the front moved on, "spread over miles was simple ordinary war garbage," he continued "clothing, food, ammunition—an immense yard sale gone crazy."[64] The task of removing debris, filling holes, and restoring a countryside "sterilized by the passage and mechanisms of war," as one journalist put it, seemed overwhelming.[65] Even in December 1944, with the front now hundreds of miles away, Normans were still reeling from the devastation. A Caen editorial declared it "the saddest Christmas we have ever known. Because we still live in a world in flames, in a murdered France, in a ravaged region. No more houses, no more roofs over our head, and grief everywhere around us."[66] On the eighth of June 1945, the same paper remembered D-day as "so beautiful and yet so cruel."[67]

The destruction would have been easier on the Normans if their victory had been assured. Part of Norman anguish in the early weeks of the campaign resulted from the uncertainty of the battle's outcome. During the very hard fighting on the Cotentin Peninsula in June and early July, villages in the region between Cherbourg and Caen were passed back and forth between German and Allied control.[68] At times the Americans were forced to retreat from villages they held, so that Normans would taste freedom only with a bitter flavor. The mayor of Sainte-Mère-Église reported to his superior that on D-day, when US military reinforcements did not arrive, "the women cried and begged: 'do not abandon us!'" The Americans reassured them "we will never abandon you, we will die on this spot."[69] According to the first US military report on the local Norman population, civilians "could not be certain that we would be able to hold our ground. They do doubt, though, of denunciations, arrests, etc. should we move out."[70]

Even after civilians were reassured that freedom—and the Americans—were there to stay, shock took a huge toll on the population. "Men and women everywhere stood crying and rocking back and forth as though in prayer," recalled John Hurkala. "Obviously they were wondering whether or not everything had taken place was true. It was."[71] In the faces of civilians returning to Caen, journalist Jacques Kayser saw "eyes overflowing with anguish and visions of horror, but also eyes that know how to say 'thank you.'"[72] "Every family had lost someone," recalled Andy Rooney. "It was true that they were being freed but at the cost of the total destruction of everything they had."[73] In Valognes, Guillaume Lecadet remembered how when the Americans appeared, "there was a little enthusiasm, but alas, a screen of terrible visions stood between us and joy."[74] The liberated also worried about loved ones caught up elsewhere in the chaos of battle.[75] After the Americans passed through his village, Jean-Pierre Launey remembered "a strange feeling invaded my spirit. We were liberated but the war was not over."[76]

Far from being blind to Norman suffering, the GIs were angered, shocked, and saddened by the effects of bombardment. Due to censorship, news of the destruction had not reached home. In November, for example, *Life* magazine refused to publish parts of a report from France that referred to "all these deaths, all these villages destroyed" by Allied bombers.[77] After American pilot Henry Hodulik jumped from his plane to safety with a Norman family near Rouen, he was horrified by the extent of nearby bombing. As his French keepers remembered, "he was ready to leave, to try and cross the line and tell Allied troops, 'You're crazy! You've bombed Neufchâtel. Where's the military objective?'"[78] "I must say, I feel sorry for the French," wrote Morton Eustis to his mother. "In order to get back their freedom, they have to see their country ravaged all over again from another direction."[79] Robert Easton imagined that Normans at Saint-Lô reasoned in the following way: "When the Germans were here they did not trouble us greatly; at least they left us our homes. Now the Americans have left nothing."[80] "It gave me a curious, displaced feeling to look at the damage that can be done," noted Jan Giles about the bombing. He was particularly saddened by the destruction of the beautiful cathedral at Carentan.[81]

The destruction was all the more painful because the GIs had fallen in love with the French countryside. Although they complained about "those bastard hedgerows"—thick bushes that presented obstacles in the breakout from the beachheads—the Americans also expressed rapture for Normandy. Even the war could not erase its splendor. "Sunrise and sunset are both awe-inspiring on favorable weather days," wrote Sidney Bowen to his wife.[82] Orval Faubus noticed "the change from one day to the next, from the grim and terrible scenes of Mortain Hill to the pretty villages and towns and beautiful countryside . . . from the stench of the battlefield to the fragrance of flower gardens along the roads."[83] "It is very beautiful country," wrote Corporal Crayton to his parents, "the birds have begun their daily practice, all the flowers and trees are in bloom, especially the poppies and tulips which are very beautiful at this time of year."[84] "The ride toward Brest was an experience that made us forget the war and the fact that we were headed for another uncertain existence," remembered

Paul Boesch. "France, so beautiful in the summer, and the Brittany peninsula, one of the more picturesque sections."[85] "I was struck by the sheer beauty of the countryside," recalled Robert Rasmus, "the little villages, the churches."[86] For Frank Irgang, the French coast was "alluring" even if "treacherous."[87] Jan Giles had only one gripe about the Norman countryside: the insects. "I know one thing for sure about France," he wrote in his diary, "They have the biggest and most mosquitoes I ever saw in my life."[88]

Both French anger and GI guilt concerning the devastation of Normandy inevitably found its way into the currency of Franco-American relations. "Their attitude was understandable," noted Frank Freese as he described the sour glares he got from civilians. "But it gave us an uncomfortable feeling and we wanted to tell them that we had no desire to be there either."[89] French signs of friendliness inspired surprise. Infantryman Charles Haug was amazed that after "we had to hurt the French people so," that they "were still able to smile and they waved at us as we drove past."[90] "In Isigny where our 72 B-26 bombers leveled the town," noted Chester Hansen in his diary on the ninth of June, "they talked when we spoke to them despite their 69–70 dead and the smoking ruins of the town."[91] Civil Affairs officers were also taken aback by civilians who "seem to bear no rancour whatever against the Allies for the suffering imposed by military operations."[92] Faubus was stunned when a Norman wounded by a bomb wanted to visit with him in a hospital.[93] French courage inspired admiration. In a letter to his mother, Morton Eustis wrote how moved he was by the sight of an elderly French couple who "sat with beaming faces on the ruins with the French flag flying above their white hair. A gallant people, I must say."[94] Raymond Gantter realized that the ruins had taught him "a proper humility." He had resented the war and the sacrifices it had demanded of him. But when he saw French civilians "kneel and start patiently to separate the whole tiles from the broken, the good timbers from the useless splinters; when they turned from their labors to smile at us and run smiling to pin flowers on our jackets—I woke up. I saw that life goes on, and that's a good thing."[95]

American soldiers and Norman civilians shared something with each other they couldn't share with anyone else. For both the war was real and they were in it together. French civilians living farther east and south would never really grasp the price paid by Normans for freedom. Similarly, no girlfriend in the United States could begin to understand what the GIs had gone through in Normandy. Herbert Enderton tried to explain it to his wife by comparing the France in the travel posters back home with the France he was now witnessing: "The winding streams running through the valleys are remembered only because our doughboys got their feet wetter there or because the artillery got stuck there."[96] The GIs' daily encounter with a "murdered France" reminded them they had come as soldiers not tourists.

Despite the hell they shared, however, the Americans and the French ultimately lived in two very different Normandys. For the Americans, it was a battlefield—a place to survive. The idea was to move through it as quickly as possible on the road to Germany and—with any luck—back home. By contrast, for the French, Normandy was home—the seat of family, the scene of childhood memories, the site of struggle and achievement. Some GIs were sensitive to such differences, for example, Jan Giles. With his buddy Mac, Giles entered one damaged house and looked at the wet, ruined sofa, the clock stopped on the mantelpiece. "I kept thinking, somebody lived here. This was somebody's home—and now look at it. I said, 'Let's get out of here.'"[97] Similarly, Capt. Dale Helm admired a small abandoned farm enclosed by a stone wall with a small well-kept house. Counting toys and beds, he guessed that the family had four children. "The smashed toys made me think how thankful I should be that the war was being fought in a country other than home."[98]

But just as often a GI could forget that Normandy was home to someone. Françoise de Hauteclocque remembers the first few moments in 1944 after her house had been bombarded. "With hearts pounding," she and her family emerged from the cellar to inspect the damage. "And what did we see? Huge gaping holes, a pile of dust, stones, bricks, and broken furniture. And in the midst of this scene of devastation, . . . an American rummaging through drawers while his friend relieved himself on the floorboards."[99] In his war memoir

Lt. Col. Claude Hettier de Boislambert begins by mourning his Norman home, destroyed except for a roof and a few bare walls stripped of everything remotely valuable. By a freak chance, he was bivouacked there with the GIs when serving as a member of the French Army. Boislambert told no one that the company was occupying his own home. But when a young officer made a fire in his kitchen with wood from his doors, Boislambert quietly asked him, "Did it ever occur to you that this house belonged to someone?" "I haven't given it a second's thought," replied the officer.[100]

The Dangerous and Incoherent Murmur of War

For much of the world, the Allied invasion was a distant display of might, a symbol of hope, and a reason to pray. For the Normans, by contrast, it was a singular mix of sounds, sights, smells, and tastes. Norman memoirs revolve around the sensory details of the Liberation—the sound of artillery, the first glimpse of an American jeep, the smell of death and decay, the taste of chocolate. What results is an extraordinarily vivid picture of hell in the *bocage*.

The Normans heard the war before they saw it. "Tuesday, June 6, around midnight, awoken by continuous bombing along the coast," wrote Jacques Perret in his diary. "Shortly afterwards, numerous planes flying overhead."[101] At four o'clock in the morning, teenagers Bernard and Solange de Cagny, on vacation in Rots, were awoken by what they thought was a terrible storm. "It took us almost a half hour to realize that no storm could be so violent, so it was probably the Allied landings on the Norman coast."[102] Farther inland that morning, Jacques Lepage also heard the noise. As a veteran of 1914–18, however, he knew better: this was the sound of war.[103] In Saint Sens, Maurice Quillien also recognized a "different sort of sound" that day. "In the preceding weeks and months, we'd heard thousands, hundreds of thousands of planes but they were at a higher altitude, and the humming lasted for hours. This was different."[104] The planes, he realized, were flying lower and reaching land targets. As the battle got underway some days later in La Haye-du-Puits, Charles Lemeland remembers "the dangerous and incoherent murmur of war" coming from every direction, "building up, slowing down, starting again, breaking out in absurd and wild starts."[105] Over the entire region, Normans heard the low rumbling of planes. They developed expert ears, and could discern the difference between the sound of a bomb as it passes over your head versus the whistle of one headed straight for you.[106] They also learned to use the sounds of artillery to determine the location of the front, and whether the Allies were advancing or retreating.[107]

It was a giddy morning. The invasion—so long awaited, so long anticipated—had at last arrived. Winks were exchanged as people shook hands.[108] The murmur of three words passed from one Norman ear to another: "C'est le débarquement!" In a matter of hours, no one would need to be told. As "the thunder of war approached," the Germans shut down the towns. Pierre Desprairies remembered the atmosphere as a strange mix of fear and hope.[109] When the first bombs hit, remembered Antoine Anne, "personally I thought my lungs were going to burst."[110] "The bombs are beginning to fall quite near us," wrote Michel Braley in his diary, "the machine gun has started to fire constantly. Because of it, we completely forgot to eat. We can no longer distinguish between the German and the American bombs. It is a constant rotation with bombs falling around the house."[111] Fernand Broeckz was paralyzed by fear that his house was going to fall down on his family. "The walls were blown open, the floorboards rose and fell. You could hear the tiles falling and the windows breaking." A bomb literally wrapped a wall around his wife.[112] In his diary of 6 June, the young Jacques Petit expressed his disbelief that he and his friends had looked forward to this moment with "romantic enthusiasm": "Huddled together, we believed our last hour to be near, and while the bombs whistle, we wait for that direct hit which would at last bring our agony to an end."[113] Remembering 1914, older men dug trenches near their houses and sheltered their families in this way. Villagers crowded into the basements of the local chateaus, not only because their thick walls offered solidity, but also because no one wanted to die alone. "Solitude was feared," remembered one civilian.[114] The only Normans exempt from the racket were the hard of hearing. Antoine Anne recalls that as the dust from one bomb cleared, he saw his deaf grandmother sitting in a chair, holding his brother in her arms, completely calm.[115]

There was no getting around the fact that the liberators were bringing the war with them. But then again, the war was bringing the liberators. The French had been waiting a long time. The signs of their arrival were sometimes quirky. Chanoine Bertreux heard someone shouting orders but not in German.[116] A serpentine trail of cigarette smoke drifting over a hedgerow provided the first glimpse of another American.[117] Still another sign was the sound of trucks and tanks. As a child, Christiane Delpierre linked the coming of the Americans with the "rumbling of motors."[118] "Down the road you could hear a constant droning," remembered Jean-Jacques Vautier. "We went to the edge of the road, our hearts beating fast. At the high point appeared a helmet, helmets, a car. Slowly the convoy descended. When the first car, a sort of 'scout car,' had come down to our level, we all burst out cheering."[119] That "scout car" or jeep made an indelible impression on the French. "Are the Americans really winning the war with these contraptions?" wondered Robert Clausse.[120] Still others considered it to be American magic—the eighth wonder of the world.[121]

There was little opportunity for formal introductions. In many cases, GIs and civilians caught their first glimpse of each other through a storm of bullets. In Remilly-sur-Lozon, Jacques Lepage at one point realized he was literally standing between the Allies and the Germans with artillery passing over his head. He evacuated his house, and when he returned, he found three dead Germans in his kitchen.[122] Auguste Couillard's home in Remilly switched back and forth between German and Allied control, at one point serving as a prison for German POWs.[123] Also in Remilly, Marguerite Pottier and her family "were between two fires because the Germans were only a few meters from us." The Americans shouted that her family should leave: "Grand Combat!!!!" they screamed.[124] In the same town, the Germans planted a bomb in the chimney of one house. In the heat of the battle, the Americans deactivated but did not remove it. When a refugee went to cook pot-au-feu in the fireplace, she got a bomb inside her pot.[125]

As the fighting moved into their backyards, Normans joined the battle. They informed Americans concerning German positions, and showed them shortcuts and hideaways in the woods.[126] Particularly in the first few hours of the invasion, as soldiers from the Eighty-Second and 101st Airborne parachuted into a wide area around Caen and Sainte-Mère-Église, civilians came forward. When two hundred GIs parachuting into Graignes fell into the marshes (flooded on purpose by the Germans), locals rescued them by boat, took them into their houses, cared for the wounded, and fished the parachutes out of the water before dawn so that the Germans would not see them.[127] Arthur and Berthe Pacary also cared for stranded parachutists in the region of Remilly by bringing them whipped cream and other provisions. "They badly needed to be cared for and cleaned," recalled the couple.[128] Marguerite Pottier's parents were relieved when they discovered *paras* hiding in their garden, as they had wondered what unknown animal was stealing their cabbage. For their part the Americans were happy to eat something else.[129] Still other Normans smuggled *paras* back to the American lines by dressing them as civilians and equipping them with maps.[130] According to Pierre and Yvonne Ferrary, two *paras* wandered Grandcamp-les-Bains in broad daylight, their guns beneath their arms, laconically asking, "the port, the port?"[131]

Still other Normans cared for the wounded. Michel Braley recorded in his diary how a badly wounded American soldier had staggered into their farm. They could not do much for him except give him coffee with eau-de-vie and show him the location of the first aid station. As he was leaving, the GI took out his New Testament and a photograph of his parents for one last look. "We tell him that we are also protestants. He thanks us and leaves. The bombs continue to rain down on us."[132] Thirteen at the time, Odette Eudes of Sainte-Mère-Église remembers that when a wounded soldier who sought shelter at their house could not walk to the first aid station, her father proposed that he carry him on his back. The soldier refused, saying that if a German took a shot, both of them would be killed.[133] Sometimes entire villages mobilized to help the Allied soldiers. Virtually all the women in le Mesnil-Vigot, northwest of Saint-Lô, devoted themselves to tending to the wounded there, even when the village was still under German control. Besides taking GIs into their farms and homes, these women carried them under German fire to a nearby hospital. One woman, Madame Dépériers, also risked her life by walking to nearby Remilly-sur-Lozon in order to get a surgical probe for a GI.[134]

Despite such shows of comradery, however, GI and civilian often met under an umbrella of mutual mistrust. The Allies worried about German ambushes, particularly in the scrappy field-to-field fighting of the early campaign.[135] They were given orders not to trust the French, and to assume that all French people were spies or collaborators.[136] It did not help that British journalists reported rumors that more than half the Normans were not to be trusted, and that they had no wish to be liberated.[137] Paratrooper Donald Burgett refused a Norman's offer of wine because "I just didn't feel like being poisoned."[138] In turn, eleven-year-old Louis Blaise was terrified when two GIs with "blackened faces and furious expressions" searched her house the morning of the sixth of June.[139] "Paralyzed by fear," the nearby Bré family also huddled together while an American searched their house.[140] Young French men who wandered around American-held beaches were arrested or interrogated.[141] Resisters eager to provide crucial intelligence were ignored or detained.[142] The schoolteacher Germaine Martin fell prey to suspicion when the GIs found on her person a map revealing the location of a German radio post. Even though, as she explained, she had picked it up by accident, she was accused of being a spy. When the Americans discovered their error, they apologized and gave her two boxes of chocolate.[143]

The French were also wary of the Americans. Frank Irgang remembers that as the Normans walked past him, "they gave me a hurried glance of distrust which made me feel unwanted."[144] Bombing had left a sour taste in the Norman mouth. German propaganda had shaped views of the Americans and British more than anyone wanted to admit.[145] By the end of June, Allied Headquarters, concerned enough to do a survey about Norman attitudes toward Americans, discovered a generally positive attitude despite some grumbling about looting.[146] In general, military officers preferred to attribute whatever coolness they experienced to "the dour and undemonstrative nature of the Norman."[147] Civil Affairs officers were warned that the Norman "is by nature reserved, a fact which may prevent too open a manifestation of welcome."[148] If the Allies "expected to find caricatures of Southern Frenchmen eager to kiss them on both cheeks," claimed one French pharmacist, they would be sadly disappointed.[149] Normans also acknowledged that they had greeted their liberators with "no wild enthusiasm but instead a dignified satisfaction as well as smiles and the shaking of hands."[150] They, too, explained this response as an effect of the Norman character. When a French soldier traveling east with the British Army noticed that the village atmosphere had suddenly become more friendly, he was not surprised to discover that his unit had left Normandy.[151] Despite the war's anguish and liberation's euphoria, noted Danièle Philippe, "most folks remained true to themselves. *Les Normands, c'est du solide!* [The Normans are tough stock!]"[152]

In fact Norman aloofness can be understood in circumstantial terms. As we have seen, during the summer of 1944, the Allies were far from winning the war. Fearful of reprisal if their villages fell again to the Germans, Norman civilians had the sense not to talk to either side.[153] Only after they witnessed the massive numbers of Allied troops, tanks, and guns being unloaded onto the beaches did they believe the Allies planned to stay. "Very soon they were opening up to us," noted one military report, "not only their hearts, but all their possessions."[154] "The civilians began to realize that we were there for good," remembered Edward Rogers. "French flags appeared, flowers, fruit and eggs were given to us as we passed villages and farms."[155]

Meanwhile, Norman stoicism was on stunning display. A young couple, Juliette and Georges, planned to marry at Sainte-Mère-Église on the sixth of June. Despite the landings, they pressed on with the ceremony, and were attended by an American captain and two lieutenants.[156] The journalist Alan Moorehead found a Norman railway ticket master at his post in a railway station, ruins all around him.

"There have been no trains here since Tuesday," he conceded.[157] Still another Norman peasant complained to the Allies that for several nights he had trouble sleeping because of a bomb that had landed on his bed. Could they come by sometime soon and deactivate it?[158] Locals doggedly milked their cows and churned their butter, even if it meant walking across battlefields.[159] One peasant was quite intent on planting his green beans despite bombs falling nearby.[160] Lt. Col. Francis Sampson noted one farm woman who didn't miss a stroke milking one of her herd, all while the bombs fell around her.[161] Still another *Normande*, when warned of the war in her backyard, turned to her daughter and urged her to milk anyways. "It will be a little bit earlier than usual," she conceded, "but when we are finished, these American gentlemen will have cleaned out the corner."[162] In fact, the Normans paid a price for such forbearance: a woman and her son were killed when she refused to stop doing her cleaning at the public laundry, even while guns fired all around them.[163] So close to the battle did the Normans come that the GIs sometimes suspected them to be German spies.[164]

If the GIs admired the Norman countryside, they fell in love with the "wonderfully clean and beautiful little" children.[165] "Don't believe I ever saw children any handsomer than the French children are," wrote Giles in his journal. "I've not seen a real ugly one yet."[166] The well-known journalist Ernie Pyle described the region as "certainly a land of children. . . . And I'll have to break down and admit that they were the most beautiful children I have ever seen." In fact, Pyle was more impressed by the children than the adults. "Apparently they grow out of this," he speculated, "for on the whole, the adults looked like people anywhere—both good and bad."[167] When he arrived at Le Havre, Joseph Edinger came to the same conclusion in his diary: "Coming out we all noticed the French people themselves. Most of them are short and somewhat stocky. They aren't very good looking, the women, but the children are beautiful. They must change at or in their adolescence."[168]

Predictably the very first Normans to open their hearts to the GIs were these children. Fifteen-year-old Bernard Gourbin remembers the wink he got from a GI fighting outside his window.[169] Parents cringed at their children's lack of reticence with soldiers.[170] Nevertheless the GI lap became a valuable piece of real estate for the smallest Normans. It did not hurt that the soldiers had big pockets bursting with candy and chewing gum, pockets that Gilles Bré noticed right away on D-day, even while the scary Americans were furiously searching his house.[171] Children appeared with large eyes and empty spoons at the windows of makeshift mess halls.[172] They could depend on the GIs to take more than they needed for dinner, then share food.[173] With hearts aching for their own families, the Americans did everything they could to protect children from harm. As Norbert Koopman's unit was passing through Saint-Lô, they came upon about two dozen children under the care of nuns. "The children were frightened by what was happening," remembered Koopman. "They didn't know if we were friend or foe. We stopped and comforted them. It was sad to see these children so upset."[174]

Norman children remember the American soldiers during the summer of 1944 as "demi-gods haloed with a kind of supernatural prestige," who showered them with love and attention. With the GIs, remembered Charles Lemeland, twelve years old in 1944, "it was the wonderful world of laughter, play, and permissiveness: candy galore, the thrill of getting inside tanks and other fascinating machinery and touching all those levers and pedals."[175] Norman children also learned skills from the GIs, like how to play gin rummy and make scoubidous.[176] A fatherless child of six crippled by polio, Francine Leblond lovingly remembers an American parachutist whom her parents hid from the Germans. Calling her "Francisca" after his hometown of San Francisco, the GI would take her in his arms, carry her around the yard, and show her American planes through his binoculars. "When he left, I was inconsolable," remembered Leblond.[177] Christine Delpierre also remembered crying like "a girl abandoned by everyone" when the GIs left, despite all efforts by her father to cheer her up.[178] For Norman children as well as adolescents and young men, the war was a great adventure, the most exciting thing that had ever happened to anyone ever.

The parents and adults also had vivid memories of the Americans. They were dirty and dusty; they looked tired; their teeth were quite white.[179] "Big children, somewhat primitive but very nice," was how Françoise de Hauteclocque described the GIs.[180] And they *were* big— "tall as a building," "giants," "huge devils," and "solid as bombs."[181] Also, they looked like cowboys, with their colts slung on their hips.[182] Most surprisingly, they did not look at all like each other. The bewildered Comtesse de Tocqueville remarked in a letter to her husband that "Americans of all coats and colors" had invaded her chateau.[183] "What a mix of races!" exclaimed de Hauteclocque. "It is common to meet a soldier whose father is Greek and mother German. And yet they all come together under the star-spangled banner."[184] Danièle Philippe was astonished to realize that the first two Americans he met were Italian and Scandinavian. What then was "American"?[185] Finally, there were the boots. "Their yellow shoes are superb!" enthused Madame Destors in her diary.[186] Long-deprived of leather by the Germans, Normans could not take their eyes off American boots, with their soft uppers and heavenly rubber soles. Unlike the clicking of German boots, they were deliciously silent when the GIs marched through town.[187] Jacques Petit was ecstatic when he found an abandoned pair of American boots at an old camp. "They fit me like a glove!" he gushed in his diary. As for those "old clodhoppers with wooden soles," they soon found their way to the back of his closet.[188]

The Odor of Death

Liberation had a smell as well as a sound and a sight. It was the smell of death. Cows, horses, sheep, and goats were strewn across the fields of Normandy, stiff and bloated "under swarms of feasting flies," and emitting horrible smells.[189] The Normans, predominantly small-farm owners, grieved these animals not only as their means of livelihood but also as members of their family. They buried them while smoking two or three cigarettes at a time in order to cover up the smell of putrefaction.[190] As they worked, other peasants came searching, hoping to reclaim their own cows or sometimes to steal them by claiming ownership.[191]

The "pestilential odor, the odor of death" also emanated from the bodies of soldiers. As one GI put it, "the most horrible aspect of infantry combat cannot be depicted in pictures or adequately described in words. It is the smell—the piercing, penetrating, ever-present, sickening stench."[192] That smell was particularly traumatic for children such as Christian Letourneur who had to walk past hundreds of corpses at Carquebut: "step by step we passed in front of these rows of bodies. Never has a field seemed to me so big! It was so hard and I wanted so much to leave!"[193] When nineteen-year-old Monsieur Morin went down to the beach near St. Laurent-sur-Mer in order to see the landings, "a noxious odor infiltrated our nostrils, an odor of spoiled meat which poisoned the air all around us." The smell, he discovered, emanated from a long line of body bags in the process of being buried.[194] Eleven years old at the time, Marcel Jourdain remembers plugging his nose and turning away from what he described as a "chef-d'oeuvre de la guerre": an enormous pit filled with stagnant water, German bodies, and the corpses of animals, including a horse staring into space with its mouth wide open.[195] Bodies lay abandoned in the embankments on the side of the road, in fields and under trees in orchards, in and around houses.[196] Eleven-year-old Louis Blaise remembers emerging from his house after the bombs had stopped only to trip on the dead bodies that lay strewn all around.[197] Below Christian Letourneau's bedroom window passed American trucks "from which, sometimes, the leg of a dead soldier would emerge."[198]

The Normans treated the bodies of German and American soldiers very differently. The bodies of dead Germans aroused feelings of anger and bitterness; they lay exposed for several days and were often kicked around.[199] Those blackened with decomposition presented an ugly irony. As French journalist Jacques Kayser put it: "the blond Aryans, newly dead on French soil, had been transformed into horrendous negroes."[200] Children, in particular, robbed the corpses of German soldiers.[201] While a German body was left face up and bereft of belongings, an American one remained face down, a bouquet of flowers on his back.[202] American deaths were mourned by Normans.[203] GI bodies evoked in them empathy and gratitude. Caught between the lines, Monsieur Le Bourg and his son Bernard walked around bodies in a field saluting the "ten American soldiers who have already died for us."[204] In recounting the campaign fifty years later, one anonymous civilian remembered foremost the sight of a dead American soldier "having come to the Norman earth to pay with his life for the freedom of others."[205] Despite the "stinking atmosphere" at the landing beach, Monsieur Morin was not distracted from the fact that "these young soldiers have come from distant American lands where they could have very well lived in peace. By hundreds and thousands they have lost and continue to lose their lives in the name of freedom."[206]

Many French people took risks to give American soldiers a proper death and burial. During the battles of the seventh of June, a Norman priest discovered some GIs behind bales of hay near Emondeville, north of Sainte-Mère-Église. "They were in the process of dying right in front of my eyes. I did not know what to say to them. And then I remembered the 'Our Father' which I had learned in English. I recited it kneeling in front of them."[207] Even when the village of Gorron was under Nazi control, the unmarked grave of an American soldier was heaped with flowers, and a crown of laurel leaves adorned with a tricolor ribbon. The *Gorronnais* had risked imprisonment to pay their respects.[208] The same phenomenon occurred at Thieux, north of Paris. Four Americans had been killed nearby when a plane was shot down. The Germans forbade a mass or flowers to commemorate the death. Nevertheless a thousand people attended the burial, and the caskets were covered with flowers.[209] Normans often buried American soldiers themselves while awaiting the authorities. One village buried sixty in a common grave, blessing each individually with holy water.[210] In liberated areas, thousands of Normans attended commemoration events. At one such event in Sainte-Mère-Église, the mayor assured the Americans present that the mothers of the town would care for the graves of "these boys who had died for the freedom of France."[211] In the Argentan region, an ambulance driven by an American woman was attacked by the Germans on the road. The woman was killed as were the wounded she transported. Even after the bodies were taken away, the ambulance remained, and was for a very long time covered with flowers.[212]

The Liberation had other smells—gunpowder, tire rubber, gasoline, machine oil.[213] If your farm was next to an infirmary or a field hospital, you awoke to the smell of ether.[214] But besides the smell of death, the scent most remembered by Normans was a pleasant one: the sweet honey aroma of cigarettes.[215] Blond or blended cigarettes were new to the French, who had been deprived of any kind of tobacco throughout the war. The perfume of cigarettes heralded the American arrival.[216] According to Jacques Perret, the "curious perfume of their Camels, their Lucky Strikes, and their Chesterfields" became the "aroma of peace, linked for a long time to the presence of Americans in France."[217] "The perfume of luxury cigarettes has entered the town," observed one French journalist. "You breathe it everywhere: in the streets, in the houses, in the shops."[218] "Ma première américaine, une *Lucky Strike!*" remembered Jacques Petit, an adolescent in 1944.[219]

If cigarettes were the smell of liberation, candy and chewing gum were its tastes. As convoys passed by, the GIs handed out chocolate, gum, and cigarettes cartons, particularly to children and pretty girls.[220] The GIs also gave children the run of their uniforms, notorious for hiding secret reserves of candy. As a result, the sons and daughters of Normandy came home with pockets bulging with chocolate, bonbons, and chewing gum.[221] Once word got around that Americans were a reliable source of such *délices*, a GI could scarcely set up a tent without setting off a stampede of children.[222] For the most part, the parents of these candy marauders found such begging shameful. Yet many adults also learned to salute the Americans and give the V for Victory sign in order to receive chocolate and cigarettes.[223] Chewing gum was new to France, and at first Norman children could not grasp the concept: does one just keep on chewing it? Six years old in 1944, Marcel Launay wondered if the gum would cause his teeth to fall out. He hardly cared, and put it under his pillow every night to preserve

it for the next day's chewing.[224] In a few weeks time, the children became connoisseurs, with some preferring spearmint and others favor-
ing Juicy Fruit.[225] The GIs also passed out oranges when they were
available. One Norman took an orange for his four-year-old daughter,
simply because "she has never seen the color."[226]

The Land of Parley-vous's

The Normans and the GIs got to know each other in August. By the
start of that month, the Allied Army had gained control over the Cotentin Peninsula, and held a front line that stretched from Avranches
to Caen. As the front grew to the south and east, the Americans moved
into Norman cities and towns, requisitioning property and working
with local officials through the Civil Affairs branch of the US Army.[227]
Large groups of GIs bivouacked in camps near Norman towns. As
they were given short day or evening passes, they began to interact
with civilians. From the start, such contacts were awkward for the
Americans. They struggled to learn new words and to understand
French customs. The irony of their situation consisted in this: while
they were conquerors of a mighty army, they were also newcomers
trying to find their way.

For starters, there was the French language. No other barrier did
more to generate anger and misunderstanding between the Americans and the French. At best, language obstacles robbed the GIs of
friendship; at worst, they deprived them of life-saving intelligence.
"The Land of Parley-vous's," as Corporal Alvin Griswold called it,
was capable of transforming the mighty liberating army into a group
of hapless stutterers.[228] Even the most confident GI—the one who had
taken "French III" or "French IV" in high school—found himself up
against a wall in Normandy. "I had taken 4 yrs. of French and thought
I could speak very fluently," remembered Roger Foehringer. His first
encounter with a Norman peasant proved him otherwise. "It was certainly very embarrassing because my buddies expected me to 'Parle
vu France' excellent, but I just didn't have it."[229] "Wish I'd studied

French a little harder in H.S.," wrote Joseph Edinger wistfully in his journal after recounting his efforts to become friends with a French family.[230] A great part of the problem was the speed with which the French spoke their language. "Even if I could make the people understand me," wrote Giles in his diary, "I couldn't understand them. They talk too fast."[231] "A rapid babble of incoherent French sounds" was how Fred Wardlaw described two Norman women conversing.[232] Another problem was the tendency of the French to make distracting gestures when they talked. According to the Texan Bill Quillen, "these God-damned Frenchmen. If you'd cut the sons-of-b——s hands off they couldn't say a single damned word."[233]

Awkward situations resulted. When Joe Hodges met a pretty French girl, he tried to say "How do you do?" in French but instead came out with "How do you want to do it?" for which he got a slap across the face.[234] Failure to communicate led to a cheese tragedy in one Norman town. American sanitary officials in pursuit of a putrid smell found it emanating from a storehouse. When they opened the door, they staggered back as their nostrils met the olfactory force of ten thousand ripening Camembert cheeses. Acting quickly, the officials secured some gasoline, saturated the building, and set it on fire, all while the cheese maker made frantic gestures in a futile effort to convey the fact that the smell was just right.[235] Joseph Messore remembers that as his infantry division moved into Paris, the guys remarked rather loudly about one woman whom they considered flat-chested. Much to their surprise, she looked directly at them and said in perfect English (she was an English teacher), "I'm sorry, but this is all I have."[236] Like any other frustrating problem, the language issue eventually landed in the lap of comedians, notably Bob Hope in his traveling USO show. "I was talking to this G.I. the other day," joked Hope, "who told me he and a couple of friends of his were walking down the street in Paris with a few French beauties on their arms. Well, one of the soldiers cuts loose with this big, loud fart. His buddy says, 'Hey, it's not very polite to fart in front of the girls!' And he said, 'Ah, that's okay. These girls don't understand English!'"[237]

For the average Joe, French products and places were a challenge.

The famous perfume became "Chinnel #5."[238] Joseph Messore reported being flown to "Rheins" and then "Le Horve."[239] As for Reims, Andy Rooney declared it a terrible choice for the German surrender because "its name is almost impossible for any non-French-speaking person to pronounce."[240] One GI strategy was just to make up their own names for places rather than try to pronounce them. Béziers morphed into "Brassieres"; La Haye-du-Puits became "Hooey da Pooey"; Isigny, "I seen ya," and Sainte-Mère-Église, "Saint Mare Eggles."[241] Talking about a battle meant referring to "St. Something-or-other."[242] Still other French words and phrases the GIs adopted enthusiastically. "Dear Kids," wrote Aramais Hovsepian to his brothers, "Bon jour, mes amis, comment allez vous? Je suis tres bien, merci. Boy, you're talking to *Frenchy* now!"[243] "Cherchez la femme" was an honored GI phrase, as was "c'est la guerre," which, Jack Plano thought, "seemed to cover anything and everything bad that had happened to the French since 1940."[244] One of the GIs' favorite songs carried the refrain "Hinky Dinky Parlez Vous!"[245] Chester Jordan remembers during his first days in Normandy that he had his "first exposure to the word 'BEAUCOUP.' There were beaucoup Germans, beaucoup planes, beaucoup artillery, beaucoup tanks, and beaucoup miles. I got the drift that it meant many but I was not about to ask for a definition."[246]

To cope with their fractured French, the GIs used several strategies. One, according to Andy Rooney, was "shouting English louder and louder until the French understood."[247] Another was to learn the language. In July *Stars and Stripes* notified its readers that a staff assistant from New Orleans would be offering French classes at the Club Victoire in Cherbourg "for Joes who want to improve their 'parles vous fanvais.'"[248] Nobody got very far with the phrasebook because it did not teach grammar.[249] The GIs thumbed through it "in order to find the dialogue necessary to obtain the kiss of a woman," but it focused on tedious things like medical aid and enemy troop activities.[250] Usually someone in a company could teach some basic French. For Jan Giles that meant "eggs," "wine," and "every form of 'amour.'"[251] In order to trade with the locals, the GIs sometimes had to resort to pantomime. When a peasant did not understand the English word "egg"—a torturous *œuf* in French—a member of Peter Belpulsi's company had to put his hands under his armpits, cluck, and pretend to lay an egg.[252] Bill Mauldin caught the scene in one of his cartoons. (See figure 1.2.) The GIs were vexed by their inability to master French, even as their mastery of France was being achieved. They may have

"The word for eggs is '*des œufs*'."

FIGURE 1.2. Bill Mauldin cartoon. "The word for eggs is 'des oeufs.'" From *Stars and Stripes*, 13 September 1944. Used with permission from Stars and Stripes. © 1944, 2012 Stars and Stripes.

been the liberators, but they sounded like two-year-olds trying to spit out a proper sentence. One of Andy Rooney's American colleagues amused himself by going up to French people on the street and saying to them "Vous parlez bien français." Surprised, they would look up and graciously say "merci!"[253] By making the French into tourists in their own country, the joke played on the GIs' discomfort with their own "outsider" position.

Although they may have appeared to enjoy the upper hand, the French struggled, in turn, with English. There was a big difference, Danièle Philippe discovered, between the English he had learned in school and the language spoken by the GIs.[254] Despite having won the English prize six years in a row, Jacques Petit could not understand one word they said.[255] Children contented themselves with learning phrases such as "chocolate if you please."[256] After befriending several GIs, the child Christiane Delpierre came to the conclusion that English was "an apparently easy language dominated by the word 'OK.' No problem getting that."[257] Spelling "chewing gum" was another matter; it became everything from "swing-gamme" to "chouine-gomme" on paper.[258] There were awkward moments for the French as well. When Jean-Jacques Vautier of Saint-Lô visited a field where the GIs had camped, he saw a tomb marked "Old Latrine." Thinking "Latrine" was an American family name, he made the sign of the cross and paid his respects to the "old" man. As he walked away, he saw another tomb—and another and another—with the same name. "Stupeur!" he thought, realizing the "tomb" was actually the remains of a GI toilet.[259]

When civilian and soldier could not understand each other, they found other means to communicate. Sharing pictures of girlfriends and family became common. For one young French man from Caen, such an exchange in an American barracks was pleasantly illuminating. "When I showed them, in turn, the photo of my fiancé, the high whistles emanating from their lips were enough to convince me that in terms of pinups, my Jeannine was in an international category."[260] In his combat journal, Lee Otts recorded an evening sharing pictures and wine with a French family. "It was wonderful being with them," he concluded, "even if I couldn't understand them."[261] Perhaps the most touching example of linguistic resourcefulness concerns two priests in Carquebut, south of Sainte-Mère-Église. A week after D-day, the carnage from the battle with the Germans was accumulating where the US Army lined up bodies in a field. In the effort to give these men a decent burial, the French pastor from the region joined forces with an American military chaplain. The two priests quickly realized they could barely communicate, since the pastor spoke no English and the chaplain no French. To get the job done, they decided to speak Latin, having both learned it at seminary.[262]

French Girls Are Easy

The adage "first impressions count" was never truer than in Normandy. For the Normans, the first impression of the US military was the might of its war machine. It was an accident of war that the Allies unloaded an army big enough to conquer a continent on the shores of Normandy. Nevertheless, they did, and it "stupefied" the Normans.[263] "It is an unbelievable sight," noted Monsieur Morin as he caught his first glimpse of the landing beaches a few hours into D-day. "Never have I seen so many boats; whether you look right or left, they are everywhere."[264] Cécile Armagnac noticed the difference between the German occupied zone, "motionless, practically deserted," and the American zone, "overflowing with materiel and men in motion!" "It's just unimaginable," said her friend Brouzet over and over.[265] As the war moved east, literally thousands of tons of war materiel, including trucks, tanks, food, and ammunition, were transported down Norman roads to the ever-shifting front. As a result, civilians in the region got a front row seat on the equipment of the US Army. Monsieur Jacques Popineau of Gouville noted in his diary that from the twenty-eighth of July to the sixth of August, day or night the Americans did not cease to pass by with their " formidable materiel."[266] Michel Braley also recorded in his journal that "considerable amounts of equipment are passing by. Big tanks, caterpillar tractors, trucks full of men. . . .

You should see how they are equipped!"[267] According to Alfred Marie, the population of Avranches "marveled" at the enormous tanks, machine guns, cranes, and "immense platforms transporting engines which we have neither seen nor even suspected their existence."[268]

The Americans not only had equipment. They knew how to use it. When Danièle Philippe's father first went and conversed with the GIs at their camp, he came back stunned by their logistical operations. "They have an organization, these Americans!" he exclaimed to the entire family, *"C'est purement fantastique!"*[269] Civilians throughout northern France had the opportunity to witness the Allied Signal and Engineer Corps at work during the summer of 1944 as they established telephone lines and reconstructed strategic routes.[270] According to Armand Frémont, the population of Le Havre considered the American engineers who rebuilt the harbor there to be "men of genius" whose work displayed their "power of force, technique and mechanics beyond what the Havrais could even imagine."[271] *"Incroyable,* an intelligent army, I never would have believed it!" declared one Norman near La Haye-du-Puits.[272] Civilians were particularly impressed with the way in which army engineers could build a bridge across a wide river in five hours time. In one village, the local priest asked if he could be the first to cross the bridge after giving it a blessing. He then walked across, Lawrence Cane wrote his wife, "looking like a kid who's just gotten a big box of candy."[273] The arrival of the Americans suggested a new future. "Stupefied by the incomparable means and organization of the Americans," Jean-Pierre Launey declared that "a new world order had come to be born and established."[274] Bernard Gourbin could not agree more. Watching the "fabulous" equipment being loaded off boats at Omaha Beach, he concluded that the Americans were "representatives of a new world which had come to save the old one. . . . At this instant, witnessing this enormous accumulation of power, I became aware of great changes which were going to take place in the world."[275]

If the Normans associated the army with the future, the Americans linked Norman society to the past. To them France was a vestige of a primitive era. "Everything seems old in Normandy," wrote

Ernie Pyle in *Stars and Stripes*. In Cherbourg, Pyle found nothing but old and worn buildings and was not ashamed to admit he liked the "regular and nice" Californian copies of Norman architecture better. In fact, Pyle admitted, looking at the Cherbourg originals, "I felt, before catching myself, that they had copied our California Norman homes and not done too good of a job."[276] In his journal Giles also noted that "the buildings, what's left of them, look like they'd been here since time began."[277] "You really should see some of these places these people over here have as homes," wrote Charles Taylor to his wife. "Most of them are made of mud or cement, rock with shale roofs or straw thatched roofs."[278] Even the traditional Norman castle failed to impress. *Stars and Stripes* reported that "life in an old chateau in France sounds romantic but the American soldiers who have tried it say they prefer a cottage on Kalamazoo."[279] One had to be "either a wizard or a lizard" to be comfortable in "these old hundred-room moss collectors" where "History—with a capital 'H'—crawled out of the woodwork at you." To make matters worse, "the sanitation system would interest the Society of Antiquarian Plumbers." Worst of all was the "seedy old character with a stained yellow mustache, smoking a cigarette by some rose bushes." He turned out to be the owner of the castle.[280] So much for the aristocracy.

One stereotype generated during the First World War was that the French were primitive in their work and bodily habits.[281] That prejudice was only reinforced in 1944. Once again, it was an accident of war that the Americans, landing in Normandy, began to define "Frenchness" in a rural, peasant culture rather than a cosmopolitan, urban one like Paris. Nevertheless the GIs quickly came to the conclusion that the entire nation lived in a time gone by. For one thing, they assumed that war expediency measures were the norm. Because gasoline was not available, peasants were forced to rely on nonmechanized methods of farming even if they did own a tractor. "They were years behind us in their farming; some even used oxen," concluded a shocked Leroy Stewart.[282] In a letter back home, Red Cross volunteer Angela Petesch voiced the same opinion: "They are way behind the times—the women still wash clothes in the little streams and pound the garments with stones; the cows and pigs and chickens still live in the same building as the family."[283] Normandy was not even archaic; it was beyond time altogether. "We marched through a village where the people lived like their great, great, great-parents did," remembered Anthony Harlinski.[284] David Ichelson considered them downright primitive: "Their homes were made out of dried mud with thatched roofs, and the pigs and chickens were allowed to run around the kitchen. They wore crude wooden shoes when working out in the fields until dark, and their evening meal was soup and bread with an apple for dessert."[285] Allan Lyon was particularly shocked by the lack of plumbing and the fact that the Normans relieved themselves with the animals.[286] For Charles E. Taylor, it all looked like something out of a fairy tale. "There is a family of French people that live in the big house to my rear," he wrote his wife. "You would laugh to see them for they sure look funny with their patched clothes and wooden shoes. Yes, they wear shoes just like you used to read about the Dutch wearing. I want to send a pair home to you, but there seems to be no extra pair around here."[287] Taylor's condescension was complete. For him Norman shoes represented nothing more than a fantasy souvenir of an antediluvian age.

As a sign of a primitive culture, animal manure became a GI preoccupation. "They're a hundred years behind in their ways, too" wrote Giles in his journal. The cow stables, he complained, were right next to the kitchen, where the smells of urine and manure became suffocating.[288] He was particularly appalled by "the manure pile in front of everybody's doorstep." Infantryman Karl Clarkson was amazed to see peasants clean out the toilets soldiers were using, take the contents, and spread it on their field. "But that is the way it was, and all the French towns looked and smelled alike."[289] Chester Hansen noted his impressions of Normandy as he rode through the countryside by jeep: "Foul smell of the yards and the manure. Bad sewage."[290] Ironically by the end of the war some Americans eventually came to prefer the Germans because, even though they were the enemies, at least they were clean.[291]

GI condescension toward "primitive," "dirty" Normans echoed

American imperial thinking in Hawaii, the Philippines, and Puerto Rico, where US officials also considered "natives" to need "civilizing" through education and hygiene.[292] "Would be good," wrote one lieutenant in Normandy to his wife, "to be back with civilized people once more."[293] Central to the GI view of the French as uncivilized was their attitudes toward the body and sex. For example, French toilets or *pissoirs* offended the GIs because in the absence of any enclosure, you just walked up to a wall to relieve yourself.[294] Not only that, French women would greet you while you were doing it.[295] "People would walk by you," remembered Karl Clarkson, "but as they were French and that was their way of life it meant nothing to them."[296] "People who build *pissoirs* in the open on the streets are people I don't even pretend to understand," wrote Giles in his diary. He was particularly horrified by a French man who "cut loose with women passing right beside him.[297]

Again like "native" peoples of the US imperial past, Normans seemed to have no shame. One day while taking a small break in a Norman village, infantryman David Ichelson was stunned by a man who waved to a woman while urinating against a wall: "As a true French Gentleman, he took his hand off his penis and used it to tip his hat to the lady and greet her in French, while holding his penis with the other hand and continuing to urinate." Like many GIs, Ichelson had heard about such "broad, philosophical attitudes, and tolerance" before he got to France. "We also heard that what we considered sex perversion was normal for them." But even the deeply imbedded association of the French with loose morals had not prepared him for this.[298] Even in enclosed men's rooms, the GIs were embarrassed by the presence of a woman attendant, or the fact that women often had to pass through to get to the women's rooms.[299] Chester Hansen told the story of a GI engineer doing a job at an airfield while hundreds of French civilians looked on. When he went to relieve himself at the makeshift toilet, a young French woman peered over the canvas and "chatted merrily to him in French." Embarrassed and unable to understand her, he simply stuttered "Wi, wi," but then to his horror, "she promptly came around, entered and sat down at a hole

next to him."[300] Then there was the apparent ease with nudity. Paul
Boesch recalls a time when he and his men went swimming naked on
a beach near Brest in the late summer. He was appalled by one French
man who continued to walk his "pretty young mademoiselle" on the
beach right by all the naked men. "The only explanation I could hit
upon was that the Frenchman must have been sure of his own physical proportions."[301]

Such stories pose the problem of determining if the GIs were imposing on the French their own preconceptions that women were
"easy" and without shame. In the last days before the invasion, remembers Sergeant Dargols, a US army officer of French origin, the
GIs overwhelmed him with questions about pretty French girls.[302]
Soldiers landing on Omaha Beach brought an army *Pocket Guide to
France* that intoned "France has been represented too often in fiction
as a frivolous nation where sly winks and coy pats on the rear are the
accepted form of address. You'd better get rid of such notions right
now if you are going to keep out of trouble."[303] In fact, the *Guide to
France* had it right that "respectability" was still the imperative for the
vast majority of French women. While the tight religious and moral
grip on sexual behavior relaxed considerably during the interwar period, standards of modesty remained high, particularly for the urban
middle class. Sexual pleasure became more accepted in courtship and
within marriage, and adultery was also less condemned. But many
women considered gynecological exams distressing and insisted on
lights off in the bedroom. Even in rural areas such as Normandy, nudity or sex in public were widely scorned as scandalous, especially for
women.[304] The schoolteacher Marcelle Hamel-Hateau remembered
how the "unleashing of sexual energy" among the GIs was a "shock"
to the Normans given their "austere or at least reserved and discrete
sexual mores."[305]

To some extent, then, the GIs must have been seeing the Normandy they wanted to see. It was not simply that Americans were
stuck in their old Puritanical morality. By the mid-twentieth century,
the Victorian restrictions of sexual continence and self-control had
largely disappeared from white middle-class American society, partic-

ularly among the younger generation. Heterosexual pleasure and sexual satisfaction were defined as important for personal happiness as well as a successful marriage. Nevertheless, as was the case in France, some traditional rules remained. For women "going all the way" was considered acceptable only in the context of love and commitment. Parents were expected to be sexual guardians who imposed limits, particularly for daughters. When Jordan's unit stayed for the night in a liberated village, some of his men accepted the "hospitality" of two local sisters for the night. "They found it disquieting at first because they were sharing a bed room with MAMA and PAPA but since it didn't seem to bother the host they got on with their business." What amazed the young Jordan was that not even a girl's parents cared to toe the line.[306]

For the Americans sexual desire was still something to be restrained, lest it overwhelm rationality and moral self-discipline.[307] Given these rules, the GIs were inclined to read their apparent absence in France as a sign of immorality. French sexual attitudes became an obsession for them. French women were called "sign language girls" because, it was believed, they could be seduced by a simple set of hand gestures.[308] Parisian girls were considered downright aggressive. When Chuck Taylor got lost in Paris, he was relieved to see a priest who could help him. "I was glad to see him," he wrote his wife, "for I almost got picked up—you know these French women."[309] Those GIs who entered through Marseille in the late summer were shocked by the sexual practices of this old port town, notorious for its sex trade. "You'd probably like to know something about the 'famous' French girls," wrote Keith Winston to his wife, "I find the French a highly immoral people by our standards. It's said there are 41,000 licensed prostitutes in Marseille—so if that figure is correct—it appears that almost every woman in the city is a whore."[310]

As we shall see in the following chapters, the GIs saw sexual promiscuity as a metaphor for the archaic and immoral nature of French society. Such a narrow view of the French obscured the truly diverse relations soldiers enjoyed with civilians, who became comrades, friends, adopted children, and even saviors in the weeks after the landings. Nevertheless, American soldiers privileged a set of sexual practices—nudity, seduction, intercourse—as defining the essence of Frenchness. Sexual looseness and lack of bodily shame combined with Norman huts and oxen as irrefutable evidence that the French were uncivilized and in need of social and political management. American prejudices held that so-called sexually excessive peoples (such as "native" societies of the imperial past) were lacking in the rational self-control necessary to maintain a democracy. Because the US military perceived French sexual practices as primitive, debates about sexual management also became contests over the French capacity for democratic self-rule. Moral condescension influenced military policy at all levels of decision making. Confronted with the strange language and practices of "a faraway land," the GIs clung to old stereotypes of the French. While such prejudices helped them to manage French cultural differences, they also had real political consequences. To see the US refusal to recognize French sovereignty as a matter of military expediency or political conflict is to miss the full complexity of the situation.

2

The Myth of the Manly GI

THE FAMILIAR IMAGE of an ecstatic American GI surrounded by adoring French women has become an icon of the liberation of Europe in 1944 (See figure Intro. 2.) Shot in the golden era of photojournalism, the GI photo demonstrates how profoundly photography shapes national memory. As visual cliché, its only equal is the Iwo Jima photo, which appeared on millions of posters in the later war years.[1] (See figure 2.1.) The Iwo Jima image represented American heroism in the Pacific theater in the same way that the GI photo represented the "good war" in Europe. Both images provided Americans with reassurance about their aims in the war. Both demonstrate how photographs are endowed with the creative strength to shape our understanding of specific periods.

The GI photo and the myths it generated at the time of the liberation of France form the subjects of this chapter. The photograph was replicated in a thousand guises in the years 1944–45. It appeared some days after the Normandy landings in the military newspaper *Stars and Stripes*, then more widely in the American mainstream press. By 1945 it had come to stand for victory in Europe. As propaganda, it constructed a deceptive banality in American war aims.

The photo drew its strength from several sources. First was its ability to be both particular and general.[2] Because the photo was carefully promoted, an individual GI (never the same soldier) came to represent the US military, even the nation. The photo also gained force

FIGURE 2.1. Iwo Jima flag raising. © AP Photo/Joe Rosenthal.

from the widely held belief that photography told the "truth" of what it saw.[3] The happy embrace of French women really did happen: the camera had seen it. Finally, the photograph hid its origins, becoming an isolated—and therefore transcendent—moment in time.[4] The viewer never learned where the embrace took place, who snapped the picture, or how it fit within the narrative of the Liberation. Anonymous and unfettered by specificity, the photo was free to produce a myth: the manly GI landed on the shores of France, and like a knight in shining armor rescued women from the jaws of Nazism, for which they were very grateful. The knight was duly awarded with kisses. In propaganda of this kind, the Normandy campaign was understood in traditional gender terms as manly men rescuing helpless women. The photo offered a myth of the GI as a virile protector who arrived on French shores merely—and the *merely* is important—to rescue French women.

Obviously the liberation of France was more complicated. Here myth describes a type of speech, both visual and textual, which is able to transform history into idealized form. Myths, like photographs, lose the memory that they once were made. They organize a world that is without depth or contradictions; they purify, simplify, and de-politicize.[5] The GI photo mythologized the American mission in Europe by presenting it as heterosexual romance. Sustained by gender roles that were themselves idealized—the manly knight, the damsel in distress—the romance neutralized tensions concerning French national sovereignty. As we have seen, the Allied leaders initially planned to install a military government in France and shunned Charles de Gaulle, refusing for months to recognize him as a sovereign leader. In creating the image of the manly GI, military propagandists steered the soldiers away from such political complexities, instead portraying the war as just another opportunity for guys to meet girls. In doing so, these propagandists exploited sexual fantasies about France already imbedded in the American mind and now revitalized to make war aims in the ETO more appealing to the GIs. Back home, the photo had yet another effect, which was to help erase the more troubling elements of the American presence, among them, the violent crimes committed by the GIs against French civilians. Finally, the photo encouraged the GIs to identify as global leaders at a time when American stewardship of Europe was just beginning.

Here's What We're Fighting For

The emergence of the GI photo was linked to the rising popularity of photojournalism, made possible by two technological advances in the 1930s. First, there was the development of half-tone technology, which enabled the inexpensive production of high-quality photos in magazines and newspapers.[6] Second was the creation of the thirty-five-millimeter camera. With its faster shutter speed and drastically reduced size, this camera made possible the photographic "candid." In response to these developments and the growing popularity among Americans for news as pictures, *Life* magazine debuted in November 1936, and its rival *Look* six weeks later.[7] The Second World War was the first war in history to be covered by photographers working side by side with soldiers in combat.[8] The manly GI image was part of this revolution in photojournalism. Its wide dissemination did not negate its candid appearance: GIs everywhere appeared to be receiving spur-of-the-moment kisses.

While the GI photo would eventually find its way to *Life* magazine, it first emerged in the military newspaper *Stars and Stripes*. Considered to be the most important of the GI gazettes, *Stars and Stripes* was produced specifically for the troops in Europe with the sanction of the US government. Its mission, as stated in the first issue, was to provide "a symbol of the things we are fighting to preserve and spread in this threatened world. It represents the free thought and free expression of a free people." Clearly, *Stars and Stripes* was intended to serve as propaganda. At the same time, however, by the express request of Gen. Dwight Eisenhower, commander of the European operation, *Stars and Stripes* was not to swerve too far from the truth about the war. Only honest papers, Eisenhower believed, could maintain confidence in the high command.[9] With its conceit of realism, photojournalism was key to the *Stars and Stripes* approach to reporting the war. The paper's photographs, in particular, looked "honest" even if they catered to the military's idealized version of the war. Andy Rooney, who reported for the paper, only noticed the "jingoistic quality" of the headlines when he looked back at it fifty years after the war.[10] The impact of *Stars and Stripes* as an instrument of propaganda cannot be overestimated. It was widely read by the GIs throughout the European theater, and when scarce, often passed from hand to hand.[11]

The first prototypes of the GI photo began to appear in *Stars and Stripes* only days after the landings in Normandy. These photos featured troops being greeted by ecstatic women and children. A typical caption read: "Everywhere Allied troops advance, they are greeted joyously by the liberated French. Here an old French woman and her family give a welcome to Americans passing through a Normandy village."[12] In the months that followed, some version of the photo continued to appear in the paper. Despite variations, two visual elements were constant. First, the categories of "French" and "American," "rescued" and "rescuer" were secured through gender differences. The US military was male, and France, female. Second, the American incursion onto French soil was consistently envisioned in sexualized terms: as an opportunity for sexual conquest.

Let us take each of these visual elements in turn. Here, *la française* represents a nation abandoned by its men. This visual effect resulted, in part, from demographic realities. By early 1944, two million able-bodied French men were residing in German labor or prison camps; countless others were officially in hiding, engaged in covert Resistance actions, or preparing to fight in northern Africa. France was largely a nation of women, children, and elderly people. "The younger men weren't anywhere around," noticed infantrymen Peter Belpulsi and Orval Faubus.[13] In the American press, the journalist Doris Fleeson said of the Norman countryside: "I was struck again as I often was in France by the absence of men. Only the very old were seen in any numbers."[14] Demographic realities aside, however, the prevalence of women in these photos had an important symbolic effect, which was to present the occupied country as a defenseless land, devoid of men, and populated with women who needed protection. That scenario not only set up the American mission as "rescue," but also portrayed France as "feminine" and submissive to military incursion. Here was a landscape made for American heroism.[15]

The identification of the French nation with a woman followed a common trend in twentieth century propaganda. Modern Western nations were gendered particularly in wartime or for colonial conquest.[16] In US military culture, "pinups" performed the same symbolic function during the war. Female pinups were common in *Stars and Stripes* as well as on fighter planes and tent walls. In an age when

such ideals as "freedom" and "democracy" had become largely mean-
ingless to the GIs, pinup women came to symbolize what they were
fighting for.[17] "Amid the smoke and stink and dead seriousness of
war," the caption of one *Stars and Stripes* photo read, "she's linked
us with the country we love—the goofy, funny, wise-cracking, happy
country that can produce the world's best tanks, . . . the best cheesecake."[18] (See figure 2.2.) As the pinup suggests, nationalism was eroticized in heterosexual terms even before the GIs arrived in France. If
Rita Hayworth symbolized the nation, *l'amour* with *la française* could
easily stand for foreign relations.

A second visual constant of *Stars and Stripes* photojournalism was
the mapping of sexual relations onto American war aims. For example, in one image titled "Here's What We're Fighting For," American
objectives in Europe were produced both visually and textually as a
guileless drive to make women happy. (See figure 2.3.) The caption
reads: "Lots of G.I.s who never thought much about Freedom before
learning about it from the smiles and happy tears of Folks who'd lost
it for four black years. . . . If we fight as hard to keep the good will of
liberated peoples as we did to win it—there's hope for happier days."[19]
The soldier is instructed to understand the meaning of freedom as an
adoring smile on every woman's face. The purpose of the war is to
keep those French girls "nuts" about the Yanks. This sexualization of
wartime aims domesticated the US mission by transforming it into a
joyful, consensual union. A closer look at the photograph reveals it to
be a composite of women's faces, clumsily pasted together, with arms
and hands often drawn to create the effect of a crowd of women. *Stars
and Stripes* was clearly determined to create a happy female crowd,
even if one did not exist.

While the newspaper doggedly focused on heterosexual romance,
the closest bonds forged between GIs and civilians were arguably with
children. As we saw in the last chapter, children were often the first
to open their hearts to the GIs. On the mantles of countless Norman
homes were shots of ecstatic children, their eyes eclipsed by huge helmets, nestled in the arms of a smiling soldier.[20] Such photographs,
however, were not to be seen in *Stars and Stripes*, where the Norman

───── *An Editorial* ─────

Cheesecake, Watermelon and Corn

CHEESECAKE is newspaper lingo for pictures like this—gals, legs and corny stuff like the watermelon and the ice.

* * *

We don't know whether or not we could have won this war without cheesecake, watermelon and corn. We don't know whether cheesecake shortened the war by as much as a single day.

* * *

All we know is that pictures like this—of gals with flirty-flirty eyes, toothpaste smiles, snazzy gams and all the trimmings have given us a lift in some pretty grim times.

* * *

We dont' know who this particular piece of cheesecake is. But she and a lot of gals like her have adorned the insides of tanks, the cabs of trucks, the dashboards of jeeps, the cockpits of planes. Amid the smoke and stink and dead seriousness of war, she's linked us with the country we love—the goofy, funny, wise-cracking, happy country that can produce the world's best tanks, the best planes —the best cheesecake.

* * *

When the history of this war is written, the infantry, the cavalry, the Engineers and all the rest will come in for their full share of well-earned glory. There will be statues to the heroes and Memorial Day parades. But the record won't be complete unless somehow, some way, we acknowledge the rôle of cheesecake in winning the war.

* * *

History may forget. The War Department may never award a citation. Congress may never confer honors.

* * *

Only the guy who has lived on Spam knows how much he owes to cheesecake, watermelon and corn.

FIGURE 2.2. "Cheesecake, Watermelon and Corn." From *Stars and Stripes*, 18 September 1944.

invasion was seen in erotic rather than parental terms. The US military knew that the average Joe equated France with brothels and pretty women. Sex was how they were going to sell the Normandy campaign. In this sense, the soldiers were literally *seduced* into fighting the war.

Here's What We're Fighting For

THE French are nuts about the Yanks. This picture gives you the idea. Lots of GI's who never thought much about Freedom before are learning about it from the smiles and happy tears of folks who'd lost it for four black years.

* * *

Let's not kid ourselves. The honeymoon won't last forever. Some franc-happy gogetters will start gypping GI's and some dumb Joes are going to do things to disgrace our Army and get the French sore.

* * *

But most of us will stay on the ball. If we fight as hard to keep the good will of liberated peoples as we did to win it—there's hope for happier days.

* * *

War has a long list of entries on the debit side of the ledger—lives, money, misery. On the credit side there's this—the love and gratitude of one people toward another. It's the chance of a lifetime—and our kids' lifetime.

* * *

Let's not piddle it away.

FIGURE 2.3. "Here's What We're Fighting For." From *Stars and Stripes*, 9 September 1944.

At the liberation of Paris, the myth became even more erotically charged. As is well known, the capital was freed from German control by the French Resistance, whose street-to-street fighting was reinforced by General Leclerc's Armored Division. General Eisenhower ordered the Americans to follow behind Leclerc as the French victors made their triumphal entrance on 25 August. Hence Paris was liberated by its own people with the support of the French Army.[21] However, in *Stars and Stripes*, the liberation of Paris was a wholly American event for which the French demonstrated their gratitude with an orgy of kissing. While Ernie Pyle noted that "everybody kissed you—little children and old women, grownup men and beautiful girls," the paper focused on erotic relations between the GIs and young Parisian women.[22] According to one infantryman interviewed by the paper, the *parisiennes* "wait at street intersections for a jeep to pause. That's the signal for all hell to break loose and the kissing starts. 'If this is war I love it.'"[23] One photo with the caption "Savee Jitterbug Mademoiselle?" featured a GI dancing with a French woman surrounded by a crowd.[24](See figure 2.4.) Still another picture of French women on a US tank was titled "Gay Paree welcomes Americans—and how!" and carried the following caption: "Laughter and kisses, flowers and wine welcomed the small contingent of American troops who entered Paris early yesterday morning . . . three G.I.s, newly arrived in the French capital, cement Franco-American relations [with a kiss] atop a tank."[25]

Paris itself was eroticized in *Stars and Stripes*. An article titled "Paris, Beautiful, Beloved of Man" likened the city to "a woman to give man

You may not speak French, and they don't savee English, but Cpl. Rosario Talliente, of Brooklyn, demonstrates there's a universal language as he teaches French cutie to jitterbug in streets of liberated city. GIs on sidelines provide music.

FIGURE 2.4. "Savee Jitterbug Mademoiselle?" From *Stars and Stripes*, 24 August 1944.

affection and love," and urged the reader to "take a good look at her: no matter what the Germans have done, she'll be worth looking at."[26] The paper also declared Paris to be "our Favorite Pin-up Girl. . . . She might remind them of that great, wonderful, shining moment when humanity realized it again was free."[27] Also erotic were the lessons in French taught to the GIs in the pages of *Stars and Stripes*. Readers could learn various phrases in French and German, supposedly in order to communicate better with liberated populations. The difference between what was considered essential German and what was considered essential French was revealing. Readers were taught such German phrases as "Kein Zigaretten! [No cigarettes!]," "Waffen niederlegen! [Throw down your arms!]," and "Antreten! Vorwarts! [Line up! Forward!]." By contrast, crucial French phrases included "Vous êtes très jolie [You are very pretty]," "Vous avez les yeux charmants [You have charming eyes]," "Je suis un général [I am a general]," "Je ne suis pas marié [I am not married]," and "Vos parents sont-ils chez eux? [Are your parents at home?]"

The American eroticization of the Liberation becomes still more evident if we contrast it with accounts of the same events provided by French daily newspapers. A study of six Parisian dailies that managed to get out a paper during the last days of August reveals how differently the Liberation looked to French eyes.[28] While pictures of soldiers on tanks and trucks also appear on the front pages of French newspapers, here they are "the boys of Leclerc" and members of the French resistance. Only one photograph in these six newspapers portray a French woman kissing an unequivocally American soldier. In all other instances, the men enjoying the "famous" French embrace are either vaguely identified as "libérateurs" or are clearly French soldiers.[29] In *Le parisien libéré*, there is not even a mention of interactions between Americans GIs and French women until 30 August, several days after the Americans entered the city. This same day, *Ce soir* describes the scene at the place de l'Opéra in this way: "The boys of Leclerc have trouble advancing in the crowd which is applauding them. They are sunburnt, exhausted and immensely happy. And on their rough cheeks, the sunburn nearly disappears under the marks of red lipstick."[30] In *Ce soir*, it is the French men who are favored with a kiss. "A cloud of Parisiennes jumped on us and kissed us right on the lips" was how one French soldier remembers his entry into Paris.[31]

In general, however, these French newspapers display little by way of eroticism. For the Parisians the Liberation was a family reunion, not a scandalous affair. *Le parisien libéré* describes the event in this way: "Certainly we know what a major role the Americans have played in the battle for France, and what rights they have gained in our country. But they wanted Paris first to taste the pure joy of a family reunion realized after a long separation."[32] The French papers also produce an air of normalcy by promoting the institution of marriage. As early as 29 August, *Ce soir* presented the first couple to be legally wed at a Parisian *mairie* after the departure of the Germans.[33] When Franco-American contact is represented in these Parisian dailies, it also takes a more familial form. For example, several photographs and articles focus on the American provisioning of Paris. On 27 August, for example, *Le franc-tireur* informed its readers that the Allies were bringing in three thousand tons of food and supplies every day, and "we are going to eat chocolate!"[34] Rather than kissing the French, the Americans appear to be giving them something to eat.

Some Iowa Girls Didn't Like That Kissing in Paris

Because Americans had long imagined the French to be a "sexy" people, *Stars and Stripes* drew on old cultural prejudices in shaping their banalized version of the mission in France. This rhetorical manipulation had a significant political effect, which was to neutralize tensions with the struggling French state and to naturalize rising American hegemony on the European continent. The photography in *Stars and Stripes* equated territorial and sexual conquest. The myth it produced was a fantasy of sexual control and virile achievement. It reassured the GIs of their manhood by giving them the girl at the end of the fighting day. That reassurance was nowhere more urgent than on the battlefields of Normandy. As historians have argued, manliness acted as a state of *becoming* rather than *being*: always in question, never quite attainable.[35] American men suffered severe challenges to manhood in the 1930s and early 1940s, including the Depression and mass unemployment.[36] Although the war provided the GIs with a chance to showcase their virility, the effort was by no means straightforward. Among other things, the soldiers were uneasy about the loyalties of their wives and girlfriends back home. Critic Susan Gubar has shown how Allied propaganda "spoke directly to servicemen's fears of their women's betrayal."[37] The GIs had a special name for a letter from a woman declaring her heart as gone astray—the dreaded "Dear John."[38]

How could sexual loyalty and the manliness it conferred be secured in these turbulent times? That question haunted the GI photo as it made its way into the mainstream of American mass culture, appearing in *Life* magazine in September of 1944. Here the photo changed meaning, becoming a symbol not of French gratitude but of male sexual infidelity abroad. Ralph Morse's version of the GI photo caused a sensation, and became "one of the most widely published of all war pictures" according to *Life*'s editors.[39](See figure 2.5.) Sensing a good story, the *Des Moines Register* sent out a reporter to get local women's reactions to the photo, which would supposedly evoke their envy and anger. The results were broadly reported, including a sequel in *Life* claiming "Some Iowa Girls Didn't Like That Kissing in Paris." (See figures 2.6 and 2.7.) The article featured seventeen Iowa women, only one of whom appeared to be a traditional mother holding her child. The other sixteen were photographed at their desks or jobs in smart suits, crisp blouses, and starched uniforms. The effect produced was a veritable icon of the 1940s American working woman—a testimony to the unprecedented number of young women, both single and married, who were earning a living outside the home.

Despite their cool professional demeanors, however, these girls were hot under the collar about that kissing in Paris. If the French women were smiling, the American women were frowning. "I want him to save his kisses for me," complained Mrs. Hubert Hanson.

Soldier and girl meet on the hood of a U. S. half-track in Chartres. Soldier kisses girl (*above*). Then he fumbles with package to offer girl a cigaret (*below*). U. S. soldiers seldom have any more than a fleeting acquaintance with French girls. Reason: units move too fast or towns are declared off limits.

FIGURE 2.5. "Soldier and Girl." From *Life*, 4 September 1944. Photo by Ralph Morse. © Getty Images.

"When I saw those pictures I was glad he isn't in the Army," confessed Mrs. William Evans. "I don't like what goes on on top of tanks," commented Wilma Hawkins.[40] Striking to the reader is the contrast between how these women look (savvy, cool, and professional) and what they have to say—old-fashioned jealous grousing. The women's

MRS. RONALD MASON, 24, and Ronald Jr., 10 months, live in Des Moines. She maintains that she would be too excited over Paris' freedom to care if her husband were kissed by a French girl. Her husband is stationed in South America.

MRS. JACK BENNETT, 28, drugstore clerk in Des Moines, has a husband who is somewhere in France but she is cool and confident. "That kissing stuff didn't bother me much. I don't think those French women have anything that I haven't got."

BERNADINE FINESTEAD, 20, of Granger, Iowa, is a bookkeeper. Bernadine has a boyfriend who is an artilleryman in France. She remarks wistfully: "I imagine that the boys enjoyed it. It was all right to kiss them if they wanted to be kissed."

BERNADINE GARTON, 24, Des Moines waitress, isn't married and doesn't have a boyfriend overseas. But she still has her doubts about those first days in Paris. "All this kissing and stuff doesn't mean anything maybe, but you never know."

VIRGINIA CHASE, 23, an OPA secretary, has a boyfriend in France, is willing to look at it from the French girls' point of view. But, "I can't believe that they kiss over there just like we shake hands . . . that was an awfully big handshake."

SONJA NANSEN, a 17-year-old counter girl, has a boyfriend who is in Australia, so she isn't the slightest bit interested in Paris. "But," she asks, "did you see where two shiploads of wives of American soldiers came back from Australia?"

FIGURE 2.6. From *Life*, 25 September 1944.

NORA SCHUCK, 25, is library clerk from West Point, Iowa. She has no boyfriend overseas. Remembering the legend of the old song about the mademoiselle, Nora says: "I didn't mind the fall of Paris so much as the capture of Armentières."

FLORENCE BROWN, 22, Des Moines reporter, does not admit to having a boyfriend in France. Florence sides with the boys: "Some of these women must be pretty jealous to begrudge those fellows a few kisses after all they have gone through."

ARLENE O'CONNELL, 19, who is an OPA stenographer, has no boyfriends she knows of overseas. Arlene takes boys' view of matter: "The French girls deserve a few kisses from American soldiers after seeing nothing but Nazis for four years."

MRS. WILLIAM EVANS, 19, is a stenographer from Winfield, Iowa. She is perfectly happy to have her husband "somewhere" with the Coast Guard where he will stay at sea. "When I saw those pictures I was glad he isn't in the Army," she says.

MRS. HUBERT HANSON, 19, who is clerical worker from Somers, Iowa, expects her husband to behave himself overseas and isn't worried about any of those French girls. "I want him to save his kisses for me," she says. "He is stationed in India."

MRS. JOHN W. WALLNER, 26, of Des Moines, an addressograph operator, disapproves of this French enthusiasm. Her husband is in Merchant Marine and, so far as she knows, is not in France. Anyway, she feels, "He'd better not be in Paris."

FIGURE 2.7. From *Life*, 25 September 1944.

protests, which were reprinted in several different editions of *Stars and Stripes*, reassured the GIs that they remained priority number one: no amount of independence could make these women indifferent to the adventures of their men abroad. In one *Stars and Stripes* article, a housewife from Chicago recognized her own husband kissing a Parisian woman at the Liberation. She registered her protest to readers by wielding a rolling pin.[41] (See figure 2.8.)

The same intimate gesture—a kiss—came to mean radically different things in France and on the American home front. The kisses

FIGURE 2.8. "The Buss That Backfired." From *Stars and Stripes*, 20 September 1944.

captured by *Stars and Stripes* photojournalism were expressions of joy and gratitude on the part of civilians who had waited four years for freedom. The military paper not only eroticized these kisses, but also remade them into symbols of Franco-American unity. In *Life* magazine, American sexual codes of conduct transformed these same gestures of intimacy again. Here the falsely eroticized kiss reinforced American stereotypes concerning French sexual decadence. The kiss also offended strict American moral codes concerning extramarital sex. As it was repackaged by *Life* magazine, the photo inverted GI fears concerning sexual faithfulness: now it was sweethearts and wives who had to be anxious. At the root of that inversion, of course, was the sexual double standard: male, but not female, sexual infidelity was encouraged. Nevertheless, the mainstream American version of the photo allayed GI fears about sexual infidelity and reinforced manly confidence.

We Had to Hide the Women

As the GI photo entered the American press, it promoted a troubling deceit. Despite the happy faces of civilians in the photo, they often experienced the American presence as a burden or a hazard. Although civilians greeted the Americans with joy on D-day, trouble was not far behind.[42] Carpet bombing and ground combat left thousands of civilians starving and homeless, with relief efforts slow in coming. A flourishing black market lined the pockets of the already well-supplied Americans, leading to resentments among the French.[43] Looting was a serious problem.[44] The liberators drank too much, made too much noise, drove their jeeps too fast, and engaged in street fighting and thievery. Jeep accidents were a common occurrence, resulting in the deaths of hundreds of civilians, including small children.[45] Last but not least, the GIs went after the local women. A common Norman joke went, "With the Germans, the men had to camouflage themselves, but when the Americans arrived, we had to hide the women."[46] By late summer 1944, scores of women throughout the Norman countryside had claimed to be sexually violated by American soldiers. Fear and panic were felt throughout the region.[47]

Such allegations subsided once the front moved east to Germany, except in Paris and other cities where American soldiers took leave. Parisian police records from 1944 to 1945 document soaring rates of theft and personal assault at the hands of American soldiers. French civilians were assaulted on the street, in bars or cafés, and even in their homes. The motive for violence was sometimes robbery, sometimes nothing at all—a sad side effect of alcohol abuse and the war's brutalization.[48] From one end of the city to another, the GIs wielded their guns and fists to get what they wanted, whether it was cognac, money, or women. The violence was overwhelmingly American, with little or no trouble from the Canadians and British allied forces.[49] By September 1945, the violent GI had become such a cliché that a notorious French criminal claimed to have been attacked by American soldiers as a ploy to cover his dealings with the Gestapo.[50]

Given the large number of soldiers in Paris at the time, including hundreds of deserters hoping to exploit the anonymity of France's biggest city, an increase in crime was not surprising.[51] More shocking was the dramatic rise of violent crimes in cities where the US Army had a significant presence, namely, Cherbourg, Le Havre, Reims, and Marseille. Le Havre, the busiest port for the Americans in terms of the movement of troops, is a case in point. Violence against the civilian population reached its peak in the summer of 1945. On 11 June, for example, the police blotter included six incidents of breaking and entering, two with assault and two with theft, as well as four other assaults and two other thefts—all at the hands of the American soldiers. In addition, the same day three Havrais sustained injuries when hit by American jeeps.[52]

The citizens of Le Havre were outraged. Complaining of "crimes of all kinds, committed day and night," one citizen wrote an angry letter to the mayor, Pierre Voisin: "Attacked, robbed, run over both on the street and in our houses, this is a regime of terror, imposed by bandits in uniform."[53] "Have we survived the bombardments of the liberating allies only to be killed by American soldiers?" asked another Havrais, Monsieur LeBras.[54] Workers at a local Tanning Company petitioned the mayor for greater security, claiming that their wives and children were being "terrorized by the nearly daily crimes taking place near their homes."[55] Another petition by 110 Havrais living near American camps demanded better lighting because of incidents of violence.[56] As late as October, Voisin was still complaining to the American commander concerning eight assaults on the night of 28 October. "The population is increasingly upset and worried by this state of affairs," Voisin informed the commander, Colonel Weed.[57] The American public was made aware of the situation in December. In *Life* magazine, journalist Joe Weston quoted a Havrais café owner, who had been recently assaulted by an American soldier: "We held our arms outstretched to take our liberators into our hearts. We accepted the gift of liberation as one great friend accepts a gift from another great friend. Today my hands have dropped to my sides and my heart has become of stone. We expected friends who would not make us ashamed of our defeat. Instead there came incomprehension, arrogance, incredibly bad manners, and the swagger of conquerors."[58]

These kind of complaints were not confined to Le Havre. A more general survey of the French population in October 1944 revealed its belief that the Americans were pretentious and scornful of the French.[59] In other cities where the American troops had a major presence, violence was a problem. In August 1944, drunk American GIs in Brittany destroyed bars and homes while demanding cognac.[60] The following summer Marseille authorities reported that women on the streets were frequently assaulted. Civilians suffered attacks even in their homes.[61] Similarly in the Moselle a father coming to the rescue of his daughter, herself the victim of a GI's "overly persistent attention," was seriously wounded.[62] Police reports were also filled with stories of American assault, theft, and rape. A gendarme in Rouen recounted how a drunk American officer forced himself into a civilian man's home and demanded to have sex with his wife. When refused, the officer fired several shots of his revolver.[63] In Cherbourg, soldiers forcibly entered houses in search of alcohol, shooting their guns and endangering lives in the process.[64]

The Marne, another northeastern area with a major troop presence, suffered from street fighting, theft, destruction of property, and sexual assault. The violence began in December and escalated throughout the summer and fall of 1945.[65] Towns in the area, such as Reims, Mourmelon, Suippes, and Châlons-sur-Marne, were overwhelmed by American soldiers who "want to do nothing but drink and cavort with women" about whom they have an "aggressive and improper attitude," according to local officials. Afraid to go out at night, the Rémois described the American presence as "a second Occupation which is becoming as unbearable as the last one."[66] They complained of "acts of banditry and terrorism" committed by the GIs.[67] By August, the US military and French police were deemed so ineffective in controlling violence in Troyes farther south that small armed bands of former Resistance members assembled in order to prevent "the bad manners and assaults which American soldiers dish out to our women and girls."[68] In Châlons-sur-Marne, according to one French official, Franco-American relations leaned toward "mute hostility" due to GI "boorishness, lack of education as well as their behavior, particularly towards women."[69]

Even this brief survey of Franco-American relations during the years 1944–46 belies the notion of a simple American "rescue" of the French. In garrison towns and large cities, American GIs made life miserable for French civilians by drinking too much, acting as a magnet for prostitutes, and visiting upon the innocent a violence they had learned in war. "Greeted with great transports of joy at the debarkation," remembered Resistance fighter Maurice Chevance-Bertin, "they nevertheless managed to sour their reputation by behaving as if they were in a conquered country."[70] Ironically Franco-American relations broke down precisely over the same issues that had been foregrounded by US military propaganda: sexual relations with female civilians. While many GIs developed sincere and respectful relationships with French women, many others pursued them as a prize for conquest. Neither GIs nor their loved ones back home read anything about the troubling violence occurring in France. Even after the war, the image ingrained in the American mind remained the happy rescue of a female nation.

Take a Look at Tomorrow

Finally, the unquestioned authority of the male in sexual romance legitimated a newly dominant American presence in "female" France. To assume that authority, American soldiers needed only to eliminate their sole competition: French men. For this reason, *Stars and Stripes* consistently denigrated French masculinity. A July 1944 article, for example, presented Free French sailors as weepy over separation from their girlfriends, whom, they feared, had forgotten them. (Unlike their American counterparts the sailors enjoyed no reassurances about sexual infidelity back home.) In reaction to the Normandy landings, "one of the least emotional soldiers on the ship could not stop his tears and went to his cabin and stayed there."[71] While the Americans were fighting, the French were weeping.

Neither did *Stars and Stripes* take seriously what was arguably the icon of French manhood at the Liberation: the French Forces of the Interior (Forces Françaises de l'Intérieur, or FFI) or resistance fighter. *Stars and Stripes* consistently portrayed them as buffoons. In one *Stars and Stripes* cartoon, for example, the manly GI image has been recast in order to insult French men.(See figure 2.9.) Two soldiers enjoy an orgy of kisses while a third dreads the embrace of an FFI member, whose girlish excitement and eager lips suggest femininity, possibly even homosexuality.[72] The French man has plenty of ammunition—sharp knives, guns, a cache of bullets—but none of this adds up to manliness. Instead we have a chubby man whose belt of bullets looks like a loopy necklace. The equation of a gun with one's manhood is explicit in this cartoon: a condom is wrapped around the driver's gun. (The GIs used condoms to keep their guns clean.) In contrast to the "erect" gun of the soldier in the back, the driver's gun falls limply to his side. The French man threatens even the manhood of the GI he accosts.

FIGURE 2.9. *Hubert* cartoon, by Sgt. Dick Wingert. From *Stars and Stripes*, 14 October 1944. Used with permission from Stars and Stripes. © 1944, 2012 Stars and Stripes.

Coverage of the Liberation also served to mock French men. In late July, *Stars and Stripes* featured a photo of seven Cherbourg women with their heads shaved, titled "They Loved Nazis." These women, explained the caption, "received their reward when loyal Cherbourg Frenchmen celebrated Bastille Day by rounding up a truckload of girls who favored the Germans with their charms. Their hair shorn, the shame-faced women were paraded through the streets."[73] The *tonte* ritual, as it was called, was repeated throughout France in thousands of newly liberated villages and cities. Young women who had engaged in sexual relationships with the Germans were brought into a public area where their clothes were ripped and their heads shaved.[74] Historians have seen the ritual as an attempt on the part of French men to restore domination over women's bodies, thus recuperating their masculinity and "the virility of the nation itself."[75] However, the *tonte*, which was widely covered by the American press, also maligned French men by drawing attention to the fact that the Germans had not only defeated their country but also snuck into their beds.

The *tonte* was a distinctly visual event. Its aim was to disgrace a woman by parading her through the streets so that her face would be known to anyone who cared to look out their window. The *tonte* was massively photographed by thousands of witnesses and bystanders.[76] Sometimes sold as postcards, these photos rationed shame and honor by humiliating the victim and exonerating those around her. At Chartres, the famous photojournalist Robert Capa shot a posed photograph of shaved women standing side by side with other civilians.(See figure 2.10.) In its setting and grouping, the photo is a macabre version of the nineteenth-century family portrait. The disgraced posed together with family and other unknown people, composing the collectivity that was liberated France.[77] Once again, as in French newspapers, the Liberation was billed as a family reunion, a metaphor that denied the politics tearing the nation apart. One of Capa's most famous photographs in the same series showed a shaved woman carrying a "German" baby, and suffering the scorn of the crowd. Appearing in *Life* in September 1944, it became, in the words of Fabrice Virgili, the "emblem" of the head shavings at the end of the war.[78] (See figure 2.11.)

Was it only coincidence, then, that Capa's photograph appeared in the same issue and article of *Life* that published Ralph Morse's GI photo? (See figure 2.5.) At first the two photographs appear to have nothing in common. Morris's GI kissing a French woman was a symbol of victory. Capa's *tondue*, on the other hand, served as a symbol of defeat. The first photograph celebrated intimacy across national boundaries; the second condemned it as shameful and humiliating.

But the fact that the two photographs made their American debut side by side also tempts comparative analysis. Both photos became iconic of the Liberation.[79] Both offered a significant deceit about the war, one that was accepted because it was politically expedient at the time. For the French, the widely distributed photographs of the *tontes* created the impression that collaborators could be easily identified and punished. The power of the image lay in its denial of the diffuse and profound nature of French collaboration. Likewise, the power of the GI photo lay in its denial of the complexities of the American military presence. Furthermore, both images figured the French na-

FIGURE 2.10. Eure-et-Loir, Chartres, 18 August 1944. © Robert Capa/Magnum Photos.

FIGURE 2.11. Chartres, 18 August 1944. © Robert Capa/Magnum Photos.

tion as a woman, and used sexual intimacy as a measure of national status. For *Life* readers, French women became either rescued princesses or shamed tarts. What did *that* say about the French? Unlike those savvy but faithful American girls, these women were symbols of what could go wrong when their men were away. Their husbands and boyfriends were incapable of either protecting them or keeping them under control. Worse still, French men were being cuckolded again, this time by the Americans only one page of *Life* away.

Neither did *Stars and Stripes* overlook such an opportunity to denigrate French masculinity. In a Bill Mauldin cartoon, a GI takes a photo of the *tonte* scene, then declares he wants to "send this home an' scare my gal outta foolin' around wit' garrison sojers." (See figure 2.12.) By using his camera, the soldier appropriates the French attempt to prevent sexual infidelity. (Mauldin was once again playing on GI fears

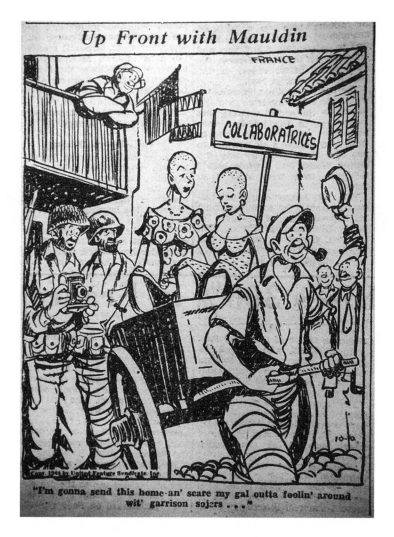

FIGURE 2.12. Bill Mauldin cartoon. "I'm gonna send this home an' scare my gal outta foolin' around wit' garrison sojers." From *Stars and Stripes*, 24 October 1944.

concerning their gals back home.) But a closer look at the cartoon reveals that the virilizing work of the *tonte* has not been accomplished. The French man pulling the cart, as well as the other French bystanders, are ineffectual, insipid figures. The only "manly man" here is the GI in the rear smoking a cigarette. Furthermore, with their low-cut dresses, protruding breasts, and flirtatious, even lewd postures, the

French women don't appear to be feeling adequately humiliated. The French men remain cuckolds unable to control their women, and by extension, their own nation.

Stars and Stripes rationed manliness to American not French men. In doing so, it rationalized a new role for the United States—as the protector of a nation without men. "This picture is a crystal ball," reads the caption of one photo editorial,

> Look into it and you see a vision of tomorrow. You see the world coming to America for help and leadership. The worried, pleading, hopeful look in this old man's eyes will be in the eyes of the world. The question on his lips will be on the world's lips. "What shall we do?" he asks. "Where can I get food? Where can I get work? How can I pull my family together . . . ?" These are the big questions. We can't duck them. We don't know what this Civil Affairs officer is telling the old man. Neither do we know what America will tell the world. All we know is this! That America is you and me and the folks back home. That the world trusts us, respects us and is looking to us for the signals. That, like it or not, you and I and the folks back home must give the world its cue.[80] [See figure 2.13.]

Here an "old man" symbolizes both the past and the future. The once mighty but now prostrated European patriarch turns to America for guidance in a brave new world. Old Europe has been reduced to an elderly man pleading for survival. The American assumption of power is banalized at every turn. The invasion is once again cast in terms of a rescue. The American nation is described as "the folks back home." The GI assumes the mantle of power only reluctantly. He is motivated not by power but by charity. Whether he "likes it or not," he is the only manly man left and so must identify as a ruler.

We have seen how American military photographs, cartoons, and newspapers contributed to a myth concerning the manly GI. Such a myth demonstrates just how central gender norms were to how the Americans defined their mission, their nation, and their ally France. As well as capturing the joyful moment of liberation, the manly GI image engaged the soldiers' sexual fantasies and eroticized American

Take a Look at Tomorrow

THIS picture is a crystal ball. Look into it and you see a vision of to-morrow.

* * *

You see the world coming to America for help and leadership. The worried, pleading, hopeful look in this old man's eyes will be in the eyes of the world. The questions on his lips will be on the world's lips.

* * *

"What shall we do?" he asks. "Where can I get food? Where can I get work? How can I pull my family together? What should I do to put our life in order?"

* * *

These are big questions. We can't duck them. We don't know what this Civil Affairs officer is telling the old man. Neither do we know what America will tell the world.

* * *

All we know is this! That America is you and me and the folks back home. ' That the world trusts us, respects us and is looking to us for the signals. That, like it or not, you and I and the folks back home must give the world its cue.

* * *

The future of the world depends on whether you and I and the folks back home have the wisdom, sincerity and size to do the job right.

* * *

If we haven't, well—a soldier's job is never done.

FIGURE 2.13. "Take a Look at Tomorrow." From *Stars and Stripes*, 9 September 1944.

war aims. It oversimplified and depoliticized the Franco-American re-lationship by defining the landings as an opportunity for romance. For "the folks back home," the myth erased from view the violent crimes that the GIs imposed upon French civilians. Finally, for the US military, it legitimated a new dominance in France by defining its presence there in familiar heterosexual terms. As *Stars and Stripes* would have it, French men had failed their manly role, which was to rescue and protect their women. Instead the GIs had to step up to do it. Only the Americans, then, were fit to run the nation. The soldiers and the folks back home would have to give the world its cue.

3

Masters in Their House

THE US MILITARY PRESS narrated the Liberation as romance by photographing American soldiers kissed by young French women, then mythologizing such embraces as *the* central GI experience. Shots of GIs as "rescuers" of a female nation domesticated the American military mission in France. In addition, the unquestioned authority of the male in heterosexual relations helped to legitimate American governance over French civilians. But where were the husbands and boyfriends of those women freed by the GIs? In fact many of these men were absent—living in German labor and prison camps, fighting with the Allies, or in hiding with the Resistance. Nevertheless, even from a distance, how did French men respond to the American "rescue" of their country?

"Badly" would be the answer given by historians, who claim French men suffered a "crisis of masculinity" during the Second World War. The 1940 defeat and the German occupation, they maintain, undermined masculine authority.[1] Equally traumatic was forced exile to German camps, where roughly two million men passed the war years battling famine and exhaustion.[2] While these experiences were no doubt trying, they cannot be adequately understood within a generalized notion of masculinity in "crisis." The trope of "gender crisis," overworked to the point of semantic collapse, imparts little meaning here beyond our commonsense intuition that military defeat is "hard" on men.

Rather than lean too heavily on the rhetoric of crisis, then, let us specify which norms of manhood were violated during the war years—what I will call *gender damage*. What *exactly* did French men suffer in having to cede male prerogatives first to the Germans and then to the Americans? The defeat of 1940 meant the failure of a duty and the loss of a privilege. In his own mind, the French man had been unable to fulfill his task as *chef de famille*, which was to protect home and family.[3] Enshrined in the Napoleonic Code, the French republican *chef de famille* acted on behalf of others who supposedly could not act for themselves. He exercised his civic rights on behalf of the women and children for whom he was materially responsible.[4] (French women did not vote until 1944.) Precisely this role as protector, French men believed, they had ceded when they could not defend their families. Furthermore, as a corollary to this failure, one that sprang from its shame, French men also feared they had lost sexual possession over their women.

Novels written by army veterans and ex-prisoners churned with humiliation and anger concerning the German assault on the French home. Images of homelessness—the pillaged house, the abandoned mattress, the vagabond refugee—abound in this literature.[5] The invaded home lies at the center of the occupation's most popular novel, Vercors's *Le Silence de la mer*. Its action takes place entirely within a home quartered by a German officer, a billeting meant to symbolize the occupation itself.[6] Of all shames visited upon the young French soldier in defeat, none was more painful than his failure to safeguard the home, equated with the nation itself.[7] The soldier Rabaud in André Chamson's *Le Dernier Village* (1946), for example, understood "the disaster in its full meaning" only when he recalled a young woman in a village his unit was forced to leave to the Germans. Although she claimed not to be afraid, her eyes told Rabaud another story. "The worst humiliation for a soldier," he lamented, "is to abandon your country's women to the whims of the conquerors." In recalling the incident, he felt "an animal jealousy of savage proportions."[8] That animal rage lasted five long years, as humiliation, anger, and fear ate away at the male soul. "What do we do? Are we then no longer men? What good are we?!" ask the soldiers in Jacques Debû-Bridel's *Déroute*.[9] Disgrace in defeat, loss of honor, impotence in the face of the enemy, humiliation concerning women's sexual infidelity—these were the makings of wartime gender damage.

Long after the signing of the armistice in June 1940, the battle between French and German men continued on another front line—the French female body. For the French as well as for the Americans, the war had been sexualized in both aim and effect. In fascist and antifascist propaganda alike, the "enemy" became he who would ravage women as booty. In this literature, the purpose of war was to prevent sexual violence against women. Such propaganda—another expression of the complex ways in which modern nations are gendered—had its roots in the First World War.[10] Hoping to boost military recruitment in 1915, Allied governments used the alleged German rapes of Belgian women to create an irrefutable moral imperative for war.[11] In this way, sex as a trophy of conquest became part of twentieth-century industrialized warfare.[12] That notion operated most famously in April 1945 when victorious Russian soldiers engaged in widespread rape in Berlin, the purpose of which was, at least in part, to humiliate German men.

But throughout the war on both fronts, command of geographical territory signaled command of sexual territory. When soldier Jean Dutourd in *Les Taxis de la Marne* sees his first German in Brittany, he felt "a crazy anger, the despair of a man who learns that the woman he loved has given herself to another."[13] At the core of such despair lay the recognition that the victors were not only powerful but also attractive. Veteran novels abound with French women who run after German and Austrian soldiers.[14] Such promiscuities were not lost on men imprisoned in Germany. According to Fabrice Virgili, a "malaise" settled over the entire German camp system due to anxiety concerning sexual betrayal on the part of wives and girlfriends back home. They were right to worry. Infidelity became so common that the prisoners were dubbed "the army of cuckolds."[15]

The links between sexual and geographical conquest lay at the heart of male anguish. They were perhaps most evident in the *tonte*

ritual at the Liberation, in which young French men publically humiliated women who had supposedly had sexual dealings with the
Germans. As we have seen, the *tonte* was an attempt to regain virility
by reestablishing dominion over women's bodies; it also complicated
whatever sexual relations might develop between these women and
the GIs.[16] Its effect, then, was to reappropriate women's bodies from
both German and American soldiers. Like land, a woman's sex was
territory to be recovered. In this way, sexual possession of the female
body became inextricable from national sovereignty. This larger political meaning of the *tonte* helps make sense of its violence. "What
do you give a shit if I have declared my ass an open city?" asked one
woman to an FFI member about to shave her head.[17] He might have
answered that, in fact, he cared a great deal. In his mind an open city
and an open set of legs amounted to the same thing.

In the first weeks after the Liberation there were many losses to
mourn. France had declined in both military prestige and international status. The nation's transportation, communication, and in-
dustrial networks had all been badly damaged. Rationing was strict
and would continue for months. Grief over such harsh realities took
place not in a vacuum but, by an accident of history, at the moment
the Americans arrived to "rescue" the French people. Male mourning over lost honor and power coincided with contact with American
soldiers.

With their disdain toward Gallic manhood, the GIs compounded
French grief. Resistors, prisoners of war in German camps, slave
laborers, soldiers fighting with the allies, civilians in large garrison
towns—all these men felt the slap of GI condescension. Contempt
surfaced only days after the invasion. "From the kick-off," a Civil
Affairs officer reported on his unit, we "made the French feel they
were masters in their own house."[18] Such pretensions of the French
as "masters" suggested, of course, the opposite. Like the Germans,
the GIs enforced the unstated but unrelenting rules of manhood: if
the French could not protect their houses and families, they did not
deserve to be masters of their homes. Still another American officer
wrote his wife from Normandy that he was "taking advantage of ev-

ery French house I can since the French had neither the wits nor the courage to take care of their own country."[19]

For French men, such contempt swelled the sting of defeat, making its pain rise higher. But no hurt was greater than GI advances on local women. As it had for the Germans, the victory bestowed upon Americans certain privileges. "Just a few weeks ago," Robert Easton wrote his wife from Normandy, "the Germans were using these roads, buildings, fields, chairs, tables, toilets, women, and now we are."[20] In describing this transfer, Easton made no attempt to separate "women" from other kinds of property now under American control. Women also counted among the spoils of war. In journals, memoirs, and novels, French veterans of the army and Resistance, as well as ex-prisoners of German camps, expressed anger at American encroachment on their sexual prerogatives. In such texts, the erotic sounded in the territorial register. Trauma about loss of sexual domination could not easily be separated from fears concerning loss of national prestige. GI advances on French women represented not only an encroachment on the *chef de famille*, but also a violation of national sovereignty.

The Trauma of Liberation

On the eve of the liberation of Paris, one journalist anticipated the arrival of the Americans in this way: "Just outside our doors is the free world! We are going to know penicillin, the film Gone with the Wind, the latest Huxley. It is an intoxicating moment."[21] The observation suggests just how shut off from news French people were until 1944. Censorship or imprisonment kept them ignorant throughout the war, with only the radio—difficult to find and dangerous to own—as a voice from beyond German confinement. As a result of this isolation, when the Americans arrived, the French had not yet absorbed the wider implications of their defeat. "It must be remembered," reported US Army Intelligence (OSS) to Allied military headquarters in October 1944, "that ordinary Frenchmen are still almost completely ignorant of . . . the extent to which many people outside France had written France off—as a great power."[22] Through contacts with the GIs, French men began to realize that their nation was no longer held in the same esteem. In this sense, the French "crisis of masculinity" was much more than a domestic matter, as historians have assumed. To be properly understood, male gender damage must be placed within an international context, namely, the war's impact on French global status and the heavy presence of American soldiers on French soil.

In 1944, French men were forced to rethink their position in the world. According to Andrew Knapp, they "suddenly had to learn to live in the second rank in a world dominated by the new superpowers."[23] While in the early twentieth century, the French Army had been widely respected, its rapid defeat in 1940 led American political leaders to conclude that France was no longer a major power.[24] This supposed fall from grace was belied by the fact that France gained many fruits of victory in 1945, among them, a permanent seat on the United Nations Security Council and an occupation zone in Germany. In addition, although the French Empire emerged from the war greatly weakened, it was more or less intact. Nevertheless, in the last months of the war, France was not represented at key diplomatic meetings at Dumbarton Oaks and Yalta. The consensus of American politicians and diplomats, solidified by President Roosevelt's personal aversion to Charles de Gaulle, was that France should no longer be included among the top-ranking powers. The US government blamed the 1940 defeat not only on military failure but also internal weakness, including a breakdown of the nation's moral fiber in the face of economic depression and fascism. Roosevelt compared the country to a child "unable to fend for itself," and dependent on the guardianship of the Allies.[25]

For the French, geopolitical decline was a bitter pill to swallow. As the historian Crane Brinton unsympathetically put it in December 1943: "all kinds of statistics show that France is, in fact, no longer a first-rate power. These Frenchmen simply cannot admit that fact. For them, France has *got* to be *la grande nation*."[26] Some months later, when Brinton was in contact with "the little people" in northern France, he changed his mind somewhat, noting that there was "no talk of reestablishing *la grandeur de la France.*" Nevertheless, he continued, "these people are not wops, they are proud, they show here and there signs of inferiority complex, and they are certainly deeply wounded by their defeat."[27]

French sources confirm Brinton's views. Some French people were indeed in denial, and were shocked not to be invited to Dumbarton Oaks. One prominent diplomat responded to the affront by smarting at the "propensity of some to 'declassify' France as a great power and demote her to the ranks of a second-rate nation."[28] "The notion that France could be held apart from Allied discussions concerning the future of Germany—it didn't even cross our minds," fumed another.[29] Diplomatic exclusions brought into focus a brave new world. "Is this then the humiliation of the defeat," asked a Norman paper, "which is going to live on in our international standing?"[30] "France has been kept from the victory, she has lost her glory, even her right to glory, her hope in glory," wrote journalist Louis Martin Chauffier.[31] Widespread "bitterness" concerning France's "weakened" position was reported throughout the northern regions.[32] In the summer of 1944 when Charles de Gaulle's government was not yet formally recognized, many civilians feared that the United States had come to colonize rather than liberate their country.[33] Assuaging national pride became de Gaulle's specialty. The new leader was quickly burdened with French hopes to raise their heads high among the world's nations.[34] As one Norman police chief put it, "only General de Gaulle can give to France the status she merits among the great powers."[35] "Too many calumnious caricatures, too many odious images have been made of our country," editorialized a Paris paper. "Because of this no Frenchman who has heard the simple, strong and honest words of the President of the provisional government of the Republic has not felt a profound emotion."[36]

The Liberation was a humiliating moment for the French. Deliverance brought freedom but also a coming to terms with unpleasant realities. Because of this fact, even the simplest of contacts with

Americans was complicated by the trauma of liberation. As the *chef de famille* who had enjoyed exclusive civic rights on behalf of women and children, the French man felt the shock of degradation most painfully. The nation, after all, had been his to lose. "However much they want to make us doubt ourselves," argued a Resistance paper, "we know that we are a major nation. And a major nation takes its own destiny into its hands, out of pride as well as shame."[37] A crushing double grief—for manhood and for the *grandeur* of France—emerges in this editor's defensive tone. The sting of American contempt would only exacerbate the problem.

Cowards and Hooligans

Anthony Harlinski remembers discovering a new sport as he landed in Marseille with the Thirty-Sixth Division. He and his buddies would throw packs of cigarettes to the crowd and watch the men wrestle with each other over them. "That fighting among men over handouts didn't give a good first impression of Frenchmen."[38] But Harlinski didn't need cigarettes to decide what he thought of the Gallic male. Like countless other GIs, he arrived with ready preconceptions. *Le français* was little, volatile, and oversexed. In short, he was a girl. If France was a "feminine" nation, as *Stars and Stripes* would have the GIs believe, it was not just because of the women. "All the manly French men must be prisoners in Germany," wrote Lt. Robert Easton to his wife, "because I see none or almost none." Nine months later, he had not changed his mind: "They are effeminate, wordy, nervous, excitable with a large helping of the gigolo and I cannot greatly like them."[39] Because the GIs considered the French to be girlish, they did not take them seriously. In April 1945, a private wrote his parents that even though the French were "good guys," they all seemed crazy. Every single one, he wrote, was "an individual scream."[40] Like women again, French men were considered hopeless with machinery. Much fun was made of their bungling when merging train cars; they were also considered a danger behind the wheel.[41] "Some of you may not

"Some of you may not come back. A French convoy has been reported on the road."

FIGURE 3.1. Bill Mauldin cartoon. "Some you may not come back. A French convoy has been reported on the road." From *Stars and Stripes*, 14 September 1944. Used with permission from Stars and Stripes. © 1944, 2012 Stars and Stripes.

come back," warned a commander to his troops in a Bill Mauldin cartoon. "A French convoy has been reported on the road."[42] (See figure 3.1.)

To understand the mercilessness of GI condescension here, we have to keep in mind that manliness was at a premium in the army at the same time that it was severely threatened. On the one hand, manliness was considered the elixir necessary to withstand both the material and psychic challenges of battle. On the other, it faced its supreme challenge in the war's chaos and death. In other words, the GIs were just enough threatened in their own manhood to withhold sympathy for anyone who had, in their opinion, failed the fire. And those who had failed were French soldiers. Because military prowess and national status were mutually determinate, a second-rate nation was a nation of second-rate fighters and therefore second-rate men.[43]

Americans widely disrespected the French Army, partly because of its protracted struggles in the First World War, but mostly due to its appalling performance in 1940. The US Army *Pocket Guide to France* tried to disabuse GIs of their notion "that France was a pushover because she fell after six week's Blitzkrieg." The French Army, they were reminded, held out against the Germans four long years in the First World War.[44] Nevertheless the Maginot Line became the object of many a GI snicker. "While we respected the British soldier, we didn't respect the *poilu*," remembered Robert Peters. "Hadn't they abandoned their vaunted Maginot line?"[45] The French, the GIs felt, had been comically unaware of how Hitler had transformed the execution of war.[46] Moreover, the GIs were resentful that the task of defending the country had fallen to them. Infantryman Leroy Stewart begrudged the fact that the French "felt like it was our duty to do the fighting for them."[47] When Jack Sacco found out that Leclerc's troops would be the first to enter Paris, he was indignant: "We felt as if the French army, through its own ineffectiveness, had played a major role in allowing the Nazis to take over France in the first place. Furthermore, as we were fighting through *their* country to liberate *their* people, *their* military was either getting in our way or nowhere to be seen."[48]

Fighting with the French Army didn't change anyone's mind. In North Africa, Americans were shocked by the static defensive strategies of the Free French.[49] Their pay was ludicrous, even worse than the British.[50] And it did not help that they were several inches smaller than the GIs. Much joking was made of the fact that fully a quarter of American deliveries for French Army uniforms had to be returned because they were too big.[51] In France, the GIs often fought side by side with the French Army. Military historians estimate that US-supplied French divisions fighting in Normandy reduced American combat needs by eight to ten divisions. Nevertheless the GIs scorned these troops as expensive handouts pandering to French pride.[52] In his diary, officer John Toole wrote patronizingly that "goodhearted Uncle Sam arranges it so that French units are always the first to enter their big cities like Paris and Marseille and now Strasbourg."[53] The GIs also complained that French soldiers looted German corpses and drank too much wine.[54] Gossip among SHAEF (Supreme Headquarters Allied Expeditionary Forces) commanders damned the incompetence of the Second French Armed Division, which, according to aide Chester Hansen, "is supposed to have gone to pot on the way in to Paris, arriving there half drunk with the wines passed to them on the roadside by the well-meaning natives. Speculation has it they will go into the west side of Paris and never emerge from the east."[55]

GI reviews of the Resistance were more positive. Unified under the aegis of the FFI, Resistance groups fought with Allied forces from the first minutes of the invasion. For the GIs, the resistance fighters were the last French men standing.[56] According to one combat surgeon, Resistance members had "never surrendered and never compromised; some of them died under torture rather than betray comrades." In short, they "set an example of bravery and loyalty."[57] American infantryman described them as "very effective," "masters of infiltration," "tough and determined," and "merciless. Most had lost family members."[58] To Civil Affairs officer John J. Maginnis, they at first appeared "nondescript" and "unmilitary looking" with their odd assemblages of clothing and weapons. However, Maginnis soon noticed their "tough resolute faces" and realized they had "fought the enemy from the inside as best they could during the past many months."[59] In the south, the "maquis" won the full respect of the commanders who praised their bravery, enthusiasm, and discipline as well as their knowledge of the enemy and the terrain.[60] The GIs traded weapons with these men, exchanging their guns for prized German souvenirs.[61] These were men the Americans recognized as men.

Nevertheless American historical memory of the Resistance is decidedly mixed. On the one hand, General Eisenhower estimated the strength of the FFI in Normandy to be the equal to a full fifteen divisions.[62] On the other, its contribution is rarely acknowledged in American military accounts. No doubt that oversight results, at least in part, from an American desire to grab all the glory. But *résistants* also did not escape the GI stereotype of the volatile French male. For one thing, they were considered foolhardy in their approach to fighting. "Hard for them to take an order from us," remembered John Bistrica. "There were times when they stuck their neck out and got in trouble because they wouldn't listen to us."[63] They were "free spirits" and didn't take discipline too well," agreed another infantryman.[64] GI memoirs are filled with images of the FFI "running around, frantic and excited."[65] Civil Affairs condemned the FFI as "young hooligans" and "irresponsible elements" posing the threat of "rowdyism."[66] "At present they are more or less disciplined," reported one Civil Affairs officer, "but one only has to see them careening about on the front mudguards of their cars with rifles between their knees to realize that with the removal of the enemy, their energies will have to be directed and controlled before the discipline disappears."[67]

Many SHAEF officers wanted to disarm the FFI altogether.[68] A nervous man became a dangerous one when he had a gun, as did many *résistants* during the summer of 1944. SHAEF headquarters equated the "excitability" of the FFI with a threat to public safety. To military aide Chester Hansen, the *résistants* looked "savage with their guns."[69] As for the French, such concerns bewildered them. When a Breton resistant asked the GIs for a jeep to transport a captured German, he was warned not to kill the prisoner on the way. "Where did the Yankees hear that we execute our prisoners?" wondered the resistant. "I don't know one case of this happening." Perhaps, he surmised, the Germans had dirtied the reputation of the Resistance. But why were the Americans listening to the Germans? "In any case," he lamented, "the atmosphere is far from friendly."[70] Another problem was that the Resistance was believed to be run by communists. In September army intelligence spread rumors that a full-scale communist revolution was about to occur in Paris, fueled by "the more violent and disreputable elements of the FFI."[71] The French political situation also helps to explain American censure of the FFI. In the days after liberation,

French towns were convulsed by violence against collaborators. The FFI played a leading role in this *épuration*, purging governments of Nazi sympathizers and replacing them with its own people. Vicious as well as violent, these purges took place on the streets where they were seen by countless GIs.[72] During the occupation, collaborators had engaged in a full range of dirty dealing, from getting fat at others' expense to betraying resisters. By 1944, then, some scores needed to be settled.[73] At the same time, these acts of revenge were ugly to watch. Not only was collaboration shameful, but its vengeance released hideous amounts of pent-up rage.

However justified *épuration* was from the French perspective, its fury fed American stereotypes of Gallic volatility. As one GI put it, "they don't screw around with lawyers, these guys."[74] In the American view, the *épuration* transformed courageous FFI fighters into crazy hoodlums. By mid-August, Civil Affairs was reporting that "bands" of the FFI were "roaming the countryside," taking "threatening attitudes towards civilians."[75] Chester Hansen described them as "still bouncing about the streets armed with their rifles, sten guns and carrying grenades that made them look dangerous. Great problem in disarming and controlling them for they are excitable and volatile in their present condition, intoxicated with the excitement of the situation."[76] Similarly after the liberation of Paris, members of the FFI were described as armed "gangs" engaged in looting, intimidating and even torturing civilians suspected of collaboration."[77]

Such disapproval in no way expressed sympathy for collaborators.[78] In the American view, friendship with the Germans had not only been cowardly, but worse still, it had not worked. The Germans still brutalized the nation, leaving it for dead.[79] At the same time, however, the GIs also considered some forms of violence, in particular those aimed at female collaborators, to be unjustified. The GIs frequently witnessed "hair-lined streets." The *tonte* rituals, in which the FFI publicly humiliated women, were deemed "harsh," "indecent and vicious," "degrading," and "a form of lynching."[80] Lawrence Cane wrote his wife that the *tontes* reminded him of the Zola scene in *Germinal* when the mining women castrate the company storekeeper. "Zola knew his people," Cane wrote with no trace of irony.[81] Capt. Dale Helm was shocked to see people in Le Mans roaring with laughter at a woman on the street with no clothes and her hair shaved. With approval he noted that his chaplain had wrapped her in a blanket and taken her away by jeep.[82]

The *tonte* violated another unspoken but unbending rule of manhood: do women no harm. Dragging a woman out in public, stripping her clothes, beating and shaming her—these acts violated the tenet that women—all women—deserved male protection. Samuel Marshall remembers one sergeant who, upon witnessing a *tonte*, "was over there in a bound, kicking the hell out of the three men and shouting at the top of his voice, 'Leave her alone, goddamn you, you're all collaborationists!'"[83] Despite strict orders not to get involved, scores of GIs came to the aid of these women.[84] Their anger sprang not only from some unstated code of chivalry but also cynicism concerning the honesty of the FFI. "They were showing much bravado," Donald Lyddon remembered thinking as he witnessed a *tonte*. "We wondered how brave they had been one week previously."[85] Finally the *tonte* was just plain embarrassing. It suggested that French men could not control their women sexually except through acts of violence. It was an act of desperation as well as revenge.

The Resistance spoiled its reputation with the American army by committing acts of violence against collaborators. The GIs witnessed not one, but two, FFIs in action in 1944. One fought the enemy courageously; the other humiliated women in town centers. The GI logic went something like this: these men had failed to protect their homes and families; they had lost honor and mastery of their house. Now they were trying to regain it by taking out their frustrations on women. The Americans did not bother to explore the reasons for French military failure; nor did they consider the possibility that they might not have done better in similar circumstances. GI manliness was too fragile for such empathetic gestures. How much easier, then, to dismiss the French as failed men and frustrated cuckolds. As for the FFI, its members had only one consolation: the Americans had absolutely no idea what they had been through. Yves Cazaux got it right when he wrote in his secret journal: "They do not appreciate in the least the extent of moral and material anguish our population has endured."[86] American derision of French men may have shored up GI manliness, but it also revealed their naïveté.

They Were Men

Despite American contempt for French men, members of the FFI expressed confidence in their manhood, particularly in hindsight. "THEY WERE MEN," wrote C. L. Flavian in his memoir of the same title, "in the most noble and virile sense of that term, they were men in their courage and in their scorn for those not like them."[87] As Flavian noted here, *résistants* found their manhood through disdain for others, and "those not like them" certainly included the GIs.

Deriding American bravery on the battlefield had the desired effect of restoring French manliness. "The Americans were not very courageous, they were afraid," remembered one *résistant* of the battle at Metz. "As soon as they heard there was shooting, they retreated and it was we who took the first line."[88] A Finistère *résistant* agreed that the Americans would attack with their tanks, then retreat, leaving the FFI to hold the line.[89] FFI memory dwells on the key intelligence it passed on to the GIs as well as crucial delays in German troop and supply movement effected by their acts of sabotage.[90] Former *résistants* frequently narrated the liberation of towns and villages as an FFI affair with minor support from the Americans.[91] When the FFI were ostracized from the battle, it was usually, in their opinion, because the Germans considered the Americans to be the less-feared enemy.[92] Still other resistance fighters expressed frustration that the Americans consistently allowed the Germans to fall back and regroup rather than encircling them, attacking, and claiming a decisive victory, as the FFI would have done.[93]

Besides the obvious advantages of claiming military superiority, *résistants* had other reasons to be scornful of the Americans. First, dramatic differences in training separated the two groups and led them to quarrel over strategy and command when they fought together. Verbal and even physical confrontation over such issues was not unusual.[94] The FFI was accustomed to fighting the enemy in spontaneous, guerilla attacks. By contrast, the GIs preferred to use artillery, which took time to move and focus on targets. For this reason, as we have seen, the GIs viewed the FFI as rash and foolhardy, and *résistants* looked down on American military tactics as too slow. Resistors also resented American commanders who did not understand or respect their tactics, particularly considering their sometimes intimate knowledge of the terrain.[95]

Second, there were stark contrasts in supplies and resources. While many *résistants* lived hand to mouth in the woods, the GIs were well armed and well supplied, sometimes obscenely so. Asked what the FFI thought of the GIs, infantryman Raymond Huntoon replied, "I believe they thought we were spoiled brats with big mouths. We had to prove we were worthy."[96] Huntoon was right. As one *résistant* put it, "they had everything and we had nothing."[97] When chocolates or cigarettes were distributed to the GIs, the FFI would look on with resentment, their mouths watering.[98] For one *résistant*, meeting the GIs was an "encounter between modern soldiers who lacked for nothing and our own sundry group, armed with this and that and dressed in every color of the rainbow."[99] The contrasts were too much to bear for some FFI, who used their well-honed survival skills to sneak off with quantities of American food, cigarettes, and gasoline. They justified such thefts by claiming that the GIs were spineless and did not care. But of course they did, and the FFI soon became known in some quarters as scoundrels and thieves.

The starkest contrast between the two groups lay in the stakes of the battle. The war was much more immediate to the *résistants*. They had land to recapture, shame to live down, and manhood to recover. As a result, they were sensitive about who exactly *was* liberating France. In Jean-Louis Curtis's *Les Forêts de la nuit* (1947), an English teacher prepares for the liberation of his small town by proposing a phrase of greeting for the GIs. At first he comes up with "welcome to our American saviors!" But that greeting, he decides, "would have been an insult to Captain Figeac and the *maquis* [i.e., the French Army and the Resistance]." Instead, then, he settles on the phrase "welcome to our American friends!"[100] The teacher's second thoughts here suggest that some French people had a thin skin about the idea of an American "savior." French soldiers also found it insulting when they were mistaken for Americans, particularly when the civilians were disappointed to realize they had made a mistake, no doubt because of the chocolate and cigarettes doled out by the GIs.[101]

These sensitivities on the part of *résistants* no doubt sprang from unacknowledged (or acknowledged) shame concerning defeat and wartime collaboration. Some months before he died, the *résistant* Claude Monod praised "the moral significance of the FFI" as "the true representation of the rising up [*levée en masse*] of the French people against the invader." In contrast to the army of 1940, he argued, the FFI made do with nothing and demonstrated enormous discipline. Who would not be impressed, he asked, by "the confidence, the enthusiasm, the warrior spirit of these men?"[102] Monod's praise was as sincere as it was strained: he was not only praising the French warrior, but summoning faith in him. In escaping the legacy of defeat, neither Monod nor any other *résistant* could rely on the help of the Americans. Every day the GIs witnessed death all around them; every day they had to reconquer their own fears. In a very real sense, there was just not enough manhood to go around. The struggle to master manhood preoccupied both the GIs and the FFI. Neither group could afford to be generous. Belittling the manhood of the other had the tonic effect of confirming one's own. That trick of self-affirmation became indispensible for both parties, literally giving them the courage to continue. But as a result, they never came to trust each other.

I Am Going to Become a Man Again

For different reasons, the GIs also failed to appreciate the anguish felt by male political prisoners and forced laborers.[103] As the US military entered Germany during the winter of 1945, it began to liberate scores of camps where French men (along with people from other nations) had survived the war as *deportés* and forced workers. Unlike the chivalric "rescue" of French women immortalized in the GI photo, the freeing of men in Germany went unrecorded by the American military and mainstream press. No doubt this is because, in contrast to the events in Paris, this liberation offered no erotic spectacle.

On the contrary, it was a story of broken manhood. For the prisoners, liberation was a climactic event about which they had fantasized for years as they endured hunger, cold, squalor, and hard labor at the hands of the Nazis. Held captive at Buchenwald for nineteen months, Marcel Conversy thought about liberation in this way: "I am going to become a man again. It was as if I was leaving a tomb."[104] "We had been prisoners for five years," remembered one detainee. "Now the liberators had arrived . . . we rushed and crushed the American soldiers, yelling and throwing ourselves on them. We shouted, we laughed, we shook, we cried."[105] "I could not be sure whether my dream was coming true or whether I was still dreaming," remembered Aimé Bonifas. "When we long await and earnestly yearn for the fulfillment of a fantasy, we dare not believe that our desire is being realized."[106]

But the liberators, it turned out, were largely unsympathetic. An imprisoned French spy for the British intelligence service, Jacques Bureau was shaken by how very few GIs "seem moved by having liberated us."[107] A French worker in Bavaria tried to embrace his rescuer by speaking English and touching him on the shoulder. The GI pushed him away, his face "closed."[108] André Nidub also recalls the "extremely cold" greeting he received from the GIs when he arrived in the American zone.[109] The Americans were in a hurry, unwilling to take a moment to celebrate. André Castex confessed to having his pride wounded on this score, and he resolved not to forgive the Americans for having "spoiled the much-awaited moment of the Liberation."[110] Still another detainee remembers the "shocking" conditions in which he was liberated, that is, "with pistols and machine guns threatening us in the face. And we had awaited them as friends."[111] In his journal

Edouard Daladier described his first American as having "a crude face and rude manners."[112]

In many cases the Americans treated the detainees no differently than the Germans who one hour earlier had made their life a living hell.[113] "Scoundrels or victims—they put them on equal ground so that we could wash out the dirty laundry between us," noted one prisoner.[114] When the GIs liberated Georges Caussé, he was shocked to notice that they "smiled at us not unlike how they had just done with the little Gretchens."[115] Many German men, in fact, received a better greeting. Because the GIs recognized them as military men, they traded cigarettes with them for Nazi souvenirs.[116] Jacques Bureau skulked away after one "large Texan" explained to him that "he had not come for them but to liberate his brothers the Germans, led astray by a foul leader who had abused them."[117]

American nonchalance became a measure of condescension. Like many other prisoners, Caussé described the GIs as "phlegmatic, constantly chewing their gum."[118] "A gum chewer from Kansas," was how Foncine described his liberator.[119] Paul Finance remembered "two American policemen casually gazing at traffic passing by and laconically chewing their gum without deigning to look at me."[120] "Seated in their Jeeps," remembered Jacques-Alain de Sédouy, "or leaning casually against their vehicles, chewing their chewing-gum, our liberators look at us with an air of friendly superiority. Despite the warmth of the encounter between them and us, there is a huge distance created by their power, wealth and victory."[121] At a time of profound trauma for these French men, GI insouciance was a stunning—and sometimes stinging—display of power. "Hello Frenchman, yes, Frenchman" the GIs would singsong while distributing biscuits.[122]

Also painful were the contrasts between the Americans and the detainees. The latter called the GIs "Amerilots" because they seemed to have *a lot* of everything.[123] In his journal, André Michel recorded how angry he was to see the Americans allow large quantities of bread, eggs, butter, and jam to go to waste. "It is solely to maintain their economic superiority that the USA has won the war!"[124] Charles-Henri-

Guy Bazin also believed that the "Amerilots" were in the war for a selfish reason, namely, to inundate Europe with "their inedible beans and degenerate music."[125] Even the physical differences between the two groups evoked agonizing contrasts. Liberated prisoner Brigitte Friang remembered admiring "the beauty of these large blond boys" in American uniform. It formed a wondrous sight for her "after so many months of crooked bodies with their twisted, decayed limbs."[126] The visual contrast between the well-fed American men and the starving French survivors called attention to their differing grasps on manhood. The GIs dwelled in an alien world of victory and physical comfort; they seemed to be winning the war without trying.[127]

The US Army had several good reasons for not putting forward a friendly face to the liberated in the winter and spring of 1945. First, American ignorance concerning the French conscripted labor program (Service du travail obligatoire or STO) led the GIs to suspect the prisoners of collaboration.[128] Second, as was the case with the FFI, language difficulties hampered communication. Rescued while trying to escape a camp, Aimé Bonifas remembered, "I wanted to give some sign of friendship but they did not appear to understand."[129] Paul Wicker fell into an awkward silence with his liberator after struggling to express his joy and thanks with his "very poor English."[130] Third, the GIs were often overwhelmed by the horror of the camps and struggled to contain their emotions. Conversy remembers the Americans at Buchenwald as "dignified, closed, correct," but also noticed that they angrily crashed a group of German bicycles with their tank.[131] Fourth, inevitably, some individuals in the camp were dangerous and criminal, and they soured the reputation of the whole.[132] Fifth, fear of contagion kept the Americans at a distance from the liberated prisoners; typhus and other diseases were rampant in the squalid camps. Many prisoners' first memory of their liberators was being hosed down or showered with disinfectant.[133]

Finally, because the SS and other German officers destroyed prisoner dossiers before ceding the camps, the Americans had no way of knowing who the men were or why they were there. Robert Cardot was an exception, simply because in his case, the SS did not have time to burn such documents before surrendering the camp. As a result, he was formally recognized by both his French and American liberators for his resistance work. "They saluted me. Due to my exhaustion and emotion, for the first time since my arrest, I let myself cry, with the large tears rolling down my emaciated body."[134]

For their part, the French tried to convince themselves that the American *froideur* did not matter. "After all, what does that mean to them—that we are French?" Caussé asked himself. "We are liberated, isn't that the important thing? What do we take ourselves for anyways—conquerors?"[135] Lessafre tried to rationalize the situation: "These men have come from the other side of the Atlantic and camped out on unknown land without seeing or understanding anything. Their goal is to occupy a piece of land: the bipeds they find along the way do not interest and even embarrass them."[136] Dufaut took the high road, discouraging his comrades from viewing the Americans as "demi-Gods": "I have made myself more than a man: a superman, a hero. I am proud. I am the equal of any of them, these American soldiers. Let's get rid of our complex. . . . Come on, aren't I a demi-God as well?"[137]

As in the battle between French and German men, the female body formed a front line demarcating liberator from prisoner. The GI who freed prisoner Charles-Henri-Guy Bazin called him "Frenchie" and screamed, "Paris . . . *jolies filles!*" Bazin turned to his friend and grumbled "France, for the Americans as well as the Germans is Paris and women."[138] One important measure of American power in French prisoners' eyes was the GIs' ability to command the favors of women in Germany. As an ex-prisoner noted, not without bitterness, "the white American soldiers are popular with the beautiful German women who do not lack for blond cigarettes or chocolate."[139] Dufaut remembers hearing music and laughter one night in the work camp where he remained after liberation. He and his comrades realized that it was the "Yankees" having an "orgy." "Glued" to the window, the men watched a gaggle of Americans having sex with three Russian and Polish women whose sighs of pleasure filled the night.[140] While some felt their "desire growing," still others considered the sight infuriating. "We haven't endured what we have endured," fumed one, "for the pleasure of seeing an ex-gangster from Chicago panting in the arms of a Ukraine peasant!"[141] This mix of anger and envy described the response of many French men to the sight of GIs enjoying the privileges of conquest in Germany. André Michel was particularly angry when the Americans scored with the French women in his camp.[142]

Not everyone, it should be noted, had a bad memory of the liberators. Dufaut fondly recalls how a GI made him crepes with one hand while manning a machine gun with another.[143] "Never has hospitality been provided with such an abundance of affection and generosity," remembered the statesman Léon Blum of his time with the Americans.[144] Prisoners appreciated American cigarettes, chocolate, sugar, coffee, milk, chewing gum, and corned beef. After several weeks with the Americans, returning to a rationed France proved difficult. Like the Normands, the detainees were enormously impressed with American military power, and often noted the equipment, technology, and materiel in their diaries and memoirs.[145]

Even when Franco-American relations got off to a good start, however, they often soured in the days and weeks that followed, as the French, itching to get home, saw no progress in their repatriation. "Ah! Those brave Americans!" remembered Charles Joyon, "how we loved them that blessed day of 29 April! If only that marvelous remembrance was the sole one in our memory."[146] When prisoners pressed the GIs for information or a schedule, they were told to "wait and see."[147] Once again, the Americans had excellent reasons for not focusing on repatriation during the spring of 1945. The required transportation equipment was crucial to the war effort, and typhus and other diseases were again major concerns.[148] Nevertheless "exasperation, feelings of revolt, even of hatred" surfaced among the prisoners, according to one detainee.[149] Bazin remembered an ugly incident in an Eisenach camp when an officer wrongly charged the prisoners with theft of American supplies. Enraged, they accused the Americans of their own form of pillage: "they allowed us to be crushed and now they are coming for the spoils!" In response, the American commander screamed, "America does not need *you!*"[150] Fed up, many French prisoners tried to escape, only to be brought back "Texas-style" by GI cowboys using their weapons.[151] As early as December 1944, the US military began to put notices in local newspapers advising French prisoners to await the proper authorities instead of trying to get home on their own. "Stay in your camp," the notice instructed, "there you are now the masters."[152] As in Normandy, the Americans assured French men they were now the masters of their house. The language implied these men's desire to recuperate their manhood as well as their freedom—to become masters once again. At the core of the repatriation fantasy was the welcoming woman whose attentions would herald the recovery of male authority "They are waiting for us in France!" exclaimed one prisoner. "A group of young women will distribute food, wine and cigarettes on the journey."[153]

Intolerable Encroachment on French Sovereignty

This type of recuperation would in fact prove elusive. Once the euphoria of the return passed, the *rapatrié* once again often had to face the grim reality of a changed situation. According to one Norman woman, the *rapatrié* returned only to find that he had lost his place, and that "his marital and paternal authority had been compromised by his too-long absence, during which his wife learned to liberate herself, to make do despite difficult conditions of life, to manage alone."[154] As a result, ex-prisoners would reach home but often not yet enjoy mastery of their house. The presence of thousands of American soldiers throughout northern France only exacerbated that sense of displacement. When Paul Finance returned after three years in a German camp, he found his house overrun with GIs eating and sleeping. Two jeeps were parked up against his family's restaurant so that he could only enter through the back door. Only with great effort was he able to find his family inside.[155] "We were undergoing a second occupation, that of the American army," noted Louis Eudier when he finally reached home in Le Havre in May of 1945.[156]

Sexual control over women once again created a front line of tension between *rapatriés* and American men. In Paris particularly, French
men had to endure countless photographs taken of their wives and
girlfriends with GIs.[157] When the army invited women but not men to
local dances, the police spent the evening calming male tempers at the
door.[158] In bars and cafés, the GIs propositioned women right in front
of their husbands or boyfriends.[159] Others would ask "how much?"
even if the woman was with a man. Predictably such inquiries would
end with a French fist in a GI face. Fights between men over women
were common during the summer of 1945. An incident at a dance in
Châlons-sur-Marne was typical. A woman refused a GI's invitation to
take a walk, insisting that she was with her husband, soon to arrive
on the scene. When the husband did appear, and told the soldier to
get lost, the GI instead attacked the wife and tore her dress. A brawl
began between the two men.[160]

In the GI mind, the French girl was fair game. The Americans had
won the war, liberated the women, and now deserved the sexual prerogatives of conquest. In 1946, *American Mercury* described the scene
this way: "Nattily dressed, well-fed American soldiers in skin-tight
Eisenhower jackets, knife-creased pants and lustrous boots, strut
along the avenues of convalescent Europe. Crowds of hollowed-
eyed Buchenwald graduates, tatterdemalion local soldiers and war-
wounded make way for them on the sidewalks."[161] The Amerilots
were handsome, well-dressed, and rich. How could the local girls
resist?[162] As one GI put it, "in France we have cut in on French soldiers
and civilians because we have more money, better clothing, jeeps, as
well as plenty of coffee, chocolate and cigarettes. Some Frenchmen
take it so seriously that they threaten to cut the girls' hair if they go
out with Yanks."[163] Once again, French men were using the *tonte* ritual
as a way to recuperate lost sexual territory, this time with the Americans. Warren Eames remembers how French soldiers of the Second
Armored Division resented them, "probably because of our mingling
with their women."[164]

The Americans trespassed on French privilege when they presumed to be the lovers and protectors of local women. "A woman

only need to have a slightly labored expression and the Americans will do everything for her," wrote a frustrated Jacques Kayser. "It's an intolerable encroachment on French sovereignty." Kayser could not help but notice that the women's cries, fruit, kisses, and flowers were always for the American troops. "We are barely noticed. When we get out of the car, the crowd does not surround us, and barely questions us." In Normandy, Kayser was particularly enraged to see that the same girls who had taken up with the Germans were now waiting tables for the GIs, "and already the Americans are chatting with them, offering them cigarettes."[165] The shamelessness of the shamed outraged many French men. "It is really my right to be indignant about these women," wrote one columnist, "outraged to see them out with the Americans."[166]

In areas where the army established permanent bases, such as Normandy or the Marne, sexual tensions between French and American men became a serious problem. In Epernay, for example, GIs on the town with girls were jeered by male civilians.[167] In Le Havre, Pierre Aubéry, French liaison to the Americans, remembered boiling with anger when the GIs showed little interest in anything but sex with French women, least of all getting to know men like himself.[168] "The plebeians—the lowly, the poor, the needy, the disarmed in the eyes of the Americans—that was us, the dockers, the Frenchmen." Aubéry's resentment intensified as the dockers were forced to witness "the flood of Americans, black and white, surging through our streets, assaulting our restaurants, beginning fights, [and] taking away our girls, who are themselves quite willing and delighted." Witnessing such a sight, Aubéry reflected, "we no longer know in what world we live, and if there is anything left of the routines, safety and ideas of the past."[169] Anger and bewilderment also pervade Gilles Morris's memory of a "desperate, unruly, chaotic" Le Havre in 1945. The American troops had overrun the town, consuming excessive amounts of alcohol, and committing theft, rape, and physical assault on a daily basis. Women could not walk the streets alone; sexual relations occurred in broad daylight under the eyes of children. The local girls flocked to the large camps north of town, where the American soldier was "jumping on, even raping, anything which fell under his dick . . . as a function of his liberator's sexual prerogative [*droit de cuissage*]."[170]

In wartime, sexual access to local women symbolized victory or defeat.[171] These French men expressed anger in two overlapping registers. First was personal frustration about sexual competition. The sight of Americans taking away French girls evoked a world in which male authority, already damaged by the war, had vanished altogether. In such a world French men were ghosted. The Americans refused to recognize them as comrades, and the local women ignored them as men.[172] But grief could be heard in a second, more political register as well. The "girl problem," as *American Mercury* called it, signaled a new subservience to the American conquerors. The refusal of the GIs to recognize French men *as men* was interpreted by the latter not only as a personal affront but also as a painful signal of postwar national decline—"an intolerable encroachment on French sovereignty." If the military used heterosexual romance to mythologize the American mission, French men fixated on such romances as a way to reconcile themselves with a brave new world.

PART TWO

Prostitution

4

Amerilots and Harlots

IN NOVEMBER 1944, the journalist Pierre Aubéry returned to his hometown Le Havre. The city, he discovered, had been rebuilt as a major supply port for the US military. Because Aubéry spoke English, he got a job on the docks as a liaison to the army. On one visit to his American commander's office, Aubéry noticed a box brimming with "foodstuffs wrapped in shining, multicolored cellophane. There is candy, chewing gum, toothpaste, razor blades, and inevitably, packages of cigarettes." The box, he wrote, "gave me, even more than my proximity to the GIs, the intense sensation of being close to America and of America's presence among us. In this country of abundance and comfort, I felt far away from France."[1] Aubéry's description evokes the power of American commodities during the years 1944–45. In a starving Europe, American wealth inspired awe and envy. It shaped a novel identity for the United States as a global power, and reinforced a new sense of inferiority, born of the war, among the French.

American riches took the measure of Gallic misery. After visiting his commander, Aubéry wandered into an empty mess hall and glimpsed a glossy magazine on the table. America was a nation in living color. Aubéry contrasted the magazine with the badly printed, grayish French newspapers. "Having just left our dirty, worn, tired world of the everyday," recorded Aubéry, "where we lack everything and are as miserly as the most humble, this ship had all the lure of abundance and luxury."[2] Aubéry was not alone in seeing French scarcity in American prosperity. "After the rationing, the rutabagas, the sawdust biscuits sold in the stations," Gilles Morris recalled, "these well-fed Americans threw away barely-touched turkey thighs or slices of bananas." No wonder, he concluded, so many French people "succumbed to the American myth during this era."[3]

Bounty lay at the center of that myth. Among civilians, the United States became virtually synonymous with wealth. This myth of abundance was far from novel. The notion of plenty had structured the idea of "Americanness" for centuries.[4] Following the First World War, the French increasingly both recognized and resented US wealth. Anti-Americanism became firmly grounded in fears that the French people would have to submit to rising American economic power. In one 1931 polemic, for example, they were portrayed as beggars and prostitutes seeking financial and sexual favors from the new "Rome," the United States.[5]

Even if not new, however, the myth of American abundance gained new force during the war years. On the one hand, the French were emerging from one of the most somber periods of their history. The Germans imposed "occupation costs" on the nation, siphoning off its supplies of dairy, produce, meat, and coal, among many other things. Women spent hours every day queuing for bread and whatever else could be had in the meager shops. During the wartime winters, many civilians strove, above all else, not to freeze to death.[6] On the other hand, there were the Americans with their abundant rations, coffee, chocolate, and cigarettes. To its soldiers the army distributed enormous quantities of such things as well as soap and other toiletries. While K rations were by no means gourmet cuisine, they were readily available. As these commodities began to circulate in the black market, they became nationalized as symbols of US affluence. The heaving GI supply store formed a painful contrast to the empty shelves of French grocers. For Aubéry and other French civilians, GI supply materialized American superiority and encouraged French awe.

But the most important product drawing lines of privilege between the two peoples—sex—was French, not American. "In France," remembered GI Jack Plano, "everything was in short supply except alcoholic beverages, bread as only the French could make it, and women."[7] While at first it may seem odd to think of a woman as a commodity, Plano did not consider prostitutes to be any different from brandy or bread in this regard. Neither did *Panther Tracks*, a GI newspaper that presented this "menu" of prostitutes in Paris: "An especially vivacious and well-rounded harlot might demand a price of 600 francs. However, the price scales downwards for fair merchandise and mediocre stock. Some fairly delicious cold cuts can be had for 150 and 200 francs."[8]

During their time in France, the GIs bought an extraordinary amount of sex. Prostitution became a widespread phenomenon during the years 1944–45 because sex was the one good not available at the local military store. Comprised of the contact of flesh and the exchange of bodily fluids, the sexual encounter between soldier and prostitute could not have been more intimate. At the same time, however, such intimacy became deeply politicized as it crossed national borders. Prostitution was defined by power and money: a soldier paid a woman to subjugate her body for his personal pleasure. From that privileged relationship, a GI was taught not only to use a French woman for his own ends, but also to exert control over French civilians in general. Sex as a commodity nurtured an arrogant, even imperialist attitude among the Americans who bought it. The fact that the GIs came into contact with prostitutes more than any other single type of French person made the political impact of sexual commerce more significant.

The prostitute not only taught the GIs power in their relations with civilians, but she also reinforced that dominion through the perceived disgrace of her own self-merchandising. Prostitutes were widely seen as debased; civilians watching them offer their services to "foreigners" felt humiliation. A traditional figure of moral depravity, the prostitute who solicited German soldiers during the war had come to denote the dishonor of the occupation. Even after the Liberation, the mere sight of a prostitute continued to remind civilians of their status as a conquered people.[9] The shame of her commerce became the shame of the nation. In this way the prostitute delineated new asymmetries of power at a key transitional moment.

Erfing with the Peasants

As commodities neither GI surplus nor the prostitute can be understood apart from what Stephen Ambrose has called "the greatest black market of all time" during the liberation era.[10] Beginning in 1940, French market relations adapted to wartime conditions through *le marché noir*. The British journalist Alan Moorehead described the wartime black market as "the acknowledged system of social economy."[11] At first innocently, then more deviously, GIs used their access to army supplies in order to take advantage of *le marché noir*. In doing so, they made it even more vibrant than during wartime.[12]

The black market was a complex system that operated on many different levels simultaneously during the war.[13] First, it consisted of the wine, meat, and other French delectables taken by the Germans to supply their various branches of the military service.[14] Second, it represented a "parallel economy," which offered large firms resources unobtainable through official channels. Finally and perhaps most importantly, *le marché noir* functioned on a more personal level, servicing a ravenous population. Wine, potatoes, oranges, chocolate, onions, tomato purée—in short, anything and everything—could be bought for a price, usually a high one. Cash was only one means of exchange; civilians favored tangible goods that would not lose value with inflation.[15] Throughout the occupation, they viewed the black market as a necessary evil and even a form of resistance. Without some dietary supplement to rationed foodstuffs, they reasoned, their daily caloric intake meant starvation.[16] Nevertheless the black market was morally ambiguous inasmuch as it attracted criminals, led to price gouging and fraud, and favored the wealthy elites.

As the Germans retreated, civilians turned to the Americans for food.[17] Nourishment came two ways: in large government shipments, and in more haphazard exchanges with individual GIs. Deprived for four years of basic necessities, urban French civilians in particular were amazed by the sheer quantity of American food, made visible to them as soldiers passed through towns and villages in northern France.[18] Army mess halls served large quantities of bread, fruit, meat, soup, and condensed milk. No child ever left a mess hall hungry.[19]

But the quality of GI food proved no less a source of wonder. For one there was margarine, a butter that—miraculously—did not melt in the sun. For another, there was peanut butter, described lovingly by Marie-Madeleine Jacqueline as a delicious "jam with peanuts."[20] White bread was also a marvel, particularly in comparison with the leaden gray variety most Normans had been eating.[21] The young actress Simone Signoret was in awe of K rations: "everything—meat pie, cheese, powdered lemonade, chocolate, candy and chewing gum—had on its wrapper the exact number of vitamins and calories required to sustain the life of an American citizen."[22] "There was magic in what they served me," recalled Christiane Delpierre of her breakfast as a child with the GIs. The Americans could make milk appear without cows simply by pouring hot water over white powder! Coffee—*real* coffee—was created from tiny little brown granules! And best of all, an omelette could be cooked without breaking eggs![23]

Because these things were easily obtainable at an army PX (supply store), a brisk trade between GIs and civilians began the first day of the landings. Unlike many other civilians, Norman peasants were not without chips to play. Dairy products, beef, and alcohol—all were impossible to find in army stocks.[24] "The local French farmers were the first we dealt with," remembered David Ichelson. "We traded them soap and cigarettes for eggs, chickens and cider."[25] Peter Belpulsi recalled old fat stewing hens and cream for his coffee, all for "our much-not-wanted spam."[26] Lawrence Cane managed to go out and find an entire cow to feed beefsteak to his unit.[27] Toward the end of the summer, the peasants also traded for gasoline in order to harvest crops with their tractors.[28] Frank Freese marveled at how his buddy Coradino Gatti managed to wrangle hard cider from a peasant "with a little high school French and a lot of Italian charm."[29] "So the people of France had plenty of soap and cigarettes and we had plenty of beverages and food," concluded Mark Goodman. "The old law of Supply and Demand was operating again."[30]

A particularly elaborate market developed for eggs. The Americans called bargaining for them "erfing" after *œufs*, the French word for eggs.[31] Some GIs liked to punch holes in the egg and suck; others preferred to cook them in a mess kit "at odd moments between bullets."[32] Ernie Pyle bragged about the large size of Norman eggs, "about every fourth one as big as a duck egg." He would rise at dawn to prepare some on a Coleman stove for his fellow journalists "in real Normandy butter—fried, scrambled, boiled or poached, as suited the whims of their respective majesties."[33] Among peasants, word quickly got around that the GIs hankered after eggs. When Peter Belpulsi's tank stalled somewhere on the Brittany Peninsula, a local rushed out to give him eggs and shout "Bonjour!"[34] One Norman woman even tried to use them to pay for dental work for her daughter.[35] Nineteen forty-four also proved to be a banner year for mushrooms, and the GIs also bargained those to cook with their eggs.[36] They created such a strong demand for local products that officials complained the Americans were disrupting local economies and depriving hungry civilians of food.[37]

Of the "four Cs" (cigarettes, chocolate, chewing gum, and Coca-Cola,) the American cigarette became by far the most prominent in European market culture. This is not only because so many Europeans were smokers, but also because cigarettes could be readily divided into units, ideal for bartering and sale at every level of transaction.[38] The GIs obtained them easily at the local PX for fifty cents a carton, the same price as in the States.[39] The war was big business for American tobacco companies. The military counted twelve million men; each smoked an average of thirty cigarettes a day. President Roosevelt had declared tobacco an essential wartime material, so that those who grew and processed it enjoyed various military exemptions in production and distribution.[40] The war is also widely recognized as the moment when Europeans gained the taste for "blond" or blended American cigarettes, soon to become the world standard.[41] "I always made a big hit in a town when I would open a pack of cigarettes and start to give the people a free smoke," recalled Leroy Stewart. "They all liked our cigarettes so much better than what they had."[42] Cigarettes became such a part of GI life that the large army residential camps throughout northern France were named after popular brands of cigarettes—Lucky Strike, Philip Morris, Herbert Tareyton, and Old Gold. Collectively they were known as the "cigarette camps."[43]

Blond cigarettes became so closely linked to the Americans that they served as a reliable sign that the GIs had arrived. Early in the morning of the sixth of June, Fernand Levoy found a pack of Luckies in a field in Montebourg, north of Saint-Mère-Église. He used them to alert the people of his village that le débarquement had finally happened.[44] In the first weeks after the landings, cigarettes served as tokens of friendship—the means by which the GIs established personal relations with civilians. Anthony Harlinski remembers that as the GIs entered Norman towns, they scattered cigarettes "like a carpet of flowers strewn in our wake." To pretty girls, they gave "extravagantly," and to the older men, they gave "with generosity."[45] Robert Ryan, a sergeant in the First Medical Battalion, claimed that relations with civilians remained "on excellent terms 90% of the time thanx [sic] to 'cigs.'"[46] Abbé Dufour, the curé of Lorey, pointed out in his diary that the Liberation could be quantified by the number of cigarettes passed out by the Americans in his small Norman town.[47] Paul Boesch traded his cigarettes to kids for fresh eggs, "though we generally lost out in the swap" he remarked good-naturedly.[48]

Cigarettes bridged the silence between two peoples who spoke different languages. In September, L'avenir du Nord noted that while the Americans did not speak French, the distribution of cigarettes "sufficed to fulfill the role of words."[49] Exchanging gifts of calvados for cigarettes in the town of Fleury, recalls Christianne Denis, definitely broke the ice between soldier and civilian, putting smiles on every face.[50] Even those who did not smoke took up the habit.[51] Fifteen-year-old Jacques Nicolle from Coutances was shocked to see his mother with a cigarette in her mouth.[52] Erotically charged and deliciously sensual, the cigarette also became a singular object of French desire. It encouraged flirtation between GIs and French women. Civil Affairs officer John Maginnis had "a little sort of joke that became a ritual" with a local leader of the FFI, a young woman named Jacqueline: "She always greeted me with 'Major, I love you and have you a cigarette?' I always asked 'Do you really love me or is it my cigarettes that you love?' She always answered 'Major, I will always love you as long as you have cigarettes.'"[53]

Finally cigarettes provided a thrilling first example of American bounty. After gazing upon pack after pack of Chesterfields and Old Golds, Michel Béchet recorded in his diary that "we had to bow before such a display of material wealth."[54] Paul Finance remembers the moment when, barely able to believe his good fortune, he received his first pack of Luckies: "Not only have they come to render a sacred service," he enthused, "but they've also offered me a pack of cigarettes!"[55] As a child, Jacques-Alain de Sédouy also felt awe the first time he witnessed American riches: "Like the white men who debark with their trinkets in the midst of an African tribe," he recalled, "the soldiers generously distributed chocolate, cigarettes, candy and chewing gum into the hands extended towards them."[56] Sédouy's framing of the American arrival through the metaphor of the colony implies a less genial sort of market exchange that would soon emerge.

Don't You Owe Us Something?

As the euphoria of the Liberation dissipated, American surplus changed in meaning and effect. The chocolate and cigarettes that had inspired joy and comradery now began to produce hostility between soldiers and civilians. In simply human terms, the Americans sought gain from their advantage, and the French increasingly resented that fact: the disparities in wealth were simply too great for generosity and gratitude to prevail over greed and anger.

Even in their generosity, the US military humiliated the French. Because the army was mobile and well supplied during the summer of 1944, it disposed of large surpluses of meat, soup, bread, cake, and condensed milk without formally offering it to the French. Civilians were not above foraging garbage cans and dumps for American leftovers to eat, trade, or sell. The fact that most assigned the task to their children suggests they found it demeaning. When an American officer in Normandy offered to feed the local peasants' pigs with garbage, they appreciated the gesture until they saw the quality of food being thrown away. Rather than feed it to their animals, they decided to keep it for themselves, but not without embarrassment.[57] For a people who took such pride in their cuisine, eating American garbage could not have been easy.

Also degrading was beggary. Children, in particular, solicited the GIs for food and cigarettes. Such pleading inspired pity in GI Keith Winston, who wrote his wife that "seeing boys as young as our little Neil begging for money or something to eat. Tears come to my eyes."[58] But older civilians found such practices demeaning. "They are judging us, and the least detail can make a difference," warned the Rennes paper *Ouest-France* in August. "Various groups, children only one among them, sometimes gather around the trucks, hands eagerly extended. . . . These gestures are not French."[59] "We see all too clearly," wrote *Le Journal de la Marne*, "that despite the ringing declarations and nice compliments, they consider us politically weak. This is why, when children beg, it gratifies the [US] feeling that France no longer has any power in the world."[60] In the Marne police admonished civilians who indulged in such behavior because it gave the Americans such a "poor impression of the French mentality."[61] Begging had to be stopped because it signaled painful changes. "You know there are Americans on the street when you see a gathering of people swarming around them like flies with a piece of sugar," sulked the Parisian daily *Le Franc-Tireur*. "In 1918 it was the reverse: the Americans were crazed for 'souvenirs' and asked for them everywhere."[62] In Le Havre as well, the sight of "pushy children who bug [the GIs] for chewing gum or cigarettes" was considered an embarrassment. "Are we a nation of beggars?" asked *Havre-éclair*. "We have been conquered; we are the vanquished of 1940; we remain the weak ones, and for years nothing will enable us to forget that."[63] By 1945, GI generosity fed the fear that France had become a nation of beggars. For civilians, American handouts increasingly symbolized the humiliation of defeat.

The meaning of army surplus began to change for the GIs as well. Sometime during the summer of 1944, the GIs discovered that their chocolate and Luckies were, in fact, valuable commodities. Chocolate and cigarettes lost their status as gifts and became instead monetary units. Revenue began to define market exchanges. Walter Brown figured out that he could buy a carton of cigarettes for fifty cents, then barter each and every cigarette for the price of one dollar. "That was a good profit so we made good use of them," concluded Brown.[64] In a letter to his parents, Capt. John Earle also noted that he could buy cigarette cartons for fifty cents and sell them for as much as fifteen dollars. "Needless to say I brought quite a supply with me."[65] Cigarettes could be traded for pretty much anything and would buy more than either francs or invasion money.[66] Two or three packs of cigarettes brought about a quart of wine, remembered infantryman Anthony Harlinski. Three nights in a broken-down Paris hotel cost battalion surgeon Bill McConahey a total of seven packs of cigarettes.[67] "For a pack of cigarettes," claimed Peter Belpulsi, "a G.I. in Paris didn't have any trouble to find a prostitute to spend a night in bed with him."[68] Medic Keith Winston wrote his wife that he was on his way to Paris with seven cartons of cigarettes in order to buy her a trinket or two.[69]

Slowly but surely, army surplus products became tools of corruption. In October a Civil Affairs report complained of a flourishing black market for cigarettes in Paris promoted by "undesirable elements" of the American infantry.[70] Cigarettes were sold openly in Rouen city center.[71] The cigarette market became a central complaint of the French police, who believed it had "stained the honor" of the army.[72] Upon arriving in Paris on leave, the first thing Jack Capell and his buddies did was "to convert our cigarettes into French currency" with the black marketeers, who swarmed military trucks entering the city.[73] It was a dirty business, marred by frequent brawls and thefts. Because the marketeers could not safely keep the large sums of money they earned, they spent it right away on prostitutes, feeding yet another illegal market.[74] In towns like Reims and Le Havre, where

American supplies arrived in enormous quantities, local civilians only had to know which GI to approach. Some specialized in chocolate and coffee, others in cigarettes, and still others in clothes, silk stockings, and shoes.[75] Gasoline was scarce, but wealthy civilians in French towns began to drive their cars again, fueling them with black market gas.[76] Because the MPs kept a close eye on the docks and supply stations, this type of trading had to be done with discretion, often in the back rooms of bars and cafés. German prisoners of war and African American soldiers became notorious as dealers because they had access to stocks when unloading ships and driving supply trucks.[77] Although both French and American authorities officially opposed the black market, neither had the manpower to shut it down.[78]

As army supplies transitioned into currency, they radically deteriorated Franco-American relations. A tiny item appearing in the Parisian daily *Ce soir* in September 1944 suggests exactly how cigarettes, for example, provoked a new wariness between soldier and civilian. Called "Bien Joué" ("Well-Played"), it told the story of two GIs in the Café de Flore. A waiter serving them "discretely mentioned that he was a poor Frenchman, deprived of cigarettes." The GIs gave him a pack. Ten minutes later, however, they witnessed the waiter selling that pack for 175 francs. Furious, they asked for the bill. Although it came to 140 francs, the GIs gave him only 50. "In flawless french," one said: "Here you go, I think you've already paid yourself adequately."[79] The joke here turned on the exploitation of cultural stereotypes. The waiter had taken the customary GI gift of cigarettes, and transformed them into currency. To do so, he exploited the stereotype, established the previous summer, of the needy civilian. In response to the waiter's duplicity, the Americans also exploited a stereotype of themselves—as the clueless GI unable to understand French. The vulnerabilities that soldier and civilian had used to forge a friendship— American naïveté and French neediness—were now transformed into instruments of deception. *Ce soir's* tone was still playful—this was a game "bien joué"—but it also left the reader with a bad aftertaste. Something profound had changed.[80]

As the *Ce soir* example shows, civilians were not beyond making a quick franc at GI expense. Again the reasons for such dealings were deeply human: if the GIs were profiting from market exchanges, why shouldn't the French as well? But there was no end of complaining among the soldiers about how "the French are gypping us" on brandy and perfume.[81] "Things are awful in price," wrote John Earle to his family. "Jewelry is just out of the question. As much as I like to send you gifts I hate to just support the French and throw my money away."[82] "Paris was a big city and all they were after was your money," agreed James Coletti.[83] Fraud was considered even more offensive. Ichelson was furious when a salesman convinced him to buy some pornographic postcards, which, it turned out, were rural landscapes. "The Frenchman had completely bamboozled me, which I thought should have been a capital offense after all I'd done for France."[84]

Ichelson's complaint reveals yet another kind of market logic that, although rarely stated, nevertheless permeated GI interactions with civilians. The logic went something like this: the United States had paid for French freedom with American lives. Now the French citizen owed a return on that blood debt, payable to soldiers who had survived. "The feeling of a portion of the military that it has 'liberated' France and has 'something coming' as a result," led to great resentment, according to Civil Affairs.[85] The Red Cross specialist Getty Page described the mind-set this way: "See, aren't we wonderful? We have liberated you. Don't you owe us something?"[86] This GI attitude charged even the most mundane transactions with explosive feelings. Leroy Stewart, a veteran of the Battle of Normandy, was furious when a Parisian barber demanded a tip for a haircut. "Here he was a young Frenchman living safe and comfortable in Paris while I was going through hell for his country."[87] Resentment arose particularly when civilians were seen to be making a profit from the American presence. The GIs guarded their market advantage as a prerogative of their war sacrifice. Cultural condescension also justified their gains. As we have seen, the GIs believed they were bringing the "gift" of civilization to the primitive, dirty, and oversexed French people.

By 1945, then, American surplus had shifted far from its original meaning as a token of friendship and had become instead a source of corruption and resentment. This transition occurred at all levels of the American army, even the highest ranks. Cigarettes, for example, were used by the Judge Advocate General's Office to compensate civilians who had been victims of GI crimes, including murder and rape. Such a payment appalled the Breton writer Louis Guilloux, who worked as an interpreter for the US Army. Guilloux saw the cigarettes as a tool of manipulation on the part of the US military meant to keep civilians from seeking further damages.[88] Once offered to bridge silence between soldier and civilian, the cigarette was now being used to seal silence on the part of victims. For French men like Guilloux, it had become shorthand for American imperiousness.

French People Have Sold Themselves to No One

Like the cigarette, the prostitute both symbolized and shaped the balance of power between soldier and civilian. Because sex was inseparable from the black market that developed in the fall of 1944, it became a commodity akin to cigarettes or chocolate. When Aubéry, for example, went down to the docks in Le Havre, the GIs promised him anything from their army supplies for a "Mad'moiselle."[89] Gilles Morris also recalled the GI obsession with "Mam'séelle Zig-Zag!" and described the central market in Le Havre as a shady place where army surplus was traded for "tainted bottles of alcohol with prestigious labels, bottles of Chanel perfume, pornographic photographs, or the address of some girl, pretty if possible."[90]

Both prostitution and the black market were semi-legal, mobile forms of consumption that operated in dark alleys, back rooms of bars, and hallways of hotels. Both thrived on a subculture of local knowledge. Both were officially condemned yet widely embraced. Finally, both operated on several different levels of exchange. Both a prostitute and a marketeer could be either a "casual" one-time merchant or a full-time "professional." French authorities frequently mentioned prostitutes and le marché noir in the same breath. An official in Marseille, for example, complained that the presence of American troops on the Côte d'Azur had engendered "a worrisome outbreak in the black market and clandestine prostitution."[91] Similarly, a Parisian policeman reported that the Opéra quarter was overwhelmed by dealers and prostitutes "the first to solicit and purchase goods, the second to offer their charms."[92]

Because of these links between the prostitute and the black market, the GIs bartered for sex no differently than they did alcohol and cigarettes.[93] Money was measured in terms of sex. On a day when Ichelson passed through France on his way to Switzerland, the government was handing out four hundred francs to every American soldier. "Four hundred francs wouldn't buy much in France," grumbled Ichelson, "except maybe two cases of gonorrhea."[94] Trading army products for sex was common GI practice throughout Europe.[95] Infantryman Bert Dansky remembered how German, Russian, and Polish women would sell sexual favors for cigarettes and K rations.[96] William Meissner was shocked when some German children approached him saying, "Hey, G.I., you wanna (make love) my mamma? She virgin."[97] "Then there were the vagabond girls," remembered battalion surgeon Bill McConahey, "who loitered along the highways, some even carrying blankets, and who would walk into the woods arm-in-arm with any G.I. who was interested. Their price was a cigarette, a stick of chewing gum, a piece of chocolate, or perhaps nothing."[98] The GIs called such prostitutes "Hershey bars" because they sold their bodies for chocolate.[99] "I once had two Hungarian girls proposition me for a five cent Hershey Bar," remembered Ichelson, "they were sisters and were willing to sell me their favors for half of the Hershey Bar for each of them. This has got to be the world's record for a cheap piece of ass. Two and a half cents each."[100] Another former GI speculated in the 1970s that "present-day Europe is full of respectable, petty-bourgeois women who have, at least once in their lives, flung back their legs for the price of a loaf of bread."[101]

French women were no exception. When Walter Brown arrived in the big city, "women chased us all over the place. When we went into cafes to eat they came in and sat near us asking us to sleep with them for cigarettes."[102] Sex could also be had for a pack of chewing gum.[103]

A prostitute arrested near Cherbourg confessed to coming there from Paris because she was told "it was possible to have shoes, cigarettes, chocolate and other provisions."[104] Many female civilians who were not prostitutes also engaged in sex for certain products. GI Robert Peters was shocked after his buddy Siever had sex with a French woman. "'You're married,' I said. 'I don't understand.' 'It don't matter,' he said. 'She wants soap and cigarettes. I want a f—.'"[105] While these kinds of sex trades began improvisationally, they again led to a well-developed sex market throughout northern France.[106]

Despite their appreciation for services rendered, many GIs viewed French prostitutes with contempt.[107] Robert Peters recalls them as "lurid females" whose "faces glared with make-up" in the fading light of the Champs-Elysees.[108] Ichelson remembers a long line of soldiers outside Camp Lucky Strike one night. At its head was a French-speaking black soldier arguing with a French woman about the price of a blow job. "What a way to make a living!" he sneered, "That girl is going to have lock jaw and a sour stomach when she finishes this day's work."[109] With equal disdain, Thomas Saylor was reminded of the French women who tried to solicit his money in a bar: "A lot of them [wanted] cigarettes, a lot for the money. . . . They were all over the place. In the bars, you find them all over. All kinds of them. Some of them were half-naked there for you. They touch you, right there in the bar. But me, I keep my money safe and sound."[110] Civil Affairs officer John J. Maginnis was in Carentan when ten prostitutes from Cherbourg were "dumped" on him. Maginnis's annoyance reached a peak when the prostitutes successfully escaped all his efforts to confine them. Fed up, he sent them "bitterly protesting" to a refugee camp. "One can stand just so much in the way of monkey-shines from people like them," he grumbled.[111]

The urban spectacle of prostitution reinforced the American view, already confirmed in Normandy, that the French were a depraved people. The army manual 112 Gripes about the French had the GIs posing this question: "How do the French themselves feel about all the streetwalkers? How can they close their eyes to all the immorality?"[112] Many GIs wrote home about the quantity of prostitutes on the

streets in Paris and other cities where they took leave.[113] As he moved
deeper into France, Jack Plano could not help but notice "the number
of young girls around selling sex." He was also shaken by the age
of these women, which he estimated to be no more than twelve or
thirteen years old.[114] Bert Damsky tried to convince himself that the
high numbers of prostitutes was merely "an outgrowth of the war."[115]
112 Gripes about the French hastened to explain that many girls could
not otherwise live on their wages. But many GIs simply concluded
that French women were "easy pick-ups" and generally "immoral."[116]
René Loisel, a docker in Le Havre, remembers how the Americans
"really scorned us, and made a habit of saying that in France, the men
were all idlers, the children all beggars, and the women all whores [*et
les femmes des p*—.]"[117] When Arthur Miller took up residence in Paris,
he grimaced at the pretty girls swapping Luckies for a grope in the
dark, and concluded that French dignity had collapsed.[118]

American contempt for prostitutes spilled over into disrespect for
the French generally. In his diary of 18 September 1944, Chester Hansen (military aid to Omar Bradley) noted the aggressive prostitutes he
encountered in Paris. When he danced with a woman, she stunned
him by asking, "You will sleep with me tonight, no?" From this encounter he concluded, "French people have sold themselves to no
one and no one is impressed by them."[119] Presumption drove Hansen
to believe the French were obligated to "sell" themselves in the first
place. But more important, he conflated a sexual proposition with a
broader bid for national recognition. Similarly, connected in his mind
was his rejection of the prostitute and his disdain for the French generally. In this way, a Parisian prostitute became the jury for an entire
people.

Military officials at all levels of command generalized about the
French "selling themselves" in this way. According to the historian
Frank Costigliola, Americans consistently imagined the French during this period as "wayward" women. Among the Western Allies,
sexual commerce came to signify a broader French plea for approval
that, in turn, reinforced American self-importance.[120] Army chaplain
Renwick Kennedy witnessed Americans "judging whole populations

by the few harlots, drunks and black marketeers they met."[121] "It isn't fair to judge a nation on the business principals and communicability of the world's oldest profession," commented Ichelson, "but we saw more French whores than we did French statesmen."[122] Ichelson's remark reminds us that Charles de Gaulle's defiance in the face of defeat was not the only image of Frenchness afforded the American soldier. The GIs' encounters with prostitutes—arguably more frequent than with any other French type—radically shaped their view of the French as an immoral, subservient people.

Au Temps des Boniches

Sometime in the summer of 1944 it began to dawn on civilians that the GI notion of "Frenchness" was not solidifying in the Louvre. "The word France in Europe and throughout the world is linked to the idea of a brothel!" complained social conservatives.[123] Throughout northern France, newspaper editors pleaded with their readers to give the GIs "the impression of a disciplined people. . . . And also of a people dignified and proud, conscious of their splendid past and the promise of the future."[124] Given "the fast, liberated manners of certain women," scolded *Journal de la Marne*, Americans were getting an impression of France that was "not flattering" at a time when their opinion mattered more than ever.[125] The mayor of Reims lamented that "a taste for pleasures and the unknown" was leading to a troublesome "abandonment of principles" among the youth of that town.[126] The police in nearby Châlons-sur-Marne also worried about "the regrettable generalizations that could be made about French women."[127]

From the French perspective, the GI presence in towns and cities had transformed the sexual attitudes of young women. Social workers heralded a new type of amateur prostitute who sold her body because the Americans had given her "the illusion of an easier life," making her reluctant to pursue serious work. "A greedy attitude" had overtaken women, insisted Alfred Scheiber. "Tempting arguments" such as chocolate and cigarettes helped the GIs turn even honest women into bad ones. The result: women of all classes, seemingly undeterred by old prejudices, were prostituting themselves—and not strictly out of economic need.[128] "The arrival of the Americans with their 'Camels,' their 'chewing gum,' and their chocolate," agreed the Parisian police, had caused an "outbreak of uncontrolled prostitution."[129] The lure of American commodities was leading a whole new class of women into the business, making the prostitute "much more difficult to define."[130] As the physician Jean-Charles Bertier put it, clandestine prostitution "recruits its personnel from all classes of society; and by that fact, is indefinable."[131] These dire warnings suggest that the threat posed by the new prostitute lay in her ability to blur two sacrosanct distinctions: between economic need and commodity desire, and between the prostitute and the respectable woman.

The liberation of Paris brought yet more pleas for ladylike behavior. "Mademoiselle ou madame," demanded *France libre*, "do not give our allied soldiers the impression of a perverse, dissolute Paris. As they enter a city whose greatness and heroism they know and admire, do they need to be greeted by a swarm of young women whose modesty has flown away with the winds of freedom?"[132] A few days later, *Le populaire* joined the call for decorum: "do we want to produce even a shadow of justification or a semblance of truth to this propaganda which does not flatter the French woman's reputation?"[133] Even in the bourgeois press the reputation of the French woman came under attack. The women's magazine *Marie-Claire* described how one young woman named Nicole wished her English was better so that she could "lurk around Americans to beg for cigarettes or a piece of chocolate." "*Véritable* young women of France," the magazine instructed, "leave to your fathers, fiancés and brothers the task of showing to Americans the gratitude in our French hearts."[134] Charles de Gaulle showed his concern about the matter by denouncing a group of female FFI members wearing transparent blouses (made of parachute silk) as lacking "respectability, solemnity and discipline."[135]

Women who "shamelessly offered" themselves to soldiers were sometimes dubbed *boniches*, a perjorative for "maid." These women were often daughters of "good" families who chose to frequent the

GIs as girlfriends and "fiancés." Like the Japanese *panpan*, the *boniche* was born of the specific conditions of the postwar period.[136] During the American occupation of Japan, the *panpans* openly prostituted themselves to the conquering hero, in the process "unsettling" the Japanese, according to John Dower, because they served as "striking symbols of the whole convoluted phenomenon of 'Americanization.'"[137] In the same way, the French *boniche* symbolized the "Americanization" of France as well as the loss of respectability traditionally invested in the figure of *la jeune fille*.

Fears about sexual behavior and national reputation were rooted in the occupation. A columnist for the *Journal de la Marne* struck a sensitive note in 1945 when he accused women seen with Americans on the streets of Reims as being no different than wartime whores and *tondues*. He was soon receiving a flood of protest in the mail, and was ultimately forced to apologize publicly to his readers about his accusations.[138] Throughout the war, prostitutes represented the humiliation of defeat. "What shame we felt," recalled Alfred Scheiber concerning prostitutes in Lyon who offered their charms occupying German soldiers.[139] Prostitutes were supposed to have benefited from the Germans by choosing to cooperate "horizontally." Wartime resisters dismissed them as *collaboratrices* who had relinquished the right to be French.[140] A large proportion of prostitutes, it was rumored, were married to French prisoners in German stalags.[141] The myth of the prostitute-wife transformed sexually available women into objects of disgrace and anger.

Even after the Liberation, as we have seen, the sexual behavior of women remained pivotal in determining national identity and reputation. At stake here was a contested Frenchness. Many journalists felt the GIs were not encountering the right *type* of women, what Pierre Aubéry called "the authentic French population, which had quietly borne its suffering during the war years."[142] For such an image journalists drew on the devout mother. The well-known writer Georges Duhamel described her in this way: "I am thinking of a woman whose face is framed with white hair, and whose expression is veiled by worry, and who said to me this morning: 'We are going to have to be patient throughout the night as we wait for our husbands and sons.'"[143] What a pity, agreed Jean Vanier of *Havre-éclair*, that the Americans lack other images of the French people, for example, "the mother of the family, tending to her children with great attentiveness, exhausting her health and strength to make ends meet."[144] Traditional gender roles served up nostalgia as *la France profonde*. To visually present the French people to an American audience in *Life* magazine, the novelist Vercors chose a poster featuring a young girl. "It is France, as light dawns. As she shields her eyes against the bright sun, her hand still bears the mark of the nail which held her crucified. . . . She is not joyful. She is proud."[145] Vercor's image of France as a suffering female Christ formed a mirror opposite to the so-called *fille de joie* greeting GIs on the streets. The pride and suffering of an entire people went missing when the prostitute offered her charms to the new conquerors.

During the months after the landings, commodities such as cigarettes and sex became central to how the French and Americans came to understand each other. From their pockets the GIs produced enchanted things: Hershey bars, chewing gum, Lucky Strikes. Only gradually would the magic of these things dissipate—as they became vehicles of American corruption and power. Just as army surplus came to stand for US wealth, so too did the prostitute become nationalized as a symbol of French immorality. To the Americans, the prostitute taught the lessons of authority and control; to her compatriots, she provided a model of dishonor and servility. In this way, she drew sharp lines of privilege between those soldiers who could enjoy her body and those who had to stand by ashamed as they did. As for the *boniche* making herself a slave to American luxuries, she also affirmed the new American equation of greatness with material wealth. Her greed heralded the encroachment of US capital, a world where a Hershey bar and a woman's body differed little except in the price they commanded on the market. Like the common whore, then, the *boniche* took the measure of national decline. She was scorned but also feared. A culture was turning its back on itself in the rush for the gaudy American future.

5

The Silver Foxhole

THE LIBERATION OF PARIS was a precarious time for a prostitute like Marie-Thérèse Cointré, who had plied her trade with the
Germans. In August 1944, a neighbor invited her to go out to welcome Charles de Gaulle. "If you want to get a punch in the mouth,
that's fine, but I'm not going!" she replied. Cointré knew all too well
that the French Resistance or FFI was publicly shaving the heads of
women who had slept with Germans during the occupation. In the
turbulence of the Liberation , the FFI sometimes failed to make the
distinction between a professional prostitute and a French woman
guilty of "horizontal collaboration."[1] Cointré did consider "hustling
up" a member of the FFI to showcase her "patriotism," but in the end
she was too scared to venture out. Instead she spent the next three
months hidden in the safety of her apartment. Lack of food on the
table forced her to reconsider her prospects. "Why not do some business with the Americans?" she asked herself. Why not indeed? While
she managed to find "Mr. USA" at the train station in Montparnasse,
her first impressions were far from favorable. "Two hundred, sometimes three hundred francs, but what bastards!" she complained to a
colleague. "They do not shut up about how 'the frauleins f— better
than you' and 'what is all this talk about Paris and French women?'"[2]

For Marie-Thérèse, the liberation of Paris meant little more than a
well-timed change to a new clientele. Such an easy switch belied the
tremendous changes taking place outside her door. Increasingly her

city had been seen as "the brothel of Europe" as Hitler liked to call it. "Talk about Paris and French women" among the GIs had made the City of Light the favored destination of soldiers on leave.[3] By eroticizing the campaign as an opportunity for romance, military propagandists gave the GIs a fresh motive for fighting the war in France. Once encouraged, however, the GI libido was impossible to contain. Prostitution became endemic as did high venereal disease rates and sexual assaults on civilian women. Although all of France was eroticized in the GI imagination, Paris became the ultimate fantasy of total libidinal satisfaction. As a result, both the Parisian sex industry and Parisian society generally underwent dramatic changes.

"Paris," remembered Roger Foehringer, "by gosh that was the ambition of every American soldier to get to PARIS."[4] The lucky ones arrived on leave; others pleaded with their commanders when their camp was nearby; the rest had to "get lost" on their way somewhere and "wind up" there.[5] For soldiers who grew up in rural America, Paris was *the* city of light—the biggest, most fantastic place they had ever visited.[6] The GIs called it "the silver foxhole." For Peter Belpulsi leave in Paris was "a journey through Paradise." Charles Taylor wrote his wife about a memorable dinner at the "ritzy" Café de Paris: "We enjoyed the place for it was full of 'oui, Monsieur,' and mirror-perfect waiters."[7] "They could take a big patch of cow manure and dress it up to look like a beef steak dinner," claimed Walter Brown, "and you wouldn't know the difference, only the taste."[8] A walk along the Seine that "brought me in view of the famous Notre Dame cathedral with its architectural flying buttress" was the highlight of Belpulsi's trip.[9] The Eiffel Tower (Eiffelt for Murray Shapiro and Eiffle for Bert Damsky) was inundated with GIs craning their necks.[10] *How to See Paris: For the Soldiers of the Allied Armies* became a trusted guide. (Ironically, the book instructed them to "find the old and picturesque Jew's district" in the Saint-Paul quarter.)[11] More disappointing was the Louvre, where Leonardo da Vinci's *Mona Lisa* had been packed up and hidden away.[12] "The sightseeing was pretty limited," remembered William Brunsell.[13]

But most GIs did not give a damn about the *Mona Lisa*. They

came to Paris for one reason and one reason only: sex. As GI Charles
Whiting put it, they "rolled into Paris" ready to "make whoopee."[14]
Gen. Omar Bradley remembered how one of his majors "anticipated the fever that seized the US Army as it neared Paris" because
the soldiers had been "raised on the fanciful tales of their fathers in
the AEF [American Expeditionary Forces]."[15] One GI on a truck to
Paris shouted joyously, "We're all going to get laid, French style!"[16]
"Ooh-la-la! Paree, here I come! Wine, women & song! That's for me!"
was how the boys in one platoon described their upcoming visit. Soldiers came back reporting that "it's ooh-la-la. Just what we've heard—
everything—and all to be had."[17] "Wicked" was how William Mc-
Conahey described the city: "pretty girls could be picked up almost at
will if one so desired." McConahey portrayed Paris as a "wide open"
city, and he was right.[18]

An estimated 40 percent of GIs who contracted venereal disease
did so in Paris.[19] "Parisianisation" for one GI inspired this little ditty:

A naughty little soldier
Who was sweating out rotation
Got a three-day pass to Paris
For some real recreation.
But after he was finished
And returned to his old station
He had to go on sick call
For some rehabilitation.[20]

GIs called the VD they contracted in Paris their "souvenir of Gai
Paree."[21] While smaller French cities—Le Havre, Marseille, Rouen,
and Reims—also became gold rush towns for French prostitutes, it
was Paris that became the center of a new sex industry.[22] The army
set aside ten thousand hotel rooms in Paris for GIs on leave there, a
number by no means comprising the number of soldiers in the city at
any one moment.[23]

For one hundred years, prostitution had been legal in France under
a system of *maisons closes* or *maisons de tolérance*—brothels supervised

by medical personnel and the police.[24] Prostitutes or *filles soumises* could practice their trade either on their own or in a legal brothel as long as they received regular exams for venereal disease.[25] Long after systems of legal prostitution had been abolished elsewhere in Europe, the French one persisted.[26] During the German occupation, the *maisons de tolérance* operated with efficiency, but when the Americans arrived, they were overwhelmed by demand. As a result, clandestine prostitutes like Marie-Thérèse were given new business. A new type of sex worker took to the street, and sexual labor became chaotic, illegal, and unprofessional. In the absence of the old system of *maisons*, liberation Paris became a scene of sexual chaos, one that left prostitutes poor and unprotected. Without pimps, police, and doctors to order their world, they suffered violence and disease as well as arrest and imprisonment. But sexual commerce was not completely disordered. A new culture of prostitution emerged in Paris with its own language, urban geography, and protective practices. Despite an official ban on prostitution by the US War Department, the army quietly acquiesced in this new culture, accommodating its practices.

The Nazi System

Postwar changes in sexual labor had their roots in the German occupation. No sooner did the Germans arrive in Paris in 1940 than they established their own brothels under the supervision of the Wehrmacht Sanitary Service. The Germans preserved the most lavish Parisian houses (122 rue de Province, Le Sphinx, Le Chabannais) for the Gestapo, and consigned lesser seats of pleasure to SS officers and soldiers.[27] Prostitutes were the objects of violent police repression on behalf of the German occupying government. While the system was not as coercive as that set up by the Japanese in Southeast Asia, the Germans forced many French women who were already prostitutes to become part of the Nazi system, where they were kept under strict medical supervision to assure their venereal health.[28] In cooperation with the French Bureau of Hygiene and Police, the German Sanitary

Service largely succeeded in keeping a personnel file on every prostitute in France. Once a woman was declared infected by a soldier or police official, it was impossible for her to continue work. Contaminating a German soldier with venereal disease was a crime punishable by a jail sentence.[29]

While prostitutes were thought to have lived through the occupation drinking champagne and betraying resisters, in fact the opposite was often true. While many sex workers did cooperate with the Germans, many others joined Resistance efforts or refused in small ways to go along with the German authorities. For this reason it is too simple to say that prostitutes were inclined toward either "collaboration" or "resistance." Prostitutes such as Geneviève Lagarde gave new meaning to the phrase "kiss and tell" by offering her favors to the Germans, then their secrets to the Resistance.[30] By custom, a policeman would not enter a French bedroom once a prostitute had closed the door with a customer, the reason being that to interrupt a man at a "certain moment" was believed to cause psychological damage.[31] As the British spy Roxanne Pitt discovered in Paris, prostitutes used this loophole to hide Allied airmen who had dropped into enemy territory. The brothels also had secret exits and passages that saved the lives of many Allied fugitives. According to Pitt, on one occasion, a British airman too shy to act as a client chose instead to dress as a prostitute; the plan backfired when a French customer took a liking to him.[32]

Marie-Thérèse's adventures during the war are in many ways typical. She escaped the German brothels for a while in 1942 by signing a contract for labor service in Germany, working as a prostitute in Berlin, and then as a laborer in a factory in Hamburg.[33] The firestorm of July 1943, which she miraculously survived, drove her back to Paris.[34] There she worked in the legal brothels from time to time, suffering through the humiliating medical visits. Still a fierce desire for independence drove her to build her own business on the street, particularly after the liberation.[35] She became a *clandestine* or *fille insoumise*, according to the lingua franca of the French police. Unregistered with the French government, she carried no *carte* with her medical record.

In this way, she evaded medical supervision, and worked the streets illegally. As a *fille insoumise*, Marie-Thérèse was the wave of the future. In December 1945, the famous abolitionist Marthe Richard would observe that "the women in the houses and the women *en carte* represent only a depraved minority in the presence of an ever-growing number of clandestine prostitutes."[36] The next year *Libération soir* would agree that "in the immense flock of prostitutes, only a feeble minority haunt the *maisons de tolérance.*"[37]

Toward Clandestine Prostitution

The GIs encouraged this process of "disenclosure" by overwhelming the legal *maisons*. In April 1946, just as the last Americans were leaving Paris, the *maisons closes* finally shut their doors. Historians have understood the demise of the French system as an effect of corruption during the German occupation. The madams and pimps who made the system work, they argue, caused it to collapse following the war because they had collaborated with the Germans—servicing their sexual needs in exchange for stolen champagne and black market luxuries. After the liberation, these *collabos* were unable to recover either morally or politically, and thus the system came to be condemned by social reformers, communists, and crusaders such as Marthe Richard who pushed through its abolition first in the Parisian municipal council, then in the National Assembly.[38] In April of 1946 what came to be known as the Marthe Richard Law declared all regulated brothels closed, including 180 houses of pleasure in Paris alone.[39]

There is no doubt that the system of legalized prostitution emerged from the war morally and politically degraded. But by attributing the system's failure to domestic politics alone, historians have overlooked the flood of Americans knocking on brothel doors. At first during the jubilant August days of the Paris liberation, sex could be had in abundance—for free. Standing out on a Parisian balcony with several reporters, looking down as French women threw themselves at the liberating soldiers, the well-known journalist Ernie Pyle famously

remarked, "Any G.I. who doesn't get laid tonight is a sissy."[40] Heterosexual sex became a symbol of liberation, and for many GIs, it was
difficult to make the transition from consensual to commercial sex.
They resented having to pay for what they once got free. As David
Ichelson said later on of the French, they "put a very high price on a
common commodity you can get free in Germany. They are grateful
for their liberation, but feel like equals and do not intend to kiss our
asses for very long."[41]

Parisian brothels were also overwhelmed in the first days of liberation. One of the highest priorities of the US military was to segregate
them. On 2 September 1944, the provost marshal of the Seine base
section (covering Paris and its suburbs) arrived in the city with the
French police. Making the rounds, the men selected certain *maisons*
for the officers, certain *maisons* for white enlisted men, and certain
maisons for "negroes."[42] The chief surgeon arrived three days later to
declare all brothels off-limits to GIs, mostly to reduce already-soaring
rates of venereal disease. But the whorehouses hardly closed their
doors. As the months passed, they were neither properly policed nor
medically supervised because the old regulatory system, now once
again under the control of the French state, was struggling to get
back on its feet. Despite themselves, the French authorities had to
admit that the Nazis had run the system with great efficiency.[43] Once
the Germans departed, the government scrambled to recruit the necessary personnel, but it lacked the funds to make regulation work
with any semblance of effectiveness.[44] Some US captains sent military
police to stand outside the brothels in question, in collaboration with
the French gendarmerie.[45] While the GIs made elaborate efforts to
enter these houses of pleasure, including stealing civilian clothing, in
general it was easier and faster for them to seek out streetwalkers. An
army survey report from February 1945 estimated that only 5 percent
of the GIs contracted VD from brothels.[46]

As illegal demand outstripped legal supply, clandestine prostitution
became the principal means of selling sex. Only occasionally in GI
memoirs do we hear about "whorehouses," the finest of which were
reserved for Allied officers. The only kind of brothel patronized by

GIs was the *boîtes aux soldats*, called *abattoirs* or "slaughterhouses" before the war. As "factories of love," the *boîtes aux soldats* represented the lowest rung on the legal ladder of brothels and a kind of mass production of pleasure.[47] The abolitionist Marcel Pinard noted that one thousand to fifteen hundred men could pass through in a day, forcing a woman to take on fifty to sixty customers.[48] Still another abolitionist put that number at sixty to eighty.[49] *Les abattoirs* were notorious for serving North Africans for as little as six francs a "turn."[50] Under the American regime, the *boîtes* were also segregated by race, with soldiers paying a different price and choosing a different woman depending on whether they were "white" or "colored."[51] During peak periods, long lines of GIs snaked down the staircase, outside the door, and around the block.[52] After the liberation of Metz, a sign went up on a brothel on the Quai de l'Arsenal: "The establishment is lacking in personnel. Clients are kindly invited to prepare themselves with their hand."[53]

But for the majority of GIs, sex took place in the cheap hotel room. When asked to note the source of his contagion on a VD report, one soldier remembered his hotel room vividly: "first to left on first landing using stairway straight ahead when facing bar."[54] Such rooms existed in the so-called *hôtels de passe* run by managers with a long list of women a telephone call away.[55] Hotel managers were under pressure from the ministry to require identification from guests, supposedly to ensure honesty when signing the register. However, the hotel industry ignored this measure.[56] Prostitutes rented rooms on a daily or weekly basis, using the adjoining bars and cafés for customer pickup.[57] Many, like Marie-Thérèse, were fundamentally homeless and itinerant, moving between Paris and other GI camp towns to make their living.[58] After the tide receded, the madams in the old *maisons* had lost their clientele to a younger, cheaper generation of prostitutes, who fiercely protected their independence and were not interested in the legalities and protections of the old arrangement. In this way the GI invasion and the changes in sexual labor it provoked contributed greatly to the demise of the old regulatory system.

The New Prostitute

For the most part young, inexperienced, and poor, the Parisian prostitute was more vulnerable than she had ever been. During the war, historians believe, it had been married women, in particular the wives of French prisoners of war, who out of economic desperation had serviced the sexual needs of the Nazis.[59] Now a new generation took to the street. Remarking on the youth of this new generation, Richard referred to them as "enfants," as did Gaullist commissaires in 1945.[60] The police also called them "très jeunes filles."[61]

While it is difficult to find accurate statistical information about prostitutes during the chaotic postliberation days, French police and prison documents, as well as US Army records, suggest that these women were, in fact, young, unmarried, and childless.[62] Prostitutes arrested as they emerged from hotels with GIs were usually between twenty and twenty-four, almost never over thirty, and overwhelmingly single.[63] The vast majority (80.6 percent) of GIs filling out army venereal disease reports also described their sex workers as under thirty years of age.[64] Prostitutes entering La Petite Roquette prison were a little older than those women recorded in arrest records, probably because they often were "repeat offenders." Nevertheless, almost half were in their twenties or younger.[65] Even those who practiced in the *maisons closes* were extremely young, having obtained their registration by filing false papers.[66] GI Jack Plano was shocked by the youth of French whores: "As we moved deeper into France, one of the things that amazed me was the number of young girls around selling sex. These girls, most of them obviously from Paris, appeared to be no more than perhaps twelve or thirteen years old, yet had somehow or other been able to filter through the fighting lines in order to reach potential American customers."[67]

Women arrested for prostitution were dangerously far from home and family. Police arrest records suggest that only about 19 percent of them were born in Paris. Most had been born in the French provinces (both small towns and rural areas); and still others came from other

European countries (Belgium, Poland, Germany) and the French colonies.[68] A Belgian woman who was beaten to death by a GI in 1946 had come for the express purpose of prostituting herself.[69] Still others arrived with different ideas in mind. The press speculated that young girls came from the provinces at a very young age to be maids and housekeepers, but eventually fell into prostitution with the GIs for cigarettes and chocolate.[70] When women did register *métiers* with the authorities, they typified the range of work open to lower class or poor rural women: maid, seamstress, hairdresser, *femme de chambre*, barmaid, waitress, cook, housekeeper, florist, and concierge.[71] Only rarely does one see schoolteacher, typist, or telephone operator.[72] Women in the hotel and restaurant trades came into daily contact with the GIs, and were frequent converts to the more lucrative way of making a living. Prostitution also furnished employment for female refugees arriving in Paris from liberated parts of Germany or Poland during the last months of the war.[73]

It would be a mistake to think that only poor women engaged in prostitution. On one roundup in Marseille, a prostitute protested: "This doesn't happen to the rich women who have no need of hotels because they have apartments!"[74] Although more poor than rich women practiced prostitution, they were also more likely to be arrested. Lack of local family ties as well as poverty made them more vulnerable. Nineteenth-century Europeans had believed that some women were "naturally" lazy and thus prone to earn their living in bed. Such prejudices lingered in the war and postwar years. In a letter to the prefect of the Marne, a local medical inspector described prostitutes as "vicious and lazy women who have freely chosen their way of life."[75] Similarly, in the preface of a well-known 1946 book on prostitution, Dr. E. Rist of the Académie de Médecine expressed his opinion that "certainly there are, and always will be, born prostitutes, instinctive perverts whose fall no moral or pedagogical barrier can prevent."[76]

Although poverty drove prostitutes to make a living on their backs, they strove to look "rich" in appearance. During her months in Berlin, Marie-Thérèse wore nice dresses and high-heeled shoes both to attract men on the streets and to fool her landlady into believing that she was a respectable woman. American GIs often recalled in vivid terms the clothes prostitutes wore. When asked to describe physically their "sexual contacts" on an army VD report, they remembered, above all, a flowered hat, a blue and pink dress, a light blue coat, a chubby maroon brown skirt, a black suit with a white blouse and a purple turban, or a light red dress.[77] Not all prostitutes were beautiful, of course; one GI remembers his sexual contact having a "flat face."[78] But when Chester Jordan witnessed an armored division blow up a German train, he was impressed with how several prostitutes were dressed when they emerged from the fire and smoke: "They were coughing, screaming, and crying which could be expected, the strange thing was the way they were dressed in fancy flowery dresses, high heel shoes and enough make-up to last the war."[79] Civil Affairs officer John Maginnis had to be told that the four "well-mannered" and "good-looking" girls who helped him shop for perfume for his wife were, in fact, prostitutes.[80] Robert Seale was also surprised when he saw a madam who had gotten cozy with his friend Stosh. Although he expected her to be "some painted-up-crude floozy," she was in fact "well-dressed and attractive and impressed Pas and me with her command of several languages."[81]

Despite prostitutes' attempt to keep up appearances, however, even the most austere of moral conservatives had to admit that if a woman earned a living from her body, it was because of poor economic opportunities. While working-class women traditionally suffered meager wages, they particularly did so after the war. The French economy was in desperate shape at this time, kept afloat only by American aid and loans. The Germans had stripped the nation of its riches, and the Allies, in turn, had destroyed the infrastructure of French industry, down 40 percent from prewar levels.[82] In the fall of 1944, coal production was only 43 percent of 1938 levels.[83] Ports, railway tracks, and factories all had to be rebuilt. The tourist and luxury industries, long a backbone of the French economy, were moribund. Sources of family economic support were cut off because of separation from spouses and parents or the imprisonment or death of these relations. There was no end in sight to wartime scarcity, and the rationing system would be in effect until 1947. Fuel and housing shortages, particularly in the cold winter of 1944–45, were other burdens to bear.

In these difficult circumstances, many women turned to prostitution. "We see parading under our eyes former workers, former office employees, women who had a profession but who, finding their salary inadequate and weary of fighting against poverty, let themselves slide down the road which led to us," noted one social worker. Her assistant agreed: "Money is our great enemy."[84] Police officers' comments in the arrest registers also provide eloquent testimony to the power of money in sexual commerce. One woman "acknowledges that she practices prostitution, her sole means of existence . . . Her mother is in Limoges and her father has been deported to Germany." Still another is "separated from her husband, her thirteen-month-old child is at her parents' house."[85] Sometimes the prostitutes speak in their own words: "I make a living from prostitution; I am without work"; "I've been without work for two months so I prostitute myself in order to supplement my needs" or "because I am without any resources."[86] Detectives investigating the murder of a prostitute killed by a GI could not help but notice that she lived "difficilement." Although she was infected with syphilis, "her means did not allow her to care for herself. She rarely gave herself over to drink, and ate little."[87]

GIs also noticed the poverty of these women. As Jack Plano put it, "there was very little in the way of employment opportunities, so women in great numbers went into the oldest business known."[88] An army manual titled 112 Gripes about the French explained the "abnormal" number of prostitutes on the streets in this way: "Many girls who cannot live on their wages take to the street. Thousands of French women have lost their sweethearts, husbands, homes. The same thing is happening all over Europe."[89] GI Murray Shapiro regretted questioning a prostitute in Pigalle about why she sold herself. While he was probably wondering whether the motive was still gratitude, "in answer to my question she held out one hand, rubbing her thumb and forefinger together. 'Money' she said. I felt quite stupid. What a naïve, ridiculous question to ask."[90]

Danger on the Rue Pigalle

As a commercial transaction that took place between a young, poor female provider and a male client with a gun as well as cash in his pocket, this form of prostitution intensified an already considerable imbalance of power between the Americans and the French. The system privileged the GI by giving him access to cheap, readily available sex. In terms of venereal disease contamination, he ran no greater risk buying sex on the street than in the brothel.

Prostitutes gained certain advantages as well, for example, greater mobility and autonomy. Increasingly they refused to take on pimps or *maquereaux*, "mackerels."[91] Harassed by her pimp when she returned from Germany, Marie-Thérèse paid him fifty thousand francs to buy her freedom. Typically, he had begun as her "boyfriend," then gradually had become her employer. "A man approaches you, asks you to 'get married,'" she explained. "If you don't say 'no,' he will take you out dining, dancing, make love. Then he tells you you are in debt to him for these things. And you have to work it off; he makes it a high sum so it is very hard to work it off at once or over a small period."[92] Yet *souteneurs* or *demi-sels*, as they were called, increasingly had trouble putting women at their mercy and in their debt.[93] For one thing, they suffered from a bad reputation, having often gotten mired in the Gestapo during the war. As a result, *les classiques professionnelles* who worked for a pimp were more rarely found on the street. According to one social worker, by war's end 90 percent of prostitutes worked only for themselves.[94]

Sex workers were happy to be free of the procurers who exploited them. Yet the pimps had served one important purpose: they had protected their women from the violence of the streets. While the new system may have liberated prostitutes from their keepers, it left them vulnerable to the rough world in which they lived. Marie-Thérèse was shrewd about the new hazards of her profession. Both times she traveled to the GI camps in Rouen, she went with another prostitute; she also hired an American pimp to protect herself and her companion. "And yet I was still afraid, because I said to myself. One hit in the face . . . and they can steal all our money." When her partner got her purse stolen, Marie-Thérèse's response was first annoyance ("I told you not to bring your purse!") then fear. "My baby cheri, nice guy, nice guy," she sputtered to her pimp as she gave him a little more money "so that he would protect me well."[95] Her opinion of the Americans, as we have already seen, was decidedly mixed. They drank too much, for one thing, and they often refused to pay or even stole money as well as perfume and cosmetics. "You had to keep an eye on your purse with those bastards. It's sad to say, but I missed my Fritzes, who were gentler with women. I was not the only one to say it; all the women thought they same as me, only they did not always say it."[96] The general opinion among prostitutes in Montmartre was that if the Americans were "good boys," the Germans were more "correct" and "disciplined." They had preferred fellatio so they could keep an eye on their watches.[97]

The Americans also brought to Paris the brutality and violence they had learned on the battlefield. Charles Whiting put it best: "The men whored. They got drunk. They fought. Their tempers were short, and after the [front] their nerves weren't so good. They were quick, very quick, to take offense."[98] Four cases of prostitutes brutally murdered by the GIs highlight the dangers women faced in the seedier neighborhoods in Pigalle and the area around the boulevard Bonne Nouvelle.[99] The four victims fit the general profile of the prostitute on the street. Three were single, under thirty, and recently arrived in Paris, one from Hungary, one from Belgium, and one from the provinces; information for the fourth was lacking. Two were clandestine; one had been legal only a few weeks, and the fourth, although *soumise*, had been avoiding the police for weeks because she was ill with syphilis.

All four women suffered extremely violent deaths. The first, Elisabeth, was strangled after a fight for money with a GI who would not pay. After killing her and stealing her jewelry, he spent the evening taking another prostitute to the movies. The second woman, Henriette, was given two thousand francs by an American soldier to accompany him to a hotel. When they arrived at the room, she began to undress.

He did not. Instead he approached her, embraced her, then kicked her in the abdomen. He drew out a knife and stabbed her twenty-nine times, according to the police. Unable to recover the two thousand francs he had given her, which she had hidden in her panties, he finally left.[100] As for the third woman, Marie, the police concluded from the position of her body (legs apart, head on bed), that she suffered a deadly blow to the head, then was strangled for refusing to have anal sex with a GI. Evidence proved that she had been forced to do so anyways. The fourth woman, Renée, was shot in a hotel room by a GI. On the stairs they had passed two other prostitutes who saw his drawn gun behind her back and promptly called the police. By the time they arrived, however, a shot had rung out and the soldier was jumping out the window of the hotel. Renée died soon after.[101]

But prostitutes were not defenseless, and they did take measures to protect themselves. For one thing, streetwalkers often hustled in pairs. Orval Faubus remembers being "accosted" by Parisian prostitutes in twos and threes.[102] Sisters also joined forces on the streets.[103] In the provinces as well prostitutes worked in teams. When one Le Havrais complained about a house of prostitution on the rue Fulton, police discovered a line of thirty GIs and two French women having sex on the floor of a bombed-out building.[104] Marie-Thérèse picked up a partner when she traveled to the GI camp in Rouen. She did so as much out of sexual desire as the need for protection. Frequently women working together were lovers as well as business partners. In general, though, prostitutes viewed each other as associates first, and friends or lovers second.

Prostitutes also looked out for each other. A police corruption report demonstrates solidarity between prostitutes. When crooked agents threatened to arrest two streetwalkers unless they came up with two thousand francs, they are able to borrow it in a few minutes time.[105] Even when they were not "friends," prostitutes knew the intimate details of each other's lives. Police interviewing streetwalkers who knew Elisabeth found out that she had been suffering from eczema, that she was saving her money, and that she had been drinking too much. By talking to women who worked in the same neighbor-

hood as Marie, police discovered that she had eaten her last meal—
two glasses of white wine and a sandwich—alone and depressed at
the café Sans Souci on the rue Pigalle. These women also told police
that Marie was a petty thief and that she had no *habitués* or regular
customers. Prostitutes favored *habitués* because other streetwalkers
could identify them if problems arose; an *habitué* allowed prostitutes
to protect each other. At the end of the day, however, mistrust won
out over friendship. The police used women as undercover agents to
ferret out clandestine prostitutes. For this reason, the women were always on their guard with each other. When a "girlfriend" at the Gare
St. Lazare kept asking Marie-Thérèse if she was *en carte* she knew it
was time to change her beat.[106] Given the competition and suspicion
between prostitutes there was a limit to their bonding. In the end they
were very much on their own.

Many sex workers carried guns in their purses and depended on
the police for safety.[107] Two policemen were called to a hotel on the
rue Étienne Marcel one evening about some trouble between GIs
and management. The Americans had come looking for two girls. A
fight had broken out, and the GIs threatened everyone with a hatchet
and a bottle. By the time the police appeared, one manager had been
severely wounded on the face, and the hotel guests had been "terrorized." The police themselves received bites and other wounds
when they tried to restrain the suspects. To the relief of everyone,
the American military police soon came on the scene.[108] Generally,
the MPs, referred to as "snowdrops" because of their white helmets,
could be relied upon to quiet down the GIs and command the situation.[109] To the French, these men looked like giants. As the street-
walker Violette de Barbès wryly observed, "no doubt you couldn't
get into the Military Police if you were less than six feet four and
220 pounds."[110]

Given the imbalance of power that existed between the American
conquerors and the liberated French at this time, the wartime transformation in commercial sex was almost certain to favor the male
clients. Throughout the winter of 1944–45, in particular, civilians were
confronting hunger and deprivation. These wartime realities fed a sex

industry that, in terms of the poverty, low wages, and labor conditions endured by the urban population that supplied it with workers,
resembled textile manufacturing in mid-nineteenth-century England.
At the same time, however, prostitutes were never forced into the
kind of sexual slavery that prevailed on the eastern front.[111]

Nor were streetwalkers angels themselves. One hotel owner told
the police that a prostitute who had been murdered had "the unfor-
tunate habit of ripping off her clients, particularly Americans passing
through."[112] In November 1945, an American soldier filed a complaint
concerning a prostitute named Anne who had relieved him of sixteen
thousand francs after he spent the night in her company.[113] Women
who emerged from hotels with GIs and were caught by the police
often had in their possession stolen money and watches.[114]

Sexual Geographies

There is no doubt that as the American GIs arrived in Paris and began
to seek out women, they encountered an unruly, often violent world.
But even in the chaos of a system without pimps or legal supervision,
the GIs bought a great deal of sex in a strange city in a very short period of time. (The average GI leave was sixty to seventy-two hours.)[115]
Although the *maisons* were officially off-limits, the Americans knew
where and how to find women for sex.[116] Despite the language barrier, they could ask for sex in French and even bargain for price. How
did they do it? For obvious reasons, the GIs were quick studies when
it came to sex. In addition, however, a new but surprisingly well-
organized culture of prostitution emerged in the days after liberation,
one that made Paris into a lean, mean sex machine, able to service the
sexual needs of thousands of GIs on a daily basis.

Although GIs and prostitutes could not meet in well-known brothels with fixed addresses, they could rely on a set of streets, train stations, and parks that were already well-established places to find sex.
Even GIs who had never been to Paris before, and most had not, could
benefit from word of mouth concerning which neighborhoods would

yield willing women, as well as which brothels were for officers, for white men, or for "colored." Specific locations and neighborhoods that had been centers of sexual labor continued to be so. When Marie-Thérèse decided to seek out "Mr. USA," she knew exactly where to find him: the train stations at Montparnasse and St. Lazare. The stations were long-established sites for buying sex; the Gare du Nord and Gare de l'Est were also easy pickings.[117] All four stations were in neighborhoods packed with *hôtels de passe* where rooms rented by the hour. Pigalle, the boulevard Bonne Nouvelle, and Montmartre were also customary spaces to buy sex. Murray Shapiro described the rue de Jean-Baptiste Pigalle as "one long prostitution street."[118] "Pig Alley swarmed with whores, professional and amateur," remembered Charles Whiting. "There were young women of all shapes and sizes, ugly and pretty, in dyed rabbit-fur jackets, too-short dresses, and wooden wedge-heel shoes, their bare legs painted brown with the seams carefully drawn in with an eyebrow pencil."[119] The Folies Bergère, a favorite entertainment spot for the GIs, also teemed with women selling their charms. Jack Capell remembered a dozen in the space of one block, some of them not too healthy: "they were deathly thin and went into frequent spells of uncontrollable coughing."[120]

Prostitutes also came to the GIs, moving into the touristy parts of the city where they tended to gather, on the Champs Elysées and *les grands boulevards*, particularly the boulevard Haussmann and the avenue de l'Opéra.[121] Robert Peters remembered venturing out to the Champs Elysées at twilight and seeing "lurid females with leather purses" who gathered around military buses even before their doors opened.[122] Streetwalkers also clustered around the special hotels that lodged GIs on leave, among them, the Grand Hôtel and the Hôtel de Paris in the Opéra quarter.[123] Leroy Stewart remembered cleaning up the best he could before arriving at a "big hotel in the heart of Paris" that the army had taken over.[124] As Paris became an established vacation center for the military forces, the American Red Cross made available a number of hotels and clubs. By the end of the war, a GI on leave would usually be housed in one of fourteen such Red Cross hotels; he need only step outside his front door in order to purchase sex.[125] Prostitutes also crowded the GI camps in or near Paris, in the Bois de Vincennes or at Versailles.[126] Working independently, these women "specialized" in Americans, even black Americans. One chambermaid at the Hotel d'Amérique remembered "a perpetual line of Americans" outside a prostitute's room. "Never a civilian . . . never an Algerian or an individual of this type."[127]

In these sexual spaces of the city, cafés, nightclubs, and bars were the most popular meeting places. The owners of such establishments would not take money for providing a rendezvous, but they would charge mightily for other "services," such as a noon and evening meal.[128] *Stars and Stripes* reported on 16 December 1944 that dancing in all bars, cabarets, nightclubs, and dance halls was prohibited in order to "curtail the activity of 'uncontrolled prostitutes' who have been flourishing since the liberation of Paris."[129] The women would crowd the GIs' favorite nightspots. "The Lido and the Casino were the places to be in Paris," remembered David Ichelson. "The women lined up and the madames came along to ask if you would accompany their 'daughter' in, as unaccompanied women were not allowed."[130] If a GI arrived alone, he would make an overture by treating a woman to a drink. After light conversation and negotiation, they would fix a price and she would provide her services, usually in a *hôtel de passe* above the bar or nearby where she was a known quantity.[131] Waitresses were often propositioned.[132] Bartenders had lists of women to call if a GI knew to ask.[133] GIs would proposition a woman or fondle her breasts even when she was with a French man; a fight would often ensue.[134]

Ballrooms and "dancings" were also reliable pickup spots; here a GI initiated a "pass" by asking a prostitute to dance. Many street-walkers went there to *lever des américains*, as they called it.[135] Many others met their *habitués* there, particularly after the war when the soldiers were not rushing back to the front. Sometimes a prostitute would fulfill her duties in an alleyway, blacked-out doorway, or under a bridge. These encounters the GIs called "knee-tremblers."[136] Finally, there were the *maisons de massage*, which offered sex as one possibility among others; these were often supervised by the police as part of the legal system.[137] As chaotic as prostitution in Paris seemed, it was highly organized compared to in the French provinces where sex took place anywhere and everywhere. On one of her trips to Reims, even as seasoned a professional as Marie-Thérèse found herself doing business in a cemetery: "Unique! But scandalous really, f——ing next to the dead!"[138]

In order to communicate their desires, the GIs had to speak French, which most could not. Similarly few prostitutes spoke English even if they had learned it at school. So the two parties developed a distinctive vernacular of sex talk. Streetwalkers all had pseudonyms, and most chose names that were easy to say and hear: "Lulu," "Blackie," and every imaginable variation on "ette": Jeannette, Paulette, Georgette, Yvette, Colette, Lucette, Odette, Lulette, and Annette. Sometimes the prostitutes took on famous names ("Lili" after "Lili Marlene," or "Choo Choo" after the pinup Choo Choo Johnson). Still others assumed American names ("Susan," "Betty," or "Kate") to bridge the gap.

Nevertheless problems persisted. GIs forced to recall the names of their sexual contacts on VD reports came up with names like "Donene," "M. Monegue Cecotte," or "Miss Yoann Charrou." On these reports, it is clear that the GIs rarely knew the family name or profession of the French woman they believed had contaminated them. Similar reports for British prostitutes contrast sharply in this sense: the GIs could provide a lot more information on the British women with whom they could converse in English.[139] French prostitutes also had trouble understanding the GIs, and relied on their pocket dictionaries to make themselves understood.[140] When Marie-Thérèse and another woman traveled to the GI camps in Rouen, two American soldiers approached her yelling "Mlle Fifique, moi fiancé." She had no idea what they were trying to say to her until she realized that they were offering to pimp her and her friend by pretending to be their "fiancés."[141] When Faubus asked a Parisian prostitute, "How much English can you speak?" she responded, "Three hundred francs."[142]

The GIs did their best to learn the lingua franca of sex talk. Karl Clarkson recalled how when he stood guard with a French man, "we

spent our time trying to teach each other the others' language. He told
me that the way to approach a French girl was to say, 'Mademoiselle,
voulez-vous coucher avec moi?' If she said 'Oui,' that says it all."[143]
According to Ichelson, "Suassont neuf [soixante-neuf] was a figure
of speech, and we knew that no normal person would practice it."[144]
"Zigzag" or "zig zig" became the words used to demand sex. Both
prostitutes and GIs would approach each other asking, "Zig Zag? Zig
Zag?"[145] Pierre Aubéry remembers several GIs on the Le Havre docks
who asked him for a "Mad'moiselle" by saying "Zig Zag" and using
an obscene gesture.[146] British and American soldiers took up the word
during the First World War to denote drunkenness, probably because
of the "zigzag" way the inebriated walk.[147] It then somehow came
to stand for intercourse, underlining the close relationship between
alcohol and sex during the war.[148] Some Americans still used it to denote inebriation, a fact that could lead to painful misunderstanding.
Plano remembers how his corporal was seeing a French girl from
a "straight-laced middle-class family" in Le Mans. One night, when
the two were eating dinner at her house, the corporal tried to make
French conversation by cheerfully exclaiming, "Hier soir, beaucoup
zig-zig!" He had meant to say that he had had too much to drink, and
could not understand why the girl's parents looked mortified. Plano's
attempt to kick him under the table caused only further confusion.[149]

GIs and sex workers also developed their own system of money
exchange. During the summer and fall of 1944, the GIs frequently had
no cash. "Invasion" money was not taken seriously by the GIs, as it
"didn't seem real" and was "like a lot of hay."[150] Most often they gam-
bled it away.[151] During this period, sex was most often had for GI products such as soap, cigarettes, chocolate, and K rations. In the winter of
1944–45, however, sex increasingly became a cash business. GIs were
given money before going on leave, and the Parisians found cigarettes
and other commodities easier to obtain. What to do with all this cash
was a problem for women who were homeless, walked bad neighborhoods, and lived in cheap hotels.[152] The standard price for a "pass"
was most frequently two to three hundred francs, about five dollars
in American money at the time (twenty-two to thirty-two euros or

sixty dollars today).[153] But price could vary wildly. Ichelson remembered paying four times that for a pass, about twenty dollars, "with an optional blow job."[154] This figure infantryman Shapiro considered outrageous at the time.[155] Evidently he was not alone. An army-issued pamphlet listing 112 *Gripes about the French* included the complaint that "French women are too damned expensive."[156] A prostitute who hustled could expect to make about eight hundred francs a night or more if she knew the right places to go.[157] The GI army camps meant even more cash. When Marie-Thérèse traveled outside of Paris to various GI encampments in Orléans, Reims, or Rouen, she brought in four thousand francs a day. But this meant "servicing" thirty to forty men in the space of a few hours.

Intimate relations could be "encouraged" commercially in more subtle ways through gifts and favors. GIs often lured women into relationships by promising them silk stockings, cigarettes, and food; in response, a French woman would consider him her *habitué* or *fiancé*. Even as shrewd a prostitute as Marie-Thérèse entered into these kinds of relations with the Americans. At one point, she finds a GI who wants to marry her and protect her from her "boyfriends." Thinking that she worked in a bar as a waitress, he would prepare her dinner when she got home. "He was gentle with me, he gave me enough money," she remembered. The American, it turned out, was married and had two children.[158] Such arrangements allowed many prostitutes to evade arrest when they would describe their customers as their "amis" or "fiancés."[159] Even if the police were not fooled, such cases were difficult to prosecute.

Prostitutes passed on American cash and cigarettes to the police, whom they affectionately called *les poulets* or "the chickens," a common slang word. Corruption was rife. Making sure that the local cop on your beat had a steady supply of cigarettes meant that he would give you advance notice when the roundups were going to happen.[160] Cops became local personalities with names like "Bébé Rose" and "Lapipe." They became pimps in the sense that they organized the neighborhood and provided protection from the police.[161] If business was bad, *les poulets* would sometimes accept sexual favors in lieu of cigarettes or cash.[162] Neither were the MPs on the straight and narrow. Shapiro recalls how in Nancy, jeep patrols of MPs would regularly police the *boîtes à soldats*. But because the schedules of such patrols were made well known, GIs could easily disappear at the appropriate moment. Long lines would melt away, then reappear suddenly once the jeeps had surveyed the area.[163]

Cooperation between GIs and prostitutes ensured a steady supply of sex. Americans were "provided" with civilian clothing so that they could enter into *maisons closes* off limits to the military.[164] Somewhat valiantly, American GIs tried to shield French women from arrest and imprisonment. If a prostitute claimed she was "une amie" or "une fiancée" of a soldier, he played along. A gendarme in Yvetot complained that an attempt to repress debauchery in the area was thwarted when "the prostitutes changed tactics. In order not to be controlled, they made soldiers their escorts."[165] A Marseille prostitute's claim that her escort was her fiancé of two months was disproven when she could not tell police his name.[166] If GIs planned to spend an evening with some woman, they would become "angry towards the guard who tried to take away their delectable merchandise," as one policeman put it.[167] At about 11:30 p.m. on 1 July 1945, French policemen attempting to round up two prostitutes had to confront a group of hostile GIs gathered around to fight them, and threatening to use their guns.[168] French Police reported getting beaten, shot, and having their pistols stolen on several occasions when rounding up prostitutes.[169] They had trouble convincing witnesses to testify, because the latter feared reprisals from pimps and American soldiers.[170]

The GIs became so notorious for hiding prostitutes in their jeeps and getting into fights with the French police that the MPs were forced to join the French police on roundups.[171] According to one journalist, the MPs "only had to appear on the scene, roll their shoulders, and rest their hands on their Colts, and the protests would stop."[172] Another method used by gendarmes and MPs was to go from hotel room to hotel room, asking both the man and the woman if they knew the name of the other. If they did, the MPs would politely say "Excuse me" and go on to the next room.[173] Undercover police learned to patrol the entrances to hotels and catch women as they came out, rather than went in, with Americans. There was decidedly less resistance from the GI if the prostitute was arrested *after* services had been rendered.[174]

Hunger Borne of the Hovering Presence of Death

GI sex began as a gift, free for the asking. Increasingly, as we saw in the last chapter, it became a commodity linked to corruption and bad faith. Demanding sex at a fast food pace, the GIs changed the rhythm and movement of the city. To accommodate soldiers, streetwalkers used not only the old geography of sexual labor but also a newly developed one—touristy bars, American hotels, and Red Cross clubs. GIs and prostitutes also invented a distinctive language for sex, giving novel meaning to such terms as *zigzag, fiancé, habitué,* and *poulet.* Finally, by bartering cigarettes or chocolate for sex, they created their own exchange system. This new culture of prostitution was quickly accepted not only by the GIs themselves, but by the American and French officials who accommodated it. The result was the collapse of the old regulatory system. Contributing to this breakdown were not simply the numbers of soldiers demanding sex at any time—nor the rapidity with which they wanted it. A uniquely American impatience with preordained systems was also important. The GIs were just not willing to put up with fussy "old world" regulations and hierarchies. Nor did they feel any need for discretion, given how far they were from their girlfriends, wives and parents back home. The *maisons closes* had been designed to facilitate the illicit satisfaction of sexual desire in as unobtrusive way as possible. Instead the GIs encouraged a form of sexual trade that was wildly democratic, boisterous, and garish—in short, quintessentially American.

This new way of doing business proved to be surprisingly efficient, so much so that it brought down the system that had ordered sexual commerce for well over a century. By deinstitutionalizing sexual labor and creating a new sex market flooded with young, homeless, single women, the GIs undermined the notion of sex as a profession that had grounded the *maisons closes*. After they departed, the system lay vulnerable to attack because of its proven irrelevance as well as its corruption. Social reformers who had campaigned against it for decades suddenly found it easy to shut down. In addition, the Americans had brought penicillin to the European continent. The "magic bullet," which was in widespread use by late 1944, reduced the number of days necessary to treat gonorrhea from twenty to five. Inasmuch as the old regulatory system was geared to the prevention of venereal disease, its purpose and its medical protocols were now also outdated. Because government regulation was never revived, prostitution in France was definitively transformed into a free market system, one that would still be structured by brothels and pimps, but never again by the state.

Paris during the winter of 1944–45 was a unique world. For many soldiers, it was a dream destination, an erotic paradise of women. Their experiences stage-side at the Folies Bergère, drinking champagne in the Lido, or taking a prostitute to a Montmartre hotel fulfilled their expectations of "gay Paree." The world of Paris and the world of combat were in every way opposite: one was a pleasure dome of light and satisfaction, the other a world of darkness, death, fear, and suffering. And yet, as Walter Brown remembered, the two worlds were intimately connected: "The few moments a man could snatch with a woman seemed somehow islands of sanity in a world gone mad. Or maybe sometimes bizarre and desperate sex were only an extension of that madness."[175] The combat world shadowed the GIs during their stay, affecting their every action and response to the city.

Wartime writings express an emotional as well as physical desire for sex among infantrymen. Their longing explains why sex was so successful as a tool of military propaganda. In his journal, Raymond Gantter spoke of a "hunger born of the hovering presence of death and the wild desire not to die unsatisfied, with a body still fierce and full and unused."[176] Similarly Nat Frankel remembered that "the sexuality of the dogface in Europe was neither flamboyant nor sentimental, nor was it callous. There was great desperation in it and considerable satisfaction, but just as often it began with terrible yearning."[177] Aramais Hovsepian wrote his father that "French girls are easy to get what with American cigarettes and chocolate and us being heroes in their eyes, and I'm not going to be so choosey [*sic*] from now on, and get my fun where I can get it while I'm alive."[178] "Anything that will take the edge off and let you forget for a little while, even an hour or two, there's a war on and tomorrow Graves Registration may be putting a tag on you," agreed Sgt. Janice Giles.[179] GIs on combat duty wore flashes of green felt; the prostitutes headed straight for them when they descended from buses because they had the reputation as the ones most interested in sex.[180] There was the war and there was Paris; nothing else lay in between. The war gave Paris meaning, and Paris made the war bearable.

6

Dangerous Indiscretions

IN SEPTEMBER 1944, while leading the Twenty-Ninth Infantry Division across Brittany to liberate France, the American Gen. Charles Gerhardt decided that his boys needed sex. So he instructed his chief of staff to start a house of prostitution.[1] The task went to the St. Renan Office of Civil Affairs, the military section assigned to provide the needs of the liberated civilian population. Asa Gardiner, the local Civil Affairs officer, called upon his contacts in the French police force, who produced a pimp named Morot. The pimp, in turn, recommended four prostitutes currently refuged nearby. Gardiner and Morot rode an army jeep to interview them, and on the way back Gardiner asked Morot to manage the business. For the actual brothel, they billeted a house outside St. Renan that had recently been vacated by the Germans. The French woman who owned the house was given no payment, nor informed of the exact use to which her property would be put.[2] A few days later, as Morot moved in with the prostitutes, Gerhardt approved the sign for the establishment reading "Blue and Gray Corral, Riding Lessons 100 Francs."[3] When the "Corral" opened for business on 10 September, twenty-one GIs, transported by jeep from the bivouac area, waited patiently in line.[4] After five hours of business, the brothel was shut down by the assistant provost marshal on the recommendation of the division chaplain.[5]

The Corral was not the only "GI whorehouse" established in France. An estimated dozen divisions started their own brothels there and in

Italy during the years 1943–45.[6] As early as 6 July 1944, one month after D-day, brothels in Cherbourg were being run indirectly by and for US soldiers, including those designated strictly for "negroes."[7] The creation of such establishments resulted in great part from the fact that, as the Brittany case makes clear, the French were happy to help. Given his soldiers' expectations of France, Gerhardt thought the best he could do was to ensure the medical safety of their sexual pursuits. The general's chief of staff later defended the brothel by arguing that "the situation in which this division was operating and in the French communities in which we were located that it would be desirable to endeavor to control social relations between our men and the French people rather than to allow promiscuous social relations to obtain."[8] Purged of army jargon, that statement meant that the soldiers fully expected to get some "action" in France, and Gerhardt wanted to keep it clean and safe. Like many US commanders, Gerhardt held that male sexual activity was healthy for battle. As Gen. George Patton most famously put it, "if they don't fuck, they don't fight."[9]

Both US military and French officials believed that sexual fulfillment was necessary for male physical vigor. Given this commonality, one might assume that the two sides would have easily cooperated on the regulation of GI sexual activity. Not so. Prostitution became a point of contention between the two nations during the US military presence. In particular, authorities clashed over the problem of venereal disease, which became a grave problem among the GIs. Army officers blamed French women for infecting US soldiers with venereal disease.[10] In order to keep their men battle ready, they began to manage the health and mobility of such women, seeking to control their proximity to US soldiers. In the army officers' view, the necessarily complete command of the GI's body gave them dominion over the French woman's body as well.

The US military insistence on sexual management of this kind sprang from contempt of the new French government that was struggling to reestablish control after the Liberation. Prostitutes, the army believed, were infecting soldiers in alarming numbers. But because of bureaucratic inefficiency as well as their own sexual depravity,

French officials were unwilling and/or unable to do anything about it. This disrespect for French authorities emboldened US officers to deny them political autonomy over a broad terrain of social welfare administration. The US military used the regulation of the French female body not only to ensure the health of its fighting force, but also to demarcate and consolidate its power in the years 1944 to 1945. In addition, by defining the French nation itself in prostituted terms, the US military naturalized its dominance of power relations in the European theater.

The conflicts that arose between the US Army and the French government over commercial sex anchored larger struggles for authority and revealed the willingness of the Americans to flex their new muscles as a global power. At the heart of the quarrel was the issue of discretion. Soon after D-day, military officers realized that they could not control GI sexual activity in France. In order to keep such activity medically safe, the officers ended up condoning it privately while condemning it publicly. The War Department prohibited such brothels as the Blue and Gray Corral because it could not keep such establishments from being observed by journalists, in other words, exposed in the American press. Above all, the army wanted to "protect" the American public from such sexual indiscretions. As a result, GI promiscuity took place in parks, cemeteries, streets, and abandoned buildings in cities. Sexual relations became unrestricted and public; sexual intercourse was performed in broad daylight before the eyes of civilians, including children. Locals in cities like Le Havre and Reims condemned such public displays as scandalous and degrading.

The army sham concerning sex signaled a fundamental disrespect toward the French people that led to bitter conflict with their government officials. In the summer and fall of 1944, the American military blamed local governments for soaring rates of venereal infection among GIs but gave them little or no power to do anything about it. Then, as the war drew to a close in 1945, the army increasingly ignored the serious social and medical effects of continued GI promiscuity in urban areas. While at first glance sexual relations may seem to be a minor issue in debates between French and American leaders over who would run the country and how the war could be won, in fact the management of GI sex in France became a subtle but vital transfer point for the growth of American political power in Europe.

The full importance of the conflicts over prostitution can only be understood within their historical context of French political instability. As we have seen, the Americans were not receptive to attempts by the French state to "prove" itself and assert political autonomy.[11] De Gaulle struggled against the Allied leadership to install his own *commissaires* in Normandy and seize control over France. Besides being "illegal" in this sense, de Gaulle's government lacked resources and international legitimacy. The United States did not recognize de Gaulle as a sovereign leader until October of 1944, and meanwhile controlled much of French economic and social life on the grounds that such supervision was necessary for the execution of the war. Hence GIs in France sought out sexual encounters with women whose national status and autonomy as French citizens had been called into question by the US military invasion. During this transitional moment, the American control of sexual relations produced critical differences between liberator and liberated. Control of sexual commerce became a means for the US military to claim its authority over the French nation at the dawn of the Cold War.[12]

Health Is Victory

Franco-American conflicts over venereal disease reveal the wider moral assumptions of American society and the military during World War II. In particular, they expose the hypocrisy at the heart of the US Army's policy toward sex. The army did not really care if a GI had sex with a French woman. What it did care about—a great deal—was that a soldier not contract a venereal disease. According to the US Army in the European Theater of Operations (ETOUSA), VD posed a very real threat to the endurance of the troops in the European theater of war. "In the face of the impending battle," wrote Cdr. Jacob Devers to all units in December 1943, "the loss of manpower from venereal disease cannot be excused. Each soldier who contracts venereal disease betrays the United States Army as completely as one who willfully neglects his duty."[13] By likening VD to betrayal, Devers freighted sexual behavior with the weight of treason. Given these high stakes, promiscuity became a topic of paramount military concern during early 1944 as American troops trained in England for the invasion of the Continent. Officers at Supreme Headquarters Allied Expeditionary Forces (SHAEF) in London grappled with the high rate of venereal disease among GIs who had fought in Sicily and southern Italy.[14] Besides high-ranking generals, those officers included senior medical consultants as well as the staff of the army's Preventive Medicine Division, in particular, officers from its Venereal Disease Control branch.[15]

Their concerns had been long in coming. The official policy of the War Department was the repression of commercial prostitution.[16] But as the number of men in training grew rapidly after 1941, the sex trade flourished around American army bases.[17] In 1941, the US Congress passed the May Act, which outlawed prostitution near army camps. But the law was slow to be implemented, and as American soldiers began fighting on foreign shores, the inadequacies of the program became painfully obvious.[18] Controlling sexual promiscuity among GIs in North Africa proved to be near impossible: venereal infection became the largest single medical problem in that theater of war.[19] In Italy, almost all classes of women resorted to prostitution in order to put food on their tables.[20] By April 1944 the VD rate in Italy was estimated to be 168 cases per one thousand men, more than five times the acceptable standard set by the War Department.[21] SHAEF medical planners realized that promiscuity could threaten the success of the Allied mission.

A close look at how medical planners "explained" the high VD rate in Italy in a series of widely circulated SHAEF memos reveals the complex notions of gender and race that underwrote their understanding of the disease. The "availability of brothels" in Italy had been, in the planners' opinion, enough to arouse the soldiers' "normal instinct" for sex. One division surgeon reported that "prostitutes from

Naples descended upon our encampment by the hundreds, outflanking guards and barbed wire. They set up 'business' in almost inaccessible caves in the surrounding bluffs. Many of them gained entrance into the camp by posing as laundresses."[22] Italian women, then, were viewed as agents of infection who "descended upon" the camp, "outflanking guards" and arousing men like so many parasites swarming down. The surgeon failed to specify who let the "laundresses" into the camps, or why the prostitutes figured it was worth their while to occupy "inaccessible caves." In this way, medical planners demonized women as seductresses who created sexual demand, and exonerated the GIs from any responsibility in the spread of venereal infection.

As was the case in Italy, SHAEF medical officers assumed that women in France would act as agents of venereal infection At a Civil Affairs planning meeting just before D-day, the officers considered what was required to prevent GI venereal disease "as the result of infection from the civilian population," from whom the GIs would have to be "protected."[23] They recommended that such women "be rounded up and deported from the occupied area" because, they believed, nothing would deter them.[24] Before they even set foot in France, SHAEF medical officers were assuming their right to manage the mobility of French women. The soldiers in these scenarios are cast as the prey of women who insidiously arouse their desires. Despite conforming to the Victorian dictates of self-control, the men are unable to rise to the sexual challenges of these exceptional circumstances.[25] In this way, prostitution symbolized the fragility of masculine sexual control and hence masculinity itself—at a time when manliness was necessarily equated with strength.[26] The legacy of the Depression, shell shock, and Nazi propaganda had already undermined American virility in the war years. As symbols of compromised manhood, sexual commerce and VD anchored diffuse anxieties about American masculinity, resolve, and endurance.[27]

If medical officers considered white men to be the innocent quarry of Italian women, they defined African American men as sexual aggressors. Racial prejudice inverted the gendered logic of contamination: European women became victims rather than agents of contagion. "European womanhood has been warned concerning the attendant risk to association with the American negro," wrote Sgt. Walter Bonner, self-described as "colored" in an ETOUSA memo outlining VD control "for colored units." "We as a race," he urged, "can no longer afford to be termed 'immoral,' 'oversexed,' 'animalistic' and the like, but we shall always lay ourselves open to the accusation as long as we continue to furnish the smallest reasons for such assertions."[28] Although Bonner spoke from the standpoint of "race pride," the very notion of a "special" program for black soldiers stigmatized their behavior.[29]

The army believed that venereal rates were higher in all-black units. Because of poor medical care and a number of other factors, black registrants to the army did have a higher VD rate.[30] Whether or not a disproportionate percentage of black soldiers became infected during their service is less clear because inconsistencies in VD reporting made statistics on the subject unreliable. For example, if a division had a high VD rate, a commanding officer, when forced to explain himself, might blame the rate on black units.[31] Whatever the statistical reality, African American soldiers became a symbol of perversion within the US military. Army racial prejudice legitimated harsh regulations restricting their freedom of movement. In this way, army sexual control also secured the internal boundaries of race between the GIs.

Venereal disease became inseparable from anxieties concerning Allied strength, masculinity, and interracial sex. Despite this heavy symbolic load, SHAEF planners had no new ideas for reducing it. As was the case in the North African and Italian campaigns, they made a two-pronged effort to educate and coerce.[32] Army statistics on male sexual behavior estimated that 15 percent of the soldiers would choose continence, while another 15 percent would insist on having sex *no matter what*. The remaining 70 percent, for whom sexual promiscuity was believed to be a question of peer pressure, became the target of the army's education efforts.[33] Education was aimed entirely at men. Women who enlisted in the Women's Army Corps were not required to complete sexual education, nor was any WAC ever given an army-

issue condom.[34] SHAEF refused to see American women in the same
way that they viewed their European counterparts—as shameless and
aggressive. Entrenched views no doubt informed this refusal, but the
army was also not eager to convey the notion that it had let thousands
of WACs loose on the world to experience sexual adventure.

Many officers maintained that ignorance alone explained the high
venereal infection rate among soldiers in Italy.[35] To address this problem, the army issued an arsenal of pamphlets, posters, and such films
as *Health Is Victory*.[36] These materials recast the seductive woman of
the night as a source of danger and death. In GI literature generally
the whore became a symbol of mortality, and many soldiers did come
to fear venereal disease.[37] Bert Damsky remembers how boys refused
French prostitutes who came to their tents at night because they
were "afraid of contracting a vernereal [*sic*] disease."[38] Robert Peters
became so paranoid about getting infected that he put his finger as
well as his penis inside a French prostitute in an attempt to control
the situation: "As I approach orgasm, I strike a wart!"[39] But such fears
were mostly inspired by other soldiers' experiences rather than antivenereal education. Thomas Saylor refused all French women's advances "because I was scared of what you'd get. Guys got disease . . .
I don't monkey around."[40] Jack Plano remembers how eight of his
friends came down with the "clap" after a night with the same French
woman. After that, he realized, "there were dangers involved, enough
to scare me out of engaging in any kind of playing around."[41]

Besides education, SHAEF sought many methods, including coer-
cion, to prevent GIs from getting VD, or "crotch rot" as it was often
called.[42] Intramural football was encouraged. Beer was shipped from
England because it was thought to be less libidinous than wine.[43]
The army issued free condoms, six per soldier per month.[44] Raymond Gantter remembers that just before he and his fellow infantry
boarded the ship for France, his sergeant stopped at every tent to give
them all a "generous" supply of condoms."[45] Once in France, GIs received condoms along with their food rations, a fact civilians found
shocking.[46] Regular medical exams for gonorrhea, dubbed "pecker
checkers" by the GIs, were imposed.[47] SHAEF also constructed "pro"

(prophylactic) stations where soldiers submitted themselves to sanitary treatment after sex. The stations could be found near brothels, army camps, and Red Cross clubs in French cities.[48] Finally, SHAEF declared French brothels off-limits, established curfews, and curtailed the sale of alcohol.[49] While at first a GI who got VD risked having his pay docked, eventually contraction of the disease became exempt from punishment for the simple reason that the army wanted everyone to get treated.[50]

The Sex Act Cannot Be Made Unpopular

Despite SHAEF's vigilant planning, once the GIs landed on French soil, sex became a big problem. In September 1944, Chief Surgeon A. W. Kenner sent word to SHAEF headquarters that unless something was done quickly, there would be "a dangerously high incidence of venereal disease among our troops, entailing serious loss of fighting efficiency."[51] Headquarters was receiving news from all over France that infection rates were reaching "unsatisfactory proportions."[52] By December, the venereal rate among US troops on the Continent was nearly 200 percent higher than it had been in September.[53] The soaring rate of infection signaled the army's incapacity at every level to regulate sexual relations between GIs and French women. This failure stands out as an exception in an army known for its strong leadership and discipline among the rank and file. It is hard to think of any other issue of command in the European theater where the military had its rules so widely ignored. The military "problem" of sex, then, is distinguished by its intractability. Why was sexual promiscuity so widely allowed, particularly when it was known to lead to disease?

In fact the poor results should not have been surprising. Although SHAEF officers did not want to admit it, the overriding lesson of the Mediterranean campaigns was that sex was out of their control. One military study found that 50 percent of married soldiers and 80 percent of unmarried soldiers had intercourse at some point during the war. As one humbled medical officer put it, "the sex act cannot be made unpopular."[54] In addition, the specific circumstances of the Normandy campaign contributed to the dramatic growth of infection. Prostitution in France was a legal business. In addition, the rapid progression of the First and Third Armies across northern France during the summer of 1944 led to unsupervised contact between soldiers and civilians. Military police had no time in any one area to ban brothels, set up pro stations, or monitor the hygiene of French women.[55] Because supplies could not be well organized behind such a quickly moving army, condoms and pro kits were often scarce. Even sleeping accommodations were improvised. Thus the GIs had plenty of opportunity to get carnally acquainted with French women.

Furthermore, SHAEF's preventive measures proved difficult to implement. Apparently, such unit-based tactics as "Rolls of Dishonor," "Iron Crosses," and "Gunmetal Eight Balls" had been ineffective. The men no longer noticed the antivenereal posters, and with a few exceptions had dismissed the early pamphlet literature.[56] The army-issue condoms generated an endless stream of complaints. Predictably the GIs considered them "too small." In addition, they were "so damn thick you can't enjoy yourself"; nevertheless, "half of them bust" or "came off during relation." For some reason, the GIs also disliked the fact that the closed end had a constriction about three centimeters back, so that the tip drooped at the front.[57] Many of the soldiers found condoms more useful for covering their rifle butts in order to keep mud out.[58] Some of the preservatives ended up in the hands of Norman children, who used them as balloons, mortifying their parents.[59]

No more successful were the pro stations, which became an object of particular loathing among the GIs. After urinating and washing himself with green soap, a GI was to apply two handfuls of bichloride of mercury to his entire genital area. Then he injected Protargol, a disinfectant, into his urethra, and held it there for five minutes. Finally he covered his entire genital area with mercurial ointment.[60] Murray Shapiro distinctly remembered his first self-treatment: "I followed directions precisely and wound up almost fainting on the floor. If this was the price to be paid for such an encounter, I could forgo it, which

I did from this point on."[61] Prophylaxis was messy, painful, public, and embarrassing. It took the joy out of sex, and soldiers avoided it.

Finally the army also tried—and failed—to trace sexual contacts. For every venereal case discovered, the unit surgeon was to fill out a report providing data on the woman involved.[62] The aim was to create a list of infected prostitutes who could then be apprehended. The Germans had successfully developed such a data bank during the occupation, but that was when the legal brothel system was operating fairly well.[63] By contrast, the US military faced a sex market of nonprofessional women. Particularly in Paris, where two out of three cases of VD were contracted, prostitutes were young and single, living in cheap hotels, and operating under false names. Such circumstances crippled the tracking system. The French police added to the problem by refusing to take action unless the army had established a sure identification; they simply did not have the personnel to follow up every case.[64] Still another setback lay in the fact that soldiers were often drunk when they had sex. In such cases the best they could remember of their "significant sexual contact" was "Paris? Hotel?"[65]

The liberation of Paris in late August 1944 raised a host of new problems. On 2 September, the provost marshal of the Seine base section (covering Paris and its suburbs) arrived in the city with the French police. The two men selected certain *maisons* for officers, certain for white enlisted men, and certain for "negroes." Although the chief surgeon arrived three days later to declare all brothels off-limits, the "unofficial" policy prevailed, with brothels organized by race and rank.[66] Very quickly Paris became a Sodom of sexual pursuit. Enterprising women from all over France flocked to the big city to offer themselves for sexual delectation. In smaller towns as well, the army had trouble keeping GIs out of French brothels. The American military police worked closely with the French police in order to guard the brothels and keep prostitutes away from military camps. Signs in both French and English declared the *maisons* "off-limits," and the French police threatened to close down any house found to be servicing soldiers.[67]

Still when there was a will, there *was* a way. The GIs considered fines for entering brothels (by one report, sixty-five dollars) as nothing more than an amenity fee for sex.[68] In order to slip by the MPs stationed in front, they dressed in borrowed or stolen civilian clothes. Some pretended to speak only French, a plausible strategy since many French Resistance and military men were also dressed in American uniforms.[69] Such efforts had the makings of a French farce, a fact not lost on cartoonist Bill Mauldin, who sketched a scene for *Stars and Stripes* in which a GI tries to evade the rules by declaring "No parlay Eenglish."[70] (See figure 6.1.) While well-known brothels were heavily

"No parley Eengleesh."

FIGURE 6.1. Bill Mauldin cartoon. "No parley Eengleesh." From *Stars and Stripes*, 30 October 1944. Used with permission from Stars and Stripes. © 1944, 2012 Stars and Stripes.

policed, many smaller ones, disguised as residential houses, flew under the MP radar. Others camouflaged themselves as bars, restaurants, or "athletic clubs." The Cherbourg provost marshal reported that as soon as the MPs declared a building off-limits in that city, the prostitutes simply moved to another of the many abandoned houses. One captain stated that he "would need an MP for each GI who is after what he wants."[71]

The GIs were obviously a determined bunch. Infantrymen who faced death every day were not easily scared by the threat of a curable infection. But the problem of sexual promiscuity went deeper than GI tenaciousness. At bottom it resulted from the army's basic lack of will in carrying out the War Department's repression of prostitution. Nowhere was the spineless nature of army policy more evident than in a key memo circulated 2 May and used in subsequent months as a classic statement of War Department policies.[72] It began by forbidding commanders from abetting prostitution in any way. However, it then ordered them to distribute condoms "to military personnel desiring them whenever such personnel leave the unit area on duties or on leave whenever they may be exposed to venereal infection."[73] By insisting that soldiers be supplied with condoms "whenever they may be exposed to venereal infection," the circular really meant "whenever they may be having sex." But if officers were not supposed to encourage prostitution, why were they authorized to hand out condoms? Issuing free condoms, providing pro stations, not penalizing diseased soldiers—such policies had the effect of normalizing the promiscuity the military was suppressing—in other words, encouraging the problem they were created to manage.[74] They thus sent a mixed message to unit commanders already comfortably noncompliant on the issue of sex.

In the absence of any structural controls, SHAEF was forced to leave the matter of sex in the hands of the acting commanders.[75] Officers were to model good behavior, keep statistical records of the VD rates in their units, and record in writing that they had given "sex morality" lectures to their men.[76] But if SHAEF headquarters was making officers confirm in writing that they had given sex morality lectures, clearly it was not convinced the officers would do it. And they would be right. At least in the North African theater, according to one army history, there was an "almost universal lack of understanding of the problem" among line officers. Because such officers were often denied promotion if their units had a high VD rate, they concealed cases and distorted their reports. Much of the initial educational program in North Africa was directed toward command, where progress was considered slow.[77] American officers in France were no different. GI John Dunn remembered that the general commander of the Eighty-Second and 101st Airborne units "who was a very religious man by the way, not a bad person . . . really believed that one way to keep the animals quiet was to have a house of prostitution." For this reason, according to Dunn, he made both prostitutes and a pro station available to them.[78] In recalling his commander's approach to sex, Dunn failed to distinguish between what was legal (pro station) and illegal (prostitution). The contradictions at the heart of SHAEF instructions to commanders provided them just the loophole they needed in order to give the male libido free reign.

Officers often ignored the "off-limits" order. Most famous among them was Gen. George Patton, who believed that a little whoring on the part of his men never hurt anyone. While in Palermo, Patton established a medical team for the six largest brothels.[79] French interpreter William Brunsell, stationed at Verdun, was first ordered to tell the madam at the local brothel to close her doors. But when Patton's army took over the area, Brunsell had to retrace his steps and request that madam get the girls back from Paris.[80] Other officers were also adamant that brothels should keep their doors open.[81] A 1944 report of the Preventive Medicine Division admitted that "unfortunately in many areas, the local American commander has been unable, or unwilling to assist in the policing problem involved."[82] SHAEF's frustration here begs the question: Why weren't officers taking responsibility for venereal disease control? Why were they so nonplussed at disobeying orders on this matter? Clearly a parallel, unspoken set of rules operated alongside SHAEF directives, ones that were widely embraced among officers despite being contrary to military policy.

According to one insider, the vast majority of officers believed that War Department policy on prostitution was "neither logical nor effective." While "individually and privately" many men favored prostitution, "collectively and officially" they had to call for rigorous repression.[83] This double maneuvering doomed SHAEF's efforts to curb venereal disease.

Quarreling with Life

General Gerhardt's efforts to start a brothel in Brittany provide an exceptionally detailed view of such double-dealing. When forced to face an investigator, Gerhardt insisted that the Corral "was not officially a house of prostitution of the 29th Division, I don't believe—we will have to check on that."[84] Rather Gerhardt wanted to call it "an extracurricular activity," and his chief of staff, Edward H. McDaniel, preferred the term "controlled rendezvous for disciplinary reasons."[85] Only eventually did Gerhardt concede that the Corral was a brothel, but only to insist that its purpose was to "protect the health of the troops."[86] The argument was dishonest. As the inquiry went on to show, neither the general nor his staff had given the prostitutes adequate medical attention before opening the Corral. When the investigator asked Gerhardt how often the prostitutes had been checked by medical officers, the general responded "just once, prior to combat."[87] In fact, Gerhardt did order the acting division surgeon, Gerald A. Logrippo, to examine the prostitutes the morning the brothel opened. The women were in poor health. Two had bad tonsils, one had a bad ovarian tube, and one had signs of lung problems. Moreover, Logrippo could not rule out gonorrhea and syphilis until test results came back. Nevertheless, when the physician tried to tell Gerhardt the bad news, he was waved off and told "that will be all right." Gerhardt was content to just visit the "ladies" and make "cheerful remarks" to them. ("Damn nice girls, they were" was how Gerhardt later described the four prostitutes.[88])

Gerhardt's motive in starting the Corral was obviously not to protect the health of his men. In fact he was trying to squirm out of the charges by catering to army anxieties concerning VD. He and his staff also played on fears concerning rape, probably for the same reason. Gerhardt also justified the Corral by the fact that in September 1944, "a great number of statements were being broadcast as to rape cases et cetera, et cetera."[89] Gerhardt implied that the Corral was instituted to prevent rape—a rationale that was on the minds of many an officer at the time because the army was investigating several charges of rape in the Norman countryside.[90] After the *maisons* had been declared off-limits the previous July in Cherbourg, so many rapes were reported that the military police considered opening them once again.[91] However, the bored "et ceteras" at the end of Gerhardt's statement betray an indifference to the reality of sexual violence. His concern about rape appeared to be no more sincere than his worries about hygiene.

Off the record, Gerhardt explained the brothel in very different terms. As a commander, Gerhardt had a reputation as a "skirt chaser" who "identified strongly with the sexual drives of his men."[92] That identification emerged clearly in a letter Gerhardt wrote to his commander, Omar Bradley (a letter Gerhardt probably did not think would become part of the official record). Here Gerhardt argued that his men were "preoccupied" with sex because they were "removed from feminine contact," and under the influence of eroticized pinups and cartoons.[93] Gerhardt's real fear was that his men would turn to homosexuality to satisfy their desires. "The question of perversion," he wrote Bradley, had emerged because soldiers found continence impossible and turned to other available outlets for sex.[94] Raising the specter of "perversion" was a strong argument in a rabidly homophobic army, but it never surfaced in the official report.

Evidence suggests that Gerhardt was not alone in his concern that forced continence would lead to so-called perverse sexual behaviors. Contemporary medical literature related cases of men who turned to other men out of desperate need, then grew "to like it," becoming "fixed" homosexuals who never "revert" back to "normal."[95] Historian Alan Berube estimates that sex between men during wartime service was high because many GIs assumed that they could get venereal disease only from a woman.[96] Homosexuality was, in fact, one way around venereal infection, but in a homophobic army, it presented even worse dangers. Men who committed sodomy ("cornholing") or fellatio were often shipped to a stockade and given dishonorable discharges; some were sent to prison for long terms.[97] GI Robert Peters remembers how when an older GI named Wisher got caught in a pup tent engaged in fellatio with a platoon sergeant, the commanding officer said this to his men: "You know the penalty for putting another man's cock in your mouth? You rot in prison for life. You'll get f—ed good there."[98]

The contrast between Gerhardt's public testimony and his letter to Bradley can be explained by how the military handled the male libido: privately affirmed, officially denied. In private, Gerhardt naturalized male sexual desire to be as inevitable as the tides. This approach allowed him (conveniently) to deny accountability for his actions. Men, Gerhardt believed, wanted sex and would sleep with each other if they did not otherwise get it. The general also expressed such views in a talk to assembled chaplains in October. Again on this occasion, he could not know that his comments would become part of the public record. To this group, he again naturalized the male libido: "It is our duty to advise against [sexual intercourse], but you still have the question of human beings. . . . It is my business to not quarrel with life."[99] For the public record, Gerhardt expressed his views on "life" and "the question of human beings" only obliquely. At one point in the official investigation, he explained to the investigator that "this division has been overseas for two years, and that is quite a long time . . ." "To go without sex" was Gerhardt's unstated conclusion. It was common knowledge that GI promiscuity rates rose in proportion to length of time in combat.[100]

At every turn, military policy on sex fluctuated between official regulation and unofficial disregard. At the most profound level, that awkward vacillation had to do with the army's growing pains. Up until 1941, the "regular" army had been a comparatively small, tight-knit group, in which a "hush hush" culture of silent loyalties and gossip had operated fairly well.[101] As the threat of war grew larger, the army

grew exponentially, and the management of men and information became infinitely more difficult. GI promiscuity was still publicly denied
and privately acknowledged, but in an age when soldiers numbered
by the millions and journalists traveled with divisions that arrangement was increasingly strained. The result was a set of contradictions:
brothels were "off-limits" but segregated by race; sex was condemned
but condoms made available; homosexuality was reviled but always
threatening; prostitution was banned but covertly organized. Also
operating here was a coded language that enabled officers to speak
to each other about sex under the new glare of publicity. That code
controlled sexual knowledge and, as a consequence, allowed unfettered promiscuity.

Operating in a Place Like France

As a final argument for the Corral, Gerhardt and his officers maintained that the division was in France. "It was felt that in the situation
in which this division was operating and in the French communities
in which we were located," argued McDaniel, "that it would be desirable to endeavor to control social relations between our men and the
French people rather than to allow promiscuous social relations to
obtain." In secular terms that statement meant "we were in France
and the boys really wanted to have sex." At another point in his testimony, McDaniel again reminded Lineman the division was "operating in a place like France."[102] By that, McDaniel meant not only that
the soldiers expected to get some "action" in France, but also that
the local police, who understood such matters, would be happy to
cooperate.[103] McDaniel's argument, in other words, was that trying to
control a soldier's sexual behavior in "a place like France" was tantamount to making him eat raw carrots in a steakhouse.

Inasmuch as the officers could shift the responsibility for infection
onto the French, they had yet another excuse for ignoring the War
Department's prohibition on prostitution. From the very beginning
of the campaign in northwest Europe, US military officers blamed

high rates of venereal infection on the fact that they were "in a place like France." As one French historian has put it "the Americans considered the French to be nothing more than . . . happy lushes leading dissolute lives."[104] A GI expressed a widely held view when he described the nation as "a country without morals."[105] In fact, of course, France was a nation struggling to recover from defeat, occupation, and war. In his war memoirs, Charles de Gaulle enumerates the many obstacles on the road to reconstruction. The Germans had robbed the nation of its riches, and the Allies had destroyed its ports, railway tracks, roads, and factories. While the French people were ecstatic about liberation, they were also deeply troubled by political discord, labor tensions, and the ghosts of collaboration.[106]

As a result of this economic and political disorder, the state's regulatory system of prostitution operated very badly.[107] Prostitutes avoided the required medical exams by becoming itinerant or disappearing when medical personnel showed up at the *maisons*. These women were not unwise to evade government medical care, even if their health was at stake. The treatment awaiting them was at best ineffective, and at worst physical torture. Examinations were given under poor lighting and in unsanitary conditions. Often no effort was made to wash the speculum between internal examinations, or for that matter, to change the linen and the pot of Vaseline.[108] The sickest of the women ended up in locked hospital wards, where nuns did their best to wage a battle against alcohol, foul language, and lesbian sex.[109] Even if women were healthy when released, they soon became ill again, either because they had been recontaminated or because they could not afford the medications to treat their illnesses. If a woman was arrested several times, or if she was proven to be corrupting minors, she would be tried and sent to prison. There she ate and slept in filthy cells aside thieves and murderers.[110]

SHAEF medical planners were made aware of the failings of this system, which in their minds reinforced prejudices about French sexual decadence. In a well-known 1941 polemic against brothels near US Army bases, two military doctors argued that "unless vigorous Federal action is initiated, we may sink to the level of France in our tolerance of prostitution."[111] An army-issued guidebook titled *Pocket Guide to France*, which warned the GIs against winking at or slapping the backsides of French women, also cautioned them not to trust the French regulatory system: "don't be fooled. No system of examination has ever made a prostitute safe. Her health card means absolutely nothing."[112] Commanders and soldiers found it particularly frustrating that French law forbade the incarceration of prostitutes if they were not infected.[113] At a public health meeting between French doctors and Allied medical officers held in Rouen in September 1944, the Americans complained that a Bayeux prostitute, known to be "infectious," had been arrested by the police, given a "cursory" medical inspection and released, then subsequently infected five other men. While the Americans blamed the French for high VD levels, they refused to give them control over tracing prostitutes.[114] In short, the French were given full responsibility and no power.

"Operating in a place like France" meant presuming control over the prostitute's body while blaming the French for infection. One medical officer described the spread of venereal disease in this way: "Any prostitute may become *infectious* immediately after contact with a diseased patron and may transmit infection to an indeterminate number of subsequent visitors before the disease can be detected in her."[115] This officer failed to acknowledge that a French prostitute who comes in contact with a diseased patron has to become *infected* before she becomes *infectious*. The male role in the transmission of disease was, as in the Italian case, completely effaced. SHAEF's perception that all French women who came in contact with the GIs were prostitutes only worsened the problem. In November, headquarters advised officers that troops in French cities should be "briefed as to the dangers of infection lurking in the 'pick-up' type of girl in those towns."[116] According to US public health reports, such "pickup" girls had replaced prostitutes as the main source of contagion back in the States.[117] The military assumed that the situation would be the same in France.

It was only one step from blaming the "pickup" girl for infection to condemning the French as a whole. If France was a nation of erotic pleasures, as so many American officers believed, venereal disease was its ugly underside, and the French had no one else to blame but themselves. As we have seen, the fact that GIs had more contact with prostitutes than with French people from other walks of life amplified the political impact of their relations with them. In both popular American culture and in high diplomatic and military circles, the whore came to articulate "Frenchness" itself. SHAEF's frustration with state regulation and its inability to see French women as *infected* as well as *infectious* also had a significant impact on Franco-American relations. Besides reinforcing American prejudices about France as decadent, the "problem" of VD inspired condescension, invited American intervention into French affairs, and naturalized the army's "right" to manage the civilian population.

Scandalous and Intolerable Public Spectacles

In 1945, conflict over prostitution reached its most climactic battle in the Norman port city of Le Havre, where discretion about commercial sex became paramount to both the local mayor and the military commander. For the French, the spectacle of prostitution at the town center was intolerable not only because it was indecent, but also because the prostitute signified national humiliation.[118] The Americans were equally focused on the issue of visibility, in this case on shielding sexual labor from the eyes of the American public. At the root of the struggle was discretion about sex, an issue made more complex by the army's double-dealing concerning promiscuity.

By 1945, Le Havre was home to hundreds of prostitutes. Liberated by the Allies on 6 September 1944, "the 16th Port," as the Americans called it, became the gateway to the European theater. Between October 1944 and 1945, some four million soldiers embarked or disembarked there.[119] Large "cigarette camps" for GIs with names like Philip Morris and Herbert Tareyton were constructed just north of the town. Soon the prostitutes were flooding into the city from all over France.[120] Le Havre's legal system of prostitution was in crisis even before the GIs began to arrive. The port town suffered greatly from bombardments during the summer of 1944.[121] Roughly 85 percent of the city was destroyed.[122] The *maisons closes* were not spared. During the night of the 14–15 June, Allied bombs completely destroyed the six *maisons* on the rue des Galions. On 5 September, another bombardment destroyed fourteen *maisons meublées* that were authorized to receive registered prostitutes. Le Havre was left with only two such houses on the rue Haudry.[123] Without the actual infrastructure of the *maisons*, it became very difficult to regulate prostitution in Le Havre.[124] The situation echoed that in Paris with the legal system broken, and prostitutes working in a "clandestine" or independent manner. They gained the cooperation of less principled members of the community by sharing profits.[125] In January, local officials obtained a legal "arrêt" to end the flow of women into town.[126] It did little good. Prostitutes arrived by train and fanned out into public spaces, only to be arrested, taken to the hospital, and treated—all at the expense of the municipality.

The flood of GIs transformed Le Havre into what one resident called the "Wild West of France" with the MPs as the "crazy sheriffs."[127] The prostitute was a difficult presence. The trade in sex was noisy, obtrusive, and linked to violence. Some of the sex trade was carried out behind camp walls.[128] Prostitutes were smuggled in, with MPs charging an entrance fee. Some of these MPs became full-time pimps, allowing the prostitutes to enter in exchange for a share of their earnings. As late as January 1946, a morning raid of an American camp turned up 124 women who had to be escorted from its confines. From the prostitute's perspective, it was an excellent way to do business: free lodging, abundant American food and cigarettes, a steady stream of customers, and no French police.[129] The camps became a haven for illegal commercial sex, particularly because the camp officers often chose to close their eyes to the goings-on.[130] But much of the sex trade was carried out throughout the city. Although legal brothels were "off-limits" to GIs, they operated under the eyes of the local provost marshal, who would periodically inspect them.[131] Unlike Paris, Le Havre had no elaborate system of hotels. With the *maisons* destroyed and the hotels in ruins, the prostitutes settled for makeshift places to do business, including the Montgeon Forest north of town, as well as scattered cemeteries, parks, and damaged buildings in the city center. Receiving tips from neighbors, the police would find small groups of prostitutes servicing scores of GIs in abandoned houses, often in rooms not even closed off from the rest of the house.[132]

It wasn't long before the Havrais began to complain. Particularly outraged were those who lived near the camps and had to endure the daily sight of GIs having sex with French women.[133] "These things are happening in full daylight right in front of children or other people who happen to be near," complained one civilian about the prostitutes plying their trade in a park.[134] "At certain times the American soldiers form a line down the staircase and into the corridor of the house," another one told the police. "They urinate along the walls and in the hallways, and they attack any women who happen to live there."[135] Still others protested the noise. Because the *maisons* operated covertly, the GIs had to shout up at windows in order to gain entrance. But because the brothels were not marked, men often knocked on several doors before finding the right house. Night after night, one local resident complained, soldiers came banging on his door shouting words that "left nothing to doubt" about the nature of their mission. The neighborhood, he lamented, "is becoming impossible for women and young girls."[136] A local tanning company petitioned the mayor for greater security, claiming that the workers' "wives and children are terrorized by the nearly daily crimes taking place near their homes."[137] Still other townsfolk complained that the GIs had made two holes in the cemetery wall, one as an "entrance," the other as an "exit." As a supervisor noted, "both operated continually, day and night, compromising the morality of the cemetery."[138]

In Le Havre, the mayor, Pierre Voisin, responded vigorously to his constituents' complaints. Although the city's politics customarily veered toward socialism, Voisin, elected by popular vote in May 1945, was a right-leaning businessman with a reputation as an effective administrator.[139] He sent out extra police to patrol key streets and parks, sealed up holes in the cemetery wall, and kept an eye on

suspect houses.[140] Despite these efforts, however, there were insur-
mountable problems. The prostitutes were mobile and flush with
cash. There were too many of them and not enough police or medical personnel to ensure the safety of the community. By the summer
of 1945, the situation had become critical. The end of the war brought
into town thousands of bored GIs waiting to go home. In addition,
the warm weather facilitated outdoor sex. Voisin began to step up
his complaints to the American commander of Le Havre operations,
Col. T. J. Weed, with whom he had a cordial, mutually respectful relationship.[141] The mayor called a meeting with Weed on 29 August in
order to discuss what could be done about prostitution.[142]

Much of what happened at this meeting we know through Voisin's hand, as he wrote Weed a letter the day after summarizing their
discussion. He began by reviewing the problem. Citizens of his town
were witnessing scandalous scenes. The prostitutes risked contaminating large numbers of soldiers and civilians. Out of the seventy-five
prostitutes arrested in August, he noted, thirty-three were infected.[143]
The complete repression of prostitution was not feasible, because if
the GIs did not find women to satisfy their desires, they would rape
"honest" women. (French authorities, like their American counterparts, widely considered prostitution to be a deterrent to sexual violence.[144]) Finally, attempts to put prostitutes onto trains headed out
of town had not worked: the women simply disembarked at the first
station and took cabs back into town. To solve the problem, then,
Voisin proposed that the Americans create a restricted zone, forbidden to the public and "convenient" to the camps. Here tents would
be set up where soldiers could visit prostitutes under the watchful
eyes of police and medical personnel. While Voisin was aware that
such a solution might upset some "perfectly respectable principles,"
he believed that "one must choose the lesser of two evils" in these
"exceptional" times.

Voisin's proposal was hardly revolutionary. He was suggesting that
the Americans establish a system of regulated prostitution very similar to France's own (and not unlike the Blue and Gray Corral). By tradition, the French Army had attached brothels to their regiments.[145]

Nor was his proposal the first to be made to the Americans. In October 1944, after formal charges of rape were brought against scores of GIs in Cherbourg, the police in that city wrote the US military urging them to establish a brothel for their soldiers.[146] In 1917–18 as well, French authorities had tried—unsuccessfully—to convince American commanders to organize or at least condone regulated brothels.[147]

Voisin was primarily interested in discretion: he wanted to remove GI sex from the public eye. Discretion was an unstated rule in French sexual relations. Traditionally a variety of sexual practices were tolerated as long as they were carried out privately. Concealment lay at the foundation of the French brothel system: the *maisons closes* were called that because the madams were told to keep the shutters *closed*. Nor were prostitutes to practice their trade near sensitive public areas such as schools and churches. Similarly, Voisin intended for the prostitutes to set up business in tents adjacent to the cigarette camps to the north of the town. This location may have been "convenient" for the soldiers, but its real aim was to keep the GIs away from residential neighborhoods and the town center. In short, the goal was to keep sex out of sight. In Voisin's words, "scenes contrary to decency take place day and night, not only in private homes, disturbing peace and quiet in various neighborhoods, but also in the squares, gardens, walkways and ruins of damaged buildings. The fact that youthful eyes are exposed to such public spectacles is not only scandalous but intolerable." To Weed, Voisin made it clear that it was "absolutely imperative to make sure that acts contrary to decency do not happen just anytime anywhere in the view of just anyone."[148] The traditional French demand for discretion was heightened by the symbolic role played by the prostitute in the postwar era. If the whore had come to represent defeat and collaboration, she was best kept out of sight.

Voisin's proposal fell on deaf American ears. Weed's response did not even engage the question of a sex zone and presented the crisis as Voisin's alone. "This serious situation," he wrote, will affect "the morality and security of your young people and the health of the entire community." American soldiers appeared nowhere in Weed's scenario. Instead of taking responsibility, he flattered the mayor in a patronizing way: "The decision to curtail the prostitution which at present prevails in the port region will demand all the vision and delicate judgment which I know you have." Finally, he declared that the "formidable" task of ushering thousands of soldiers in and out of Le Havre demanded all his time and energy. In other words, not only was he not accountable for the problem, but he could not be bothered to fix it.[149] Weed's letter suggests that did not care about the American impact on the community of Le Havre. A few days later, a high-ranking French police official, in touch with the American provost marshal, confirmed for Voisin what the latter no doubt already knew: "the American authorities are hostile to the creation of what could be called 'regulated army brothels.'"[150] The American military instead pledged to send in forty American doctors to treat women.[151] There were also promises of a floating hospital, anchored in the port and supplied by the Americans.[152] Both these promises addressed the same predicament: local venereal wards were overflowing. In Voisin's very careful record of correspondence, however, no evidence exists that the Americans made good on either promise.[153]

A Theater of Military Debauchery

Since American authorities never wrote to Voisin on the issue of the army brothels, we are left to speculate why they were so "hostile" to his proposal. Of course, on the face of it, the issue came down to following War Department rules. But as Gerhardt's case suggests, obedience was not paramount when it came to prostitution. Furthermore, regulated prostitution was already a reality in the Pacific theater, namely, in Hawaii, where it was overseen by the military, local police, and government.[154] Why, then, were brothels not officially established in France?

Brothels in Honolulu provide an instructive example. "Hotel Street," as the district there was called, existed for many years prior to the war because of cooperation between the military, police, and government. Located near a large military base, "Hotel Street" attracted thirty thousand visitors a day at its peak of operation during the war. With Taylorist efficiency, the soldiers were ushered in and out of small rooms where they had sex in hygienic conditions; the prostitutes received regular checkups and good medical care. The military was happy with the system because it kept venereal disease rates low; the white elite favored it because it kept the seedy sorts out of their neighborhoods; and the police supported it because they thought it prevented sexual violence. It also worked because representatives from each of these three groups—the military, the elites, and the police—knew and trusted each other to keep the arrangement working effectively. Nevertheless, Hotel Street was a delicate sexual ecosystem. Despite the fantastic wealth that the prostitutes accumulated, they were not allowed to enter certain elite neighborhoods of Honolulu. For this reason, they remained in the city only about six months. When the women began to rebel against these restrictions and buy property in wealthy areas, the brothels were promptly closed down.[155]

Circumstances in Honolulu differed sharply from those in France, and these contrasts are illuminating. One important difference concerns the matter of race. Was the American military command more tolerant of prostitution in a US territory with a nonwhite population? While race undoubtedly played a part in the regulation of sex, the majority of prostitutes working on Hotel Street were white women from San Francisco.[156] In buying property, these women violated class as much as racial boundaries, as these neighborhoods were inhabited by an indigenous elite. Nevertheless other circumstances worked in favor of tolerance in the Hawaii case, namely, that it was a permanent arrangement with a history of cooperation between the military, police, pimps, and prostitutes. For example, the provost marshal knew all of the madams by name.[157] In France, by contrast, French police and US military officials did not even speak the same language. Nor did these military officials respect local medical and police authorities. Bonds of trust might have been established over time, but conditions rendered that process impossible. Honolulu was a US military base, but Weed had no incentive to do long-range planning. The war in Europe was over; the boys were going home, and particularly after

the victory in Japan, the military had lost its motive for preventing venereal infection. Furthermore, unlike Hotel Street, where prostitutes
received good medical attention, the French system was teetering on
the brink of collapse. By the summer of 1945, medical planners had
gotten a close look at state regulation and wanted no part of it.[158] In
the meantime, penicillin began to be widely used in the European
theater. SHAEF headquarters looked upon its use with some ambivalence because it created a "false" sense of safety. Nevertheless it was
a turning point inasmuch as army doctors could cope with venereal
infection without having to bother with the French at all.

Finally, military commanders had one overriding incentive *not* to
regulate. Like the French, they were supremely attentive to the issue of discretion. The military insisted on keeping French sexual labor invisible, not only from War Department officials, but also and
even more importantly, from the American public back home. In a
May 1945 memo to all commanding officers, Adj. Gen. R. B. Lovett
argued that if the army was found guilty of condoning prostitution in
overseas theaters, the War Department would "be open to the charge
that it is supporting conditions inimical to the health and welfare of
troops. The eventual result might be public scandal with the families
of military personnel charging the War Department with an unfor-
givable violation of trust in neglecting to care for the physical and
moral well-being of its personnel."[159]

Fear of scandal lay at the heart of all the military double-talk about
sex. As Sarah Kovner describes the military's approach to sex work in
postwar Japan, "policy back home and on the ground were two different things."[160] The official line had to be respected in order to "protect" the US public. Photographs of the pro stations that populated
French cities and military camps were censored throughout the war.[161]
Robert Seale remembers another GI brothel, the "Idle Hours Athletic
Club," which was closed because it "would not be appreciated by the
soldiers' wives and loved ones in the states."[162] GI Murray Shapiro
once observed how the MPs policed the *maisons* at precisely sched-
uled times, allowing all parties to evacuate and avoid arrest. When
Shapiro asked an officer why this "farce" went on, he was given this

response: "to mollify civilian sensibility . . . American mothers and sweethearts are not wanting to hear of such activities being officially condoned."[163] Forced to condemn what it could not condone, the US military was also obligated to condone what it could not control.

Given this dilemma, the issue was reduced to a matter of visibility. Put another way, the problem resulted from a conflict between meanings of the private. What was kept private and hence "invisible" in the United States had therefore to become very public and "visible" in France. In this sense, the Le Havre situation instructs us that at times privacy must be conceived in transnational as well as national terms. Because any institutionalized form of prostitution made sexual labor potentially observable to the American public, promiscuity had to take place covertly. Venereal disease remained the price paid for American hypocrisy. The war had brought new sexual opportunities both back home and abroad by separating millions of youths from their families. Inevitably such changes generated anxiety concerning changing morals.[164] Beginning in the 1920s, "going all the way" had become increasingly permissible, but Victorian morality did not entirely loosen its grip, particularly among the middle class. In fact, the divide between public condemnation and private acquiescence maintained by the US military characterized much of American sexual life, with Americans often condemning pre- or extramarital intercourse in public discourse even as they made it a norm in private.[165] Military officials' attempt to keep sexual labor invisible only reproduced this general divide. The policy of secrecy also allowed the army to maintain a myth of the GI as a traditional manly man, disciplined and self-controlled.[166]

At the same time, however, the sex that had to remain hidden from Americans remained a rudely visible reality for the French. One fact seems to have escaped the concern of officers eager to maintain an unsullied image of American manhood: its cost to French civilians. In many large cities and small towns, French families could not leave their homes without witnessing what Voisin tactfully called "scenes contrary to decency." According to a French policeman in one small Norman town, "the healthy segment of the population is disgusted by such debauchery, which takes place even under the eyes of children."[167]

Le Havre was not alone in having to endure a promiscuous landscape. In the Marne region where GIs also had large base camps, "the eyes of a scandalized populace are subject to scenes of debauchery," according to local French government reports. In the spring and summer of 1945, "a crowd of prostitutes" had come into the town of Mourmelon, where for lack of hotels, they set up business in fields and parks.[168] The cemetery had become a "theater of military debauchery."[169] In nearby Châlons-sur-Marne, break-ins, fights, thefts, violent assaults, "all having either their origin or their end in prostitution," had made the summer a living hell for both civilians and policemen. The latter were "powerless because there were too few of them or they were not well enough protected" to maintain control.[170]

The frequent reference to children in these complaints not only expressed adult worry but also served to reaffirm a sense of morality, even innocence, among the civilian population. The authorities in Lison, near Caen, received letters concerning prostitutes with American soldiers around the train station there. "The children are aware of these women's love cries, and their responses to such scenes are sometimes frightening."[171] In Reims as well the residents "were complaining of the spectacle to which their children were exposed." Local authorities reported that women were being accosted on the street.[172] Here officials proposed a number of plans to the Americans: providing them with 150 prostitutes, creating special brothels, and reopening the *maisons*, which had been declared officially off-limits. They even promised to do so "as secretly as possible . . . in order not to rub up against the sensibilities of the Generals."[173] It was all to no avail, although the Americans did help reinforce the local police with a brigade of MPs.[174]

Permanent Disorder Reigns

Nor did the trouble always disappear when the Americans left for home. By early 1946, most Americans had shipped out of Le Havre

and returned to their towns and communities back home. Nevertheless, in January of that year, Voisin reported to the *sous-préfet* that one
thousand prostitutes remained in Le Havre "servicing" Americans.[175]
The women offering sex—farm girls from the area—were even more
inexperienced than during the war. They had come to town in the
hopes of finding an American husband, and ended up prostituting
themselves after their "lovers" shipped out. Because such women
were naive about health matters, they did not take precautions, and
as a result, a greater percentage of them were sick. One prostitute
was rumored to have been in the clinic no less than ten times.[176] Venereal wards were overwhelmed: a ward meant for forty was forced
to accommodate nearly two hundred. "Permanent disorder" reigned
in these wards, according to one French official: The women fought
for the beds; they tried to escape by the windows using bedsheets and
shirts; and they amused themselves by having sex with each other. To
make matters worse, although the clinics were unsafe and ineffective,
they were expensive. "The American authorities insist that the greatest possible number of these women be frequently hospitalized," Voisin wrote, at a cost of about 8.5 million francs a month. At this rate,
he argued, his entire medical budget for the year would be gone before March.[177] The mayor was writing his superior, hoping to get extra
funds, so he probably exaggerated the problem. At the same time, it is
impossible not to be struck by the unfairness of the situation. At one
of the US military's two most important French ports (Marseille was
the other), Voisin was trying to keep pace with extraordinary American demands for hygiene on a limited municipal budget.

The injustice of Voisin's position—and the uniqueness of the
French case—becomes clearer if we look at how the US military dealt
with sexual relations in other nations of the European theater. In Italy,
relations with civilian women were complicated by military fears concerning the chaos of civil war and "fraternization" with the enemy.
That was even more the case in Germany, where soldiers were warned
that women were spies, and that the disease prostitutes supposedly
harbored was "Jerry's deadliest V. weapon"[178] To a great extent, dealing with the enemy in these countries justified military control of
sexual relations. A stronger parallel to France is Great Britain. Like

the French, the British were allies who also hosted a huge American military presence. As a result of that presence, VD reached alarming levels in Great Britain as well, particularly in London and its suburbs. The crisis produced a meeting in April 1943 between American, Canadian, and British military and health authorities. As it began, the chief American representative, Surgeon General Paul Hawley, advised all involved that the British could not be blamed for the situation: "There was no more moral laxity in this country than in the United States," he argued. "The problem was one for the public health authorities."[179] Following Hawley's suggestion, a joint committee was established; it convened American, British, and Canadian health authorities to cooperate in solutions to the rising rates of VD.

One cannot imagine Hawley making such a statement about France, nor such a committee being set up to address venereal disease there. Entrenched stereotypes led US military authorities to arrogate to themselves the management of the French female body when it served them, and to abandon such management when it no longer proved necessary. The American GI did not have to worry that his VD would go untreated, nor that his loved ones might witness "scenes contrary to decency." The military approach to venereal disease in Le Havre registered a growing confidence on the part of the US government to construct—whether consciously or through inaction—asymmetries of power in the transatlantic alliance: whose health was important and whose was not, whose family would be protected and whose would not.[180] If the Americans did not worry about public prostitution in Le Havre, was it because they believed that the display of sex could not be disruptive in a society without morals? Or was it because the Havrais—as members of a community, as citizens of a sovereign nation—were simply invisible to the army?

In either case, French citizens paid the cost of American diffidence. In addition, by not taking more vigorous action to establish hygienic sex, the US military protected the "virtuous" American woman back home at the expense of the French prostitute. (This asymmetry no doubt followed in some way the nineteenth-century class division between the chaste middle-class female and the working-class harlot.)

Our last two glimpses of the prostitutes in Le Havre are images of daring and subjection. Mayor Voisin wrote to his superior in 1946 that the prostitutes infected by American GIs "preferred to tear up their cash or throw it in the sewer rather than be forced to pay their bills."[181] By refusing medical costs, the prostitutes were preventing a situation where their profits would be eaten up by medical expenses. In other words, they were preserving their business. But their refusal to pay also signaled their belief that illness was not their responsibility alone to bear. It was also an act of defiant courage.

At the same time, many of these women forfeited their health and freedom. Voisin's last effort to relieve crowding at his hospital was to find a home for infected prostitutes at the Fort de Tourneville to the north of the town. Ironically, the fort had served as American headquarters during the war and so became available as the soldiers left town.[182] Since no American floating hospital had materialized, Voisin was hoping to create a medical facility at the fort. But despite several letters to his superiors, his request was refused.[183] As the Americans bade "adieu" to France, government officials everywhere in Normandy faced the same problem: what to do with the sick women? The venereal wards were overwhelmed. French medical services in Cany Barville transported the women in vans to Rouen, only to be turned back because there was no room at the hospital. They were then taken to Le Havre, only to be redirected back to Rouen by the authorities there for the same reason. Some women were then accepted at Rouen, but the majority were sent to Dieppe. There, they were once again redirected to Le Havre. But when the women arrived in Le Havre, they were pointed yet again in the direction of Dieppe, only to be sent back from Dieppe to Le Havre.[184] An unwanted, homeless population of diseased women being shuttled from town to town— these prostitutes compromise the legacy of the American occupation in Normandy.

The US insistence on either completely controlling or completely ignoring the effects of GI sexual activity cannot be dismissed in light of the more "primary" demands of the war effort. To do so would be tantamount to either naturalizing male sexual needs or ignoring the war's chronology. In "hotspots" such as Le Havre and the Marne, the troubles associated with prostitution reached their peak *after* the war was won. At bottom the sexual exploitation of French women during the years 1944–46 was about American arrogance and the exercise of sheer power. US military officers shifted responsibility for venereal infection onto France itself, already fixed in their minds as a feminine, debauched country. Such a shift both justified their presumption of control over French women's bodies and further allowed them to avoid accountability for their men's behavior.

No less than American victories on the battlefield, sexual regula-tion lay at the heart of what the war was all about—the struggle over people and territory. At stake in the control of the French prostitute's body was not only the health of the American GI but also the ques-tion of who would manage the mobility, health, and well-being of French civilians. Furthermore, the US military's very visible violation of War Department rules was itself a display of power. French offi-cials were painfully aware of the army's duplicity on sex as well as the fact that its prudery extended only as far as the public back home. By flaunting its disregard for its own sexual and social norms in France, the US Army related a potent message concerning their opinion of the French people: that they were hardly worth good behavior on the part of the GIs. French exposure to sex—rather than its repression—became a sign of American domination.[185] All too aware of Ameri-can contempt, the French returned the favor by branding Americans as loud and loutish. Finally, then, the Franco-American struggles over sex force us to dig deeper for the roots of postwar French anti-Americanism.[186] A decade before the 1950s "ugly American," the sala-cious GI warranted French scorn for boorish indiscretion.

PART THREE
Rape

7

The Innocent Suffer

IN OCTOBER 1944, the US chief of police in the European theater of operations (ETO) presented a list of crimes committed by GIs in France to his superior, the provost marshal. At the top of the list was the offense of rape. According to the chief's statistics, 152 American soldiers had been tried for rape; of these 139 were "colored." "When we consider that only approximately 10% of the troops on the continent are colored," commented the chief, "the above figures are astounding." In this way the chief pointed out the disproportionate number of black soldiers convicted of sexual assault in US military courts. He did not offer any explanation. Instead his primary concern was the impact such crimes might have on Franco-American relations. In order to show the French people that the army was punishing sexual assault with harsh measures, the chief recommended that "public executions be held in the vicinity of the crime."[1] That last piece of advice the provost marshal followed. In the years 1944 and 1945, twenty-nine public executions by hanging were carried out in the ETO as a result of rape charges. Among those hanged by rope, twenty-five were African American soldiers.[2]

The chief had one thing right: the rape statistics in France were "astounding" in their racial character. Official military historians have chosen to remain silent about this prosecution of rape accusations, in particular their racial character.[3] More recently scholars have brought the record to light, attributing its racialized character to discrimination on the part of US military officials.[4] There is no doubt that the American army demonstrated a deep and abiding racism in its dealings with African American soldiers, and more specifically, in its prosecution of them for violent crimes.

At the same time, this explanation falls short in two ways. First, it does not take into account that the French, not the Americans, initiated the allegations of sexual violence. Despite the reputation France enjoyed among African Americans as an oasis of racial tolerance, a startling number of charges were made by civilians against "soldats de couleur," "les noirs," or "des soldats de race noir."[5] French officials were also quick to point the finger at black GIs. The mayor of Le Havre, for example, wrote on several occasions to American authorities concerning "odious acts committed by blacks in the American Army," and the fact "that numerous assaults against civilians of my City, in particular, women, have been made by the colored soldiers of the American Army."[6] Second, if the racialization of rape was a result of American discrimination, why was it worse in some parts of the European theater than others? While criminal sexual assault was racialized throughout the ETO, the problem was particularly acute in France. Seventy-seven percent of court-martial convictions for rape in the ETO concerned African American soldiers. In Germany, that figure was only 26 percent.[7]

The aim of the next two chapters is to pose the questions passed over by the chief of police in reporting his statistics to the provost: why were so many rape charges aimed at African American soldiers? How did rape become a "Negro" crime in France? And why were so many more black soldiers than whites executed for the crime of rape? I will argue that the army racialized the crime of rape by failing to account for certain key factors concerning the function and location of black units. It is impossible to determine whether a disproportionate number of black men did, in fact, commit rape. They were indeed responsible for some rapes, as evidenced by credible confessions of the accused, as well as a preponderance of physical and medical evidence.[8] In many cases, however, charges against black soldiers were based on hearsay and "sightings" produced in an atmosphere of racial hatred and fear. The US military inadequately investigated rape charges, concluded too quickly that the accused was black, arrived too easily at the identification of the alleged rapist, insufficiently probed the reputation of the accuser and witnesses, and erroneously assumed premeditated sexual violence on the part of black men.

At the same time, French civilian behavior toward black soldiers also increased their chances of being charged and convicted of rape. As we shall see in the next chapter, the black soldier quickly became a projection of civilian fears concerning the chaos of war and the tensions of military occupation. Normandy and Brittany during the summer of 1944 were places of turmoil and destruction, with French refugees as well as American soldiers invading cities and small villages. Civilians struggled to communicate with black soldiers in this atmosphere of confusion; they also too quickly identified them as sexual assailants. Miscommunication and dishonesty on the part of French civilians lay at the heart of many rape accusations.

Ultimately it was the cooperation between French civilians and US military authorities in the prosecution of sexual crimes that created a proliferation of charges against black soldiers. On the American side, this sort of collaboration operated at many echelons of army command, from platoon captain to SHAEF headquarters. On the French side as well this cooperation functioned at several different levels, from the women who brought forth accusations to the police who reported such crimes, to the local authorities who considered all black men to be rapists. In many cases in which the standard "reasonable doubt" might have won the day, it did not. In this way, the French and the Americans became deadly allies in racism.

During the summer of 1944, rape became a black crime on the western front.[9] In general, rape was probably the most widespread war crime in the European theater of war, although its violence had different meanings in various areas. On the eastern front, the German Wehrmacht committed rape with impunity as part of their aim to enslave Slavic peoples.[10] Beginning in Hungary in 1944, the Soviet military used rape as an instrument of revenge.[11] At the end of the war, thousands of German women suffered from the crime of rape, and not only from the Red Army. According to US Judge Advocate General (JAG) statistics, at least five hundred German women were raped by American soldiers.[12]

The JAG office reported two significant "rape waves" in the ETO: the first in the late summer of 1944, and the second in the spring of 1945. Both waves took place during "breakout" periods of war, in which a fast-moving front made both police control of troops and investigation of crimes more difficult.[13] In such periods, women were in relatively uncontrolled military environments and hence more vulnerable to sexual assault.[14] About such rapes the JAG Office took the sanguine view that "comparing the number of cases with the total number of men engaged in what was perhaps the greatest human project of all time, and allowing for the unnatural and extreme conditions in which many of them were placed, the record seems less black or even better than could normally have been expected."[15]

If the spring 1945 rape wave can be seen as a last paroxysm of violence against a defeated people, the summer 1944 wave is more difficult to fathom. On the one hand, rape no doubt resulted from the pressures of combat. The Normandy campaign was a brutal battle. Particularly in the hedgerow countryside along the Cotentin Peninsula, the Americans took heavy losses until their breakout in August. In such circumstances, rape became a way to assert control of territory. On the other hand unlike Berlin, the Battle of Normandy was waged in territory occupied by an allied, not an enemy civilian population. The rape wave distinguished itself in still two other ways. First, as we have seen, the greatest number of suspects were black soldiers.[16] Second, the wave was characterized by an extreme number of cases ending in a nonguilty verdict. In July, for example, 41 percent of the rape accusations were revealed at some point of the judicial process to be false.[17] Considering these two factors together, I will argue that the 1944 wave was, at least in part, a hysterical response of French women to their fears concerning black men.

The Racialization of Rape

The racialization of rape as a crime in the ETO has its roots in the segregation of the US Army.[18] While the War Department famously claimed that no distinctions were made between white and black troops other than segregation, in practice blacks in the army suffered discrimination in every aspect of their military lives. As the historian Steven Ambrose has put it, the army did "almost everything possible to insure that blacks would fail the test of combat. And when, despite everything, black soldiers did perform adequately—and often enough magnificently—the army and the public simply ignored the record."[19]

As the war cloud began to hover over Washington in 1940, black activists, expecting some degree of American engagement, struggled with the Roosevelt administration to desegregate the US military.[20] In the election of 1940, National Association for the Advancement of Colored People (NAACP) leaders such as Walter White and Roy Wilkins, as well as veterans and the black press, made segregation a subject of national controversy by staging a boycott of black soldiers against the selective service.[21] When despite these efforts, segregation remained the official policy of the War Department, Roosevelt appointed judge and civil rights activist Henry Hastie as a civilian aide to the secretary of war as a conciliatory gesture to win the black vote in 1940.[22] Until his resignation in 1943 over conflicts concerning segregation in the air force, Hastie acted as a watchdog over the treatment of African Americans in the military forces. He received and investigated the complaints detailed in hundreds of letters from humiliated, frustrated black soldiers who bemoaned unfair treatment, inadequate facilities, racist and even sadistic commanders, and excessive court-martial punishment.[23] Racial violence in and around American military camps became commonplace in the war years as black soldiers suffered every kind of discrimination at the hands of white soldiers, officers, and military police.[24]

Besides dealing with oppression and violence, African Americans

were consistently given inadequate training for war. The army assigned white southern officers to command black soldiers on the
premise that coming from the Jim Crow South, these white officers
knew "best" how to "handle Negroes."[25] Black soldiers, especially
those who hailed from the North, were often traumatized by such
officers. The son of a Harlem judge, James Watson, pleaded in a letter
to his father to use whatever influence he had to get him transferred
from a training camp in Georgia, which he described as "a state in
which racial prejudice and bigotry is rampant. The Negro is really
persecuted down here and looked upon with disdain."[26] Likewise,
powerful testimony to the degradation suffered during training is
provided by letters from black privates to a former teacher in Harlem, activist Layle Lane. "This camp, as you no doubt suspect, is a
vast prison," wrote one soldier to Lane. "In the past 36 days we have
been so thoroughly humiliated that we must be fit material for can-
non fodder."[27]

Rather than receive full basic training, black soldiers were often
sent out to do menial labor.[28] "Little chance for promotion," wrote
another soldier to Lane. "Men are dissatisfied. Dislike the prospect of
being housekeepers indefinitely."[29] Due to quota systems, very few
men had hopes of advancement. Still another private told Lane that
he planned to apply for Officer Candidate School since his IQ was 129.
It was interesting to note, he wrote, "that out of 200 colleges I could
only select A & T College in North Carolina. I was shown a clause
whereby Negroes can only go there. And at that only 500 can go per
term at this school."[30] Even those men who became officers at the
junior level were consistently passed over for promotion.[31]

In addition, as black soldiers entered the military, army policies
of segregation presented them with disconcerting questions: Which
barber shop could a black man use? Which telephone? Which part of
the mess hall? Anxiety about disobeying the unwritten rules of segregation, which varied considerably from post to post, had an exhausting effect.[32] One soldier wrote Lane about a "fatigue" that was not
"entirely physical," but instead resulted from "the insinuations that
a man of color must face in the apparency of an inevitable status-

quo."[33] Black GIs with passes into town would often get stuck on base because their white peers, allowed to get on buses first, would either leave them no room at the back or refuse to let them ride at all. Even getting into town would not guarantee a relaxing evening, as black soldiers would often looked in vain for a "colored" restaurant, bar, or theater.[34] The results were deeply demoralizing. One young soldier wrote Lane how he had just met some "very intelligent" new recruits who were "products of admirable homes." "The army," he noted with bitterness, will soon "harden them and shrink their souls."[35]

Segregational practices also poisoned base camps in the ETO. "Believe you me it's over here too," Salvador Tomas wrote to Lane from Corsica. "Those Jim Crow phobia-addicts retain their prejudices blindly against the colored man more than their distaste for the supposed common enemy."[36] A GI corresponding from England told Lane that the British girls had asked him if it was true what the white boys said: did he have a tail?[37] Blacks were sometimes refused service at British pubs because white soldiers threatened the owners with a boycott.[38]

While questions of access to resources fueled racial tensions in all theaters, the most dangerous color line to cross was, without a doubt, sexual relations with white women.[39] One soldier described to Lane the dances held in small British towns during the months before the invasion: "Whenever we go to a dance where there are also white Americans, the Negroes usually dominate the scene, for they are better dancers and have what it takes in socializing. . . . One night, the show-down came. Some of the Negroes managed to dance with the girls. The whites didn't like it. Later, during the dance, there was a racial clash. One of my friends got cut."[40] Maj. Gen. William G. Weaver remembers that while commanding a black army unit in Cheltenham, his highest priority was getting black WAC units stationed nearby to "furnish social feminine companionship for our colored troops," and thus avoid interracial hostilities.[41] Such conflicts, as we will see, emerged as a key element in the proliferation of rape accusations against black soldiers once the Americans landed in France.

As humiliating and frustrating as segregational practices could be, the greatest deprivation suffered by black soldiers was that, with a few notable exceptions, they were denied combat roles.[42] Only in December 1944 when the Battle of the Bulge radically drained American manpower were commanders "forced" to consider integrating combat units. During this crisis, black Americans were "allowed" to replace proliferating casualties on the line.[43] Otherwise, black soldiers were assigned to service units, including supply (quartermaster), ordnance, transportation, laundry, and graves registry. Perhaps the most famous service provided by black troops in France was the Red Ball Express, a five-hundred-mile supply line sustained mostly by truck because of heavy damage to railways. Driving up to thirty-six hours at a time, Red Ball drivers (60 percent of whom were black) succeeded in supplying a fast-moving front with gasoline and ordnance despite frequent encounters with gunfire, strafing, and mines.[44] In addition, using what was often the oldest, most outdated equipment in the ETO, black soldiers also unloaded boats, hung telephone lines, built bridges, provided meals, cleaned shirts, and buried bodies.[45] The last task was perhaps the most difficult. One French man remembered seeing black soldiers identify cadavers, wrap up their bodies, and save their personal effects. To brace themselves for this "macabre task," he recalled, they had to swig brandy.[46]

The fact that black soldiers operated mostly in service units was one of the keys to the racialization of rape as a black crime. Most such troops served in the rear echelons of the army that followed the frontline army as it moved east, making sure it was equipped and serviced.[47] This arrangement was formalized in October 1944, with the establishment of the Communications Zone (ComZ), a logistical agency that administered the service sector of the war effort. Some of these ComZ units, particularly those in the advance section closest to the front, were on the move, following the troops east as they advanced to Germany. But in base sections such as Cherbourg and Le Havre, ComZ stayed and established permanent supply bases. One day after the liberation of Cherbourg (26 June 1944), the GIs had already begun reconstruction of the port, where tons of ammunition, food, and other supplies were soon unloaded off boats every day.[48]

When the US Army began to keep statistics on rape accusations, they paid particular attention to charges made against soldiers operating in ComZ. Army numbers on rape in ComZ included a breakdown between black and white soldiers, with blacks overwhelming whites in terms of rape accusations, ninety-five to five. Once the theater provost marshal had received statistics from the chief of police in October of 1944, he circulated them to all theater commanders, again "inviting" their attention (as did the chief) "to the abnormally high proportion of these crimes that were committed by colored troops."[49] As we have seen, the army made much of the fact that only 10 percent of the troops were black in interpreting the "astoundingly" high rate of rape accusations among African Americans.

In reading these statistics, the army failed to take into account three crucial mitigating factors concerning black troops. First, they were disproportionately represented in the ComZ base sections because of their assignment to service units. Even if only 10 percent of the ETO troops were black, that percentage was much higher in ComZ, given the overwhelming number of black soldiers in service units. ComZ included nonblack units, such as engineering, signal, and medical. But there were many black ones as well, namely, transportation, quartermaster, salvage, engineer dump truck, signal construction, and ordnance. According to historian Ulysses Lee, the Oise base section (part of ComZ in north-central France including Reims) had a total white strength of 29,154 and a total black strength of 14,060 or about 33 percent.[50] *Stars and Stripes* reporter Alan Morrison described four out of every five port battalions (in Cherbourg and Le Havre) as manned by African Americans.[51] Seventy-eight percent of rape accusations against GIs were targeted against troops in service units, where black troops had disproportionate representation.[52]

Second, the army did not consider that the ComZ units, particularly those in permanent base sections such as Cherbourg, had by nature of their location and activity much more contact with the French civilian population than did combat units. A common complaint among the infantry was that soldiers in the rear echelons had more opportunities to meet women.[53] "White soldiers felt they were forced to do all of the fighting," an infantry corporal remembered. "Blacks were resented as they had rear echelon (safe) duties, got to go to Paris to fraternize with the women, while the whites had to do all the fighting and dying."[54] More contact meant a greater possibility that black soldiers, for all reasons we will explore, were more likely to be accused of (or commit) rape. Finally, the army failed to take into consideration that service units were not as mobile as the infantry during the summer of 1944, so that rape charges in such units could be properly brought up and examined. An infantryman could easily rape a woman in a nearby village one night and be on his way early the next morning before she had a chance to bring her complaint to the military police.[55] A black GI in a permanent section base had no such easy means of escape. Hence a disproportionate number of charges against black soldiers in service units were investigated and prosecuted.

By not taking into account these three crucial circumstances— the larger number of black soldiers in ComZ, the more intense contact between black soldiers and civilians, and the greater ability of the army to prosecute crime in geographically stable, black service units—the army racialized rape as a crime. Taking these factors into account may not have eliminated the correlation between race and rape, but it would have limited it. To explain the "overwhelming number" of black soldiers accused of rape, military officials instead drew on traditional racial stereotypes concerning black men as morally debauched. One officer in the Judge Advocate General's Office reasoned that "colored soldiers" simply "incline toward certain of the more serious crimes."[56]

Most commonly, officers explained the rape charges in terms of the supposed hypersexuality of black men. This stereotype was deeply rooted in the American South where, according to Martha Hodes, "the greater sexual ardor of black men" had been a professed belief among whites since the colonial era.[57] Such prejudices were widely embraced by officers in the US Army. Black men were believed to exhibit higher rates of venereal disease because they were "natural" rapists.[58] Military policy dictated that contact between black soldiers and French civilians be more rigidly supervised than was the case with whites, because black soldiers were more sexually aggressive.[59] An August 1944 intelligence report related how "embarrassed" French civilians were to see naked black troops running around in daylight. One American officer explained "that such was the habit of the Negroes back in the United States and therefore their customs could not be changed over here . . . he felt very sorry about the matter."[60] Alcohol, ComZ officials believed, worsened the situation by triggering black aggression, thus "turning a man into a beast. The blacks have difficulty in carrying alcohol, and when they imbibe large quantities they lose their senses."[61]

The JAG judges who reviewed court-martial decisions against black soldiers also shared these beliefs in the hypersexuality and debauchery of black men. They described alleged rapes committed by black soldiers as "orgies" and "sexual saturnalias" that revealed the assailants' "bestial lust" and "lustful desires."[62] A memo circulated by the judge advocate in November 1944 maintained that the crime of rape "discloses an entirely unique savagery and wanton disregard of any limits whatever upon measures to accomplish satisfaction of sex desire" as well as a "fundamental deficiency in character and predominant animal instincts on the part of the criminal."[63] The judges referred to one alleged rape in the Finistère as "a scene of brutal and lustful savagery finding few equals in the whole annals of American legal history."[64] Speaking of an accuser who claimed to be raped by a black soldier in Mouchard on 25 September, the judges noted that "due to the disproportionate size of their genitals [those of black men], there was no complete coition."[65]

The Problem of Identification

The racialization of sexual crime occurred in the European theater because the US military neglected to consider the unique location and function of black units when interpreting statistics concerning rape in the Communications Zone. This failure occurred due to widely held prejudices that African Americans were hypersexual and hence innately sexually violent. But the misreading of statistics on the part of US officials cannot alone account for the fact that rape became a "Negro" crime. Once charged with the crime of rape, black men were much more likely than white men to be found guilty and executed for that accusation. We must then also closely examine how French women brought forth these charges of rape and how the accused were subsequently tried by court-martial and convicted of these charges.

A critical examination of French police reports and American juridical documents suggests that while rapes undoubtedly occurred, the French women involved frequently made their accusations in uncertain, even dubious circumstances. Often they miscommunicated with their assailants or could not identify them, and in other cases their motives for bringing charges were suspect. These problems were, in turn, inadequately handled by the court-martial and judge advocate officials who prosecuted the rape cases. In many such cases, there was frequently little if any positive, corroborated evidence to support charges against black soldiers.[66] This lack of evidence can be explained, in part, by the military court system at this time, which required no legal counsel for the defendant, no formal indictment by a grand jury, and no guarantee of impartial judges.[67] In such a system, according to one military handbook, acquittal of a soldier who had "clearly" committed a crime against local civilians was considered worse than the original offense because the reputation of the army and the United States was in question. Hence there was pressure on the courts to convict even when evidence was scanty.[68]

Since rape trials most often had civilian witnesses, the accused had to be tried by the army locally—a fact that made proper legal counsel a bonus rather than a fact of life. Soldiers were tried in hastily setup military courts in small towns close to the locations of the alleged crimes. Particularly during August 1944, when the Allies were moving rapidly against the German Army across northern France, time to prepare a case became a luxury. One stunning piece of evidence that the accused were not adequately defended in court was the rapidity with which they were brought to trial. Arthur E. Davis and Charles H. Jordan, both of the 3326 Quartermaster Truck Company, were accused of raping a woman in Saint-Pierre-des-Landes on or about 10 August 1944. They were charged with the crime on 13 August, and their trial occurred three days later in Poilley (thirty-five kilometers away). The trial lasted one day, and resulted for both in a death sentence by hanging.[69] This brevity of time between charge and trial was not at all unusual. Only nine days passed between the time Wilford Teton and Arthur Farrell were charged with rape and when they went on trial for this charge.[70] Similarly, Eugene Houston was tried fifteen days after being charged. James Sanders, Florine Wilson, and Roy Anderson were tried twenty-five days after being charged; George Ferguson and Henry Rorie were given twenty-eight days between charge and trial; Leonard Bell was tried thirty days after being arrested.[71] These short periods were not in themselves discriminatory since white men accused of crimes were likely to be subject to the same. At the same time, however, the drive for a speedy trial at a local town made the preparation of an adequate defense difficult, and may have also unleashed racist tendencies that a slower, more careful prosecution of law could have restrained.[72]

If the defendant did have a spokesman, it was usually chosen for him by the commander of his unit, and was often *not* a lawyer but an officer or other military personnel. Rather than receive formal legal training, officers were given handbooks to instruct them on court-martial process, about which there was much grumbling. Ignorance and miscomprehension among officers was a major problem in military trials.[73] John Davis, a white American GI in France, recalled being called into headquarters to work on some cases because he had studied commercial law in college and done a little legal work. He had no experience in criminal law, and was surprised to find himself working on rape and rape-murder cases in which the accused were frequently executed.[74] In the fall of 1944, some army officers expressed their discomfort with the defendant's lack of a court lawyer and proposed to have an "associate Negro defense counsel" to represent accused black soldiers for major crimes. But the proposal was rejected by the Judge

Advocate General's Office, the chief provider of legal services in the army, on the grounds that it was "impractical" and would "indefensibly retard administration of justice."[75]

Lack of proper legal representation was compounded by prejudice on the part of commanding officers. After the war black *Stars and Stripes* reporter Allan Morrison noted that "colored soldiers were particularly vulnerable to prejudiced officers in the realm of the court-martial" because such officers were "convinced that every Negro was a potential rapist" and hence "willing to believe in a Negro's guilt before it had been proven."[76] Of the court-martial system, one black soldier remembered that commanders had an undue influence on the outcome of the trial when they made it clear they wanted the man found guilty—or else they would be unhappy.[77] Precisely these prejudices blinded investigators and court officials to three complex problems that arose in the prosecution of French rape cases: the identification of the accused, witness credibility, and miscommunication between accuser and accused. Let us examine each of these in turn.

The overwhelming majority of rape accusations were made in villages and small towns.[78] In the summer of 1944, few rural Normans enjoyed such modern conveniences as electricity and running water. Even in the relatively large cities of Cherbourg and Saint-Lô at that time, only the fairly well-to-do could boast such luxuries. In addition, Allied bombardment damaged or destroyed much of the utility infrastructure, and its repair was dictated by the needs of the front rather than civilian comfort. The Norman electric network was not reestablished until February of 1945.[79] As a result, the majority of Normans had to do with candles or gaslight for illumination, and it was by this light that alleged rapists were often identified. Even in broad daylight, identification would have been difficult given the fact that all soldiers wore the same uniform in the same color. But in addition, the majority of rapes throughout the European theater took place after dark.[80]

Accusers and witnesses were well aware of the problems of positive identification. They often willingly admitted that "I saw them only by the light of a simple candle," "the scene took place in darkness," or "I would not be able to recognize them because I was beside myself and it happened in darkness."[81] Nevertheless American officials dismissed the problems raised by darkness. In an incident on 26 August south of Saint-Lô, a woman claimed to be raped by a black man near her house in a field at 10:00 p.m. Only at the trial did the accuser and witnesses point a finger at the accused, James P. Rudesal, who fell under suspicion for the sole reason that he was listed out of the bivouac area during the night of the crime.[82] Private Robert Skinner was convicted in a case of rape that allegedly took place in the dark near Bricquebec on 1 August. Although the alleged victim identified the accused as her assailant, she also admitted that it was "rather dark" during the assault. According to the reviewing judge, however, "her confusion, evidently engendered by the excitement and surprise of the assault, is readily understandable and in no way impeaches her positive identification of the accused."[83] In the case of Private L. C. Williams, the reviewing judge insisted that "there was no moonlight on this night, and no light in the house. There was only a little light from the stars. The soldiers however lit matches or lighters to see their way about the house, and Monsieur and Madame Brochet saw them clearly."[84] Many other soldiers in the ETO, including Privates Davis and Jordan whose trial took place three days after formal charges, were convicted of rape and put to death even though their alleged crimes took place by candlelight or flashlight or in complete darkness.[85]

Although Norman rape accusers admitted to their failure in identifying their assailants, they often insisted without a trace of doubt that these attackers were black. French police accused black soldiers of committing all twelve rapes reported in the Cherbourg region between July and October 1944. Of these twelve rapes, seven occurred after dark and often very late at night. Some French civilians identified their assailants as black only by resorting to racist stereotypes. For example, in a case of rape near Saint Malo, which allegedly took place in the dark, the accuser could not identify the accused at the trial but insisted that her rapists were black "by their speech, large lips and shiny skins." Trial testimony also established that this woman's sight without glasses was "very weak," and that her glasses had been broken during the attack.[86]

Only two out of twelve cases of rape reported by the Cherbourg police during the first wave concluded in a positive identification, despite the fact that entire units of African American soldiers were paraded in front of accusers and witnesses. Witnesses were given three identification parades of black units in the case against John David Cooper and J. P. Wilson, in which the alleged rape took place by candlelight and flashlight only. One parade involved an entire battalion of six hundred men. Of the sixteen witnesses present at these three parades, only one identified Cooper in one parade. At a fourth, smaller parade held in Commercy, six witnesses identified Cooper, one of whom also "pointed to Wilson but wouldn't point him out because she wasn't sure . . . because he had shaved off a little growth of hair."[87] In the trial of James Parrott, Grant Smith, and William Downes, whose crime, once again, allegedly took place by matches and candlelight, only Downes was identified by accuser Marie Lepottevin, who was positive about Downes only because he was "much larger" than the others. No physical evidence linked Downes to the crime, only the fact that he was found in the vicinity of the crime. Nevertheless, he was sentenced to death by hanging.[88] In the case of Private L. C. Williams, one witness claimed to have identified the accused at the trial. However at a previous trial, this witness had pointed out the assistant defense counsel as the accused.[89] In the case of Fred Westfield, despite several parades neither accuser nor witnesses made a positive identification until the trial. A witness, Roland, could only "identify accused in the courtroom because he was alone." The accused was condemned to death solely on the basis of a ballistics test in which an expert testified that the bullets found near the accuser were fired from Westfield's gun.[90]

A telling contrast to these cases is that of Joseph Striggle, a white private in the 101st Airborne division, accused of raping a woman in Joigny in the early fall of 1945. Striggle's accuser positively identified him in an identity parade, but she was questioned repeatedly during the trial concerning the light in the alley where she was raped. On several occasions the prosecutor suggested through questioning that it was too dark for the accuser to have accurately identified her attacker.

Striggle, who was put in the vicinity of the crime by a friend, claimed to be, in fact, at a card game that night. Another private present at the game at first gave sworn testimony that he did not remember Striggle being there, and ultimately signed an affidavit affirming that fact. Despite the positive identification by the accuser, however, the court concluded that "reasonable doubt" had been established and acquitted Striggle.[91]

The case also demonstrates how court treatment of the female accuser turned on the issue of race. In cases involving black soldiers, the woman's accusations were almost never doubted. Given the perceived hypersexuality of black men, the woman accuser came to be seen as a blameless victim of a savage lust who would never "choose" to have relations with an African American. In cases involving white soldiers, however, the court was more likely to assign the burden of sexual aggression to the woman, that is, to see her as a prostitute rather than a victim. She would most likely be doubted both for her claims to resistance and her attempts to identify her assailant. In this way, racist stereotypes trumped sexism in the judicial treatment of rape.

American military authorities were mostly complicit with French civilians and officials in their assumption that rapists were almost always black. Some of the judges reviewing these cases stated their misgivings about the methods by which accusers identified their assailants. In the case of James Hendricks, for example, the judges spoke of the importance of circumstantial evidence as more "convincing" than personal identification of witnesses: "particularly is this true where the witnesses are not familiar with Negro characteristics and faces."[92] But an American military investigation of a series of rapes that allegedly occurred in Clos-Fontaine, seventy kilometers southeast of Paris, reveals an almost willful blindness to the problems of identification in the ETO. One alleged victim, Hus Stanislawa, claimed to be the victim of a gang rape by five soldiers on 31 August; the second, Zozet Lovry, charged two men with raping her in separate incidents on 2 September. Both accusers claimed that their assailants were black. Both incidents took place after dark in homes lit only by candlelight. In the Lovry case, the house was so dark that the intruder had to strike matches in order to find the woman in her bed. Neither accuser was able to identify her attacker, despite the fact that both were given identification parades involving two entire units of black soldiers. Stanislawa saw every soldier in a black unit, and was only able to narrow her choices down to nine men. According to the captain in charge, "she could not positively identify anyone, and she showed great indecision in even saying maybe."[93] Lovry explained through a translator that she could not identify her rapist in a parade of the entire unit because "they all look the same."[94]

Despite these facts, the American investigator never questioned the accusers' claims that the assailants were black. Even after neither accuser could make a positive identification, it apparently did not occur to him to carry the investigation into white units stationed near Clos-Fontaine at the time. In the Stanislawa case, one piece of physical evidence (a raincoat) linked the rape to a black unit.[95] But no such evidence existed for the Lovry rape, and in fact, one piece of evidence connected the case to a nonblack unit: the first intruder had gained entrance into Lovry's house by offering a beefsteak. As the investigator well knew, neither black unit in the area had a meal of beefsteak in the days before the crime occurred. Nor did the investigator ever question odd facts revealed by testimony in the Lovry case. According to the accuser, the attacker closed her husband in a room by threatening him with a carbine. But, as the accuser testified, the room was unlocked, so the husband supposedly chose to stay in the room for hours while his wife was raped a few feet away. In addition, moments after the alleged rapist finally left, at about 4:00 a.m., the husband went out of the house—theoretically to go to work. After her husband left, according to the accuser, she was raped a second time by another man who came in through the back window. For some reason, the first rapist had to leave by the back window, which he supposedly broke in the process of leaving, though it was never established why he did not simply use the door.[96]

The unanswered questions of the Lovry rape demonstrate how American cooperation with French charges of rape meant that key aspects of cases were never interrogated. According to Robert Lilly, military investigators in the ETO during the summer of 1944 were also "inexperienced and not able to look at evidence critically and observe clues that could be important to the case."[97] If a black soldier was found in the vicinity of the crime or missing from the bivouac area when it occurred, he was vulnerable to prosecution, imprisonment, and death.

African American soldiers were not the only racial group vulnerable to racial profiling based on identifications that took place in the dark. In a Brittany case, 1st Lt. Maurice Reeves rushed to the scene of an alleged rape one evening in time to hear the accuser, Lucie Hualla, give her description of her assailant as "short, heavy-set and dark complexioned." From this Reeves concluded that the rapist was "either a Mexican or an Indian." When Reeves returned to his camp and could not find Corporal Wilford Teton, a Shoshone Indian, he charged him with the crime, which took place late at night. In their review of the trial, the Judge Advocate Board described Teton as having "typical Indian features," including "a stolid expression." Although Teton was picked from an identification parade by some neighbors, the accuser at first claimed she could not identify her attacker because of the darkness. But she became convinced that he and Farrell were rapists because "she just knew they were."[98] Teton was found guilty and sentenced to life in prison.

The Problem of Witness Credibility

Another problem in the judicial evaluation of these rape accusations was the failure to measure the credibility of the accusers and witnesses. Individual testimony often became the deciding factor in these cases because the prosecution lacked reliable physical and medical evidence. The standard of proof for rape in the military court system consisted of two types of evidence: first, that sexual penetration had occurred, and second, that the accuser/victim had tried, to the full extent that she was able, to resist the assault. Both these standards of proof presented problems for military prosecutors. First, as regards evidence of penetration, American medical authorities often did not examine the accusers, or they did so by candlelight or several days after the incident.[99] Norman doctors failed to routinely check for traces of spermatozoa; they gave a woman an internal exam only if she claimed to have been a virgin.[100] In addition, French medical testimony in court was sometimes difficult to understand because of the language problem. In one case, for example, a doctor presented this incoherent medical observation in court: "When I examined the girl with my finger I do not see the stem with hairs at all. When I put my finger in the back the organ was ripped . . . I think there was penetration there with fecundation."[101] When there was no evidence of sexual penetration, such as the presence of sperm, military officials had nothing but individual testimony to prove that the accuser had actually been raped.[102] Even when medical evidence could prove that sexual intercourse had occurred, it often failed to establish that a struggle had taken place, which was the second standard of proof. In such cases, which were numerous in France in the late summer of 1944, the decision rested on whom to believe—the accuser claiming rape or the accused claiming innocence.[103]

The importance of establishing accuser and witness credibility is demonstrated by a Cherbourg incident, one of only two cases in the French police records in which the accuser, Madeleine Peronneau, could positively identify her assailants. She claimed to have been gang-raped by four black soldiers on the night of 10 August 1944. According to her testimony, she cried out for help after the men had been in her house for a while. She had had sex with each of them once, and they then wanted another "round." But a neighbor claimed that Peronneau was a well-known prostitute who was "drunk nearly every day" and who "received numerous American soldiers, white as well as black."[104] Prostitutes such as Peronneau were known to threaten black soldiers with charges of rape in order to extort higher fees for services.[105] Most likely what happened, then, was that Peronneau wanted to make the men pay a higher price, and when they refused, she retaliated by reporting to the police that she had been raped. The case would have looked quite different, however, if the neighbor had not testified.

For court-martial prosecutors, then, the accuser's credibility became imperative. Even women who were not prostitutes but "willing" to sleep with black soldiers, also sometimes charged them with rape in order to preserve their own "respectability." Very early one July morning, Marie Rouvrière woke her upstairs neighbor, claiming to have been raped. When the French police were summoned to the scene, they found the soldier in question, John Phenix, sound asleep on Madame Rouvrière's bed, with his clothes nearby on a chair. Upon further investigation, the police discovered that the woman's husband was out of town, and that the house showed no means of forced entry. (Phenix had entered through the window.)[106] An American medical exam failed to discover any physical evidence of sexual trauma or even penetration. In court, Rouvrière testified that Phenix had a knife, and that she locked herself in the bedroom with the soldier while he was raping her "because I didn't like to see my children know what was going on." She urged him to leave by 5:00 a.m., and when he remained asleep after dawn, she took her children upstairs to a neighbor to get help.

Phenix, for his part, testified that he had been seeing this woman for about two months, but that they had always met "at some less obvious place where no one could see us together." This was his first visit to her house. "I guess it is just her word against mine," he remarked in the trial.[107] The defense, which rested largely silent, failed to pursue a key observation in the French police report: that Phenix was "deeply" sleeping when they arrived, and was only very slowly wakened.[108] Rouvrière probably had been carrying on an affair with Phenix, but could not rouse him that morning in order to leave her house before full daylight. Desperate to hide the affair from her husband, and to save her reputation, she decided she had no choice but to claim rape. This explanation of the events was not even raised at the trial, however, and Phenix was sentenced to ten years hard labor.[109]

As the Phenix case demonstrates, rape cases often hung on whom to believe—a woman unknown to all or an African American soldier.[110] But credibility was exceptionally difficult to establish in the conditions under which court-martial prosecutors labored—a foreign country populated with displaced persons speaking a strange language during a period of war. Prosecutors were often forced to rely on the testimony of accusers and witnesses whose background was not only unknown to them, but to *anyone* present in the courtroom. What is surprising to the reader of these court-martial transcripts is how little this inability to verify the reliability of accusers seemed to bother the prosecutors.

Another key case in this regard concerned an alleged rape committed at Bricquebec, south of Cherbourg, on 23 June 1944. The accuser, Denise Quonian, was a twenty-two-year-old refugee from Cherbourg traveling with a man, Jules Lelouey. Quonian claimed to be raped at gunpoint by two black soldiers, George Ferguson and Henry Rorie, in a field near a farm where she was staying. Quonian had tried to keep the incident hush-hush. When the maid asked her why her clothes were torn, Quonian responded that she had been assaulted, not raped, and that no one needed to know about it. But the maid, alarmed by the story, contacted the police. As a result, rape charges were drawn up against the two soldiers. More than enough reasonable doubt was established in the trial. Medical examination provided evidence that while Quonian's hymen was torn, its condition "might have resulted from normal intercourse."[111]

While Ferguson's and Rorie's accounts of the day's events were consistent, those of Quonian and Lelouey were full of inconsistencies and contradictions. Quonian admitted in testimony that she had accepted five hundred francs from one of the accused, and one hundred francs from the other, and that Lelouey had also been given one hundred francs. At one point Lelouey testified that sex with "one of the boys" was consensual. When Quonian's testimony began, she denied even knowing the two soldiers; only after a short recess did she bring forth charges again. In a letter to General Eisenhower pleading clemency, Ferguson wrote, "the lady said she didn't know me until the Judge [illegible] took her on the outside of the Court room [sic] and talked to her and when she come back in the Court room she said that she knowed me. So sir I dont [sic] think that I got a fair trial." According to

Ferguson, "the God's truth" was that he "paid a French lady 700 francs to have an [sic] intercourse with her but I did not rape any girl."

Despite inconsistencies in Quonian's and Lelouey's testimony, the reviewing judges made no apparent effort to investigate their reputations. One judge did comment that Lelouey's presence "cannot be satisfactorily explained except on the ground that he was a procurer and the woman is a common prostitute," but he forced himself not to conclude this fact given lack of evidence. The woman's torn clothes, the judge reasoned, proved that Ferguson "had given away entirely to his passion" and "there was no particular reason why they should have made up a false story." In fact, however, there was. Quonian was a poor, homeless refugee no doubt prostituted by Lelouey. She told the maid a story of sexual assault in order to save not only her respectability but also her lodging situation. Since prostitution stigmatized women, its discovery would have led to her expulsion from the farm. At the same time, Quonian clearly did not want anyone to get in trouble: that is why she urged the maid to keep a secret and also why in court she at first testified that she did not know the two men. From Ferguson's perspective, she was coerced to testify against them. Despite all these ways in which the judges might have established reasonable doubt, they condemned Ferguson and Rorie to death by hanging. Because of the special plea made by Ferguson to General Eisenhower, his sentence was commuted to life in prison.[112]

In such cases, prejudices concerning African Americans as "giving themselves entirely to their passion" undermined their credibility— and hence their claims to innocence. A Cherbourg case illustrates how the prosecutors' tendency to assume that black soldiers were natural rapists influenced their decisions. A well-known prostitute who limited her clients to white soldiers testified that when she tried to close up "shop" on the night of 9 September at 10:30, a group of black soldiers sought illegal entrance and raped her. At the trial, the woman failed to identify which of the five men in the room actually raped her, one of whom escaped altogether. She identified only one soldier because of his "simian" features, despite the fact that the alleged crime took place by candlelight. Her testimony was full of contradictions and statements that were undermined by other witnesses, including her denial that she was a prostitute. At the same time, however, she expressed an explicit plea that the men not be prosecuted. Her aim, she stated, was only to have her window repaired. In reviewing the case, the judge advocates admitted that her testimony was "weak and inconclusive," but insisted that "her standard of personal morals" was "irrelevant and immaterial." As for the accused, he described their actions as an "orgy" and a "brutal, animalistic and savage endeavor to satisfy their lustful desires."[113]

The defense was silent in this case, as it was in many other court-martial trials reviewing rape accusations during the summer of 1944. When a black GI was accused of rape, his only legal defense in a court-martial trial was either his white commander or another military officer chosen by the commander. But because many white officers fell prey to prejudices about rape and African Americans, they were less likely to investigate the credibility of those women or witnesses bringing forth an accusation of rape.

The advantages of a thorough investigation for the accused are evident in the Bricquebac case of Ora B. Broadus. An aviation technician, Broadus was charged with assault on 16 July and attempted rape on 24 July in Neuilly-la-Forêt, south of Cherbourg. The alleged assault was witnessed by a French boy and two other GIs who came to the accuser's rescue. Distinctive in this case was the vigorous defense by Broadus's commander, Lt. Samuel D. Worton. The officer took it upon himself to determine the reliability of witness statements by conducting various tests. For example, he had the boy, Roger Letellier, reenact the run he made on the night of the attack after hearing the accuser's screams. While Letellier had claimed to see the accused get up and walk away from the woman, Worton concluded that Letellier was too far away from the crime scene to arrive in time to see this happen. In this way, the boy's testimony was put into doubt. In addition to Worton's efforts, the army investigated the reliability of the witnesses and the character of the accusers, one of whom turned out to be a prostitute. Broadus was also examined by a medical board to determine his sanity. Character witnesses were called forth in defense of the accused; Broadus's tent-mate described him as someone who "wrote letters and listened to the radio and played cards. That was about all he cared to do."

What distinguished this case, in addition to the more thorough investigation, was that the accused was a white man. The two alleged witnesses to the incident, besides the young boy, were African American. Not only were they not made to appear in court, but they were never even approached for a statement during the course of the investigation. Broadus benefited from the more critical approach to evidence and testimony: he was sentenced to only twelve years hard labor for attempted rape, and found innocent of charges (by a prostitute) of assault. In addition, because of "irregularities" in the trial process, the reviewing judge advocate reduced that sentence to five years.[114]

The differential treatment of black and white soldiers in the court-martial system itself led to false rape accusations against African Americans. Aware that black men suffered from a credibility problem with white officers, white soldiers framed blacks for crimes the latter did not commit—either to escape guilt themselves or out of pure racial hatred. One Norman policeman reported that the village folks "have respected the black soldiers stationed in Grainville for a long time, believing that they do no harm, and witnessing how incidents are always provoked by drunk soldiers who have a real hatred for the 'Negroes.' The fact is that girls now prefer the blacks to the whites, and as a result, several fights over them have been provoked by jealous white soldiers."[115] "If a young black fellow, eighteen years old, would get together with a British girl, sixteen," remembered black soldier Timuel Black of his time in Britain, "that girl would be encouraged to say that she was raped."[116] Alfred Duckett remembers that while he and other black soldiers were at Camp Lucky Strike outside Le Havre, "there was an almost psychotic terror on the part of white commanders that there would be a great deal of association with the white women." One night in a Red Cross station, a white MP "caught" a member of Duckett's unit talking to a French woman who was serving coffee. When this black man refused to stop talking with the woman, and instead turned away from the MP, he was shot in the back and killed.[117]

White soldiers could rape a French white woman with impunity if an African American was in the vicinity and could be plausibly blamed. In several cases, black soldiers were picked up in the vicinity of the rape, and charged on those grounds alone, without any physical evidence or witness identification to prove their presence at the crime.[118] Even a kiss or a friendly gesture could quickly escalate into a rape charge. Signal Corps soldier Jack Sacco remembers how a black GI named Copeland was accused of trying to rape a French girl, and was threatened by the other men in his unit who wanted to shoot him dead on the spot. He pleaded innocent, saying he only wanted to kiss the girl in question. Luckily, there was an interpreter nearby who was able to understand the French girl as she confirmed that Copeland was only trying to kiss her. Unfortunately, when the girl's mother saw the couple, she "ran out of the house in a frenzy" and accused the GI of rape.[119]

The Problem of Miscommunication

Besides issues of identification and credibility, court-martial prosecutors failed to deal with a third crucial issue in rape accusations—misunderstandings between black soldiers and white French women. Such miscommunication stemmed from the obvious language problems, but also basic misconceptions about racial and national character. French women were taught to fear black soldiers as violent and sexually libidinous.[120] For their part, African American soldiers had also heard from their fathers that French women were lacking in sexual inhibitions. In addition, they thought themselves to be in a country with a reputation for racial tolerance. As Robert Lilly has put it, "the image of less racial prejudice and discrimination in France, coupled with the real or imagined sexual freedom of French women encouraged some black soldiers during World War II to think that all they had to do to win sexual relations with French women was to knock on their door."[121]

Many black soldiers were less naive than Lilly presents them, and even if they weren't, the first execution would have dispelled their views. At the same time, many were not aware that rape in France, as was the case in the United States, could be defined so broadly that even an unwanted glance or accidental touch could be interpreted as a form of sexual violence.[122] Accused of raping a woman in Brix, south of Cherbourg on 1 July, Leonard Bell testified that he was only trying to help the accuser with her laundry as she walked away from the river. According to Bell, who was described by a psychiatrist at the time of the trial as a "mature, responsible, submissive-type individual," he "walked on the side and put my hand on her elbow and was helping her like you help a woman across the street. She dropped the clothes and started screaming." At the trial, the accuser admitted to always being "on guard" with black soldiers, and that she was frightened simply because "he came so close to me and fell in the river. It got me afraid."[123] Many rape accusations began as friendly gestures or unwanted sexual advances on the part of black men who did not understand the stakes of the game they were playing.[124]

In addition, many African American soldiers mistakenly identified "honest" French women as prostitutes. A large number of incidents that resulted in rape accusations began as black soldiers arrived on the scene calling out for "Mademoiselles" or "Madame Coucher [Madame Go-to-Bed]" or offering money, cigarettes, or chocolate.[125] If the women were friendly, the soldiers would then make gestures signaling their desire to have sex and pass the night.[126] Besides the supposed French weakness for sex, it was well known that many women were resorting to prostitution as a matter of desperation. GI Walter Brown remembered that soldiers counseled a new private in this way: "Back home you could get your face slapped just for lookin'. They've been brought up different over here. What with four years of war, you don't have to mess around. All you gotta do is offer 'em some cigarettes, say 'zig-zig' [code for "sex"] and you're in like flynn."[127]

Such words were often spoken by black soldiers to French women who accused them of rape. Eugene Houston testified in his trial that when he said "zig zig" to his accuser and gave her one hundred francs, she "asked him to return" later on in the day "when no one would be around." When the prosecution asked Houston how one says that sentence in French, he had no idea, guessing only "jig, jig voo."[128] In another case, witnesses testified that Tommie Davison displayed five hundred francs to the husband of the accuser, claiming that he wanted a Mademoiselle and saying "zig zig."[129] John White was cleared of rape charges as it became clear he mistook refugee Clementine Larisisien for a prostitute. According to him, she agreed to "get him some lady" for two hundred francs. When she didn't, he asked for his two hundred francs back, but she kept one hundred, supposedly saying she had no food. When a fight broke out, she charged him with rape.[130] In several cases, the accusers testified that they had been given money either before or after they had been allegedly raped.[131] One of Private Forrest Washington's friends reported to him that he had had sex with a woman in a particular house. Believing the address to be a house of prostitution, Washington went there only to be accused of raping the woman who lived downstairs.[132]

In dealing with such rape accusations, prosecutors were unable to reconstruct the crime scene in terms other than sexual violence. Because they presumed violent and erratic behavior on the part of black men, they could not envision them as either confused or engaged in more rational sexual exchanges. If black soldiers attempted to escape arrest or showed fear under questioning, they were assumed to be guilty rather than simply afraid of unfair prosecution.[133] In addition, many judges and prosecutors simply could not imagine that a woman might engage by choice in sexual relations with a black man. In the case of Richard Scott, for example, the reviewing judge scorned the accused's testimony that a wife in Octeville had consented to sex, with her husband's blessings: "the accused's story, if believed, would indicate that by accident that night he blundered into the hands of two depraved people who, not for money but from sheer desire, the one to participate in and the other to watch the sexual act, enticed a

soldier of a different race." The story, he concluded, was "too incred-
ible for belief."[134]

The Legacy of the Noose

Whether out of fear or desperation, some French women made their
accusations of rape on unsound grounds. But US military prosecutors
did not sufficiently test out these questionable areas of these cases. In
part, this failure was a matter of time and circumstance. Particularly
during the summer of 1944, army investigators and prosecutors found
themselves on a rapidly moving front in a foreign country. More important, however, this failure was due to shared prejudices between
the Americans and the French concerning the "innate" sexual violence of black men. Cooperation between the American military and
French civilians consisted in a joint failure to envision black men in
circumstances other than the violent pursuit of sexual satisfaction.
Complicity also operated through unacknowledged consent on both
sides not to interrogate critical holes in the crime narrative, doubt the
credibility of the witness, or point out the lack of accurate medical or
any other positive, corroborated evidence. This mutual complacency
accounts for why so many blacks were convicted for sexual violence.

Understanding the convictions in this way, however, still leaves unanswered several questions concerning the punishment given black
men convicted of rape. As we have seen, many more black than white
soldiers were sentenced to death for rape (twenty-five out of twenty-
nine in the ETO). How can we explain the harsher sentences given
black men?[135] In part, those rulings can be understood by the relative
expendability of black soldiers. In contrast to a white soldier, who had
received excellent training and performed important combat tasks, a
black soldier was more dispensable in relation to the war effort.[136] But
such an explanation does not wholly account for the peculiar harshness of sentences for sexual assault because, in fact, black men were
sentenced to death for rape much more than any other crime. In the

years 1944–45, 151 death sentences were imposed for the crime of rape, 64.9 percent of those sentenced were black. By contrast, 130 death sentences were given for desertion; only 14.4 percent were black.[137] Furthermore, execution by hanging presented a challenge in the land of the guillotine. The army struggled to find officials qualified to do the job and was finally forced to bring a specialist across the Atlantic. "He was a professional, stationed in Texas," remembered GI Tommy Bridges. "He'd bring his own rope. He wouldn't talk."[138]

Why, then, was rape so severely punished? And why specifically with public executions by hanging? The answer to these questions lay in the grisly links between rape, race, and noose that had taken shape in the American South at least a century before. In the decades after the Civil War, when the demise of slavery limited the means by which white supremacists could maintain the color line, sex between black men and white women became a heightened taboo. In the American South, any interaction between a white woman and a black man was considered sufficient foundation for the charge of rape. According to historian Martha Hodes, white racists "conflated black men's alleged sexual misconduct toward white women with the exercise of their newly-won political rights." Particularly in the 1890s, but also throughout the twentieth century, rape accusations against black men often led to their lynchings at the hands of violent white mobs. Lynching became a punishment for any assertion on the part of the black community for civil rights or a better life.[139]

The military hangings drew upon (but did not replicate) such Jim Crow practices. The executions were not meant to produce a local atmosphere of terror as was the case with lynching. Rather SHAEF officials had related but different aims. First, they sought to create an effective deterrent for the crime of rape among black GIs.[140] When the army adjudged a death sentence, commanders of black units were instructed to post the decisions on the bulletin boards in such a way as to "draw the attention of relatively unintelligent soldiers."[141] Military officials deemed fear of the noose among black men to be powerful enough to act as a "scare" tactic in Normandy. A pamphlet titled "Let's Look at Rape," distributed to four thousand black chaplains

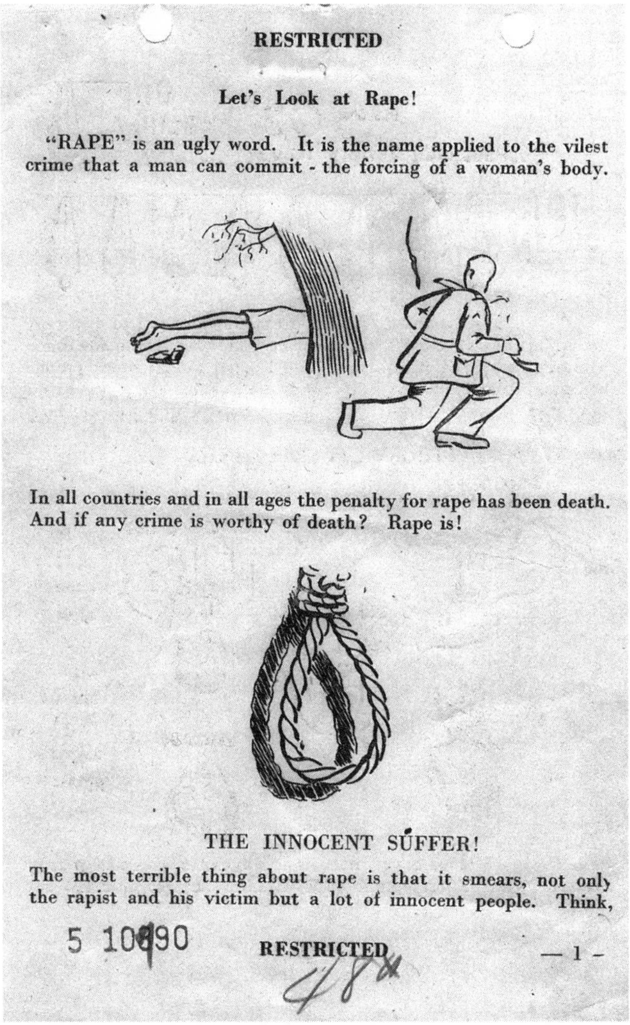

RESTRICTED

Let's Look at Rape!

"RAPE" is an ugly word. It is the name applied to the vilest crime that a man can commit - the forcing of a woman's body.

In all countries and in all ages the penalty for rape has been death. And if any crime is worthy of death? Rape is!

THE INNOCENT SUFFER!

The most terrible thing about rape is that it smears, not only the rapist and his victim but a lot of innocent people. Think,

RESTRICTED — 1 -

FIGURE 7.1. Pamphlet, "Let's Look at Rape." National Archives and Records Administration.

throughout ComZ, prominently featured a picture of a noose. (See figure 7.1.) The use of a noose to "educate" black soldiers about rape demonstrates just how racialized the crime had become by the fall of 1944. The pamphlet's iconography neatly linked the alleged sexual transgressions of black GIs in the ETO to Jim Crow mob violence. Already denied a combat role, black men were reminded that white

French women were no more their prize for victory than American ones. Like Jim Crow practices, then, the hangings aimed to protect the color line. The picture's caption in this context—"The innocent suffer!"—can only be described as ironic.[142]

Second, the army used public execution to showcase its ability to maintain law and order. Before a hanging was to occur, local military officials sent a notice of the event to the mayor of the village or town where the rape accusation was made. The townspeople were in this way invited to attend.[143] Convictions were also publicized in local newspapers.[144] The purpose of these measures becomes clear if we compare them with the execution of military justice in Germany, where not one soldier was publicly hanged. "Put simply," explains Lilly, "the rape of German women was not worth taking the life of one American soldier."[145] Why France and not Germany? By May of 1945, Germany was a broken nation without any option except complete surrender to Allied occupation. By contrast, during the summer and fall of 1944, France remained in a much more ambiguous position of power in relation to the United States. On the one hand, France was an ally whose army fought side by side with the Americans; on the other hand, it was a defeated power whose sovereignty, in the form of Charles de Gaulle's government, was not yet formally recognized. In these more uncertain circumstances, the military felt a greater need to demonstrate its power to prosecute its will.

Third, the public hangings scapegoated black soldiers for the crime of rape in order to save the reputation of the US Army. SHAEF intelligence reports in the summer and fall of 1944 demonstrate a growing inclination among military authorities to make rape a "negro" not an "American" problem. In its first missive from Normandy in late June 1944, intelligence noted without any reference to race that "there has been a good deal of misbehavior, mostly consisting of drunkenness and looting. There have been four rapes, one of which was punished by hanging."[146] When in the following weeks the problems persisted, intelligence shrugged off the problem: "It does not seem likely that anything short of severe disciplinary action will bring about any improvement in the behavior of our troops. Commanders, naturally, are loath to take such steps. It might be wise, therefore, to condition the French for the arrival of the fun-loving, exuberant American boy."[147] By mid-July, however, the US military was struggling mightily with the problems of GI promiscuity. As we have seen, clandestine prostitution was rampant; venereal disease rates were escalating, and accusations of rape were legion. Furthermore, no evidence exists that comparable problems plagued the Canadian or British troops. The US Army alone appeared to be out of control.[148]

Faced with this situation, as we have seen, the army tried and convicted a disproportionate number of black soldiers. It then used the statistics drawn from these prosecutions to present rape as a black crime. In other words, the US military used its own record of injustice to construct rape as a *fact* of racial depravity. This last twist seems to have occurred sometime in October when Norman intelligence was called upon to explain a particularly nasty article in the local Cherbourg press. On its front page, the stately *La presse cherbourgeoise* issued a "very grave warning" concerning the American troops. Accusing the GIs of pillage, rape, and murder, the paper cautioned its readers that "no place is safe—neither the roads nor even the home. A very real terror is instilling fear in our families. . . . The law of lynching will have to be harshly imposed since the authorities have proven so powerless."[149] The allusion to the "law of lynching" was particularly stinging; it pronounced the American occupiers to be so powerless that only their own Jim Crow lawlessness could solve the problem. The Cherbourg "warning" reached SHAEF headquarters thanks to the French Ministry of War, which sent a copy to General Eisenhower, accompanied by a note claiming that it "expresse[d] the sentiments not only of the people of the Manche, but of all Norman people in contact with the American troops."[150]

The response of Norman intelligence to the Cherbourg "warning" was to blame black soldiers. The October intelligence report cited provost marshal statistics, based on prosecutions in the previous months, to argue that 80 to 85 percent of the violence was committed by African Americans.[151] Not only did these statistics overlook the function and location of black units, as we have noted, but they were also directly based on a JAG record deeply flawed in its execution of justice. Nevertheless, the numbers themselves began to take on a life of their own, serving as evidence that rape was indisputably a "negro," not an "American" crime. By the beginning of November, Norman intelligence was also adopting the language of fear expressed in the "warning": "Civilians are being subjected to a minor reign of terror by negro soldiers," the report said, "and acts of mass violence may be expected at any time." By contrast, "there has been no evidence of antagonism towards US white troops, whose conduct continues to be reported as generally excellent."[152] To explain the high incidence of sexual violence, then, Norman intelligence combined provost marshal statistics with the rhetoric of terror first expressed in *La presse cherbourgeoise*. Once again French and American authorities were deadly allies in racism.

The US military could have admitted the breadth of the sexual violence problem to both the American and the French publics. Instead it chose to scapegoat black soldiers. In fact much more than the reputation of the army was at stake. The occurrence of rape undermined myths about the United States carefully cultivated in the months prior to and during the invasion. Long before an American foot made a print on Omaha Beach, the Office of War Information (OWI) was engaged in "psychological warfare" against the Nazis. The aim of the OWI was not only to counteract Nazi propaganda, but also to bring the French over to the "American way." Beginning in 1943, civilians read literature, air-dropped by Allied planes, which defined US war ambitions as the opportunity "to see our flag recognized throughout the world as a symbol of liberty and irresistible force consecrated to the defense of freedom."[153] The French also received assurances that the Americans did not "fight in order to aggrandize ourselves, to pillage or exercise the authority of a dominating power over the lives or governments of other peoples."[154]

An important theme of this propaganda was the inclusion of all minority American peoples. The idea was to present the United States as a vibrant democracy embraced by all peoples working together to achieve war goals. Photographs displayed "happy Negroes" contributing to industry, and stories boasted of Navajo Indians rushing on their ponies to join the army.[155] After the actual invasion, the propaganda machine continued in liberated towns where the Allies screened films lauding the virtues of the American liberators.[156] Again the French were reassured that their occupiers represented not only an advanced military power, but a principled government beloved by all its citizens.

Sexual violence gave the lie not only to prelanding propaganda, but also to the image of the "manly GI" so carefully constructed in *Stars and Stripes*. The specter of sexual assault transformed the Americans from a liberating people to an imperial power enjoying the traditional prerogatives of conquest. Occurrences of rape equally altered the manly GI from a knight in shining armor to an assailant instilling terror in women's hearts. Finally, such incidents reduced the so-called American rescue of France to crude pillage and unrestrained violence. They undermined the image of heterosexual romance used to help civilians accept growing American political dominance. In short, the costs of sexual violence were enormous, and had to be curtailed. If rape could be presented as the crime of a minority, it could be diminished in political effect. Exonerating white GIs neutralized the power of rape to undermine American authority. Executing black soldiers in public assured civilians that the problem of sexual violence was under control. By February 1945, SHAEF headquarters would report, not without satisfaction, that while "the misconduct of negro troops" persisted in some areas, in general, "a better understanding has been achieved by giving wide publicity to the results of Courts Martial against military offenders."[157]

"Hush Hush" in Normandy

As was the case with prostitution, a conflicting set of policies characterized the military approach to rape. Visibility was again a key issue. If SHAEF's aim was to make the prosecution of black soldiers for rape as evident as possible to French civilians, its goal was the opposite in the case of the American public. Like sexual labor, court-martial punishments for African Americans were visible to the French and invisible to the Americans. During the same week in October that *La presse cherbourgeoise* issued its "warning," the *Saturday Evening Post* ran an upbeat article about the "resurrection" of Cherbourg. Nary a word was spoken about GI sexual violence.[158] Over the next year, the American people would be constantly kept in the dark concerning the French rape accusations. Most puzzling in this regard is the silence of the black press. Although many black newspapers, including the feisty *Chicago Defender*, had pledged support—and hence self-censorship—on behalf of the war cause, black papers criticized court-martial justice in England and the Pacific theater of war.[159] But there was only silence from France.

Extreme censorship is the only explanation. Control over information represented business as usual for the War Department, particularly inasmuch as the rape hysteria possessed a racial element. Historian George Roeder describes race as "the most explosive issue" in the wartime censorship of visual images due to the fact that "millions of Americans judged every government action largely by its impact on race relations."[160] Because one of its chief aims was to portray the American people as united in a common struggle against the enemy, the Office of Censorship restricted publication of any material depicting racial conflict, including violent confrontations on US military bases.[161] Guidelines prohibited release of any information that could be used as propaganda against the US war effort. Stress was placed on compatibility between American race attitudes and the goal of winning the war. Black correspondents "of known radical character" did not receive press credentials in the ETO. Also censored were photographs of black GIs dancing with white British women.[162] The official silence surrounding the French rape accusations no doubt resulted from these restrictions, which sought to elide racial tension in order to keep Americans united behind the military forces.

That silence affected the ability of black leaders not only to serve as watchdogs on the military, but also to exploit the contradictions inherent in a war fought by a segregated military against ideologies of racial supremacy. Secrecy concerning the military way of justice became a growing imperative for the War Department during the preinvasion months, in great part because of militant actions on the part of the black community. By the summer of 1944, SHAEF headquarters was already squirming under the light of bad publicity due to public exposure of its court-martial procedures. While such procedures normally took place behind closed military doors without press coverage, a series of well-publicized convictions in the years 1943–44 had embarrassed the overseas Judge Advocate General (JAG) Offices that had prosecuted them. The result was even greater pressure to repress what was going on in France.

The first of these cases occurred in New Caledonia off the coast of Australia in the spring of 1943, when two black soldiers received life sentences for allegedly raping a white prostitute.[163] The case escaped censors when black leaders got wind of it and found multiple legal problems with the prosecution.[164] A year later an even bigger scandal in England further embarrassed the military. It concerned a black soldier named Leroy Henry who awoke a British couple in Bath late one May night. The wife answered the door, then accompanied the soldier down the road, supposedly to give him directions back to camp. When she did not return, her husband went in search of her. Found by the side of the road, she claimed to have been raped. Subsequently charged with rape, found guilty, and condemned to death by hanging, Henry claimed that he knew the woman and had had relations with her before. The only difference that evening, he argued, was that she asked for more money than usual.[165]

The case was brought to light by the British press, which made Henry's conviction a cause célèbre.[166] Besides launching a press attack on US military justice, British civilians ran a grassroots petition campaign against the conviction.[167] Ultimately the NAACP in New York pleaded for and received a stay of execution for Henry. In their own extensive coverage of the Henry case, the black press countered SHAEF's belief that strong court-martial punishment for black soldiers would shore up local faith in American authority. On the contrary, black newspapers argued, such punitive actions degraded the integrity of American democracy.[168]

The black press was playing to white American as well as a British sentiments. Early on in the war years, black leaders proposed a Double V campaign, which sought to defeat fascism abroad and Jim Crow at home. Once the war started, FDR increased his use of federal powers against lynching, justifying his actions through the argument that lynchers abetted the nation's enemies. German propaganda exploited the fact of lynching in order to argue that Americans did not really believe in freedom, at least for people of color.[169] African Americans capitalized on the troubling inconsistency between the cause of winning the war against a fascist enemy and the desire to preserve racial segregation. Such efforts did not fall on deaf American ears, particularly those of parents who had sons fighting in Germany or Japan. As the war dragged on, white men and women became aware that their sons were being sacrificed to eradicate not one but two powers whose ideological backbone was racial supremacy.[170]

By the light of this brighter cultural climate, the black press pieced together similarities between key court-martial cases in order to claim a pattern of racial discrimination. In March 1944, *The Crisis* described the defendants in the New Caledonia case as "denied adequate defense counsel, convicted 9,000 miles away from home on flimsy evidence, and given a harsh and unreasonable sentence solely because they were Negroes."[171] The cases exemplified how black soldiers "simply do not get a fair trial" when "faced with the average American white attitude toward an incident involving a Negro man and a white woman."[172] As for the Henry case, it again demonstrated that "rape by colored men, in the American military mind, is different from rape by white men."[173] "It begins to look like Negro soldiers are getting a thorough rooking in military courts on 'rape' charges," agreed Roy Wilkins in the *New York Amsterdam News*.[174] "Old southern prejudices which seem to permeate the whole army," reckoned the *Chicago Defender*, "are almost always present in court-martials to see that the Negro soldiers get sentences out of proportion to the crimes committed."[175] "The evidence was shockingly skimpy," editorialized the *Pittsburgh Courier*, "as it usually is where the accused is black and the judge and jury are white Americans, and the woman is white."[176] In this way, the black press served as watchdogs for a "Scottsboro" pattern of "railroading" black soldiers for the alleged crime of rape.[177]

By the summer of 1944, SHAEF public relations was well aware of what the black press thought about army courts-martial, and was advising headquarters to handle race relations with kid gloves.[178] Equally painful had been the visit of NAACP President Walter White to England some months earlier in January 1944. In the wake of Judge Hastie's angry resignation from the War Department in 1943, the NAACP became so concerned by reports of military injustice that it sent its president to England. An affable but strong-willed leader who had powerful connections within the black community, White could not be ignored.[179] The War Department made arrangements to "guide" him through the ETO, that is, to keep him from talking candidly to black soldiers during his visit.[180] But White was no fool, and despite all efforts to the contrary, he managed to learn a lot about what was going on in England.[181] At the end of his "tour," he made a number of recommendations to Eisenhower, chief among them the establishment of a biracial, impartial board to review trials of black soldiers.[182] "I came across innumerable instances where Negro soldiers were court-martialed, found guilty, and sentenced to long terms for minor offenses," White later recalled.[183] In 1945 he published *A Rising Wind*, a bold account of his trip that argued that the court-martial procedure was being used "to break the spirit of Negro soldiers."[184]

The army's response to White's visit suggests that during the summer of the French rape accusations, military officials were both preoccupied with and in denial about racial discrimination. Soon after White left Britain in 1944, he received a letter from Gen. John Lee, deputy commander of the ETO. In condescending tones, Lee praised White's work, reminded him of Eisenhower's "guiding philosophy" that only "if we work together," can the war be won, and urged White to demonstrate "that you are 'on the Team'—and that is all our country asks of any man or woman in this war." He went on to state baldly that "there is no Negro problem in the European Theater of Operations, United States Army, nor has there ever been a Negro problem."[185] In this way Lee managed to both deny the problem and urge White not to talk about it. When White's *A Rising Wind* appeared, Lee assigned a colonel in the JAG Office to read it. The latter's response was outrage: White was guilty of "dishonest and irresponsible journalism." His book was "reprehensible," written in bad faith, "intended to produce a profit," and would actually lead one to believe in "the existence of a definite and malicious ill-will toward colored troops on the part of white soldiers and officers" that was "obviously not the case." Nevertheless, the colonel advised Lee not to make any official protest because to do so would only incite further attention.[186] Once again the army stood at a crossroads between denial and the desire for control: it denied that there was a "negro" problem but also worried that attention not be drawn to it.

Even before one French woman cried rape in the summer of 1944, then, SHAEF headquarters had been under attack concerning its handling of judicial procedures. Its response to such criticism was to be ever more vigilant about the secrecy of its proceedings. Neither the British nor the American authorities were to leak ComZ's statistics on rape to the press.[187] Black correspondents in France appeared not to know what was going on; their newspapers focused on the heroic contributions of black men in Normandy.[188] Nor did any of the watchdogs appear to be on guard: Hastie had resigned from his post as liaison to the War Department, and White was preoccupied by the situation in England. Correspondence between these two men, as well as between White and his board of directors, during the summer of 1944, suggests that if the NAACP leadership knew about the French situation, they were not discussing it.[189] Not even the families of those sentenced to death were given notice of their relatives' impending fate. In 1945 one mother hired a lawyer to ask the army why she was never told of her son's conviction and execution, a fact that deprived her of the opportunity to ask for clemency.[190]

An opportunity for discovery did arise in July, when Brig. Gen. Benjamin O. Davis, the highest-ranking African American in the army, declared his intention to visit the ETO.[191] But SHAEF public relations had the Walter White debacle on its mind. In a memo to headquarters orchestrating Davis's every move while in Europe, SHAEF planners referred to the elsewhere-much-denied "Negro Problem" in the ETO. Knowing that the trip would garner press attention, SHAEF planners were determined to portray the army as "making no distinction between white and colored in matters of military justice, housing, recreation and assignment of duties."[192] SHAEF seems to have succeeded this time in keeping Davis in the dark, for at the end of his visit the general reassured black journalist Edward Toles that "racial relations among American troops in France are much better than they have been in England."[193]

When news of the French rape accusations finally did reach the American public, it was via the adder tongue of one of the country's most notorious racists, Mississippi Senator James O. Eastland. As part of a joint Senate Military-Naval Affairs Committee, Eastland traveled in Europe in May 1945 to compile statistics on German devastation.[194] Upon his return, he participated in a filibuster to kill the wartime Fair Employment Practices Committee (FEPC), established by Roosevelt to regulate racial equality in war industries. In this context, Eastland shared the "findings" of his trip, including the reports from "numerous high-ranking generals of the American Army" that "Negroes" had been deserters and "lazy" workers. Worse still, the senator related what he called a "hush hush" story concerning black soldiers in France:

> It was necessary during the Normandy invasion to disarm a good many Negro soldiers, I was reliably informed by a high-ranking general in Paris. Negro soldiers would go to farm houses and holler "Boche! Boche!" as if they were looking for Germans, call the men of the families out into the yards, and hold guns on them while they went in and criminally assaulted the women members of the family. . . . In the small Normandy peninsula, from invasion date to May of this year, there were 33 cases of criminal assault, 26 by Negroes, 7 by whites. . . . They constituted only one-twelfth of our army yet they had committed more than half the crimes.[195]

Although his statistics were inaccurate, Eastland's accusations echoed SHAEF memoranda concerning sexual assault in the summer of 1944. His statements contained one element of truth: rape in France was still being discussed in the form of dinner conversation among high-ranking officers.[196] The old army network of silent loyalty and gossip was reemerging in the wake of the era of mass conscription. As long as the rape accusations remained "hush hush," top military officers could continue to "understand" them on their own terms—as proof of black depravity.

Eastland's remarks created a stir in the mainstream press and, to say the least, presented a difficult moment for the army.[197] The senator never identified the "high-ranking general" in Paris. The War Department issued a statement that it had "no knowledge" of the incidents referred to by Eastland, and that it was "proud" of its black troops.[198] SHAEF headquarters had "no comment" on Eastland's reference to the Normandy rapes—except to say that no Negroes had been used as combat troops in Normandy.[199] What drew the loudest cries of outrage from the black community was not the rape charges but Eastland's disparagement of black military performance in the ETO.[200] Black editors called the senator a "drooly-mouthed Mississippian" and a "Goebbels" who had "concocted a lie so monstrous that many Americans will doubtless believe it."[201] Rather than hear Eastland's "hush hush" as a distress signal from Normandy, black journalists and leaders did not allow the message for the messenger.

The Orphans from Paris

Still another obstacle blinded the black community to Eastland's disclosures: tender veneration. The idea that France, in particular Paris, was a "safe zone" for blacks dated back to the First World War, when African Americans first arrived on French shores in large numbers. During these years, historian Adriane Lentz-Smith has argued, black soldiers clung to their belief that French civilians knew no color line, and would treat them with a respect unknown to them at home: "a utopian France came to represent, emotionally and discursively, all that the United States denied African Americans."[202] In the postwar period, Paris, in particular, became a magnet for black musicians, artists, and writers.[203] In the summer of 1944, black soldiers saw their trip across the channel to Normandy as a voyage to a land of recognition and approval. In this sense, the rape accusations caught many off guard—at home as well as in France.

African Americans' belief in their "special" relationship with the French people made the liberation of Paris for them a singular pleasure. Because New York was home to Langston Hughes, Fredi Washington, Edna Thomas, and many other black writers, artists, and musicians who had recently enjoyed the City of Light, the Liberation was celebrated in Harlem. No sooner did the Allied troops make their entry into the liberated city, declared Abe Hill of *New York Amsterdam News*, than "former Paris dwellers and visitors began to brush up their French as their hopes and joys vied with each other over the prospects of again returning to the French capitol." Even more than the food and wine, reasoned Hill, "it is the over-all feeling of real race equality in France that makes them love it. A man's place in a Parisian community is based solely on his individuality, with his race being merely incidental. A prejudiced Frenchman is a person who's hard to find." Hill called Hughes and other black artists "orphans from Paris" and "refugees" from "French liberty."[204]

In this view of the Liberation, the kisses of French women meant much more than romance or rescue. In addition, they held out the promise of full manhood.[205] "G.I. Jody [as the black GI was sometimes called] was never a greater hero," announced proudly the *New York Amsterdam News*.[206] Rumor had it that "Parisian beauties" were darkening their white skins with powder and donning zoot suits as "tan Yanks" entered the city. French youth "has turned to the colored Americans' way of doing things by wearing zoot suits and jitterbugging," announced the *Richmond African American*.[207] Paris was dancing to Nazi-banned swing music again in Montmartre, according to black correspondent Edward Toles. "Nowhere have I seen people so friendly, congenial and sincere."[208] "Paree itself we found to be all that it has been painted," related black Sgt. Peyton Gray. "Loads and loads of pretty women, and I do mean pretty, wearing flimsy, flowing, filmy dresses and above all—riding bicycles in a gentle spring wind. Needless to say, most of us swung our heads from left to right and right to left, as if our necks were nothing more than a pivot."[209] It is hard to imagine any black man making such a remark about a white American woman at this time. For black men, Paris provided the key to a forbidden erotic world, one that also opened the door to manhood, equality, and power. Because African Americans had precisely this emotional—and profoundly political—investment in France, letting go was difficult. For this reason, Eastland's remarks about Normandy sparked no expression of lingering concerns. Even a year later, the *Chicago Defender* maintained the view that "tan Yanks" were "treated by the French people, young and old, with a tolerance and friendliness seldom accorded them in the United States."[210] One correspondent in Rouen reported that he saw "Negro soldiers and French girls walking with their arms around each other in the city's streets."[211] If there was trouble, it came from the American MPs, who arrested such soldiers and "americanized" the Normans by teaching them segregation.[212] If racial attitudes had soured, insisted the *Chicago Defender*, it was due to the white, not the black GIs: "France has too great a tradition to allow it to be spoiled by the sinister influence of unenlightened Americans."[213] No doubt white Americans had brought their Jim Crow ways to France. But as we shall see, French racial attitudes were also infinitely more complex than the black press suspected.

8

Black Terror on the *Bocage*

IN OCTOBER 1944, a "Very Grave Warning" appeared on the front page of the Norman paper *La presse cherbourgeoise*. The warning cautioned French men and women that "scenes of savagery and bestiality," including "pillages, rapes and murders," were "desolating" the French countryside: "No place is safe—neither the roads nor even the home. A very real terror is instilling fear in our families."[1] "Very Grave Warning" stands as an odd exception to the paper's usually stately tenor and careful neutrality: clearly grave times demanded extraordinary measures. And grave times they were. The Cherbourg editors were responding to scores of rape charges made by Norman women. The warning characterized the fear and panic spreading throughout Normandy during the American presence there during 1944 and 1945.[2]

Stories and rumors of rape by black soldiers were legion, circulating from village to village. The sense that "no place is safe," and that "a very real terror" stalked the countryside was widely felt in northern France for the entirety of the American stay there. "The French in Le Havre," wrote one Norman in November, "are terrified by the Americans, both black and white, whom America has sent to clean up the port. They run after the women, the children, the men."[3] Also that month, the mayor of Le Havre, Pierre Voisin, informed the American authorities that his city's population was "absolutely terrorized."[4] Farther west, a Bayeux aristocrat, le Marquis de Traynel, reported an incident in which a woman, pursued by a black soldier, came to his house "in the grip of a veritable terror." Traynel targeted the American soldiers in particular: "as long as we had only British or Canadian soldiers here, we had nothing but praise for their correct behavior. But from the moment that the American army began to enter into our region, our women and girls became the prey of individuals terrorizing the region."⁵ Subsequently the chief of police in Caen reported that "an American formation composed of mostly black soldiers had become the terror of the region."⁶ The prefect of this city agreed that his constituents showed "a visible fear of black soldiers" after an alleged incident of rape. In nearby Mézidon, he reported, "negro soldiers frequently pursue women and are extremely feared by the population."⁷ In Cherbourg, female accusers claimed to be "terrorized by fright" when faced with soldiers making advances on them.⁸ At least in Le Havre, the so-called terror lasted far into 1945 when the Americans once more swept through Normandy to leave the ETO. In the late summer of that year, Le Havre's mayor was still receiving scores of angry letters from constituents claiming that women were being "terrorized by nearly daily attacks on them," and that a "regime of terror" had been "imposed by bandits in uniform."⁹

How can we explain the panic gripping Normandy during this period? Why did the French contribute to the proliferation of rape charges against African American soldiers, as we learned in the last chapter? Why did they not, like the British, protest cases in which black soldiers were being condemned on flimsy evidence? French complacency about the rape cases can be explained, in great part, by racial prejudice. Despite their reputation among African Americans for racial tolerance, many French people harbored deeply-rooted racist sentiments, largely developed in relationship to the colonized peoples of western Africa. In 1944, loss, grief, and fear intensified these attitudes. But racism alone cannot fully account for the rape accusations. In addition, the black-GI-as-rapist came to serve as a projection for a whole host of postwar French emotions, including anger, frustration, and shame. To be properly understood, then, the "terror" of

1944 must be framed by the political transition in which it took place, namely, growing US dominance over French life.

The Great Fear of 1944

The rape charges circulated Normandy in the form of rumor. Rumors spread about a variety of topics during the summer of 1944. Some concerned the Germans: for example, that Hitler had been murdered, or that the SS was parachuting behind Allied lines.[10] Refugees far from home often heard terrible rumors concerning the destruction of their villages.[11] This predilection for rumor sprang from the Normans' inability to get any reliable information about what was happening. In June and July, when French newspapers were practically nonexistent, Normans were almost completely without news. In some areas, a radio car would broadcast updates in the center of town.[12] In most cases, however, the Normans had to wait for the occasional American soldier who spoke French in order to find out about the military situation.[13]

Most pressing was news of family and friends touched by the war. Throughout the summer, *La presse cherbourgeoise* posted pleas for information, ever more desperate, on the whereabouts of missing relatives.[14] In mid-August, a Civil Affairs officer southwest of Saint-Lô was still reporting that "the population was starved for news. Since the invasion, they have been living on rumours."[15] Word traveled from mouth to mouth and in the process was amplified and distorted to such an extent that no one knew what was really true.[16] As Jacques Petit recorded with frustration in his diary, "What are we supposed to believe? . . . We have no way of sorting out the true from the false."[17]

Rumors thrive in situations where lack of knowledge combines with fear. By assigning chaotic events some sort of rumored pattern, people gain the illusion of control. Ironically, then, rumors both spread and relieve anxiety. To "know" the worse, even erroneously, helps a population feel as if it has gained some power over frightful circumstances.[18] The Normans were "good rumor-mongers" according to SHAEF intelligence.[19] Rumors of rape, in particular, raced through the region. French civilians in Saint-Lô, for example, believed the Germans had taken two twenty-year-old girls with them and raped them repeatedly before sending them home.[20] A much-repeated rumor along the Cotentin Peninsula concerned a priest in Denneville, who was shot while stopping a soldier "trying to force his attentions upon a woman."[21] The story soon reached Barneville to the east, causing concern regarding the arrival of black troops. "Throughout that area, reported SHAEF, "rumors of rape by American white and colored troops are being spread,"[22] Unlike the JAG Office that prosecuted the rape accusations, intelligence expressed doubts about their veracity, and often felt compelled to vouchsafe the credibility of their informants: "sources include the priest, a sensible and reliable person."[23]

Rumor was not a new phenomenon in the French countryside. During July of 1789, with Paris in a revolutionary fever, rural areas throughout France became caught up in a mass hysteria fueled by rumor. Fearful concerning the upheavals brought on by the Revolution, peasants spread stories concerning robbers who were hired by the aristocracy to steal grain and do violence in their villages.[24] The hysteria itself was described in a rhetoric of fear, becoming known as *la grande peur* or *la terreur panique*.[25] Although it is risky to compare phenomenon as different as the great fear of 1789 and the rape hysteria of 1944, placing the rape accusations within a longer historical framework also helps us to understand them. In particular, the comparison highlights the overwhelmingly provincial character of the 1944 charges. Police reports in the Paris region during the summer and fall of 1944 reveal that while American soldiers may have brawled and thieved in the City of Light, they were not targeted as rapists.[26] Nor were there any rapes reported in Paris by the First and Third Armies in September 1944.[27]

The fact that the rape hysteria of 1944 was not an urban phenomenon gives weight to the idea that the French provinces (in both 1789 and 1944) had their own social contagion of fear. Mostly against black soldiers, these charges can also be explained by the idiosyncratic history of African Americans in France. Although France was praised as an oasis of tolerance in the early twentieth century, historians have revealed this haven from prejudice to be limited to Paris. Brett Berliner, for example, has insisted this tolerance was a myth forged from the welcome given to no more than two hundred African Americans in Paris during the 1920s.[28]

The more general French view of African Americans largely followed from their perception of Africans, whom they believed to be savage, prone to violence, and hypersexual.[29] When African Americans arrived in France for the first time during the First World War, the French simply transferred these prejudices about Africans onto them.[30] French civilians were "instructed" about black men of the Ninety-Second Division fighting in France, namely, their "lust" for women, and their "unbridled" sexual drive. In short, they were told that every black man was a "potential rapist."[31] In the 1920s and 1930s, African Americans remained at best an oddity outside Paris. While people living in such large ports as Cherbourg and Le Havre had some exposure to non-European peoples, to meet an African American elsewhere in northern France was an event: most rural folk had never seen one.[32]

The contrast between urban familiarity and provincial ignorance regarding African Americans helps to explain why rape hysteria was a provincial rather than a Parisian phenomena. Racial ignorance was widespread among civilians in Normandy. As a child, Norman Yves Boudier remembers his surprise when he touched a black soldier "and my hand was not dirty afterwards."[33] A journalist for *Le Havre-éclair* referred to black soldiers at Camp Tareyton as "enigmatic, squatting around a fire of brushwood, dreaming of savage steppes which they have no doubt known."[34] For *normande* Danièle Philippe, the sight of men "jubilant with their white teeth in their black faces" was "so astonishing that we stood silently scared stiff."[35] "One could almost be afraid of these poor unfortunates," another Norman told SHAEF intelligence, "but they are nice and reasonable."[36]

Blackened with Americans

As civilians in northern France struggled to live with the American presence, this racial ignorance soured into distrust and fear.[37] "The place is blackened with American colored soldiers," reported one Norman to military intelligence. "They think nothing of stealing, raping and attacking in spite of the colored MPs who do not give a hoot anyway and drink with the delinquents."[38] A Cherbourgeois complained to the American military that "invasion troops abound here . . . Negroes especially, and when they've had something to drink, they behave worse than beasts."[39] Marcelle Hamel-Hateau remembered a neighbor who, traumatized when a GI raped her goat, expressed shocked that it was "not even black soldiers" who did it. For her part, Hamel-Hateau lamented the terrible racism that overcame Normandy at the time: "they [black soldiers] were blamed for all the wrongdoing of the troops."[40] Fear of African American soldiers had spread throughout the Norman region by August of 1944. In the small village of Le Pas, the Gourdin family barricaded their doors after some black soldiers came by to ask for cider.[41] "Everyone was afraid of the blacks," remembered Marguerite Gidon of Bernesq. "When you saw them, you ran to the other side!"[42]

In such an atmosphere rumor gathered speed and force. "Here too the Negroes are savages," claimed a civilian from Le Cateau: "They have already raped seven girls and even a seven- year old child."[43] Such rumors then spread east to Valenciennes, where another civilian reported that sixteen black soldiers "yesterday raped a young girl and she died. They are real brutes."[44] "The white troops are well-enough regarded," one gendarme in Cany-Barville wrote, "but the black ones are the object of a general repulsion on the part of the population due to their primitive ways with women and their notorious intemperance."[45] Perhaps because black soldiers were assigned to service units rather than the infantry, they were not seen as soldiers. "We have no more soldiers here, just a few negroes who terrorize the neighborhood," remarked one civilian in April of 1945.[46]

Among government officials, the presence of both North African

troops and African American soldiers set off cries of alarm.[47] The prefect of Calvados reported that a black soldier had hacked a woman
to pieces with an axe, then "without any shame whatsoever," raped
the corpse.[48] Authorities came to assume that any black soldier was a
rapist and vice versa. One Norman police chief reported to the prefect that allied behavior was "in general correct, except for the black
Americans." But the available record of sexual assaults in his region
demonstrates that the accused were, in fact, either unidentified, British, or white.[49] Another policeman reassured the Le Havre mayor
Pierre Voisin that incidents of assault in one area of the city had been
investigated. The citizens had drawn up a petition in which they attrib-
uted the violence to a nearby "American camp." But in his letter to the
mayor, the policeman wrote his own version of the problem, which
was that "negro soldiers [were] billeted in the camp nearby."[50] In this
way an "American" problem again became a "negro" problem.

To understand such racial hostility, we must remember how frightening it was to live in Normandy and Brittany during the years 1944–45.
Despite the racist views of civilians throughout northern France, no
rape wave took place except in these two regions during the summer of 1944. Even in Reims, where there was an enormous base camp
established for American GIs in the spring and summer of 1945, rape
was not a serious problem.[51] Rape accusations were brought forth in
Le Havre during the summer of 1945, but not with the intensity of the
year before. Within Normandy and Brittany, the location of the rape
charges formed no pattern except that they arose in predominantly
rural areas.[52] In looking for the roots of the rape hysteria, then, we
must limit ourselves to what circumstances the two regions shared
during the campaign.

That shared experience was the terror of living in a battlefield.
During the first months of the invasion, two million French citizens
became homeless as a result of bombardment and combat. As we
have seen, the destruction in Normandy was particularly horrible.
Bombed continuously for over a week, Caen was left three-quarters
destroyed, its population decimated. Saint-Lô was also left in ruins,
as was Vire, Coutances, Lisieux, Falaise, Avranches, Argentan, Dom-

front, and Alençon. Le Havre earned the dubious honor of being the most destroyed town in all of France, with 85 percent of its buildings ruined and eighty thousand left homeless. The Breton towns Saint-Malo and Brest were also heavily damaged. French fields were a scene of carnage, littered with dead cows and other farm animals, as well as the corpses of soldiers and civilians. Widespread German, then American, looting further traumatized civilians as well as depriving them of their most indispensable belongings.[53]

While liberation was sweet, what followed further disrupted civilian life. "There was an extraordinary upheaval throughout the region," remembered Madame Georges Guernier.[54] The destruction of war had brought scores of unknown refugees into villages. Like the 1789 vagrants who caused panic when they clogged roads, the 1944 refugees were strangers upsetting the rhythm of village life, only on a scale unimaginable in the eighteenth century. Collaborationists and German spies were also said to be present, lingering in American uniforms.[55] Most importantly, the Americans moved in, appropriating enormous amounts of property and dominating the roads with the movement of troops and materiel.[56]

Normans experienced the Americans as invaders of still another sort, with the towns of Cherbourg and Le Havre particularly inconvenienced. "Le Havre was literally invaded," remembered Roger Hilliquin, an adolescent at the time. "You could not stick your nose out the door without seeing a Jeep or a Dodge drive by, or hundreds of soldiers walking around."[57] *Havre-éclair* reported that the "tensions and inconveniences" of cohabitation had soured the folks in Le Havre on the Americans.[58] A refugee returning home to Cherbourg in midsummer 1944 saw it as a "completely transformed town. What a surprise to see once again the same streets now lit up and swarming with the American military."[59] "Cherbourg, murdered city," wrote Henri Dabrin in his war journal. "Everything which moves is American. Everywhere their police control everything, regulate all traffic. Nothing can delay the constant flow of their vehicles debarking. . . . There are not even any sidewalks or passageways for pedestrians."[60] In order to drive huge tanks and other vehicles through the city, the Americans had to knock down buildings and widen streets.[61] They literally re-shaped the city to accommodate their needs.

This second "invasion" further transformed racial ignorance into fear. African American soldiers were doubly threatening: not only were they foreigners but when they entered overwhelmingly white villages, they transgressed the boundaries of race. In Bayeux neighbors reviled a woman who resorted to prostitution, not only because her husband was in a German prison but also because she consorted with black soldiers.[62] Civilians in Saint-Lô neighborhoods where prostitutes did business with African American soldiers were indignant that someone would invite a black man into their streets and near their homes.[63] Black soldiers came to symbolize all that was wrong with the American "invasion." In the frightening news blackout of those long hot days, civilians resorted to rumor in order to make sense of the threats against their lives. The black-soldier-as-rapist became a communal fantasy, born of rumor. Accusations of violence against black GIs gave French civilians the illusion of control. More than an object of prejudice, the African American soldier became a projection of civilian anxiety concerning the terror of war as well as the tensions of military occupation.

Black Peril Revisited

While the rape accusations were undoubtedly racist, they were also used to vent anxieties that had nothing to do with race, even while used to articulate them. Racism is inadequate to explain the rape charges not only because of the dynamics of rumor but also the distinctly sexual nature of rape as a crime. Rape had a complex history in both France and the United States where it had operated for hundreds of years to maintain white colonial power. While lynching was not a common practice in either metropolitan or colonial France, French imperialists shared with American racists a set of fantasies concerning black sexuality as a challenge to white political authority. When civilians projected those colonial fantasies onto African American soldiers during the summer of 1944, they led to accusations of rape.

Like their American counterparts, as we have seen, the French defined men of color as hypersexual in their desires particularly for white women. North African attempts to sexually possess a white woman were seen as direct challenges to white colonial authority. As Frantz Fanon famously put it, "When my restless hands caress those white breasts, they grasp white civilization and dignity and make them mine."[64] Rumors of the rape of white women by black men in colonial societies served as a barometer for challenges to the French government, and often peaked during periods of crisis in the authority of colonial rule. Because French imperialists fantasized that colonized men were lustful toward white women—what they called *the black peril*—they felt justified in rigidly repressing them.[65] The oppression of colonized men became more challenging during the two world wars when West and North African soldiers fought on metropolitan French soil. Most famous among these soldiers were the *tirailleurs sénégalais*, originally a slave force that emerged in 1914 as the backbone of the conscripted African military force.[66] In 1940, about seventy-five thousand colonial troops fought in metropolitan France against the Germans. These soldiers were largely abandoned by their officers in defeat; thousands were massacred by the Germans; still others died in horrific conditions in German prison camps or transit stations waiting to go home.[67]

Of primary concern to the French Army in both wars was to segregate the colonial troops from the French metropolitan population. Despite the surprise French civilians sometimes expressed about American segregational practices, in fact, they had some familiarity with racial tensions in their own military. Military officials insisted on attaching to nonwhite regiments special brothels serviced only by nonwhite women. Such a move, it was believed, was the best way to prevent the rapes of "respectable" white women.[68] In April 1940, the French Army circulated a document arguing that most of the rapes committed against white women in North Africa had been by black men who had frequented metropolitan white women in the last war.[69] French officers frowned upon using white prostitutes for non-white troops because, in one officer's words, "to sexually possess a white woman, *a fortiori* paying her like a vulgar piece of merchandise, permits [a man of color] to reverse the power relation and re-write history in his own way."[70] This officer's fear that sex between a black man and a white woman could erode imperial authority suggests just how vital sex was to the maintenance of white supremacy.

If we look again at the rape charges of 1944 with these power dynamics in mind, we recognize that the accusations were imbedded in French men's efforts to deal with wartime gender damage. During the summer of 1944, French authorities were trying to recover both their manhood and their status as a great power. Rape became a degrading reminder of the defeat of 1940 and the German occupation.[71] The raped woman's body symbolized the failure of French men to protect their women from outside enemies. The black claim to the white woman's body represented not only a loss of French sexual prerogatives, but also a decline in political status.

Signs of that decline appeared everywhere in the summer of 1944.[72] The American military was moving in, requisitioning enormous amounts of property and hanging their flag on municipal buildings.[73] American intelligence reports reveal how apprehensive the Normans were concerning France's national weakness. American bombing, it was believed, was being carried out "to ruin France and make it an American colony."[74] "The economic imperialism of the great powers" was a great source of worry for the locals, according to the chief of police in Caen.[75] "Popular reaction to the manifest power of the Allied forces," reported another officer, "is the feeling of a need to restore France to a position of power and prestige through the rapid creation of a strong French Army."[76] An intelligence officer interviewing civilians in Hambye, south of Saint-Lô, reported enormous anxiety about the fate of the French: "What will be the future of France?" asked one butcher, Monsieur Nelle. "Will the Allies let her keep her colonies? We are weak now and she cannot defend herself."[77] Normans were not the only ones to experience such fears. In the Marne, for example, there were widespread fears that "the Americans want to win the war only to make us accept their economic laws at the end of the conflict."[78]

Concern about the future of France often mixed with dread concerning black troops. Although these two fears seem not to have anything to do with each other, they often appeared side by side in police reports. For example, in September 1944, one police official observed that French civilians "suffer to see that the allies refuse to allow France to take the place that its past and its innumerable sacrifices for the common cause give it the right to occupy." He then charged that "black soldiers have been responsible for serious assaults, notably in Normandy where there have been several rapes." Why would an official both record such a lament and then accuse black soldiers of rape?

A report some months later by French intelligence in Caen provides the answer to that question. In a letter to the prefect, an official described the Americans as engaged in an effort "to make France a second-rate state, a mere tributary to the Great Powers." Such was the opinion of the Normans, he argued, based on how badly they were treated by "colored" American troops stationed nearby.[79] For this official, rape on the part of black soldiers suggested France's new status as a "mere tributary to the Great Powers." Once again, sexual violence took the measure of a crisis in white political authority. The same equation between rape and power was made by civilians. In her diary of the war in Cherbourg, Suzanne Bigeon wrote: "the black Americans believe they are authorized, by their 'liberating' action, to violate numerous women, particularly in the countryside." For Begeon, the punishment dealt such rapists, "hung high and fast on trees in the court of honor," was utterly justified.[80]

In short, the racialized nature of rape as a crime heightened the sting of national humiliation. The "black peril" had undergone a devastating reversal, one that charged the rape accusations with the emotional baggage of French dishonor. The black-GI-as-rapist was *not* a colonized man of color defying white authority. Rather, in the French mind, he was the American conqueror asserting a prerogative of dominance. He symbolized exactly how much French authority had been undermined by defeat and occupation, how much power relations had been reversed, and how much history had been rewritten. The body of the raped French woman symbolized a new world of French subservience. No wonder the Normans were terrified.

Rape had been established in the European mind as a metaphor of national humiliation some years before with the "Black horror on the Rhine" propaganda campaign. To occupy the Rhineland during the interwar period, the French Army had deployed Senegalese soldiers. Although the French claimed to have made this decision for practical reasons of troop shortage, they were also engaged, according to the historian Keith Nelson, "in a subtle kind of psychological warfare" against the Germans.[81] The French must have been aware, Nelson argues, that such a deployment would be interpreted as a humiliation for the Germans. While occupation by white soldiers was degrading enough, occupation by black soldiers added insult to injury. The Germans responded with a propaganda campaign called "the black horror" that focused on the rape of white German women by Senegalese soldiers. In films and pamphlets, African soldiers were portrayed as jungle savages who raped young white German girls or forced them into brothels. Not one of the alleged incidents was ever proven, but the campaign nevertheless became an international cause célèbre.[82] When attacked in the "black horror" campaign, the French denied any intent to humiliate the Germans.[83] Now only a few years later, they had created their own black terror on the *bocage*.[84]

Is This a Special Prison for Colored Men?

Unlike the British press, French newspapers did not protest the verdicts of court-martial trials involving rape charges against African American soldiers. Nor did they appear to launch a grassroots petition campaign, as the British people did in the case of Leroy Henry. Why such silence? Where, one might ask, was the moral conscience of the average French person?

Silence on the other side of the channel had to do with historical circumstance rather than any moral lapse on the part of civilians.
For one thing there was barely an existing French press during the
summer of 1944. Even in such sizable towns as Cherbourg, Le Havre,
and Brest, journalists struggled to find the capital and newsprint to
publish a daily paper. Not until the end of August when Paris was liberated was there anything approaching a national press. The French
thus lacked a crucial means to learn about and protest the court-
martial trials. Like much else that summer, news concerning the trials circulated in the form of rumor. Even if civilians knew enough
to stage a protest, communication networks—indeed communities
themselves—had been radically disrupted by war.

Second, the French were in a different situation than the British.
By virtue of their status as a defeated country, the French were more
dependent on the Americans for food and security. To question the
judgment of the US Army in the summer of 1944 would have been at
best disrespectful, at worst foolhardy. Finally, unlike the British, the
Normans were forced to endure a war in their backyard. While civilians in northeastern France had already suffered two invasions, the
Normans had little idea what to expect of war. The death, destruction, and chaos took them by surprise. It is a sad fact of French history
that the traumas of that summer bore the fruit of a deadly racism.
But while the British struggled in many of the same ways, they did
not see their nation so destroyed and humiliated.

Nor would it be fair to interpret French silence on court-martial verdicts as complacency toward American racial practices. While some
civilians exhibited a deep-seated racism, still others were shocked at
American racial injustice. Even during the chaotic first days of the
invasion, the swiftness with which black soldiers were condemned
and executed did not escape the Norman *Liberator*, which noted the
case of a black soldier tried and condemned for rape "only six days
after the alleged crime." Although the paper's tone was respectful, the
editors were clearly shocked by the "rapidity of American justice."[85]
Elsewhere in France, SHAEF intelligence reported "French surprise
and disapproval" of American segregational practices, which were

the subject of much conversation.[86] "Hasty justice" was the subject of
writer Jean Galtier-Boissière's journal entry of 8 October 1944. Here
he recounted events surrounding a rape charge in La Charité-sur-
Loire. The military police paraded a dozen black soldiers in front of
the accuser, demanding immediate identification. When she finally
pointed a finger at one soldier, he was promptly hanged by rope right
there in her garden. Horrified, the woman screamed, "the crime is
not worth that!"[87]

French outrage also found expression in memoirs and fiction. One
Norman remembered the military police acting "not without brutality" in rape cases. With anger, he recalled the contrast between black
GIs who were hanged for rape and white GIs whose sexual assaults
went unprosecuted.[88] In his autobiographical novel about Le Havre,
Gilles Morris's character Pedro Diaz predicts what will happen when
a rape occurs: the military police will pin the crime on "a Negro who
is probably innocent." A Mexican, Diaz knows that "anyone with even
a drop of black blood in his veins runs the risk of having to pay for the
jars which, 100 percent of the time, are broken by white people." The
French police in the novel concur that "if there is too much noise in
high places, they will hang a Negro and that will be that!"[89]

Louis Guilloux's autobiographical novel *Ok, Joe* represents yet another caustic critique of military justice. Guilloux was a Breton novelist fluent in English who was hired by the US military to act as an
interpreter for witnesses in the military courts. Based on Guilloux's
diaries written during the summer of 1944, *Ok, Joe* focuses on the pre-
trial and court procedures used by the JAG Office in prosecuting GI
crimes against French civilians. Guilloux recounts one murder-rape
case in which the lawyers for the defense and the prosecution explore the crime scene together. Good friends, the two lawyers then
spend the ride home sharing their views on black men as "idiots" and
"terrible liars" who seem "always ready to go to hell for some white
woman."[90] For another case, the same lawyers visit a farm very late
at night, waking up the accuser and demanding she identify a black
suspect despite the extreme darkness.[91] She does so only with great
hesitation and only because she is frightened.

In this way Guilloux presents the military court as a travesty of justice. When he first arrives at the prison in Brittany, he asks the jeep driver: "Say Joe, is this a special prison for colored men"? "No," responds Joe, "it's the prison."[92] When Guilloux asks another soldier his view on blacks, the latter argues, "they're out of control," and "those people don't know how to act. They are incapable of self-discipline."[93] Guilloux's novel ends with a dark question mark hanging over the American mission: How could the "greatest democracy in the world" (as he sarcastically calls the United States, following military propaganda) lynch African American soldiers with moral impunity?[94]

For Guilloux, the real terror on the *bocage* was the capriciousness of American military power. As we have seen, SHAEF headquarters considered the rape accusations to be profoundly disruptive of the myths surrounding its mission, including the vitality of American democracy and the manly honor of the GI. By making rape at every level a "Negro" rather than an "American" problem, the US military engaged in racial scapegoating to deflect the impact of GI violence. But at least in Guilloux's unflinching view, the conviction and execution of black soldiers did anything but restore the romance of the manly GI. Instead military injustice exposed the ugly underside of the greatest democracy in the world. In its efforts to racialize rape and prove the fitness of white Americans to govern, the US military managed to suggest just the opposite.

Conclusion

Two Victory Days

ON 8 MAY 1945 the war in Europe ended. In Drancy, near Paris, Simone Levasseur was riding her bicycle with her friend Françoise when sirens and gunshots rang out celebrating the German surrender. As the girls pedaled down the road, Simone complained that her back hurt. They slowed their bicycles and upon inspection, Françoise noticed a small hole in her friend's jacket near her left shoulder. Simone continued a few feet, then fainted and fell off the bike. People from a nearby café hurried to the two friends' aid and carried Simone to a nearby hospital where she was given emergency surgery. A bullet had entered her back at the base of the left shoulder, then lodged in her abdomen. She died in surgery. In response to the incident, the French police opened a murder investigation. Evidence pointed to an American camp one-half mile from the scene of the accident. Witnesses reported that GIs, happy about the war's end, started shooting their guns on the railway tracks despite the area being densely populated. Although the bullet extracted from Simone's body came from an American gun, her killer was never found.[1]

Simone's killing typified the misfortunes besetting French civilians during those years. Although her death was caused by carelessness not maliciousness, her moment of victory soured into tragedy. Like countless other civilians, she was simply in the wrong place at the wrong time. Although the US military did not take away French sovereignty, they did make the nation its own battlefield, garrison, and entertainment center. The American passage left anguished traces in French literature and memoir. These traces suggest that for many French people, liberation was a dangerous and humiliating experience. While American soldiers were in no way responsible for the calamity of 1940 or the subsequent German occupation, their sometimes callous treatment of civilians heightened the sting of French shame. Dramatic changes in sexual relations also intensified French humiliation. Men returning from battle or prison interpreted GI advances on French women as a violation of their sexual prerogatives. That violation, in turn, rendered proof of diminished national prestige. For many civilians, the prostitute became a particularly visceral symbol of dishonor. Sexual relations, as they were embodied in the prostitute, provided painful evidence of French subservience to American power.

Simone's tragedy recalls to mind the Battle of Normandy the previous summer, when joy also brought suffering. But the dangers facing Simone differed from those facing the Normans a year before. In the *bocage* civilians were preoccupied with escaping the war. Now a year later, they were more worried about avoiding the Americans. That change can be explained, at least in part, by the fact that the GIs passing back across northern France in 1945 were not the same men who had made their way east a year before. Triumphant over death, they were haunted in life. Lost friends crowded their dreams; guilt consumed them. Drinking and whoring with French women kept the demons away, but only for a little while. For these men, fighting had become a way of life.

So had having the world their way—the American way. Some months earlier, as we have seen, the renowned political scientist André Siegfried had characterized the United States as ascending to a new position on the world stage. The Americans, he had argued, would have to assume their new position as "giants," that is, they would have to grow into their new role as global leaders.[2] By the summer of 1945, the GIs had done just that: they had learned to become giants. In the process, they had sometimes forgotten that the French were decent citizens of a sovereign nation.

If the GIs had learned to have the world their way, one of their schoolhouses had been the French brothel. Prostitution produced radical asymmetries of power in relations between the two nations. At the most intimate level, the prostitute taught a GI dominance by submitting her own body for his pleasure. That lesson proceeded at a much higher level as well. By managing prostitution, imposing medical hygiene, and presuming control over women's bodies, US military officials demarcated new lines of power in France. By furthering the notion that the French were decadent and immoral, prostitution enabled the US military to justify its dominion over the nation. In all these ways, the sexual exploitation of French women allowed the US military to test out the new gears of its global authority.

The US response to Norman rape charges also became inseparable from the nation's rise to power. If the army seemed negligent in its attitude toward prostitution, the case was the opposite for rape. There was no ambivalence about its costs. Here a firm resolve to address the problem led to the execution of more than one innocent black soldier. Accusations of rape threatened to undermine the myth of the American mission embodied in the manly GI. Whether well-founded or not, charges of sexual assault transformed the American soldier from a noble warrior into a sexual predator. Rape accusations corrupted the notion of heterosexual romance grounding the myth of the American rescue. They suggested what could be seen as the brutal reality of US dominance. Equally important, the allegations implied that the Americans had neither the will nor the power to establish law and order in the lands they conquered. In short, then, the costs of rape, unlike those of prostitution, were too great to be ignored.

By way of response, US officers tried to contain the damage to their reputation by scapegoating black GIs and proclaiming rape to be a "black" crime. In promoting this fiction, the US military had the full cooperation of the French people. From racist propaganda and literature concerning colonial West Africa, French civilians had come to believe, again like the Americans, that black men were hypersexual and violent. Racial prejudices encouraged women to cry rape and local policemen to press accusations. Perhaps even more important was French sensitivity to how rape, even more than prostitution, lay bare the reality of American dominion over everyday life. If French and American officials quarreled about prostitution, they cooperated on rape. As a result, innocent men went to their deaths.

A second American victory—this time over Japan—followed the French one a few months later. Its celebration in August produced a picture as compelling as Simone's story of how the war had been won. In New York City, a sailor capitalized on the giddy moment by grabbing a nurse, taking her into his arms, and planting a big kiss on her lips. Photographer Alfred Eisenstaedt stood nearby and captured the moment.[3] (See figure Conc.1.) When some days later, Eisenstadt's "Times Square Kiss" appeared in *Life*, it became the iconic image of victory in Japan.

"Times Square Kiss" takes on new meaning if we bear in mind how politicized sexual intimacy had become by the summer of 1945. Throughout the war, conquest had been eroticized: the gorgeous gams of pinup girls graced the sides of bombers; the liberation of Europe was defined as a French kiss. Ralph Morse's image of a GI embracing a French woman had caused a sensation just a year before. Now in America's greatest hour, the notorious kiss had come home to Times Square, imported by a sailor and domesticated by a nurse. Sex and romance had stood at the center of how the war was waged; now Eisenstadt's photo made it vital to how the war was won.

"Time Square Kiss" demonstrates—as does much of this study—that the history of war cannot be separated from the history of the body. The GIs landing on Omaha Beach brought with them prejudices about the French having to do with the body: French girls were beautiful as well as easy. Shame over bodily functions did not exist. Sex occurred anywhere and everywhere. Pleasure was paramount; France was a large bordello. Peasant practices regarding hygiene and sex offended GI sensibilities, reinforcing their assumptions about French society as primitive and depraved. The myth that the French were oversexed, present in American culture even today, structured the attitudes of the US military in Normandy as it attempted to determine clear lines of authority.

FIGURE CONC. 1. "Times Square Kiss." Photo © Alfred Eisenstaedt/Getty Images.

Moral judgments about the French in turn triggered political ones, chiefly, that the French lacked self-control and could not restore a modern democracy. Being "in a place like France," where all women were presumed prostitutes, allowed military officers to naturalize soldiers' sexual needs. Sex also became central to economic relations: prostitutes were considered the French commodity par excellence. In the mind of the GI, a prostitute differed little from a cigarette, save in price on the black market. Thus GIs were emboldened to believe the nation was theirs for the taking—at an affordable price. In garrison towns like Le Havre, their disregard for French social norms meant they had public sex with prostitutes and assaulted women on the streets. Women's bodies became an important means by which Franco-American relations were reordered.

This book suggests that military historians dismiss at their own risk sexual relations as an ahistorical sideshow of combat. And it compels them to rethink their narratives outside the framework of the nation-state. As historian Carol Gluck has observed, our memory of the world war has sadly left much of the "world" out. Because nation states fought the war, demanding total mobilization and the sacrifice of citizens, historiography cast within the national frame is inevitably distorted. In both the French and the American cases, the costs of "imprisoning a world war within national borders" are clear.[4] It is impossible to understand the postwar restoration of French society, for example, without taking into account the US military presence during the crucial years 1944–46. Several so-called domestic developments—the "crisis" of French masculinity, the end to regulated prostitution, the outburst of racial prejudices—can only be understood within a transnational frame. Neither can the trauma the French experienced in confronting their national decline be grasped apart from the condescension civilians suffered in their relations with the GIs. Only through their interactions with Americans did the French realize they were no longer a first-rate power.

A transnational approach to the campaign in Western Europe also has much to teach American historians. Contrary to what so many African Americans believed in the 1920s and 1930s, France was not an oasis of racial tolerance. Nor was the Normandy campaign an epic placed before destiny: it was a heroic battle fought by all-too-human beings who were not beyond behaving badly. The transnational perspective also demonstrates that the Allies were far from alone in their struggle. It dispels the view that civilians expected liberation to be handed to them on a platter, and reveals Gallic passivity to be as big a myth as de Gaulle's bromide that every French person resisted. Civilians everywhere aided the battle in ways both big and small despite the tragic losses they suffered.

Last but not least, thinking transnationally allows us to understand the campaign as a school in global ascendancy. The American rise to superpower status took place not just in Teheran or Yalta but also in the foxholes of the *bocage*. There GIs reading *Stars and Stripes* began to think of the world as "coming to America for help and leadership." The violence they visited upon French citizens arose as much from growing pains as it did from war trauma. A nation rarely acquires power in a graceful manner. One aim of this book has been to confront the giants with their trail of clumsy destruction. Remembering the "good war" has also meant forgetting as well. By affording a view beyond the national frame, historians can make the memories of the war both more truthful and more complex.

Notes

Introduction

1 Archives Municipales de la Ville du Havre (hereafter AMH), FC H4 15-6, Prostitution. For a full account of this exchange, see chapter 6.

2 See Janice Holt Giles, *The G.I. Journal of Sergeant Giles* (Boston: Houghton-Mifflin Company, 1965), 27.

3 AMH, FC H4 15-5, Joe Weston, "The GIs in Le Havre," manuscript. The article was printed in *Life* magazine, 31 December 1945. In fact, such stereotypes of the French predated 1917. See Jean Yves Le Naour, *Misères et tourments de la chair durant la Grande Guerre: les moeurs sexuelles des Français, 1914–1918* (Paris: Aubier, 2002), 205.

4 Charles Maier, *Among Empires: American Ascendancy and Its Predecessors* (Cambridge, MA: Harvard University Press, 2007), 154–55.

5 See Irwin Wall, *The United States and the Making of Postwar France, 1945–1954* (Cambridge: Cambridge University Press, 1991), 34, 195, 198.

6 AMGOT stood for Allied Military Government for Occupied Territories. On AMGOT, see Régine Torrent, *La France américaine: controverses de la Libération* (Brussels: Éditions Racine, 2004), chap. 2.

7 Most recently, Jean Edward Smith has argued that Eisenhower favored plans to include General de Gaulle and his CFLN organization in the reconstruction of liberated France. In response to Eisenhower's support of de Gaulle, the War Department sent a representative, John J. McCloy, to the White House in order to convince FDR to soften his stance against the French general. See *Eisenhower in War and Peace* (New York: Random House, 2012), 338.

8 On the French challenge to the Anglo-American bid for military government, see Julian G. Hurstfield, *America and the French Nation, 1939–1945* (Chapel Hill: University of North Carolina Press, 1986), 194–224; Wall, *The United States*, chap. 1.

9 For the conflict between FDR and Charles de Gaulle, see Charles Cogan and Andrew Knapp, "Washington at the Liberation, 1944–1947," in *The Uncertain Foundation: France at the Liberation, 1944–1947*, ed. Andrew Knapp (New York: Palgrave McMillan, 2007), 183–206.

10 Andrew A. Thomson, "'Over There' 1944/45, Americans in the Liberation of France: Their Perceptions of, and Relations with France and the French" (PhD thesis, University of Kent at Canterbury, 1996), 8. Thomson argues that AMGOT did not die out completely in 1944.

11 Coulet was the first *commissaire* whom Charles de Gaulle appointed in Bayeux. There he dealt mostly with British troops. However, Coulet soon assumed the role of regional *commissaire* for all of Normandy. In this position he dealt frequently with the Americans.

12 Archives Nationales (hereafter AN), Séries AN F1a 4005, Mission militaire de liasion adminstrative, 1944–46 (hereafter 4005), report of 27 June 1944. The clearest historical account of the liberation from the French political perspective is Robert Aron, *Histoire de la libération de la France, juin 1944—mai 1945* (Paris: A. Fayard, 1959).

13 AN, Séries F1a 4005, Documents François Coulet, report dated 1 July 1944.

14 Hurstfield, *America and the French Nation*, 207.

15 Jacques Kaiser, *Un journaliste sur le front de Normandie : carnet de route juillet–août 1944* (Paris: Arléa, 1991), 32.

16 Harry L. Coles and Albert K. Weinberg, *Civil Affairs: Soldiers Become Governors* (Washington, DC: Center of Military History, US Army, 2004), 729.

17 In *The American Soldier: Adjustment during Army Life*, 2 vols. (Princeton, NJ: Princeton University Press, 1949), 1:433, Samuel A. Stouffer argues that servicemen of the Second World War made very little effort "to give the war meaning in terms of the principles and causes involved."

18 André Siegfried, *Les États-Unis d'aujourd'hui* (Paris: Armand Colin, 1927); translated as *America Comes of Age* (New York: Harcourt Brace and Company, 1928). Siegfried is widely considered to be the founder of French political science.

19 André Siegfried, "Les États-Unis à la croisée des chemins," *Le figaro*, 26 March 1945. For more on Siegfried as an important figure in the French anti-Americanist tradition, see Philippe Roger, *L'ennemi américain: généalogie de l'antiaméricanisme français* (Paris: Éditions du Seuil, 2002), 373–79.

20 See Stephen E. Ambrose, *Citizen Soldiers: The U.S. Army from the Normandy Beaches to the Bulge to the Surrender of Germany, June 7, 1944–May 7, 1945* (New York: Simon and Schuster, 1997), 337–38; *Band of Brothers: E Company, 506th Regiment, 101st Airborne from Normandy to Hitler's Eagle's Nest* (New York: Simon and Schuster, 1992), 169–70, 263, 286–87. In *Wartime: Understanding and Behavior in the Second World War* (New York: Oxford University Press, 1989), Paul Fussell also marginalizes sexuality, treating it in a separate chapter titled "Drinking Far Too Much, Copulating Too Little."

21 See Maria Höhn, *GIs and Fräuleins: The German-American Encounter in 1950s West Germany* (Chapel Hill: University of North Carolina Press, 2002); Petra Goedde, *GIs and Germans: Culture, Gender and Foreign Relations, 1945–1949* (New Haven, CT: Yale University Press, 2003); John Dower, *Embracing Defeat: Japan in the Wake of World War II* (New York: W. W. Norton, 1999), 135–36; Mire Koikari, "Rethinking Gender and Power in the U.S. Occupation of Japan, 1945–1952," *Gender and History*, 11, no. 2 (1999): 313–35; Naoko Shibusawa, *America's Geisha Ally: Reimagining the Japanese Enemy* (Cambridge, MA: Harvard University Press, 2006), 38–40.

Chapter 1

1 Cornelius Ryan, *The Longest Day: June 6, 1944* (New York: Touchstone, 1959), 105–7.

2 This is the fatality figure provided by the US National D-Day Memorial Foundation. See http://www.ddaymuseum.co.uk/faq.htm.

3 See Robert M. Citino, "Review Essay: Military History Old and New; A Reintroduction," *American Historical Review* 112, no. 4 (October 2007): 1070–71.

4 Stephen E. Ambrose, *Citizens Soldiers: The U.S. Army from the Normandy Beaches to the Bulge to the Surrender of Germany, June 7, 1944–May 7, 1945* (New York: Simon and Schuster, 1997), 50.

5 See Ambrose, *Band of Brothers: E Company, 506th Regiment, 101st Airborne from Normandy to Hitler's Eagle Nest* (New York: Simon and Schuster, 1992), 73. By contrast, see the more inclusive Olivier Wieviorka, *Histoire du débarquement en Normandie: des Origines à la libération de Paris, 1941–1944* (Paris: Seuil, 2007). On Normans as traitors, see Ambrose, *June 6, 1944, D-Day, The Climactic Battle of World War II* (New York: Simon and Schuster, 1994), 315.

6 Ambrose, *June 6, 1944*, 214, 307, 313.

7 Ambrose, *Band of Brothers*, 253.

8 Jean Quellien and Bernard Garnier, *Les victimes civiles du Calvados dans la bataille de Normandie: 1er mars 1944–31 décembre 1945* (Caen: Éditions-Diffusion du Lys, 1995), 13–20; William I. Hitchcock, *The Bitter Road to Freedom: A New History of the Liberation of Europe* (New York: Free Press 2008), 27–28. The casualties for France throughout the entire Second World War are 217,600 military deaths and an estimated 350,000 civilian deaths.

9 Jacques Perret, *Caen, 6 juin 1944, une famille dans le débarquement* (Paris: Éditions Tirésias, 1994), 127.

10 Jacques-Alain de Sédouy, *Une enfance bien-pensante sous l'occupation, 1940–1945* (Paris: Librairie Académique Perrin, 1998), 141.

11 Jacques Kayser, *Un journaliste sur le front de Normandie: carnet de route juillet–août 1944* (Paris: Arléa, 1991), 72.

12 US Army Military History Institute, Carlisle Barracks (hereafter MHI), World War Two Survey Collection (hereafter WWII Survey), Box 99th infantry Division, John W. Baxter, "World War II Experiences," 14.

13 Aramais Hovsepian, *Your Son and Mine* (New York: Duell, Sloan and Pearce, 1950), 79.

14 Janice Holt Giles, *The G.I. Journal of Sergeant Giles* (Boston: Houghton-Mifflin Company, 1965), 40.

15 Howard H. Peckham and Shirley A. Snyder, *Letters from Fighting Hoosiers* (Bloomington: Indiana War History Commission, 1948), 119.

16 Robert Peters, *For You, Lili Marlene* (Madison: University of Wisconsin Press, 1995), 57; MHI, WWII Survey, Box 71st Infantry Division, David Ichelson, "I Was There," 64–65; Frank J. Irgang, *Etched in Purple* (Caldwell, ID: Caxton Printers, Ltd., 1949), 149.

17 Anne Frank, *The Diary of a Young Girl, the Definitive Edition* (New York: Bantam Books, 1995), 307. For the theme of "hope," see Jean-Louis Bory, *Mon village à l'heure allemande* (New York: Éditions de la Maison Française, 1945), 309.

18 Françoise Seligman, *Liberté quand tu nous tiens* (Paris: Fayard, 2000), 226.

19 Philippe Bertin, ed., *Histoires extraordinaires du jour le plus long* (Rennes: Éditions Ouest-France, 1994), Story of Yvonne (no family name given), 81–82.

20 Wieviorka, *Histoire du débarquement*, 151–55. See also Torrent's thorough discussion of the effects of bombardment on civilians in Régine Torrent, *La France américaine: controverses de la libération* (Brussels: Éditions Racine, 2004), chap. 1; and Eddy Florentin, *Quand les alliés bombardaient la France* (Paris: Librairie Académique Perrin, 1997).

21 Wieviorka, *Histoire du débarquement*, 159.

22 Jean Quellien, "Le Département du Calvados à la veille du débarquement," in *Normandie 44: du débarquement à la libération*, ed. François Bédarida (Paris: Albin Michel, 1987), 144; Régine Torrent, "L'image du soldat américain en France de 1943 à 1945," in *Les américains et la France, 1917–1947: engagements et représentations*, ed. F. Cochet, Marie-Claude Genet-Delacroix, and Hélène Trocmé (Reims: Maisonneuve et Larose, 1994), 233.

23 Jean Collet, *A vingt ans dans la Résistance, 1940–1944* (Paris: Graphein, 1999), 124.

24 Quellien, "Le département du Calvados," 145. See also Michel Boivin, Gérard Bourdin, and Jean Quellien, *Villes normandes sous les bombes (juin 1944)* (Caen: Presses Universitaires de Caen, 1994).

25 See a description of this type of propaganda in *La presse cherbourgeoise*, 20 July 1944; André Siegfried, "Pourquoi les américains font la guerre," *Le figaro*, 12 October 1944.

26 Institut d'histoire du temps présent (hereafter IHTP), ARC 074-62 Alliés (2), "Les armées de l'air américaine addressent ce message au peuple français"; *L'amérique en guerre*, 3 May 1944; *Le courrier de l'air*, 15 July 1943; Bibliothèque historique de la ville de Paris, Séries 30 Actualités, Box 28, Propagande alliée, tractes, affiches.

27 Julien Septeuil, *Jours tranquilles sous l'occupation* (Brive: Écritures, 1999), 181; Archives nationales (hereafter AN), Séries F1a 3743, Opinion publique (hereafter F1a 3743), "La vie et l'opinion des parisiens en 1943."

28 AN, F1a 3743, "La réaction en face de bombardements alliés, rapport du 1 octobre 1943."

29 De Sédouy, *Une enfance bien-pensant*, 141. The same feelings were prevalent in the south of France. See Arthur Layton Funk, *Hidden Ally: The French Resistance, Special Operations, and the Landings in Southern France, 1944* (Westport, CT: Greenwood Press, 1992), 256.

30 AN, F1a 3743, "Une opinion sur les bombardements alliés, rapport du 16 mai 1944."

31 AN, F1a 3743, "Réaction de l'opinion publique française en regard des bombardements anglo-américains," nd [early 1944]. See also Torrent, "L'image du soldat américain," 231, 235.

32 AN, F1a 3743, "L'opinion et la position des américains vis-à-vis Vichy, rapport de mai 1944," and "La vie et l'opinion des parisiens en 1943." In the secondary literature, see Irwin Wall, *The United States and the Making of Postwar France, 1945–1954* (Cambridge: Cambridge University Press, 1991), 25.

33 AN, F1a 3743, "Réaction de l'opinion publique française."

34 Andrew A. Thomson, "'Over There' 1944/45, Americans in the Liberation of France: Their Perceptions of, and Relations with, France and the French" (PhD thesis, University of Kent at Canterbury, October 1996), 59–60, 67–69.

35 IHTP, Fonds Émile Delavanay (hereafter FED), Interviews with Vincent Auriol, Eduard Froment, and Juste Evrard, all 28 October 1943. These interviews were led by the European Intelligence Department in London of people recently arrived from metropolitan or colonial France.

36 Alfred Fabre-Luce, *Journal de la France, juin 1943–août 1944* (Paris: Auteur, nd), 75.

37 IHTP, FED, Interview with Edward and René Banbanast, 6 August 1942, and Interview with M. Bouvier, 28 April 1942.

38 IHTP, FED, Interview with Captain Bucknall, 29 March 1943.

39 Augustin Maresquier, *Journal d'un exode (août 1944)* (Cherbourg: Éditions Isoète, 1994), 32.

40 ADM, 1366 W, *MT*, Claude Tatard, "Claude Bourdon, réfugiée de St.-Lô—1944 été," 904.

41 On this point, see Crane Brinton, "Letters from Liberated France," *French Historical Studies*, 2, no. 1 (Spring 1961): 4–5.

42 Georges Duhamel, "The Ordeal of Paris," *New York Times*, 17 September 1944. For a personal response to the bombing of Le Havre, see Roger Hilliquin, *Les années de guerre d'un adolescent havrais, 1939–1945* (Luneray: Éditions Bertout, 2002), 115.

43 National Archives and Records Administration (hereafter NARA), Record Group 331, Records of Allied Operation and Occupation, Headquarters, World War II (SHAEF) (hereafter RG 331), General Staff Divisions, G-5 Division, Secretariat, Numeric File, August 1943–July 1945, Entry 47 (hereafter Entry 47), Box 28, Civil Affairs Weekly Summary, no. 7, 28 July 1944.

44 Kayser, *Un journaliste sur le front*, 75. On this issue, see also Brinton, "Letters from Liberated France," letter dated 29 August 1944, 10.

45 NARA, RG 331, Entry 47, Box 28, Civil Affairs Weekly Summary no. 13, 8 September 1944; and see also Louis Eudier, *Notre combat de classe et de patriotes 1934–1945* (Le Havre: L. Eudier, 1982), 125.

46 NARA, RG 331, Entry 47, Box 28, "Report on Le Havre," 19 October 1944.

47 Antoine Anne, *J'aurais aimé vous conter une autre histoire* (Saint-Georges d'Elle: A. Anne, 1999), 65–66.

48 ADM, 1366 W, *MT*, Robert Simon, "Printemps 1944—je vais avoir bientôt 12 ans," 886.

49 ADM, 1366 W, *MT*, Témoignage de Madame Marie-Thérèse Dold-Lomet, 285.

50 Jacques Petit, *Au coeur de la bataille de Normandie: souvenirs d'un adolescent, de Saint-Lô à Avranches, été 1944* (Louviers: Ysec, 2004), 116. See also René Herval, *Bataille de Normandie: récits de témoins recueillis et présentés par René Herval*, 2 vols. (Paris: Éditions de "Notre Temps," 1947), 1:87–89.

51 Bertin, *Histoires*, 35; Petit, *Au coeur de la bataille*, 114. In *Bataille de Normandie*, René Herval refers, 1:85, to "the Passion of Saint-Lô." For a detailed description of the Allied destruction at Saint-Lô, see M. Lantier, *Saint-Lô au bûcher* (Saint-Lô: Imp. Jacqueline, 1969). See also Augustin Le Maresquier, *La Manche libérée et meurtrie* (Corbeil: Imprimerie Crété, 1946).

52 NARA, RG 331, General Staff, G-5 Division, Information Branch, Historical Section, Numeric-Subject Operations File Entry 54 (hereafter Entry 54), Box 111, "Report from the Field on Reactions of Local Population in Normandy, No. 6, 14 August 1944."

53 MHI, Templeton Payne Papers, "A Complete Change of Life—into World War II," 31.

54 MHI, WWII Survey, Box 84th Infantry Division, Freese, "Private Memories," 17.

55 MHI, Chester Hansen Collection, diary entry dated 3 August, 1944.

56 Bertin, *Histoires extraordinaires*, 34–35.

57 ADM, 1366 W, *MT*, Témoignage de Raymond Avignon, 28.

58 Bertin, *Histoires extraordinaires*, 146.

59 Hilary Kaiser, *Veteran Recall: Americans in France Remember the War* (Paris: H. Kaiser, 1994), 83.

60 Lucie Aubrac, *Cette exigeante liberté: entretiens avec Corinne Bouchoux* (Paris: L'Archipel, 1997), 146. See also ADM, 1366 W, *MT*, Carnet de Michel Braley, 105.

61 Andy Rooney, *My War* (New York: Random House, 1995), 166. See also Angela Petesch, *War through the Hole of a Donut* (Madison, WI: Hunter Halverson Press, 2006), 141.

62 Hilary Footitt, *War and Liberation in France* (New York: Palgrave Macmillan, 2004), 43.

63 ADM, 1366 W, *MT*, Témoignage de Raymond Avignon, 28–29.

64 Kaiser, *Veteran Recall*, 89.

65 Kayser, *Un journaliste sur le front*, 32.

66 *Liberté de Normandie*, 23 December 1944.

67 *Liberté de Normandie*, 8 June 1945.

68 An excellent source for the progress of the battle is Stéphane Simonnet, *Atlas de la libération de la France, 6 juin 1944–8 mai 1945* (Paris: Éditions Autrement, 2004).

69 AN, Séries F1a 4005, Mission Militaire de Liaison Administrative, 1944–46 (hereafter F1a 4005), "No. 415, Le Maire, St-Mère-Église à Coulet à Bayeux, 6 juin 1944."

70 NARA, RG 331, Entry 54, Box 111, "Report from the Field on Reactions of Local Population in Normandy, no. 1, nd."

71 John Hurkala, *The Fighting First Division: A True Story* (New York: Greenwich Book Publishers, 1957), 150.

72 Kayser, *Un journaliste sur le front*, 72.

73 Rooney, *My War*, 166, 161. See also ADM, 1366 W, *MT*, Témoignage de Madame Fenand, 342. Fenand had one brother killed and knew a family who lost all four of their children, ages sixteen, fifteen, ten, and nine.

74 Guillaume Lecadet, *Valognes: le Versailles normand aux heures tragiques* (Paris: Office d'Édition du Livre d'Histoire, 1997 [1946–47]), 240. Abbé Brunet remembers the liberation of Caen in this way: "joy to know oneself liberated, but also a return to the most terrible of realities: the ruins and the many dead bodies they contained." See François Lefaivre, ed., *J'ai vécu les bombardements à Condé-sur-Noireau* (Condé-sur-Noireau: C. Corlet, 1994), Témoignage of Abbé Brunet, 41.

75 See also Archives Départmentales du Calvados (hereafter ADC), 9 W 101, Débarquement des troupes alliés, 1944. The first folder in this dossier contains often poignant letters to the préfet from French men unable to get in touch with their relatives in the area. The letters range in date from mid- to late June.

76 ADM, 1366 W, *MT*, Témoignage de Jean-Pierre Launey.

77 Vercors, *Souffrances de mon pays* (Paris: Collections des 150, 1945), 16. The article appeared in *Life*, 6 November 1944. The original French version was published some months later. Vercors was a novelist whose *Silence de la mer* became extremely well known in France.

78 Kaiser, *Veteran Recall*, 74–75.

79 Morton Eustis, *War Letters of Morton Eustis to His Mother: February 6, 1941 to August 10, 1944* (New York: Spiral, 1945), 213. See also A. J. Liebling, *Normandy Revisited* (New York: Simon and Schuster, 1958), 125; Peter Schrijvers, *The Crash of Ruin: American Combat Soldiers in Europe during World War II* (New York: New York University Press, 1998), 200–201.

80 Robert and Jane Easton, *Love and War: Pearl Harbor through V-J Day* (Norman: University of Oklahoma Press), 241.

81 Giles, *G.I. Journal*, 34–35, 45–46. See also Hovsepian, *Your Son and Mine*, 80; MHI, WWII Survey, Box 84th Infantry Division, Wendell Albert, "For the Duration . . . and Six Months," 59.

82 Sidney Bowen, *Dearest Isabel, Letters from an Enlisted Man in World War II* (Manhattan, KS: Sunflower University Press, 1992), 73.

83 Orval Eugene Faubus, *In This Faraway Land* (Conway, AR: River Road, 1971), 248. On this point, see also Hurkala, *The Fighting First Division*, 148, and the British memoir, Charles Hargrove, *Asnelles 6 juin 1944* (Lisieux: EFE, 2004).

84 Annette Tapert, ed., *Lines of Battle: Letters from American Servicemen, 1941–1945* (New York: Times Books, 1987), 165.

85 Paul Boesch, *Road to Heurtgen-Forest in Hell* (Houston, TX: Gulf, 1962), 48.

86 Quoted in Studs Terkel, *The Good War: An Oral History of World War Two* (New York: Ballantine Books, 1985)), 38. See also Lawrence Cane, *Fighting Fascism in Europe: The World War II Letters of an American Veteran of the Spanish Civil War* (New York: Fordham University Press, 2003), 113.

87 Irgang, *Etched in Purple*, 19. See also MHI, WWII Survey, Box 5th Infantry Division, Joseph Edinger, diary entry dated 6 February 1945; and Liebling, *Normandy Revisited*, 103.

88 Giles, *Journal*, 41. For the same complaint from some of the free French who were fighting farther east, see Gwenn-Aël Bolloré, *Commando de la France libre: Normandie, 6 juin 1944* (Paris: France-Empire, 1985), 179.

89 MHI, WWII Survey, Box 84th Infantry Division, Freese, "Private Memories," 17. See also Jack Plano, *Fishhooks, Apples and Outhouses* (Kalamazoo, MI: Personality Press, 1991), 252.

90 MHI, WWII Survey, Box 28th Infantry Division, Charles Haug, "Courageous Defenders as I Remember It," 3.

91 MHI, Chester Hansen diary entry dated 9 June 1944.

92 NARA, RG 331, Entry 54, Box 28, Civil Affairs Summary No. 5, 4 July 1944. See also RG 331, Entry 54, Box 111, "Report from the Field on Reactions of Local Population in Normandy No. 7, 18 August 1944."

93 Faubus, *In This Faraway Land*, 256. See also MHI, WWII Survey, Box 28th Infantry Division, Murray Shapiro, "Letters Home," letter of 20 October 1944; and Terkel, *The Good War*, 379.

94 Eustis, *War Letters*, 213–14. See also Faubus, *In This Faraway Land*, 232.

95 Raymond Gantter, *Roll Me Over: An Infantryman's World War II* (New York: Ivy Books, 1997), 7–8.

96 Tapert, *Lines of Battle*, 228–229.

97 Giles, *Journal*, 35, 44–46.

98 Georgia H. Helm, *From Foxhole to Freedom: The World War II European Journal of Captain H. Dale Helm of Indiana* (Indianapolis: Guild Press of Indiana, 1996), 40.

99 Françoise de Hauteclocque, *La guerre chez nous: en Normandie, 1939–1944* (Paris: Éditions Colbert, 1945), 99

100 Claude Hettier de Boislambert, *Les fers de l'espoir* (Paris: Éditions Plon, 1978), 9–10.

101 Perret, *Caen, 6 juin*, 47; Herval, *Bataille de Normandie*, 1:37, 52.

102 Bernard de Cagny, *Jour J comme jeunesse* (Condé-sur-Noireau: Éditions Corlet, 2003), 46.

103 ADM, 1366 W, *MT*, Jacques Lepage, "Combats sur le Lozon," 379.

104 Kaiser, *Veteran Recall*, 73.

105 Ibid., 89.

106 De Sédouy, *Une enfance bien-pensante*, 131; Marcel Leveel, *Rails et haies: la double bataille de l'Elle et de Lison* (Marigny: Éditions Eurocibles, 2004), 82.

107 Herval, *Bataille*, 1:44, 52.

108 Ibid., 1:189.

109 Ibid., 1:54; Irgang, *Etched in Purple*, 19.

110 Anne, *J'aurais aimé vous conter*, 59–60.

111 ADM, 1366 W, *MT*, Carnet de Michel Braley, 105.

112 Herval, *Bataille*, 1:32, 121.

113 Petit, *Au coeur de la bataille*, 9–12.

114 Claude Paris, *Paroles de braves: d'Omaha la sanglante à Saint-Lô, capitale des ruines, 7 juin–18 juillet 1944* (Condé-sur-Noireau: Éditions Charles Corlet, 2007), 146.

115 Anne, *J'aurais aimé vous conter*, 61. See also Paris, *Paroles de braves*, 148.

116 Herval, *Bataille*, 1: 62.

117 Leveel, *Rails et haies*, 97.

118 Christiane Delpierre, *Une enfance normande* (Angers: Cheminements, 1999), 148–49. See also Herval, *Bataille*, 1:35, 204.

119 ADM, 1366 W, *MT*, Témoignage de Jean-Jacques Vautier, 976.

120 J. Raibaud and H. Henric, eds., *Témoins de la fin du IIIe Reich: des polytechniciens racontent . . .* (Paris: L'Harmattan, 2004), 352–53. The first jeeps were developed in the early 1940s by American Bantam, Willys-Overland, and the Ford Motor Company. On the jeep, see also Simone Signoret, *La nostalgie n'est plus ce qu'elle était* (Paris: Éditions du Seuil), 81; ADM, 1366 W, *MT*, Jacques Nicolle, "J'avais quinze ans," 811; IHTP, ARC 116, Michel Geoffroy, "Libération: visage de Paris"; Leveel, *Rails et haies*, 94; Petit, *Au coeur de la bataille*, 85; de Sédouy, *Une enfance bien-pensante*, 152.

121 Torrent, *La France américaine*, 15.

122 ADM, 1366 W, *MT*, Lepage, "Combats sur le Lozon," 379–80.

123 ADM, 1366 W, *MT*, Témoignage d'Auguste Couillard, 419. See also Bernard Gourbin, *Une jeunesse occupée: de l'Orne au Bessin; 1940–1944* (Le Coudray-Macouard: Cheminements, 2004); Herval, *Bataille*, 1:29, 165.

124 ADM, 1366 W, *MT*, Témoignage de Marguerite Pottier, 416.

125 ADM, 1366 W, *MT*, Témoignage de Georgette Leduc Le Bourg, 443.

126 In the French autobiographical literature, see Le Mémorial de Caen, Séries FN— France Normandie, Trevières, "Américains—Normands—Omaha—1944," témoignage of André Morel, 27; Hargrove, *Asnelles 6 juin 1944*, 9; Paris, *Paroles de braves*, 36–37; Herval, *Bataille*, 1:28,153, 177, 335, 337. In the American memoir literature, see MHI, WWII Survey, Box 84th Infantry Division, Freese, "Private Memories," 17.

127 Gilles Bré, *Chroniques du Jour J* (Paris: Éditions Christian, 2006), 233; ADM, 1366

W, *MT*, Témoignage d' Andreé Julien, 610–12; Frédérick Lemarchand, ed., *Vivre dans le bocage bas-normand au XXe siècle: témoignages d'un siècle: un récit à plusieurs voix* (Caen: Université Inter-âges de Basse-Normandie, 2003), memoir of Francine Morin, 388–89; Geneviève Duboscq, *Bye Bye Geneviève!* (Paris: Éditions Robert Laffont, 1978), or the English translation by Richard S. Woodward, *My Longest Night* (New York: Seaver Books, 1981); Edouard Marie, *Souvenirs d'un marin pêcheur de Chausey* (Granville: Éditions Formats, 1995); Elizabeth Coquart and Philippe Huet, *Le jour le plus fou: 6 juin 1944, les civils dans la tourmente* (Paris: Albin Michel, 1994), 32–35; and Coquart and Huet, *Les rescapés du Jour J: les civils dans l'enfer du 6 juin 44* (Paris: Albin Michel, 1999), 60–73.

128   ADM, 1366 W, *MT*, Arthur and Berthe Pacary, "Une halte mouvementée," 399. See also Francis L. Sampson, *Look Out Below: A Story of the Airborne by a Paratrooper Padre* (Washington, DC: Catholic University of American Press, 1958), 60; Marcel Jourdain, *Petites surprises de printemps* (Le Chaufour: Éditions Anovi, 2004), 105–20; de Sédouy, *Une enfance bien-pensante*, 138–41.

129   ADM, 1366 W, *MT*, Pottier, 416.

130   Herval, *Bataille*, 1:122.

131   Ibid., 1:39.

132   ADM, 1366 W, *MT*, Carnet de Michel Braley, 105. See also Paris, *Paroles de braves*, 36.

133   ADM, 1366 W, *MT*, Témoignage de Madame Odette Eudes, 333.

134   ADM, 1366 W, *MT*, Anonymous, "Deux jours de guerres inoubliables," 993–94, 997.

135   ADM, 1366 W, *MT*, Carnet de Michel Braley, 105.

136   Marc Hillel, *Vie et moeurs des GI's en Europe, 1942–1947* (Paris: Balland, 1981), 132. See also Bolloré, *Commando de la France libre*, 204; Coquart and Huet, *Le jour le plus fou*, 23; Leveel, *Rails et haies*, 103.

137   Alan Moorehead, *Eclipse* (Paris: Le Sagittaire, 1947 [ca. 1945]), 112; Harry L. Coles and Albert K. Weinberg, *Civil Affairs: Soldiers Become Governors* (Washington, DC: Center of Military History, US Army, 2004), 727–28; NARA, RG 331, Entry 54, Box 264, Analysis Sheet dated 14 June 1944.

138   Donald Burgett, *Currahee! "We Stand Alone!" A Paratrooper's Account of the Normandy Invasion* (London: Hutchinson, 1967), 95. See also William Tsuchida, *Wear It Proudly* (Berkeley: University of California Press, 1947), 45–46.

139   ADM, 1366 W, *MT*, Témoignage de Louis Blaise, 83.

140   Bré, *Chroniques du Jour J*, 61–62.

141   Béatrice Poule, ed., *Cahiers de mémoire: vivre et survivre pendant la Bataille de Normandie* (Caen: Conseil Général du Calvados, 1994), 72–76.

142   Herval, *Bataille*, 1:39.

143   ADM, 1366 W, *MT*, Carnet d'Albert Allix, 11.

144   Irgang, *Etched in Purple*, 19. See also Tapert, ed., *Lines of Battle*, 166.

145   Footitt, *War and Liberation*, 15–16.

146   AN, Séries F1a 4005. For the survey, see NARA, RG 331, Entry 54, Box 111, "Analysis Sheet, 2 October 1944."

147   NARA, RG 331, Entry 54, Box 264, "Analysis Sheet of the Rex North Article," and Entry 54, Box 111, "Report from the Field on Reactions of Local Population in Normandy, Undated."

148 NARA, RG 331, Entry 47, Box 111, "Memo to Civil Affairs, 22 June 1944," and "Report from the Field on Reactions of Local Population in Normandy No. 2, 8 July 1944."

149 NARA, RG 331, Entry 47, Box 28, "First Report on U.S. Zone of Operations in France," 25 June 1944; and see also Easton, *Love and War*, 224.

150 Lucien Lepoittevin, *Mémoires de guerres (1692–1993)* (Cherbourg: Isoète, 1994), 104.

151 Maurice Chauvet, *It's a Long Way to Normandy: 6 juin 1944* (Paris: Jean Picollec, 2004), 276.

152 Danièle Philippe, *J'avais quinze ans . . . en juin 44 en Normandie* (Paris: Éditions France-Empire, 1994), 232. See also André Hamel, *Le canton des pieux: six ans de guerre, 1939–1945 et la 9th division U.S. d'Utah Beach à Goury* (Cherbourg: Le Canton des Pieux, 1994), 117; Coquart and Huet, *Le jour le plus fou*, 17–18.

153 NARA, RG 331, Entry 47, Box 28, "First Report on U.S. Zone of Operations in France." See also Irgang, *Etched in Purple*, 54–55.

154 NARA, RG 331, Entry 47, Box 27, "Civil Affairs 21 Army Group—First General Report, 15 August 1944." See also NARA, RG 331, Entry 54, Box 194, memo dated December 1944; Schrijvers, *The Crash of Ruin*, 124–25.

155 Edward Rogers, *Doughboy Chaplain* (Boston: Meador, 1946), 158.

156 Bertin, ed., *Histoires extraordinaires*, 118.

157 MHI, Chester Hansen Collection, diary entry dated 2 July 1944.

158 MHI, The John J. Maginnis Papers, untitled memoir, 39–40.

159 MHI Chester Hansen Collection, diary entry dated 10 June 1944; MHI, The John J. Maginnis Papers, untitled memoir, 120; Coquart and Huet, *Le jour le plus fou*, 61–62, 73; Leveel, *Rails et haies*, 83.

160 Coquart and Huet, *Les rescapés*, 83.

161 Sampson, *Look Out Below*, 69.

162 Kayser, *Un journaliste sur le front*, 41. See also ADM, 1366 W, *MT*, Témoignage de Jouet Monpied, 603.

163 Kayser, *Un journaliste sur le front*, 53.

164 Wisconsin State Veterans' Museum, Box 93, WVM Mss. Folder 17, 1994, Robert Bowers, "The War Years, 1942–1945," 12–13.

165 Faubus, *In This Faraway Land*, 248.

166 Giles, *Journal*, 97.

167 Ernie Pyle, *Brave Men* (New York: H. Holt and Company, 1944), 285.

168 MHI, World War II Survey, Box 71st Infantry Division, Joseph Edinger, diary entry dated 6 February 1945.

169 Gourbin, *Une jeunesse occupée*, 110.

170 Poule, *Cahiers de mémoire*, 28.

171 Bré, *Chroniques du Jour*, 61–62. See also Gourbin, *Une jeunesse occupée*, 113.

172 Bowen, *Dearest Isabel*, 70.

173 MHI, WWII Survey, Box Fifth Infantry Division, Karl Clarkson, "The Story of G.I. Joe (Karl): A Combat Infantryman in World War II," 14. See also Bowen, *Dearest Isabel*, 87.

174 Wisconsin State Veterans' Museum, Unpublished mss., 2001, Norbert Koopman, "I Was Just Lucky: Memoirs of a World War II Private," 35. For stories concerning GIs who stopped a battle in order to protect civilians, see ADM, 1366 W, *MT*, Témoignage de Madame Geneviève Jouet Monpied, 603; and Témoignage de Madame Fenand, 342. On protecting children from harm in the south of France during battle, see Keith Winston, *V . . . -Mail: Letters of a World War II Combat Medic* (Chapel Hill, NC: Algonquin Books, 1985), 142.

175 Kaiser, *Veteran Recall*, 91. See also ADM, 1366 W, *MT*, Témoignage de Madame Lucienne Letourneau, 736; Lepoittevin, *Mémoires de guerres*, 104; Delpierre, *Une enfance normande*, 149.

176 ADM, 1366 W, *MT*, Témoignage de Madame Odette Eudes, 333.

177 ADM, 1366 W, *MT*, Témoignage de Madame Francine Leblond, 651.

178 Delpierre, *Une enfance normande*, 150–51.

179 Herval, *Bataille*, 1:46, 99.

180 Hauteclocque, *La guerre chez nous*, 107.

181 Victor Dufaut, *La Vie vient de l'ouest* (Paris: Promotion et Édition, 1969), 205; Jourdain, *Petites surprises*, 123; Duboscq, *Bye Bye Geneviève!*, 87; Perret, *Caen, 6 juin 1944*, 123; Herval, *Bataille*, 1:106, 110, 144, 146; Le Mémorial de Caen, Séries FN–France Normandie, Trevières, "Américains—Normands—Omaha—1944," Témoignage of André Morel, 27.

182 Philippe, *J'avais quinze ans*, 131; Lemarchand, *Vivre dans le bocage*, 388; Gourbin, *Une jeunesse occupée*, 113.

183 ADM, 1366 W, *MT*, "Lettres de Madame Hélène de Tocqueville," 219. See also Kayser, *Un journaliste sur le front*, 45.

184 Hauteclocque, *La guerre chez nous*, 110.

185 Philippe, *J'avais quinze ans*, 145.

186 Poule, *Cahiers de mémoire*, 22.

187 ADM, 1366 W, *MT*, Madame Colette l'Hermitte, "La Bataille de Carentan," 624; Bertin, *Histoires extraordinaires*, 149; Anonymous, *L'occupation et la libération de Saint-Clair-Sur-Elle: 18 juin 1940–10 janvier 1945; témoignages de ses habitants* (Saint-Lô: Ateliers Beuzelin/Esnouf, 1984), np; Jourdain, *Petites surprises*, 137; Coquart and Huet, *Le jour le plus fou*; Leveel, *Rails et haies*, 92–93; Herval, *Bataille*, 1:46.

188 Petit, *Au coeur de la bataille*, 94–95.

189 ADM, 1366 W, *MT*, Jean Lepage, "Combats sur le Lozon," 379, and Témoignage de Madame Fenand dit Soeur Christine Yvonne, 342; Bertin, *Histoires extraordinaires*, 81; Jourdain, *Petites surprises*, 111; Marcel Launay, *6 ans en 1944* (Montreuil-l'Argillé: Pierann, 1999), 18; Herval, *Bataille*, 1:123, 246; Hauteclocque, *La guerre chez nous*, 102. In the American memoir literature, see Bruce E. Egger and Lee MacMillan Otts, *G Company War: Two Personal Accounts of the Campaigns in Europe* (Tuscaloosa: University of Alabama Press, 1992), 20. See also Herval, *Bataille*, 1:123, 246.

190 ADM, 1366 W, *MT*, Témoignage de Jean-Jacques Vautier, 978–79.

191 ADM, 1366 W, *MT*, René Saint-Clair, "1944 La libération au pays des marais," 863; Jourdain, *Petites surprises*, 120.

192 Jack Capell, *Surviving the Odds* (Claremont, CA: Regina Books, 2007), 67.

193 ADM, 1366 W, *MT*, Témoignage de Christian Letourneur, 732.

194 Poule, *Cahiers de mémoire*, 72–73.

195 Jourdain, *Petites surprises*, 140.

196 Bertin, *Histoires extraordinaires*, 81. See also ADM, 1366 W, *MT*, Lucien Hélye, "Souvenirs de la libération," 513.

197 ADM, 1366 W, *MT*, Témoignage de Louis Blaise, 83.

198 ADM, 1366 W, *MT*, Témoignage de Christian Letourneur, 732.

199 Paris, *Paroles de braves*, 155.

200 Kayser, *Un journaliste sur le front*, 98; and also Leveel, *Rails et haies*, 122.

201 Michel Renouard and Manonmani Restif, eds., *Les malouins et la libération: combats et vie quotidienne* (Saint-Malo: Éditions Cristel, 2006), 187.

202 MHI, World War II Survey, Box 5th Infantry Division, Mark Goodman, "Unit History of Company A," 50.

203 Danièle Philippe remembers an American intelligence officer who came to her family's house one night for dinner. After eating, the officer played on the piano, and in the silence that followed, he stated flatly that he had lost his twenty-one-year-old son, Joe, on D-day at Omaha Beach. Philippe's family comforted him and shared their last bottle of champagne. Philippe, *J'avais quinze ans*, 167.

204 ADM, 1366 W, *MT*, Témoignage de Georgette Leduc Le Bourg, 392.

205 ADM, 1366 W, *MT*, Anonymous Témoignage, 1017–18.

206 Poule, *Cahiers de mémoire*, 73.

207 Bertin, *Histoires extraordinaires*, 114.

208 Michel Béchet, *L'attente: "Overlord" vécu à cent kilomètres du front* (Montsûrs: Résiac, 1994), 84.

209 Collet, *A vingt ans dans la Résistance*, 139.

210 ADM, 1366 W, *MT*, Anonymous, "Deux jours de guerres inoubliables," 993–94, 997.

211 *Stars and Stripes*, 5 July 1944. For a similar tribute in Bréhal, see *Stars and Stripes*, 7 August 1944. In the memoir literature, see Sampson, *Look Out Below*, 75.

212 Herval, *Bataille*, 1:402.

213 ADC, 13 T II/41, *L'entente nouvelle*, June 1945.

214 Jourdain, *Petites surprises*, 133.

215 ADM, 1366 W, *MT*, Témoignage de Robert Simon, 886. See also Petit, *Au cœur de la bataille*, 86.

216 "Chewing gum with a cigarette on their lips" was how the mayor of Sainte-Mère-Église portrayed the GIs while they liberated his town on the sixth of June. See AN, Séries F1a 4005. The image quickly became classic. For example, see Raibaud and Henric, *Des polytechniques racontent*, 185.

217 Perret, *Caen, 6 juin*, 127.

218 *L'avenir du nord de l'Aisne*, 10 September 1944.

219 Petit, *Au coeur de la bataille*, 86

220 Among many other possibilities, see ADM, 1366 W, *MT*, Témoignage de Dold-Lomet, 284, Témoignage de Louis Blaise, 83; and Anonymous "Le Débarquement," 1017–18; Bré, *Chroniques*, 78; Philippe, *J'avais quinze ans*, 144.

221 ADM, 1366 W, *MT*, Témoignage de Christianne Denis, 249.

222 ADM, 1366 W, *MT*, Témoignage d'Odette Eudes, 333, and Lucien Hélye, "Souvenirs de la libération," 515; Poule, *Cahiers de mémoire*, 21–22.

223 Kayser, *Un journaliste sur le front*, 129.

224 Launay, *6 ans en 1944*, 18, 37.

225 Philippe, *J'avais quinze ans*, 144, 188.

226 ADM, 1366 W, *MT*, Témoignage de Georgette Leduc Le Bourg, 393, and Docloue, "Souvenirs d'une famille," 320. See also de Sédouy, *Une enfance bien-pensante*, 153.

227 For an American view of how Civil Affairs worked with French officials, see Maj.

Don Dresden, "Grandcamp Learns the American Way," *New York Times*, 13 August 1944.

228 MHI, WWII Survey, Box 9th Infantry Division, Alvin Griswold, "Letters from Hughes."

229 MHI, WWII Survey, Box 99th Infantry Division, Roger Foehringer, "Untitled Reminiscences," 7. See also Box 71st Infantry Division, Lewington S. Ponder, "Recollections of World War II," 72.

230 MHI, WWII Survey, Box 5th Infantry Division, Joseph Edinger, diary entry dated 5 February 1945.

231 Giles, *G.I. Journal*, 28.

232 Frederick C. Wardlaw, ed., *Missing in Action: Letters of a Medic* (Raleigh, NC: Sparks, 1983), 67.

233 Faubus, *In This Faraway Land*, 325.

234 Jack Sacco, *Where the Birds Never Sing: The True Story of the 92nd Signal Battalion and the Liberation of Dachau* (New York: Reagan Books, 2003), 211. See also *Stars and Stripes*, 6 September 1944.

235 *Stars and Stripes*, 1 August 1944.

236 MHI, WWII Survey, Box 28th Infantry Division, Joseph Messore, "28th Infantry Division: A Recollection Fifty Years Later," 26. See also Box 36th Infantry Division, Anthony Harlinski, "The Purple Road Back," 4.

237 The story was retold in Sacco, *Where the Birds Never Sing*, 211.

238 MHI, WWII Survey, Box 71st Infantry Division, John Earle, "Letter to His Parents."

239 MHI, WWII Survey, Box 28th Infantry Division, Messore, "28th Infantry Division," 59.

240 Rooney, *My War*, 277.

241 MHI, WWII Survey, Box 9th Infantry Division, Chester Jordan, "Bull Sessions: World War II, Company K, 47th Inf., 9th Infantry Division from Normandy to Remagen," 161; Kaiser, *Veteran Recall*, 78; Giles, *Journal*, 57; Liebling, *Normandy Revisited*, 99; Schrijvers, *The Crash of Ruin*, 177.

242 MHI, WWII Survey, Box 9th Infantry Division, Jordan, "Bull Sessions," 65.

243 Hovsepian, *Your Son and Mine*, 79.

244 Vernon McHugh, *From Hell to Heaven: Memoirs from Patton's Third Army* (Ardmore, PA: Dorrance and Company, 1980), 26; Plano, *Fishhooks, Apples and Outhouses*, 253. On "c'est la guerre," see also MHI, WWII Survey, Box 1st Infantry Division, Leroy Stewart, "Hurry Up and Wait," 50; Schrijvers, *The Crash of Ruin*, 155.

245 Eric Posselt, *GI Songs, Written, Composed and/or Collected by Men in the Service* (New York: Sheridan House Publishers, 1944), 72–73.

246 MHI, WWII Survey, Box 9th Infantry Division, Jordan, "Bull Sessions," 41.

247 Andy Rooney, *My War*, 225.

248 *Stars and Stripes*, 26 July 1944.

249 Lepoittevin, *Mémoires de guerres*, 105; Giles, *Journal*, 28.

250 Gourbin, *Une jeunesse occupée*, 113. See also Egger and Otts, *G Company War*, 69.

251 Giles, *G.I. Journal*, 27.

252 Peter Belpulsi, *A GI's View of World War II* (Salem, MO: Globe Publishers. 1997), 94.

253 Andy Rooney, *My War*, 225.

254 Philippe, *J'avais quinze ans*, 145. See also Claude Boisse, *Jeunesse ardente, 1943–1945* (Montségur-sur-Lauzon: C. Boisse, 1997), 27.

255 Petit, *Au coeur de la bataille*, 87.

256 ADM, 1366 W, MT, Témoignage de Louis Blaise, 83, 86.

257 Delpierre, *Une enfance normande*, 148–49. See also Leveel, *Rails et haies*, 144–45.

258 ADM, 1366 W, MT, Claude Tatard, "Claude Bourdon," 904, and Témoignage de Yves Boudier, 101.

259 ADM, 1366 W, MT, Témoignage de Jean-Jacques Vautier, 979.

260 Poule, *Cahiers de mémoire*, 76.

261 Egger and Otts, *G Company War*, 62.

262 ADM, 1366 W, MT, Témoignage de Christian Letourneur, 732.

263 Alfred Marie, *Avranches: Souvenirs de l'occupation allemande, les bombardements, l'exode, la libération* (Avranches: Éditions de l'Avranchin, 1949), 179; NARA, RG 331, Entry 54, Box 111, "Summary of Findings of Civilian Investigations."

264 Poule, *Cahiers de mémoire*, 72–73.

265 Cécile Armagnac, *Ambulancières en Normandie: Cherbourg-Caen, 1944* (Faverolles, Barbery: Éditions du Moulin Vieux, 1994), 135.

266 ADM, 1366 W, MT, Témoignage de Jacques Popineau, 837. See also Jean Ably, *Interprète volant: avec la 72e escadrille de liaison américaine, France-Allemagne, 1944–1945* (Paris: B. Arthaud, 1946), 119.

267 ADM, 1366 W, MT, Carnet de Michel Braley, 115.

268 Marie, *Avranches*, 179. See also ADM, 1366 W, MT, Témoignage de Christianne Denis, 249; Claude Lesouquet, "Heugueville Souvenirs Année 44, Pont de la Roque," 725, Témoignage de Christiane Levent, 750–52; Michel Leroy, "Ma guerre 1939–1945," 704; Témoignage de Jean-Jacques Vautier, 981, Témoignage de Jacques Popineau, 837; NARA, RG 331, Entry 54, Box 111, "Summary of Findings of Civilian Investigations" and "Report from the Field on Reactions of Local Population in Normandy, No. 6"; Herval *Bataille*, 1:35, 70; Leveel, *Rails et haies*, 125. For Paris, see Edmond Dubois, *Paris sans lumière, 1939–1945; témoignages* (Lausanne: Éditions Payot, 1946), 213; Ferdinand Dupuy, *La libération de Paris vue d'un commissariat de police* (Paris: Librairies-Imprimeries Réunies, 1945), 30–31.

269 Philippe, *J'avais quinze ans*, 143.

270 ADM, 1366 W, MT, Carnet de Michel Braley, 105.

271 Armand Frémont, *La Mémoire d'un port, Le Havre* (Paris: Aléa,1997), 115.

272 Jourdain, *Petites surprises*, 139.

273 Cane, *Fighting Fascism in Europe*, 121.

274 ADM, 1366 W, MT, Témoignage de Jean-Pierre Launey, 641–42.

275 Gourbin, *Jeunesse occupée*, 126–27.

276 Pyle, *Brave Men*, 284.

277 Giles, *Journal*, 41. See also Peckham and Snyder, *Letters from Fighting Hoosiers*, 119. For the same opinion in the south of France, see Winston, *V . . . -Mail*, 152.

278 Judy Barrett Litoff, David C. Smith, Barbara Wooddall Taylor, and Charles E. Taylor, *Miss You: The World War II Letters of Barbara Wooddall Taylor and Charles E. Taylor* (Athens: University of Georgia Press, 1990), 212; Pierrette Rieublandou, *J'ai vécu le débarquement en Normandie: 6 juin 1944* (Paris: Bayard Jeunesse, 2004), 23.

279 *Stars and Stripes*, 2 September 1944. Kalamazoo River is in Marshall, Michigan.

280 Ibid. For more complaints about the castle, see Petesch, *War through the Hole of* *a Donut*, 151, 162. For a positive view of a French castle, see Capell, *Surviving the Odds*, 108–9.

281 Hillel, *Vie et moeurs des GI's en Europe*, 135.

282 MHI, WWII Survey, Box 1st Infantry Division, Stewart, "Hurry Up and Wait," 36.

283 Petesch, *War through the Hole of a Donut*, 145.

284 MHI, WWII Survey, Box 36th Infantry Division, Anthony Harlinski, "The Purple Road Back," 13.

285 MHI, WWII Survey, Box 71st Infantry Division, Ichelson, "I Was There," 61.

286 Allan Lyon, *Toward an Unknown Station* (New York: MacMillan Company, 1948), 135.

287 Litoff et al., *Miss You*, 198. See also Rogers, *Doughboy Chaplain*, 154.

288 Giles, *Journal*, 90–91. See also Egger and Otts, *G Company War*, 59; Schrijvers, *Crash of Ruin*, 230–31.

289 MHI, WWII Survey, Box 5th Infantry Division, Clarkson, "The Story of G.I. Joe," 14.

290 MHI, Chester Hansen Collection, diary entry dated 2 July 1944.

291 Harvey Levenstein, *We'll Always Have Paris: American Tourists in France since 1930* (Chicago: University of Chicago, 2004), 88.

292 See Rona Tamiko Halualani, "A Critical-Historical Genealogy of *Koko* (Blood), *'Aina* (Land), Hawaiian Identity, and Western Law and Governance," 243; Pablo Navarro-Rivera, "The Imperial Enterprise and the Educational Policies in Colonial Puerto Rico," 172; and Warwick Anderson, "Pacific Crossings: Imperial Logics in United States' Public Health Programs," 278–79, all in *Colonial Crucible: Empire in the Making of the Modern American State*, ed. Alfred W. McCoy and Francisco A. Scarano (Madison: University of Wisconsin Press, 2009).

293 Quoted in Schrijvers, *Crash of Ruin*, 229.

294 On *pissoirs*, see also Avery E. Kolb, *Jigger Whitchet's War* (New York: Simon and Schuster, 1959), 158; Daniel Glaser, "The Sentiments of American Soldiers Abroad towards Europeans," *American Journal of Sociology* 51, no. 5 (March 1946), 434; Jack Capell, *Surviving the Odds*, 214.

295 Thomson, "Over There," 56.

296 MHI, WWII Survey, Box 5th Infantry Division, Clarkson, "The Story of G.I. Joe," 8–9.

297 Giles, *Journal*, 90–91.

298 MHI, WWII Survey, Box 71st Infantry Division, Ichelson, "I Was There," 61–64.

299 US Army, *112 Gripes about the French* (Fontenay-aux-Roses: US Army, 1945), 47; MHI, WWII Survey, Box 71st Infantry Division, Ichelson, "I Was There," 199.

300 MHI, Chester Hansen Collection, diary entry dated 9 September 1944.

301 Boesch, *Road to Heurtgen-Forest in Hell*, 92. See also Schrijvers, *Crash of Ruin*, 239. On the nudity issue, see also MHI, WWII Survey, Box 70th Infantry Division, Thomas S. Higley, 1.

302 Le Mémorial de Caen, TE 243, Témoignage de Sergent Chef Dargols, 1.

303 US Army Service Forces, Army Information Branch, *A Pocket Guide to France* (Washington, DC: War & Navy Departments, 1944), 19.

304 Anne-Marie Sohn, *Du premier baiser à l'alcôve: la sexualité des français au quotidien (1850–1950)* (Paris: Aubier,1996), 80–84, 96–97, 307–10.

305 Le Mémorial de Caen, TE 277, Marcelle Hamel-Hateau, "Des mémoires d'une

petit maîtresse d'école de Normandie: souvenirs du débarquement de juin 1944," 19. Hamel-Hateau lived in Neuville-au-Plain, near Sainte-Mère-Eglise

306   MHI, WWII Survey, Box 9th Infantry Division, Jordan, "Bull Sessions," 85.

307   John D'Emilio and Estelle B. Freedman, *Intimate Matters: A History of Sexuality in America* (New York: Harper and Row, 1988), 241, 257–58, 263–64; Christina Simmons, *Making Marriage Modern: Women's Sexuality from the Progressive Era to World War II* (New York: Oxford University Press, 2009), 11–12, 57.

308   Hillel, *Vie et moeurs*, 163. Not every GI thought such practices were offensive. See MHI, WWII Survey, Box 1st Infantry Division, Bert Damsky, "Shipping Order___ APO___," 38–39.

309   Litoff et al., *Miss You*, 237.

310   Winston, *V . . . -Mail*, 113–14.

Chapter 2

1   On the Iwo Jima image as visual cliché, see Janie L. Edwards and Carol K. Winkler, "Representative Form and the Visual Ideograph: The Iwo Jima Image in Editorial Cartoons," *Quarterly Journal of Speech* 83 (1997): 289–310; John Louis Lucaites and Robert Hariman, "Visual Rhetoric, Photojournalism and Democratic Public Culture," *Rhetoric Review* 20, no. 1/2, (2001): 37–42.

2   Rhetoricians consider photography to be a peculiarly democratic visual form because it calls upon the individual to represent the whole. See Lucaites and Hariman, "Visual Rhetoric"; Cara A. Finnegan, *Picturing Poverty: Print Culture and FSA Photographs* (Washington, DC: Smithsonian Books, 2003), 118.

3   As Susan Sontag writes in *On Photography* (New York: Picador, 1973), 5, "a photograph passes for incontrovertible proof that a given thing happened."

4   Ibid., 23.

5   Roland Barthes, *Mythologies* (New York: Hill and Wang, 1972), 129, 142, 11. For more on "myth" in the Second World War, see Kenneth Rose, *Myth and the Greatest Generation: A Social History of Americans in World War II* (New York: Routledge, 2008).

6   Bodo Von Dewitz and Robert Lebek, eds., *Kiosk: Eine Geschichte der Fotoreportage, 1839–1973 / A History of Photojournalism, 1839–1973* (Gottingern: Steidl, 2001), 162, 190.

7   Finnegan, *Picturing Poverty*, 170, 242.

8   Andrew Mendelson and C. Zoe Smith, "Part of the Team: *Life* Photographers and Their Symbiotic Relationship with the Military during World War II," *American Journalism* 12, no. 3 (Summer 1995): 278–87.

9   Alfred Cornbise, "American Armed Forces Newspapers in World War Two," *American Journalism* 12, no. 3 (Summer 1995): 213–24.

10   Andy Rooney, *My War* (New York: Random House, 1995), 98. On censorship in *Stars and Stripes*, see George H. Roeder Jr., *The Censored War: American Visual Experience during World War II* (New Haven, CT: Yale University Press, 1993), 99.

11   See Jack E. Pulwers, *The Press of Battle: The GI Reporter and the American People* (Raleigh, NC: Ivy House Publishing, 2003), 407–95; Francis Caron, *Hexalogie ou mes souvenirs* (Aubenas d'Ardèche: Le Regard du monde, 1992), 73, 86.

12   *Stars and Stripes*, 24 June 1944.

13 Peter Belpulsi, *A GI's View of World War II* (Salem, MO: Globe Publishers, 1997), 80; Orval Faubus, *In This Faraway Land* (Conway, AR: River Road, 1971), 232. See also Aramais Hovsepian, *Your Son and Mine* (New York: Duell, Sloan and Pearce, 1950), 80.

14 Bibliothèque historique de la ville de Paris, Séries 30, fonds actualités, box 32, Presse américaine, Doris Fleeson, "Into the Heart of France" np, nd. See also Cecil E. Roberts, *A Soldier from Texas* (Fort Worth, TX: Branch-Smith, 1978), 45; Hilary Footitt, *War and Liberation in France* (New York: Palgrave Macmillan, 2004), 60–61.

15 French women greeting GIs with delirious happiness was a textual as well as visual element of *Stars and Stripes* reportage. See "They Don't Parlay English, but It's 'Welcome' All Right," 2 August 1944, and G. K. Hedenfield, "Beer—Ice Cold—Flows in Rennes," 8 August 1944.

16 See Mrinalini Sinha, "Gender and Nation," in *Women's History in Global Perspective*, ed. Bonnie G. Smith, 3 vols. (Urbana: University of Illinois Press, 2004), 1:229–74.

17 Robert Westbrook, "'I Want a Girl, Just Like the Girl That Married Harry James': American Women and the Problem of Political Obligation in World War II," *American Quarterly* 42, no. 4 (1990): 587–614. On pinups in World War II, see also Joanne Meyerowitz, "Women, Cheesecake, and Borderline Material: Responses to Girlie Pictures in Mid-Twentieth Century U.S.," *Journal of Women's History* 8, no. 3 (1996): 9–35; Maria Elena Buszek, *Pin-Up Grrrls: Feminism, Sexuality, Popular Culture* (Durham, NC: Duke University Press, 2006), 210–13.

18 *Stars and Stripes*, 9 September 1944.

19 Ibid.

20 Hilary Kaiser, *Veteran Recall: Americans in France Remember the War* (Paris: Author, 1994), 91. See also Archives Départmentales de la Manche, Saint-Lô (hereafter ADM), 1366 W, Comité vérité historique, *Liberté 44, la Manche témoigne: de l'occupation à la libération; les manchois se souviennent* (hereafter MT), Témoignage de Lucien Hélye, 515; Christiane Delpierre, *Une enfance normande* (Angers: Cheminements, 1999), 149; Danièle Philippe, *J'avais quinze ans . . . en juin 44 en Normandie* (Paris: Éditions France-Empire, 1994), 150.

21 Maurice Larkin, *France since the Popular Front: Government and People, 1936–1996* (New York: Oxford University Press, 1997), 116. The classic account is Dominique Lapierre and Larry Collins, *Is Paris Burning?* (New York: Simon and Schuster, 1965).

22 *Stars and Stripes*, 28 August 1944.

23 *Stars and Stripes*, 29 August 1944.

24 *Stars and Stripes*, 24 August 1944.

25 *Stars and Stripes*, 26 August 1944.

26 *Stars and Stripes*, 24 August 1944.

27 *Stars and Stripes*, 29 September 1944.

28 The six newspapers are *Le parisien libéré, Le populaire, Ce soir, France libre, Le franc-tireur,* and *L'aube.*

29 For the vagueness concerning "les libérateurs," see *France libre,* 26 August 1944. For textual accounts of the Liberation that appeared in these newspapers at the time, and which also contrast sharply with the American version of events, see Suzanne Campaux, ed., *La libération de Paris (19–26 août 1944): récits de combattants et de témoins réunis* (Paris: Éditions Payot, 1945).

30 *Ce soir*, 30 August 1944.

31 Maurice Boverat, *Du Cotentin à Colmar avec les chars de Leclerc* (Paris: Éditions Berger-Levrault, 1947), 59.

32 *Le parisien libéré*, 26 August 1944.

33 In French republican culture, such conjugality symbolized social and moral stability. See Judith Surkis, *Sexing the Citizen: Morality and Masculinity in France, 1870–1920* (Ithaca, NY: Cornell University Press, 2006).

34 *Le franc-tireur*, 27 August 1944.

35 Christopher Forth and Bertrand Taithe, "Introduction: French Manhood in the Modern World," in *French Masculinities: History, Culture and Politics*, ed. Forth and Taithe (New York: Palgrave McMillan, 2007), 5.

36 Christina Jarvis, *The Male Body at War: American Masculinity during World War II* (DeKalb: Northern Illinois University Press, 2004), 15–16.

37 Susan Gubar, "'This Is My Rifle, This Is My Gun': World War II and the Blitz on Women," in *Behind the Lines: Gender and the Two World Wars*, ed. Margaret Higonnet et al. (New Haven, CT: Yale University Press, 1987), 197–226. On the contrast between American and French women, see Elisabeth Coquart, *La France des G.I.s: Histoire d'un amour déçu* (Paris: Albin Michel, 2003), 74–75.

38 Paul Fussell, *Wartime: Understanding and Behavior in the Second World War* (New York: Oxford University Press, 1989), 253.

39 On Ralph Morse, see Roeder, *The Censored War*, 95.

40 *Life*, 25 September 1944.

41 *Stars and Stripes*, 20 September 1944.

42 Examples of such a joyous greeting are too numerous to mention here, but a sampling would include the following. In the American memoir literature, see Robert Adleman and George Walton, *The Champagne Campaign* (Boston: Little, Brown and Company, 1969), 171; Annette Tapert, ed., *Lines of Battle: Letters from American Servicemen, 1941–1945* (New York: New York Times Books, 1987), 165. In the archival literature, see US Army Military History Institute, Carlisle Barracks, (hereafter MHI), World War Two Survey (hereafter WWII Survey), Box 5th Infantry Division, Robert Russell, "World War II Memoirs," 19, and Mark Goodman, "Unit History of Company A," 41, 46. In the French memoir literature, see André Hamel, *La canton des pieux: six ans de guerre, 1939–1945 et la 9th division U.S. d'Utah Beach à Goury* (Cherbourg: Le Canton des Pieux, 1994), 116; Michel Béchet, *L'attente: "Overlord" vécu à cent kilomètres du front* (Montsûrs: Résiac, 1994), 91–94.

43 Marc Bergère, "Français et américains en Basse-Seine à la Libération (1944–1946): des relations ambivalentes," *Annales de Bretagne et des pays de l'ouest*, 109, no. 4 (2002): 203–15. See also Marc Hillel, *Vie et moeurs des GI's en Europe, 1942–1947* (Paris: Balland, 1981), 148–55, 172. In the American literature, see "The Wrong Ambassadors," *Time*, 19 November 1945.

44 The GIs referred to looting as "liberating." See MHI, WWII Survey, Box 1st Infantry Division, Leroy Stewart, "Hurry Up and Wait," 76. In general, theft was not considered to be morally reprehensible. Some rules applied. Engagement rings, for example, were not considered legal loot. See MHI, WWII Survey, Box 71st Infantry Division, David Ichelson, "I Was There," 89, and Box 85th Infantry Division, Hal O'Neill, "Looting." For the official military response to looting, see National Archives and Records Administration (hereafter NARA), Record Group 331, Records of Allied Operation and Occupation, Headquarters, World War II (SHAEF) (hereafter RG 331), General Staff Divisions, G-5 Division, Secretariat, Numeric File, August 1943–July 1945, Entry 47, Box 28, Civil Affairs Weekly Summary, no. 9, 11 August 1944; NARA, RG 331, General Correspondence, 1944–45, Entry 6, Box 11, "Looting by Troops and Relations with Civilian Population." SHAEF headquarters set up a formal commission in Normandy for the reparation of French goods stolen by GIs, politely called "irregular requisitions" by the French. See ADM, 158 W, Réquisitions américaines, 1944–46, 159–202, réquisitions irrégulières. One measure of the breadth of these complaints is that they fill up forty-three boxes.

45 For the occurrence of these accidents in Le Havre, see the *Faits divers* column of *Havre-éclair* during the summer of 1945. On 26 June, for example, the column notes that a three-year-old child had been killed by an American vehicle. For the same sort of accident in Caen, see Archives Départementales du Calvados, 726 W 16 905, "Correspondance avec les autorités militaires alliées au sujet de sepultures alliées et enemies," where an angry letter from the Sous-préfet de Bayeux complains about a jeep running over a small child. In Reims, the police chief reported on 9 February 1945 that civilians believed the Americans to be aiming at them on purpose. See ADM, 132 W 276, Mission militaire française de liaison auprès de l'armée américaine, rapport du Commissaire de Police. In this file, see also an undated document titled "Difficultés avec les américains," which describes as "frequent" "mortal accidents" with American jeeps.

46 Coquart, *La France des G.I.s*, 74. In *Naître ennemi: les enfants de couples franco-allemands nés pendant la seconde guerre mondiale* (Paris: Éditions Payot, 2009), 193–94. Fabrice Virgili notes that in early 1944 rapes by German soldiers against French women were very infrequent.

47 For a full exploration of these rape charges, see chapter 7. On GI misbehavior, see also Footitt, *War and Liberation in France*, 163–64.

48 Archives de la Préfecture de la Police (hereafter APP), BA 1822 Libération. This file contains scores of police reports, dated from December 1944 through February 1946, and concerning armed robbery and assault, allegedly at the hands of American soldiers.

49 While there are over a hundred reports of crimes committed by the Americans in the police file APP, BA 1822 Libération, not one report implicated a British soldier, and only three cases targeted Canadian soldiers. These reports represent only a fraction of alleged crimes against the GIs, as the American military police often handled problems without the French police. No arrondissement of Paris was spared from American violence, although trouble centered on the *grands boulevards* and in red light districts of the eighth, ninth, and tenth *arrondissements*. In *Liberators: The Allies and Belgian Society, 1944–1945* (Cambridge: Cambridge University Press, 2009), 243, Peter Schrijvers notes that similar types of crimes in Belgium—assault, public drunkenness, rape, and theft—were overwhelmingly American.

50 APP, Name of dossier withheld, A-1945/6 (F. 32.795). The man in question had a long police record, mostly for robbery, and worked for the Gestapo during the war. On 8 September 1945, he became seriously wounded, and when the doctor was called, he claimed to have been attacked by American GIs. The police later concluded it had been a fight, most likely resulting from a "paying of debts with people of his sort."

51 On deserters in Paris, see Jack Capell, *Surviving the Odds* (Claremont, CA: Regina Books, 2007), 213–14.

52 Archives Municipales de la Ville du Havre (hereafter AMH), FC H4 15-6, Daily Police Report, 10–11 June 1945.

53 AMH, FC H4 15-6, letter dated 8 October 1945.

54 AMH, FC H4 15-6, letter dated 26 November 1945.

55 AMH, FC H4 15-6, letter dated 10 September 1945.

56 AMH, FC H4 15-6, petition dated 19 September 1945.

57 AMH, FC H4 15-6, letter dated 30 October 1945.

58 AMH, FC H4 15-5, Joe Weston, "The GIs in Le Havre," manuscript; *Life*, 31 December 1945.

59 Régine Torrent, "L'image du soldat américain en France, de 1943 à 1945," in *Les américains et la France (1917–1947): engagements et représentations*, ed. François Cochet, Marie-Claude Genet-Delacroix, and Hélène Trocmé (Paris: Maisonneuve et Larose, 1999), 239.

60 Archives Départmentales du Finistère, Fonds Roger Bourrières, 202J9, Libération du Finistère après le 6 juin: rapports, récits, témoignages, région centre. The accounts of violence come from the diary of an unnamed member of the FFI who was put in charge of guarding the village of Botmeur. See also in this archive Fonds Alain Le Grand, 200 W 75, Attentats, sabotages, vols, actes de terrorisme, report dated 26 août 1944.

61 Archives Nationales (hereafter AN), F1A 4023, Rapports du commissaire de la Republique, Marseille, 15 Juillet 1945.

62 AN, F1c III, Préfet de Moselle, September 1945.

63 Service historique de la gendarmerie nationale, Vincennes, 027720, Troisième légion R/2 1944–45, Rouen, Synthèse mensuelle sur l'état d'esprit des populations, February 1945. There are scores of such crimes reported in the archives of the Gendarmerie nationale. A sampling would include 76 E 7 Compagnie de la Seine-Inférieur à Rouen, registres de correspondance courante au départ, 6 avril au 9 novembre 1945, report of 24 December 1944; 76 E 163 Section de Rouen, registres de correspondance courante au départ, 8 février au 22 mai 1945, report of 15 February 1945; 76E 114 Section du Havre, registres de correspondance courante au départ (R/2), 23 avril 1945 au 17 janvier 1946, letter to the Provost Marshall dated 23 July 1945.

64 Régine Torrent, *La France américaine: controverses de la Libération* (Brussels: Éditions Racine, 2004), 230–31. Torrent bases her argument on prefectural reports from Cherbourg in the summer of 1944.

65 See, in particular, Archives Départmentales de la Marne (hereafter ADMar), 16 W 266, Relations avec les autorités alliés, notes et correspondance, letter dated 6 December 1944 and report dated 13 August 1945. Scores of thefts and assaults by American soldiers are also reported in *16 W 268* Affaires réservées: incidents avec les troupes alliées. For American violence in Reims, see Daniel Pellus, *La Marne dans la guerre 1939/1945* (Le Coteau: Éditions Horvath, 1987), 159–60; Georges Clause, *Reims autour du 7 mai 1945* (Nîmes: Christian Lacour, 1997), 388–92; Jacques Pernet and Michel Hubert, *Reims: chronique des années de guerre* (Saint-Cyr-sur-Loire: Éditions Alan Sutton, 2003), 53–87; Jacques Pernet and Michel Hubert, *1944 il était une fois . . . les américains* (Reims: Éditions de l'Atelier Graphique, 1994), 67–68, 93–95, 107–9, 111–21; Jean-Pierre Husson, *La Marne et les marnais a l'épreuve de la seconde guerre mondiale*, 2 vols. (Reims: Presses Universitaires de Reims, 1995), 1:308–10, 2:76–77, 92–93.

66 ADMar, 161 W 323, Incidents franco-américains: rapports 1944–46, letter dated 26 June 1945 and letter dated 17 July 1945. For police reports of these crimes, see the same file, three reports all dated 22 June 1945, which concern assaults by GIs in a French home, backyard, and a local café. See also ADMar, 8 U 180, Rapports de gendarmerie et de police concernant des faits de guerre, report dated 15 May 1945; 162 W 355, Rapports journaliers des relations avec les troupes, 1945, in particular the report dated 22 October 1945 describing broken windows, demands for alcohol and women, and the rape of a mother of eight children, all in Reims. Since Polish and French soldiers also wore American uniforms in this area, it is possible that the GIs were being wrongly accused of violence committed by these two groups.

67 ADMar, 132 W 276, Mission militaire française de liaison auprès de l'armée américaine, letter dated 21 October 1945.

68 ADMar, 16 W 266, Relations avec les autorités alliés, notes et correspondance, letter dated 8 August 1945 from "A group of indignant fathers of families."

69 ADMar, 162 W 355, Rapports journaliers des relations avec les troupes, report dated 15 August 1945.

70 Maurice Chevance-Bertin, *Vingt mille heures d'angoisse, 1940–1945* (Paris: Éditions Robert Laffont, 1990), 170.

71 *Stars and Stripes*, 1 July 1944.

72 The origin of this cartoon could have been an incident that occurred during General Eisenhower's entry into Paris in late August. In an awkward moment, a man approached the general on his jeep and gave him a kiss. See MHI, Chester Hansen Collection, diary entry 27 August 1944. According to Hansen, Gen. Omar Bradley also was kissed somewhat awkwardly by a woman, but he bragged: "Well I did better than Ike; he had a man kiss him."

73 *Stars and Stripes*, 31 July 1944.

74 The classic work is Fabrice Virgili, *La France "virile": des femmes tondues à la Libération* (Paris: Éditions Payot et Rivages, 2000); English trans., *Shorn Women: Gender and Punishment in Liberation France* (Oxford: Berg, 2002). There were *tonte* rituals elsewhere in Europe, namely, Belgium and Italy. See, for example, Schrijvers, *Liberators*, 77–78.

75 Luc Capdevila, "The Quest for Masculinity in a Defeated France," *Contemporary European History* 10, no. 3 (2001): 444–45.

76 Corran Laurens, "'La femme au turban': les femmes tondues," in *The Liberation of France: Image and Event*, ed. H. R. Kedward and Nancy Wood (Oxford: Berg Publishers, 1995), 156, 176–77; Virgili, *Shorn Women*, 83–84.

77 Virgili, *Shorn Women*, 84, 219, 237.

78 See Virgili's exhaustive analysis of the photo in *Naître ennemi*, 176–79.

79 For the equation of the Liberation with the *tonte*, see Virgili, *Shorn Women*, 83.

80 *Stars and Stripes* 9 September 1944.

Chapter 3

1 See Michael Kelly, "The Reconstruction of Masculinity at the Liberation," and Corran Laurens, "'La femme au turban': Les femmes tondues," in *The Liberation of France: Image and Event*, ed. H. R. Kedward and Nancy Wood (Oxford: Berg

Publishers, 1995), 117–28, 155–96; Luc Capdevila, "The Quest for Masculinity in a
Defeated France," *Contemporary European History* 10, no. 3 (2001): 444–45.

2 For the figure of two million, see Fabrice Virgili, *Shorn Women: Gender and Punishment in Liberation France* (Oxford: Berg Publishers, 2002), 302. For the Service du
Travail Obligatoire (STO), see Richard Vinen, *The Unfree French: Life under the Occupation* (New Haven, CT: Yale University Press, 2006), 247–80.

3 French Swiss novelist Charles-Ferdinand Ramuz defined the "defense of the sacred" in this way: "the nation, most importantly, is a simple corner of the earth:
this is my house, my fields, my village, my family, my things . . . so I defend it
against those who would ruin the earth, set fire to the houses and perhaps take the
lives of my wife and children." See C.-F. Ramuz, "Défense du sacré," in *La patrie
se fait tous les jours, textes français, 1939–1945*, ed. Jean Paulhan and Dominique Aury
(Paris: Les Éditions de Minuit, 1947), 57–58.

4 Important studies of the *chef de famille* are Sylvia Schafer, *Children in Moral Danger
and the Problem of Government in Third Republic France* (Princeton, NJ: Princeton
University Press, 1997); and Judith Surkis, *Sexing the Citizen: Morality and Masculinity in France, 1870–1920* (Ithaca, NY: Cornell University Press, 2006).

5 For such images of homelessness, see Jean-Paul Sartre, *Troubled Sleep* [*La mort dans
l'âme*] (New York: Alfred Knopf, 1951; orig. 1947), 18–19; André Malraux, *The Wal-
nut Trees of Altenburg* [*Les noyers d'Altenburg*] (New York: Howard Fertig, 1989; orig.
1948), 16; Jean Dutourd, *Les taxis de la Marne* (Paris: Gallimard, 1956), 12. Sartre was
drafted into the army in 1939, and captured by the Germans in Padoux. After nine
months as a prisoner of war, he was released for health reasons. Malraux fought in
the battle of 1940 and was captured by the Germans. He later escaped and joined
the Resistance. Dutourd was drafted in 1940, briefly taken prisoner by the Germans, then escaped to Paris.

6 Vercors [Jean Bruller], *Le silence de la mer* (New York: Pantheon Books, 1943; orig.
1942). On the importance of the novel, see Fabrice Virgili, *Naître ennemi: les enfants
de couples franco-allemands nés pendant la seconde guerre mondiale* (Paris: Éditions
Payot, 2009), 54–56. Bruller, who fought in the Battle of France, later recounted
to an American audience, "Oh helplessness, lamentable, intolerable helplessness
of a France covered with crimes and shame!" See Vercors, "A Plea for France: A
Nation Weak and Uncertain Needs Our Understanding," *Life*, 6 November 1944;
Souffrances de mon pays (Paris: Collections des 150, 1945), 21, 41.

7 For how veteran shame is portrayed, see Sartre, *Troubled Sleep*, 109, 125, 172, 201–2,
281–82; Général d'Armée Victor Bourret, *La tragédie de l'armée française* (Paris: La
Table Ronde, 1947), 21. Bourret was the commander of the French Fifth Army in
1940. In this literature, Great War veterans scorn the younger generation, lending
legitimacy to the author's angry judgment concerning those who lost in 1940. See,
for example, the character of Babtiston in Antoine Blondin, *L'Europe buissonnière*
(Paris: Éditions Jean Froissart, 1949); Girard in André Chamson, *Le dernier village:
roman* (Paris: Mercure de France, 1946); and the veterans of Verdun haunting the
dreams of Buissières in Joseph Peyré, *Un soldat chez les hommes* (Paris: Éditions
Bernard Grasset, 1946), 23. Chamson fought in 1940 as a captain of the *chasseurs
alpins*.

8 Chamson, *Dernier village*, 240. See also Henri Macé, *44: la remontée* (Liège: Éditions
A. Maréchal, 1945), 10.

9 Jacques Debû-Bridel, *Déroute* (Paris: Gallimard, 1942), 248–49. Debû-Bridel was drafted in 1939 and fought in the Battle of France.

10 See Mrinalini Sinha, "Gender and Nation," in *Women's History in Global Perspective*, ed. Bonnie G. Smith, 2 vols. (Urbana: University of Illinois Press, 2004), 1:229–74.

11 Nicoletta F. Gullace, *"The Blood of Our Sons": Men, Women, and the Renegotiation of British Citizenship during the Great War* (New York: Palgrave Macmillan, 2002), chap. 1. For the sexualization of the Second World War, see also Peter Paret and Beth Irwin Lewis, *Persuasive Images: Posters of War and Revolution in the Hoover Archives* (Princeton, NJ: Princeton University Press, 1992); Susan Gubar, "'This Is My Rifle, This Is My Gun': World War II and the Blitz on Women," in *Behind the Lines: Gender and the Two World Wars*, ed. Margaret Higonnet et al. (New Haven, CT: Yale University Press, 1987), 227–59.

12 The custom far precedes the twentieth century according to Thorstein Veblen, *The Theory of the Leisure Class: An Economic History of Institutions* (New York: Macmillan Co., 1912), 22–25.

13 Dutourd, *Les taxis de la Marne*, 59. See also Sartre, *Troubled Sleep*, 174–75.

14 See Jean-Louis Bory's *Mon village à l'heure allemand* (New York: Éditions de la Maison Française, 1945), which won the Prix Goncourt in 1945. See also Jean-Louis Curtis, *The Forests of the Night* [*Les forêts de la nuit*] (New York: G. P. Putnam's Sons, 1951; orig.1947), 289–90. Both Bory and Curtis were drafted in 1939, and participated in the Battle of France.

15 Virgili, *Naître ennemi*, chap. 3, 193–94, 215. In the primary literature, see Jacques Perret, *Le caporal épinglé* (Paris: Gallimard, 1972; orig. 1947), 114–15.

16 Virgili, *Shorn Women*, chap. 8.

17 Antoinette Oriot, *La fille du boulanger* (Charenton-Le-Pont: Presses de Valmy, 1998), 347–48.

18 National Archives and Records Administration (hereafter NARA), Record Group 331, Records of Allied Operation and Occupation, Headquarters, World War II (SHAEF) (hereafter RG 331), Entry 47, General Staff Divisions, G-5 Division, Secretariat, Numeric File, August 1943–July 1945 (hereafter Entry 47), Box 27, RECCE Report on Cherbourg. RECCE was a SHAEF mission undertaken in late June through early July 1944 to gauge French opinion in liberated territory. For the notion that the French were "maîtres chez eux," see also *L'Amérique en guerre*, 12 April 1944.

19 US Army Military History Institute, Carlisle Barracks (hereafter MHI), Letters of Lt. Col. Bealke, letter dated 4 August 1944.

20 Robert and Jane Easton, *Love and War: Pearl Harbor through V-J Day* (Norman: University of Oklahoma Press, 1991), 224.

21 Alfred Fabre-Luce, *Journal de la France, juin 1943–août 1944* (Paris: Auteur, nd), 85.

22 NARA, RG 331, Entry 54 General Staff, G-5 Division, Information Branch, Historical Section, Numeric-Subject Operations File (hereafter Entry 54), Box 193, analysis sheet from OSS to SHAEF Headquarters dated October 1944.

23 Andrew Knapp, "Introduction: France's 'Long' Liberation, 1944–1947," in *The Uncertain Foundation: France at the Liberation, 1944–1947*, ed. Andrew Knapp (New York: Palgrave McMillan, 2007), 2, 12.

24 Charles Cogan and Andrew Knapp, "Washington at the Liberation, 1944–1947," in Knapp, *The Uncertain Foundation*, 184.

25 Irwin Wall, *The United States and the Making of Postwar France, 1945–1954* (Cambridge: Cambridge University Press, 1991), 21, 23, 25.

26 NARA, RG 331, Entry 53, General Staff Divisions, G-5 Division, Information Branch, Historical Section, Numeric-Subject Planning File, 1943–July 1945, Crane Brinton, "Memorandum on the Situation in France" dated December 1943.

27 Crane Brinton, "Letters from Liberated France," *French Historical Studies* 2, no. 1 (Spring 1961): 6, letter dated 23 August 1944.

28 Robert de Saint Jean in *Le figaro*, 22 September 1944.

29 Wladimir d'Ormesson in *Le figaro*, 15 September 1944. In October, the French chief of police, Lt. Col. Girard, noted that civilians "do not understand that France no longer occupies the place on the world stage that is its right to hold." Archives Nationales, Séries 72AJ, 384, La gendarmerie nationale, synthèse pour la période du 15 septembre au 15 octobre 1944.

30 *Paris Normandie*, 23 September 1944.

31 Louis Martin Chauffier, "Ma patrie, la langue française," in Paulhan and Aury, *La patrie se fait tous les jours*, 199. Chauffier's statement is undated in the text.

32 Archives Départmentales du Calvados (hereafter ADC), 9 W 45, Rapports du préfet, rapports mensuels et bimensuels, 25 June 1945; 9 W 53, Police, rapports journaliers, 12 April 1945; 21 W 16, Rapports mensuels du préfet: Documents préparatoires de synthèse. For the Marne, see Archives Départmentales de la Marne (hereafter ADMar), "Bulletin quotidien d'information, chapitre 1," 7 June 1945.

33 This argument has been taken up by Régine Torrent, *La France américaine: controverses de la libération* (Brussels: Éditions Racine, 2004).

34 *La presse cherbourgeoise*, 1 July and 25 October 1944. In the memoir literature, see Oriot, *La fille du boulanger*, 373. ADMar, "Bulletin quotidien d'information: la situation intérieure et l'opinion publique," 28 May 1945.

35 ADC, 21 W 15/2, Rapports mensuels du préfet: documents préparatoires de synthèse, 1944, 18 December 1944. On the issue of de Gaulle, see same dossier 5 February and 11 March 1945.

36 *Front national*, 12 September 1944.

37 *Combat*, 23 August 1944.

38 MHI, World War Two Survey Collection (hereafter WWII Survey), Box 36th Infantry Division, Anthony Harlinski, "The Purple Road Back," 6.

39 Easton, *Love and War*, 239, 339.

40 Quoted in Peter Schrijvers, *The Crash of Ruin: American Combat Soldiers in Europe during World War II* (New York: New York University Press, 1998), 43. See also MHI, WWII Survey, Box Quartermaster Laundry Company, Leslie Brown, untitled memoir, np.

41 John Toole, *Battle Diary* (Missoula, MT: Vigilante Press, 1978), 22.

42 Bill Mauldin, *Willie and Joe: The World War II Years*, 2 vols. (Seattle: Fantagraphic Books, 2008), 2:196: "The French army started tearing up the roads," Mauldin explained, "and they made our worst quartermaster drivers seem like timid old ladies." See also Bill Mauldin, *Up Front* (New York: H. Holt and Co., 1945), 107–8. See also Brendan Phibbs, *The Other Side of Time: A Combat Surgeon in World War II* (Boston: Little Brown and Co., 1987), 101.

43 Wall, *Making of Postwar France*, 12.

44 US Army Service Forces, Army Info Branch, *A Pocket Guide to France* (Washington, DC: War & Navy Departments, 1944), 6–8.

45 Robert Peters, *For You, Lili Marlene* (Madison: University of Wisconsin Press, 1995), 47.

46 MHI, WWII Survey, Box 1st Infantry Division, George J. Koch survey.

47 MHI, WWII Survey, Box 1st Infantry Division, Leroy Stewart, "Hurry Up and Wait."

48 Jack Sacco, *Where the Birds Never Sing: The True Story of the 92nd Signal Battalion and the Liberation of Dachau* (New York: HarperCollins Publishers, 2003), 201.

49 Schrijvers, *Crash of Ruin*, 43; MHI, WWII Survey, Box 1st Infantry Division, Andrew Wright survey.

50 Schrijvers, *Crash of Ruin*, 45.

51 Ibid., 42.

52 Ibid., 43, 46.

53 Toole, *Battle Diary*, diary entry dated 26 November 1944, 61.

54 MHI, WWII Survey, Box 1st Infantry Division, Warren R. Eames survey; Jack Sacco, *Where the Birds Never Sing*, 209; Phibbs, *The Other Side of Time*, 101. In the secondary literature, see Marc Hillel, *Vie et moeurs des GI's en Europe, 1942–1947* (Paris: Balland, 1981), 134.

55 MHI, Chester Hansen Collection, diary entry dated 25 August 1944. See also Andrew A. Thomson, "'Over There' 1944/45, Americans in the Liberation of France: Their Perceptions of, and Relations with France and the French" (PhD thesis, University of Kent at Canterbury, 1996), 135–36.

56 Hilary Footitt, *War and Liberation in France* (New York: Palgrave Macmillan, 2004), 106.

57 Phibbs, *Other Side of Time*, 100, 166, 185–94.

58 MHI, WWII Survey, Box 1st Infantry Division, John E. Bistrica survey and Warren R. Eames survey; Nat Frankel and Larry Smith, *Patton's Best: An Informal History of the 4th Armored Division* (New York: Hawthorn, 1978), 31; William M. McConahey, MD, *Battalion Surgeon* (Rochester, MN: W. McConahey, 1966), 86; Paul Boesch, *Road to Heurtgen-Forest in Hell* (Houston, TX: Gulf Publishers, 1962), 85; Orval Eugene Faubus, *In This Faraway Land* (Conway, AR: River Road, 1971), 254. The GIs were particularly impressed by female members of the FFI, and often tried to seduce them. See MHI, John J. Maginnis Papers, untitled memoir, 202–4, 227–8, 270; Easton, *Love and War*, 248; John Hurkala, *The Fighting First Division: A True Story* (New York: Greenwich Book Publishers, 1957), 158.

59 MHI, John J. Maginnis Papers, untitled memoir, 205.

60 See Arthur Layton Funk, *Hidden Ally: The French Resistance, Special Operations, and the Landings in Southern France, 1944* (Westport, CT: Greenwood Press, 1992), 121, 253–56.

61 See Institut d'histoire du temps présent (hereafter IHTP), typescript, Claude Collin, "L'attitude des résistants face aux 'liberateurs' américains: un mélange d'admiration et de méfiance," "Les américains en Lorraine, september 44–mai 45, Actes du colloque historique franco-américain," Thionville, 10 November 1989, 102. See also Thomson, "Over There," 75, 142.

62 H. R. Kedward, *Occupied France: Collaboration and Resistance, 1940–1944* (Oxford: Blackwell Publishers, 1985), 75.

63 MHI, WWII Survey, Box 1st Infantry Division, John E. Bistrica survey.

64 MHI, WWII Survey, Box 1st Infantry Division, William Lee survey; Lucien Guenneau, André Goacolou, and Alain Le Bris, eds., *Résistants et maquisards dans le Finistère: témoignages* (Spézet: Les Amis de la Résistance du Finistère-ANACR, 2008), 48.

65 MHI, WWII Survey, Box 5th Infantry Division, Robert Russell, "World War II Memoirs," 19, and Mark Goodman, "Unit History of Company A," np.

66 NARA, RG 331, Entry 47, Box 27, "850/2 Civil Affairs Summaries—21 Army Group"; RG 331, Entry 54, Box 194, "France Documents Copied from Hist. Files from Com Z," report dated 19 October 1944; Brinton, "Letters from Liberated France," 140; Thomson, "Over There," 142.

67 NARA, RG 331, Entry 47, Box 27, memo dated 5 September 1944; and see also Box 28, Civil Affairs weekly summary no. 13, 8 september 1944.

68 NARA, RG 331, Entry 54, Box 194, Civil Affairs report, 18 August to 23 August 1944.

69 MHI, Chester Hansen Collection, diary entry dated 27 August 1944.

70 Archives Départmentales du Finistère, Fonds Roger Bourrières, 202J9 Libération du Finistère après le 6 juin: rapports, récits, témoignages, Région Sud, Anonymous manuscript, 63. The author was a member of the Resistance group "Vengeance" in Quimper.

71 NARA, RG 331, Entry 54, Box 194, report dated 30 September 1944.

72 On the *épuration*, see Philippe Bourdrel, *L'épuration sauvage, 1944–1945* (Paris: Éditions Perrin, 2002); Peter Novick, *The Resistance versus Vichy: The Purge of Collaborators in Vichy France* (London: London, Chatto & Windus, 1968).

73 MHI, WWII Survey, Box 1st Infantry Division, Rocco Moretto survey.

74 Phibbs, *Other Side of Time*, 172.

75 NARA, RG 331, Entry 54, Box 194, Civil Affairs report 18 August to 23 August 1944.

76 MHI Chester Hansen Collection, diary entry dated 27 August 1944. For a more positive account of the same phenomenon, see MHI, John J. Maginnis Papers, untitled memoir, 195: "I had observed the FFI about town. They were having a high old time, tearing through the streets in captured or seized cars, always carrying arms and taking liberties almost at will. This was their day in the sun so to speak, the day they had been working for and waiting for, for so long. I felt that they were entitled to this moment of power and glory while the flush of liberation lasted, provided they did not get out of hand."

77 NARA, RG 331, Entry 47, Box 28, report dated 27 October 1944 and Civil Affairs weekly summary, 8 September 1944. See also RG 331, Entry 54, Box 194, report dated 19 October 1944. For a contrasting positive report, see same box, report dated 30 September 1944. In the secondary literature, see Wall, *Making of Postwar France*, 25.

78 Allan Lyon, *Toward an Unknown Station* (New York: MacMillan Company, 1948), 135.

79 MHI, WWII Survey, 452nd Quartermaster Laundry Company, Leslie Brown, untitled memoir, np; Phibbs, *The Other Side of Time*, 167.

80 For the discomfort of the GIs with the *tonte* rituals, see Archives Départmentales du Morbihan, 1 J 641, Fonds du Comité d'Histoire de la Deuxième Guerre Mondiale, Paul Rollando, "4 Août 1944: La libération de Vannes" (1944), 41. In the American autobiographical literature, see Robert Adleman and George Walton, *The Champagne Campaign* (Boston: Little Brown, 1969), 236–39; Frank Irgang, *Etched in Purple* (Caldwell, ID: Caxton Printers, 1949), 28; MHI, Charles Maginnis Papers, untitled memoir, 82; Faubus, *In This Faraway Land*, 255; Andy Rooney, *My War* (New York: New York Times Books, 1995), 213; Alan Moorehead, *Eclipse* (New York: Coward-McCann, 1945), 114 (Moorehead is British, but he describes the American response to the *tontes*); Sacco, *Where the Birds Never Sing*, 201; Ken Parker, *Civilian at War* (Traverse City, MI: Author, 1984), 88; MHI, WWII Survey, Box 9th Infantry Division, Chester Jordan, "Bull Sessions: World War II, Company K, 47th Inf, 9th Division from Normandy to Remagen," 79; Box 1st Infantry Division, William Faust survey; Box 28th Infantry Division, Joseph Messore survey.

81 Lawrence Cane, *Fighting Fascism in Europe: The World War II Letters of an American Veteran of the Spanish Civil War* (New York: Fordham University Press, 2003), 122.

82 Georgia H. Helm, *From Foxhole to Freedom: The World War II European Journal of Captain H. Dale Helm of Indiana* (Indianapolis: Guild Press of Indiana, 1996), 14.

83 S. L. A. Marshall, *Bringing Up the Rear: A Memoir* (San Rafael, CA: Presidio Press, 1979), 97. See also Francis L. Sampson, *Look Out Below: A Story of the Airborne by a Paratrooper Padre* (Washington, DC: Catholic University of America Press, 1958), 751. Many French civilians also suspected that some members of the FFI were "resistors of the last minute," meaning that they joined the FFI at the Liberation in order to cover up wartime collaboration. For a sampling of these views, see François Lefaivre, *J'ai vécu les bombardements à Condé-sur-Noireau* (Condé-sur-Noireau: C. Corlet, 1994), 166–67; Oriot, *La fille du boulanger*, 347; Bernard Gourbin, *Une jeunesse occupée: de l'Orne au Bessin:1940–1944* (Le Coudray-Macouard: Cheminements, 2004), 114; Claude Boisse, *Jeunesse ardente, 1943–1945* (Montségur-sur-Lauzon: C. Boisse, 1997), 33.

84 NARA, RG 331, Entry 54, Box 194, report 18 August to 23 August 1944; Entry 54, Box 111, analysis sheet of the Langelon Report, dated 4 August 1944. Also in Box 111, see "Summary of Findings of Civilian Investigations" dated 25 June 1944, and report dated 2 August 1944. In the French memoir literature, see Jean Leloup, *La sanglante bataille de la Seine: témoignage* (Almenèches: Humusaire, 2003), 117.

85 MHI, WWII Survey, Box 28th Infantry Division, Donald Lyddon, "My Memories of World War II," 26. See also Jack Capell, *Surviving the Odds* (Claremont, CA: Regina Books, 2007), 110.

86 Yves Cazaux, *Journal secret de la libération, 6 juin 1914–17 novembre, 1944* (Paris: Albin Michel, 1975), 294. See also Fabre-Luce, *Journal de la France*, 84.

87 C. L. Flavian, *Ils furent des hommes* (Paris: Nouvelles Éditions Latines, 1948), 11.

88 IHTP, Collin, "L'attitude des resistants"; and see also Collin, *L'été des partisans: Les F.T.P. et l'organisation de la Résistance en Meuse* (Nancy: Presses Universitaires de Nancy, 1992); MHI, WWII Survey, Box 28th Infantry Division, Charles F. Carré Jr. survey.

89 Guenneau et al., *Résistants et maquisards dans le Finistère*, 33.

90 Archives Départmentales du Finistère (hereafter ADF), Fonds Roger Bourrières (hereafter FRB), 202J 9, Libération du Finistère après le 6 juin: rapports, récits, témoignages (hereafter 202J 9), Région Centre, reports dated 15 June 1944, 27 June 1944, 22 September 1944, and Anonymous "Les Quimperois dans les Combats de la Presqu'île de Crozon." See also Jean-Jacques François and Colette François-Dive,

De la Résistance à la libération (Luisant: Durand S.A., 2001), 213; Guenneau et al., *Resistants et maquisards*, 48; Pierre Servagnat, *La Résistance et les Forces Françaises de l'Intérior dans l'arrondissement d'Épernay* (La Chapelle–Montligeon: Imprimerie de Montligeon, 1946), 141; Jean Reuchet, *Le désarroi, la souffrance, l'espoir vécu par les combattants de la Résistance de Haute-Saône* (Pantin: Éditions Crimée, 1996), 213.

91 For a good example of this kind of narration, see Claude Monod, *La région D: rapport d'activité des maquis de Bourgogne-Franche-Comté* (Saint-Etienne-Vallée-Française: AIOU, 1994), 72–75.

92 Reuchet, *Le désarroi*, 213; François and François-Dive, *De la Résistance à la Libération*, 104–5.

93 Reuchet, *Le désarroi*, 213.

94 IHTP, Fonds Émile Delavaney, testimonies of Vincent Auriol, Eduard Froment, and Juste Evrard, 28 October 1943; ADF, FRB, 202J9, Région Sud, Capt. C. G. W. Blathway, Capt. P. Charron, and Sgt. N. Wood, "Report on Word of Jedburgh Team Gilbert," 11–12; Guenneau et al., *Résistants et maquisards*, 145. There were also squabbles over confiscated German property. See MHI, John J. Maginnis Papers, untitled memoir, 202.

95 Funk, *Hidden Ally*, 149, 255–56.

96 MHI, WWII Survey, Box 1st Infantry Division, Raymond Huntoon survey.

97 See IHTP Collin, "L'attitude des resistants," 102; Boisse, *Jeunesse ardente*, 27.

98 Jean Ably, *Interprète volant: avec la 72e escadrille de liaison américaine, France-Allemagne, 1944–1945* (Paris: B. Arthaud, 1946), 22.

99 Pierre Douguet, *17 ans, résistant* (Brest: Télégramme, 2001), 173.

100 Curtis *Les forêts de la nuit*, 251.

101 Peyré, *Soldat chez les hommes*, 93–94, 139, 150.

102 Monod, *La région D*, 80–81. FFI leader of the Burgundy "D" region, Monod joined the First French Army in 1944 and was killed some months later in Germany.

103 In order to investigate the responses of these French men to their American liberators, I read scores of memoirs of French *deportés* and forced labor workers who were residing in German camps at the end of the war. Most of these testimonies have been written in the last two decades.

104 Marcel Conversy, *Quinze mois à Buchenwald* (Geneva: Éditions du Milieu du Monde, 1945), 192–93.

105 François Cochet and Maurice Vaisse, *Les exclus de la victoire: histoire de prisonniers de guerre, deportés, et STO* (Paris: S.P.M., 1992), 48.

106 Aimé Bonifas, *Prisoner 20–801: A French National in the Nazi Labor Camps* (Carbondale: Southern Illinois University Press, 1987). See also the touching liberation story of André Pontoizeau in *Dora-la-Mort: de la Résistance à la libération par Buchenwald et Dora* (Tours: C.O.S.O.R., 1947), 142.

107 Jacques Bureau, *Un soldat menteur* (Paris: R. Laffont, 1992), 349.

108 Paul Fourtier Berger, *Nuits bavaroises ou les désarrois d'un STO: chroniques 1943–45* (Romilly-sur-Seine: P. Fourtier Berger, 1999), 335. According to one ex-prisoner, the British were the same in their closed demeanors. See Paul Assens, Henri Henric, and Jean Raibaud, eds., *Témoins de la fin du IIIe Reich: des polytechniciens racontent* (Paris: L'Harmattan, 2004), 329.

109 André Nidub, *Quand les jours noirs proliféraient: ma jeunesse 1939–1945* (Paris: La Pensée Universelle, 1981), 308–9.

110 André Castex, *Au-delà du Rhin, 1943–1945* (Bidache: La Ronde, 1945), 95.

111 See Cochet and Vaisse, *Les exclus de la victoire*, 51.

112 Edouard Daladier, *Journal de captivité (1940–1945)* (Paris: Calmann-Lévy, 1991), 350.

113 Cochet and Vaisse, *Les exclus de la victoire*, 52.

114 Robert Lessafre, *Des bruyères d'Auvergne aux ronces du S.T.O.* (Paris: Les Lettres Libres, 1986), 184.

115 Georges Caussé, *Mémoires d'un tarnais S.T.O. en Allemagne, 1943–1945* (Toulouse: Graphi Midi-Pyrénées, 1997), 159.

116 Jean-Louis Foncine, *Un si long orage: chronique d'une jeunesse, les eaux vertes de la Flöha*, 2 vols. (Pouilly-sur-Loire: Héron Éditions, 1995), 2:278.

117 Bureau, *Un soldat menteur*, 349.

118 Caussé, *Mémoires d'un tarnais S.T.O.*, 159; see also Jean Damascène La Javie, *Prêtre ouvrier clandestin* (Paris: Éditions France-Empire, 1967), 194. On this issue, see also Patrice Arnaud, *Les STO: histoire des français requis en Allemagne nazie, 1942–1945* (Paris: CNRS Éditions, 2010,), 418.

119 Foncine, *Un si long orage*, 274.

120 Paul Finance, *Trois ans de ma vie, 1942 à 1945* (Riquewihr: La Petite Imprimerie, 1993), 117.

121 Jacques-Alain de Sédouy, *Une enfance bien-pensante sous l'occupation, 1940–1945* (Paris: Librairie Académique Perrin, 1998), 152.

122 Caussé, *Mémoires d'un tarnais S.T.O.*, 159.

123 Jean-Louis Querillhac, *J'étais STO* (Paris: Folio, 1991), 291. See also Lessafre, *Des bruyères d'Auvergne*, 190; Bernard Duneau, *Les insoumis du STO: épopée de la seconde guerre mondiale* (Alençon: Éditions des Vérités, 2005), 427.

124 André Michel, *Mes moires II: en liberté dans cette cage, en cage dans ces libertés* (Gentilly: A. Michel, 1995), 122.

125 Charles-Henri-Guy Bazin, *"Déporté du travail": à la BMW-Eisenach, 1943–1945* (Paris: Cubnezais, 1986), 351.

126 Brigitte Friang, *Regarde-toi qui meurs: 1943–1945* (Paris: R. Laffont, 1970), 307.

127 Michel, *Mes moires II*, 114; Raibaud and Henric, *Témoins de la fin du IIIe Reich*, 141, 312; Archives Départmentales de la Manche, Saint-Lô (hereafter ADM), 1366 W; Comité vérité historique, *Liberté 44, la Manche témoigne: de l'occupation à la libération; les Manchois se souviennent* (hereafter *MT*), Anonymous, "Le débarquement," 1017–18; Béatrice Poule, ed., *Cahiers de mémoire: vivre et survivre pendant la bataille de Normandie* (Caen: Conseil Général du Calvados, 1994), 76. In the secondary literature, see Schrijvers, *The Crash of Ruin*, 236.

128 André Chassaignon, *Retours vers la France: récits de la captivité* (Paris: Éditions Littéraires Artistiques, 1944), 153; René and Christian Taramini, *Villégiature en Thuringe: souvenirs d'un prisonnier de guerre* (Coeuvres-et-Valsery: Atelier Ressouvenances, 1999), 205–6.

129 Aimé Bonifas, *Prisoner 20-801: A French National in the Nazi Labor Camps* (Carbondale and Edwardsville: Southern Illinois University Press, 1987), 129.

130 Raibaud and Henric, *Témoins de la fin*, 329. See also Foncine, *Un si long orage*, 275; Caussé, *Mémoires d'un tarnais S.T.O.*, 159.

131 Conversy, *Quinze mois à Buchenwald*, 203.

132 Cochet and Vaisse, *Les exclus de la victoire*, 49.

133 Cochet and Vaisse, *Les exclus de la victoire*, 52; Robert Cardot, *L'abeille reste indomp-*

tée (Paris: Éditions des Écrivains, 2003), 103; Louis Eudier, *Notre combat de classe et de patriotes, 1934–1945* (Le Havre: L. Eudier, 2001), 122.

134   Cardot, *L'abeille reste indomptée*, 105.

135   Caussé, *Mémoires d'un tarnais S.T.O.*, 159. Jean-Pierre Ganter, *Une jeunesse heureuse assassiné* (Paris: La Pensée Universelle, 1994), 68.

136   Lessafre, *Des bruyères d'Auvergne*, 184.

137   Victor Dufaut, *La vie vient de l'ouest* (Paris: Promotion et Édition, 1969), 199. See also Foncine, *Un si long orage*, 275. Those prisoners lucky enough to be liberated by their own army were thankful for both its warmth of reception and its model of French manhood. See Caussé, *Mémoires d'un tarnais S.T.O.*, 160; Ganter, *Une jeunesse heureuse assassiné*, 68.

138   Bazin, *"Deporté du travail,"* 340–341.

139   Nidub, *Quand les jours noirs proliféraient*, 308–309.

140   Such women were called "DP" or "displaced person" girls. While sleeping with German women was considered fraternizing with the enemy, the GIs were free to cavort with "DP girls." See Stephen E. Ambrose, *Band of Brothers: E Company, 506th Regiment, 101st Airborne from Normandy to Hitler's Eagle's Nest* (New York: Simon and Schuster, 1992), 263.

141   Dufaut, *La vie vient de l'ouest*, 202–4.

142   Michel, *Mes moires II*, 113. See also Torrent, *La France américaine*, 231.

143   Dufaut, *La vie vient de l'ouest*, 199. See also Louis Le Bonniec, *Dans le vent de l'est, journal de route d'un déporté du travail* (Rennes: d'Oberthur, 1954), 238; Castex, *Au-delà du Rhin*, 230.

144   Léon Blum, *Le dernier mot* (Paris: Éditions Diderot, 1946), 88–89. Blum was a well-known politician who served as the French prime minister in 1936. No doubt his fame and status enhanced his treatment by the Americans.

145   Arnaud, *Les STOs*, 422.

146   Charles Joyon, *Qu'as-tu fait de ma jeunesse?* (Paris: Lacoste, 1957), 54.

147   Raibaud and Henric, *Témoins de la fin du IIIe Reich*, 352–53.

148   Michel Gerbeaux, *20 ans un deporté se souvient* (Chartres: M. Gerbeaux, 1965), 207. Some *deportés* claimed that the Russians took even longer to get displaced persons home. See, for example, Yannick Rodrigues, *Le STO en Vaucluse: une jeunesse dechirée* (Mazan: Études Comtadines, 2006), 153.

149   See Cochet and Vaisse, *Les exclus de la victoire*, 49–51; Duneau, *Les insoumis du STO*, 427; Michel, *Mes moires II*, 121; Jean-Charles, *Suivez le cancre* (Paris: Presses de la Cité, 1983), 105–6.

150   Bazin, *Deporté du travail*, 351. See also Querillac, *J'étais STO*, 291.

151   Cochet and Vaisse, *Les exclus de la victoire*, 52; La Javie, *Prêtre ouvrier*, 192.

152   Cochet and Vaisse, *Les exclus de la victoire*, 60.

153   Michel, *Mes moires II*, 121.

154   Oriot, *La fille du boulanger*, 378.

155   Finance, *Trois ans de ma vie*, 119–20.

156   Eudier, *Notre combat de classe*, 125. See also IHTP, ARC 116, untitled memoir of Michael Geoffrey, 33.

157   Torrent, *La France américaine*, 231–32.

158   Archives Nationales, Séries AJ 384, La gendarmerie nationale, synthèse pour la période du 15 janvier–15 fevrier 1945; ADMar, 161 W 323 Incidents franco-américains, rapports, 1944–46, news clip titled "Une délibération du Conseil Municipal" and

162 W 355 Rapports journaliers des relations avec les troupes (hereafter 162 W 355), undated report [August 1945]. See also Ludivine Hamel, "Les américains au Havre et dans sa région, 1944–1946: réalisations et impacts" (Mémoire de maîtrise d'histoire, Université du Havre, 2001), np; James Finucane, "What's Wrong with Our GIs Abroad?," *American Mercury*, February 1946, 195.

159 Les Archives de la Préfecture de Police (hereafter APP), BA 1822 Libération.

160 ADMar, 162 W 355, undated report [August 1945]. For two other similar incidents, see also 162 W 355, police reports dated 6 July 1945 and 27 July 1945.

161 Finucane, "What's Wrong with Our GIs Abroad?," 197.

162 Jean-Pierre Vittori, *Eux, les STO* (Paris: Temps Actuels, 1982), 216.

163 Finucane, "What's Wrong with Our GIs Abroad?," 195.

164 MHI, WWII Survey, Box 1st Infantry Division, Warren R. Eames survey.

165 Jacques Kayser, *Un journaliste sur le front de Normandie: Carnet de route juillet-août, 1944* (Paris: Arléa, 1991), 119, 164, 187. Kayser uses the word *filles* to refer to these women; *fille* is a term for a prostitute. See also "L'attitude populaire," *Journal de la Marne*, 21 September 1944; Irgang, *Etched in Purple*, 146–47; René Loisel, "Des liens avec trois GI's," *Havre libre*, 13 August 2003.

166 "Les réflexions de l'homme de la rue," *Journal de la Marne*, 24 June 1945.

167 ADMar, 162 W 355, letter dated 27 August 1945.

168 Pierre Aubéry, *Les américains au Havre* (Paris: La Bibliothèque Française, 1948), 38.

169 Ibid., 34–35, 85, 119.

170 See Morris's autobiography under the name Gilles Morris-Dumoulin, *Le forçat de l'Underwood* (Levallois-Perret: Éditions Manya, 1993), 66–68, 72; and his autobiographical novel, *Assassin, mon frère* (Monaco [Paris]: Éditions de Rocher, 1990), 10, 19–20, 107. The pseudonym "Morris" comes from "Camp Philip Morris," the GI camp where he worked. (Many of the GI camps in France were named after cigarette brands.)

171 Throughout Curzio Malaparte's *The Skin* (which became a best seller and was immediately translated into French), the Italian journalist explores how sexual relations between the GIs and Italian women both diminish Italian manhood and materialize American dominance. Malaparte describes "the virgin of Naples" who opens her legs for the price of a dollar. In long lines, the GIs queue to see her. When an American officer voices his disgust at the sight, his Italian companion angrily responds: "If you had lost the war there would be an American virgin on that bed instead of that poor Neapolitan girl." See *The Skin* (London: Alvin Redman Limited, 1952; orig. 1949), 60.

172 The GIs also did not respect the French police. See APP, BA 1822 Libération; ADC 21 W 16, Préfet report dated January to March 1945 and police report dated 5 March 1945; ADMar, 162 W 355 report dated 22 October 1945 and "Programme de mesures franco-américaines de Police."

Chapter 4

1 Pierre Aubéry, *Les américains au Havre* (Paris: La Bibliothèque Française, 1948), 14, 16–17. Aubéry was also a journalist for the local *Havre-éclair* in the years 1945 to 1946.

2 Ibid., 73, 77.

3 Gilles Morris, *Le forçat de l'Underwood* (Levallois-Perret: Éditions Manya, 1993), 74.

4 See T. J. Jackson Lears, *Fables of Abundance: A Cultural History of Advertising in America* (New York: Basic Books, 1994).

5 Philippe Roger, *L'ennemi américain: généalogie de l'antiaméricanisme français* (Paris: Éditions du Seuil, 2002), 359–60.

6 On wartime hardship, see Richard Vinen, *The Unfree French: Life under the Occupation* (New Haven, CT: Yale University Press, 2006), 223–24, chap. 7; Fabrice Grenard, *La France du marché noir, 1940–1949* (Paris: Éditions Payot, 2008), 227.

7 Jack Plano, *Fishhooks, Apples and Outhouses: Memories of the 1920s, 1930s, 1940s* (Kalamazoo, MI: Personality Press, 1991), 254.

8 John Gimlette, *Panther Soup: Travels through Europe in War and Peace* (New York: Alfred A. Knopf, 2008), 168–69.

9 For a similar situation in Japan, see Sarah Kovner, "Prostitution in Postwar Japan: Sex Workers, Servicemen, and Social Activists, 1945–1956" (PhD diss., Columbia University, 2004), 24–25; and Kovner, "Base Cultures: Sex Workers and Servicemen in Postwar Japan, *Journal of Asian Studies* 68, no. 3 (August 2009): 777–804.

10 Stephen E. Ambrose, *Citizen Soldiers: The U.S. Army from the Normandy Beaches to the Bulge to the Surrender of Germany, June 7, 1944–May 7, 1945* (New York: Simon and Schuster, 1997), 337.

11 Alan Moorehead, *Eclipse* (Paris: Coward-McCann, 1974), 112.

12 Grenard, *La France du marché noir*, 256, 258, 261–63.

13 For the origins of the black market in 1940, see Dominique Veillon, *Vivre et survivre en France, 1939–1947* (Paris: Éditions Payot, 1995), 478–79.

14 See Philippe Burrin, *France under the Germans: Collaboration and Compromise* (New York: New Press, 1996), 279–80.

15 Vinen, *The Unfree French*, 223–25.

16 Veillon, *Vivre et survivre*, 180.

17 On this transition, see Robert Mencherini, "Les américains à Marseille," in *Marseille et les américains, 1940–46*, ed. Musée d'Histoire de Marseille (Marseille: Musée d'Histoire de Marseille, 1996), 45.

18 Elizabeth Coquart, *La France des G.I.s: histoire d'un amour déçu* (Paris: Albin Michel, 2003), 68.

19 Ludivine Hamel, "Les Américains au Havre et dans sa région, 1944–1946: réalisations et impacts" (Université du Havre, Mémoire de Maîtrise d'histoire, 2001), interview with Max Bengston, np.

20 Archives Départementales de la Manche, Saint-Lô (hereafter ADM), 1366 W, Comité vérité historique, *Liberté 44, la Manche témoigne: de l'occupation à la libération; les manchois se souviennent* (hereafter MT), témoignage of Marie-Madeleine Jacqueline, 572.

21 Mémorial de Caen, Séries FN–France Normandie, FN 61 Trévières, "Américains-Normands-Omaha-1944," témoignage of Madame Renée Porrée, 9.

22 Simone Signoret, *La nostalgie n'est plus ce qu'elle était* (Paris: Éditions du Seuil), 82.

23 Christiane Delpierre, *Une enfance normande* (Le Coudray-Macouard: Cheminements, 1999), 150. See also ADM, MT, Carnet de Monsieur Albert Allix, 11; témoignage of Monsieur Yves Boudier, 101.

24 "Calvados was the true coin of exchange," noted Norman Marcel Leveel, author of *Rails et haies: la double bataille d'Elle et de Lison* (Marigny: Éditions Eurocibles,

2004), 141. See also René Herval, *Bataille de Normandie: récits de témoins recueillis et présentés par René Herval*, 2 vols. (Paris: Éditions de "Notre temps," 1947), 1:183; Hilary Kaiser, *Veteran Recall: Americans in France Remember the War* (Paris: H. Kaiser, 1994), 79.

25 US Army US Military History Institute, Carlisle Barracks (hereafter MHI), World War II Veterans Survey Collection (hereafter WWII Survey), Box 71st Infantry Division, David Ichelson, "I Was There," 61. On the purchase of eggs, see also John Toole, *Battle Diary* (Missoula, MT: Vigilante Press, 1978), 19.

26 Peter A. Belpulsi, *A G.I.'s View of World War II* (Salem, MO: Globe Publishers, 1997), 94.

27 Lawrence Cane, *Fighting Fascism in Europe: The World War II Letters of an American Veteran of the Spanish Civil War* (New York: Fordham University Press, 2003), 90–91.

28 Service Historique de la Gendarmerie Nationale, Vincennes (hereafter SHGN), 76E6 Compagnie de la Seine-Inférieur à Rouen, registres de correspondance courante au départ (hereafter 76E6), report dated 19 October 1944. See also 76E6, report dated 2 August 1945; and 76E 113 Section du Havre, registres de correspondance courante au départ (R/2), report dated 10 August 1945.

29 MHI, WWII Survey, Box 84th Infantry Division, Frank Freese, "Private Memories of World War II (A Small Piece of a Big War)," 17.

30 MHI, WWII Survey, Box 5th Infantry Division, Mark Goodman, "Unit History of Company A," 48.

31 Janice Holt Giles, *The G.I. Journal of Sergeant Giles* (Boston: Houghton-Mifflin Company, 1965), 80.

32 Ken Parker, *Civilian at War* (Traverse City, MI: Author, 1984), 94; Annette Tapert, ed., *Lines of Battle: Letters from American Servicemen, 1941–1945* (New York: New York Times Books, 1987), 165. See also Toole, *Battle Diary*, 19.

33 Ernie Pyle, *Brave Men* (New York: Henry Holt and Company, 1944), 285.

34 Belpulsi, *G.I.'s View*, 94. On eggs as a gift, see also Edward K. Rogers, *Doughboy Chaplain* (Boston: Meador, 1946), 158.

35 Béatrice Poule, ed., *Cahiers de mémoire: vivre et survivre pendant la bataille de Normandie* (Caen: Conseil Général du Calvados, 1994), 28.

36 Claude Boisse, *Jeunesse ardente, 1943–1945* (Montségur-sur-Lauzon: C. Boisse, 1997), 36.

37 Grenard, *La France du marché noir*, 261. Grenard notes that officials were too "intimidated by their liberators" to actually regulate or stop the barter.

38 Vinen, *The Unfree French*, 225; Veillon, *Vivre et survivre*, 178.

39 MHI, WWII Survey, Box 71st Infantry Division, David Ichelson, "I Was There," 93.

40 Richard Kluger, *Ashes to Ashes: America's Hundred-Year Cigarette War, the Public Health, and the Unabashed Triumph of Philip Morris* (New York: Alfred A. Knopf, 1996), 112–13.

41 Hamel, "Les Américains au Havre," interview with Mr. Adam, np.

42 MHI, WWII Survey, Box 1st Infantry Division, Leroy Stewart, "Hurry Up and Wait," 49.

43 On the cigarette camps, see Jean-Claude Marquis, *Les camps "cigarettes"* (Rouen: Éditions Médianes, 1994); Valérie Moulin, Daniel Baccara, and Jean-Michel Harel,

Le Havre 16th Port of Embarkation, Northern District Normandy Base Section (Le Havre: Éditions USST, 1997), 28–29.

44 Association historique et culturelle de Montbourg et son canton, *Montebourg se souvient, 6 juin–19 juin, 1944* (Condé-sur-Noireau: Éditions Corlet, 1994), 55.

45 MHI, WWII Survey, Box 36th Infantry Division, Anthony Harlinski, "The Purple Road Back," 8.

46 MHI, WWII Survey, Box 1st Infantry Division, Robert Ryan survey.

47 Abbe H. Dufour, *La guerre chez nous: souvenirs, Le Lorey, 1940–1944* (Coutances: Imprimerie OCEPS, 1986), 43.

48 Paul Boesch, *Road to Huertgen: Forest in Hell* (Houston, TX: Gulf Publishing Company, 1962), 73.

49 *L'avenir du Nord de l'Aisne*, 10 September 1944. See also Jacques Pernet and Michel Hubert, *1944 il était une fois . . . les américains* (Reims: Éditions de l'Atelier Graphique, 1994), 40–41.

50 ADM, 1366 W, *MT*, témoignage of Christianne Denis, 249.

51 ADM, 1366 W, *MT*, témoignage of Madame Dold-Lomet, 284.

52 ADM, 1366 W, *MT*, Jacques Nicolle, "J'avais quinze ans," 811. Nicolle started to smoke when the soldiers arrived, giving it up definitively a year later. He put it this way: "my smoking was historical."

53 MHI, The John J. Maginnis Papers, untitled memoir, 227–28.

54 Michel Béchet, *L'attente: (Overlord) vécu à cent kilomètres du front* (Montsûrs: Résiac, 1994), 85.

55 Paul Finance, *Trois ans de ma vie, 1942 à 1945* (Riquewihr: La Petite Imprimerie, 1993), 117.

56 Jacques-Alain de Sédouy, *Une enfance bien-pensante sous l'Occupation, 1940–1945* (Paris: Librairie Académique Perrin, 1998), 171. See also Bernard Festoc, *La vie à Airel et Saint-Fromont pendant la seconde guerre mondiale* (Périers: Imprimerie X. Garlan, 1994), 89.

57 Danièle Philippe, *J'avais quinze ans . . . en juin 44 en Normandie* (Paris: Éditions France-Empire, 1994), 193. For the same situation in Reims, see Georges Clause, *Reims autour du 7 mai 1945* (Nîmes: Christian Lacour, 1997), 329.

58 Keith Winston, *V . . . -Mail: Letters of a World War II Combat Medic* (Chapel Hill, NC: Algonquin Books, 1985), 107.

59 *Ouest-France*, 9 August 1944.

60 *Journal de la Marne*, 22 August 1945.

61 Archives Départmentales de la Marne (hereafter ADMar), 130 W 9, Rapports mensuels sur la situation générale adressées par le Sous-Préfet au Préfet septembre–décembre 1944, report dated 11 September 1944.

62 *Le Franc-tireur*, 28 August 1944.

63 *Havre-éclair*, 12 August 1945. See also Jacques Kayser, *Un journaliste sur le front de Normandie: carnet de route juillet-aôut 1944* (Paris: Arléa, 1991), 44, 129.

64 Walter Brown, *Up Front with U.S.* (np: W. Brown, 1979), 563.

65 MHI, WWII Survey, Box 7th Infantry Division, John Earle, Letter to his mother, 9 March 1945. See also Box 36th Infantry Division, Harlinski, "The Purple Road Back," 9.

66 MHI, WWII Survey, Box 1st Infantry Division, Karl Clarkson, "The Story of G. I. Joe (Karl): A Combat Infantryman in World War II," 14.

67 William M. McConahey, MD, *Battalion Surgeon* (Rochester, MN: Author, 1966), 176.

68 Peter Belpulsi, *A GI's View of World War II* (Salem, MA: Globe Publishers, 1997), 174. See also Thomas Saylor, *Remembering the Good War: Minnesota's Greatest Generation* (Minneapolis: Minnesota Historical Society Press, 2005), 246.

69 Winston, *V . . . -Mail*, 178.

70 National Archives and Records Administration (hereafter NARA), Record Group 331, Records of Allied Operation and Occupation, Headquarters, World War II (SHAEF) (hereafter RG 331), Entry 47, General Staff Divisions, G-5 Division, Secretariat, Numeric File, August 1943–July 1945 (hereafter Entry 47), Box 28, Civil Affairs Miscellaneous Reports, report dated 27 October 1944.

71 Grenard, *France du marché noir*, 261.

72 SHGN, 76E162, Section de Rouen, registres de correspondance courante au départ, reports dated 15 November 1944 and 15 December 1944. In SHGN, 76E6 Compagnie de la Seine-Inférieur à Rouen, registres de correspondance courante au départ, see reports dated 19 October 1944 and 2 August 1945. See also SHGN, 76E112, Section d'Elbeuf, registres de correspondance confidentielle au départ (R/4), report dated 13 October 1944; and 76E113, Section du Havre, registres de correspondance courante au départ (R/2), report dated 10 August 1945.

73 Jack Capell, *Surviving the Odds* (Claremont, CA: Regina Books, 2007), 212.

74 Marc Hillel, *Vie et moeurs des GI's en Europe, 1942–1947* (Paris: Balland, 1981), 156.

75 For Le Havre, see Hamel, "Les américains au Havre," interview with Max Bengston," np; Aubéry, *Les américains*, 52–54; Moulin et al., *Le Havre 16th Port of Embarkation*, 31, 35. For Reims, see Clause, *Reims autour du 7 mai*, 391. Marseilles was the other port town that became a major center for black market activity.

76 NARA, RG 331, Entry 47, Box 28, Civil Affairs Miscellaneous Reports, report dated 27 October 1944. The MPs established a system of checks at the main outlets of Paris, where a test was made of the gas in the tank. If the car was found to be running on Allied gas supplies, it was confiscated for a month, and its owners were prosecuted. About 10 percent of cars tested were caught with Allied gas and prosecuted.

77 On the subject of African American soldiers and the black market, see Aubéry, *Les américains*, 34–38. For German POWs, see Laroque Lucie, "Le Ravitaillement des Havrais de 1939 à 1949" (Université du Havre, Maîtrise d'histoire contemporaine, 2001), 105.

78 Lucie, "Le Ravitaillement des Havrais," 105–6.

79 *Ce soir*, 8 September 1944. For a similar situation, see *Journal de la Marne*, 6 September 1944.

80 The GIs also began to engage in trickery around the sale of cigarettes. Just as they were leaving a train station, for example, they would sell cigarette cartons emptied of their contents and filled with sawdust. As the train left the station, they would get a big laugh watching enraged French men discover their error. See Andrew A. Thomson, "'Over There' 1944/45, Americans in the Liberation of France: Their Perceptions of, and Relations with France and the French" (PhD thesis, University of Kent at Canterbury, 1996), 187; and also Hillel, *Vie et moeurs*, 156.

81 *112 Gripes about the French* (Fontenay-aux-Roses: US Army, 1945), 21, 68–69.

82 MHI, WWII Survey, Box 71st Infantry Division, Earle, letter with unclear date [1945], np. See also MHI, Payne Templeton Papers, "A Complete Change of Life—into World War II," 63.

83 MHI, WWII Survey, Box 71st Infantry Division, James J. Coletti, "It Made a Man

Out of You," np. For other commentaries on the outrageousness of the prices, see Judy Barrett Litoff, David C. Smith, Barbara Wooddall Taylor, and Charles E. Taylor, *Miss You: The World War II Letters of Barbara Wooddall Taylor and Charles E. Taylor* (Athens: University of Georgia Press, 1990), 236, 240.

84 MHI, WWII Survey, Box 71st Infantry Division, Ichelson, "I Was There," 63–64.

85 Harry L. Coles and Albert K. Weinberg, *Civil Affairs: Soldiers Become Governors* (Washington, DC: Center of Military History US Army, 2004), 747–48.

86 Robert Adleman and George Walton, *The Champagne Campaign* (Boston: Little Brown, 1969), 225.

87 See MHI, WWII Survey, Box 1st Infantry Division, Leroy Stewart, "Hurry Up and Wait," 76.

88 Louis Guilloux, *Ok, Joe* (Chicago: University of Chicago Press, 2003; orig. 1973), 81.

89 Aubéry, *Les américains*, 34–35.

90 G. Morris, *Assasin, mon frère* (Paris: Éditions de Rocher, 1990), 19–20; Morris, *Le forçat de l'Underwood*, 71.

91 Archives Nationales, F1a 4023, Rapports du commissaire de la République, report dated 15 June 1945. See also Mencherini, "Les américains à Marseille."

92 Archives de la Préfecture de la Police, Paris (hereafter APP), BA1822, reports dated 4 June 1945 and 1 July 1945. See also Michel Renouard and Manonmani Restif, eds., *Les malouins et la Libération: combats et vie quotidienne* (Saint-Malo: Éditions Cristel, 2006), 192.

93 MHI, WWII Survey, Box 1st Infantry Division, Warren R. Eames survey. The historian Louis Chevalier has noted how prostitutes were rich with cigarettes and dollars in this period. See his *Les ruines de Subure: Montmartre de 1939 aux années 80* (Paris: Éditions Robert Laffont, 1985), 82.

94 MHI, WWII Survey, Box 71st Infantry Division, Ichelson, "I Was There," 64.

95 See Leonard D. Heaton, *Communicable Diseases Transmitted through Contact or by Unknown Means*, vol. 5 of *Preventive Medicine in World War II*, 9 vols., (Washington, DC: Office of the Surgeon General, Department of the Army, 1960), 5:245; Hillel, *Vie et moeurs*, 147.

96 MHI, WWII Survey, Box 18th Infantry Division, Bert Damsky, "Shipping Order___APO___," 45.

97 MHI, WWII Survey, Box 71st Infantry Division, William Meissner survey.

98 McConahey, *Battalion Surgeon*, 174.

99 Peter Schrijvers, *The Crash of Ruin: American Combat Soldiers in Europe during World War II* (New York: New York University Press, 1998), 182.

100 MHI, WWII Survey, Box 71st Infantry Division, Ichelson, "I Was There" 93–94.

101 Nat Frankel and Larry Smith, *Patton's Best: An Informal History of the 4th Armored Division* (New York: Hawthorne Books, 1978), 77.

102 Brown, *Up Front*, 562; Gimlette, *Panther Soup*, 27.

103 MHI, Chester Hansen Collection, diary entry dated 8 September 1944.

104 ADM, Séries 3 U, Justice, Fonds du Tribunal de première instance de Cherbourg Procès-verbal (hereafter Séries 3 U), report dated 14 November 1944. See also APP, Registres de commissariats, CB39.98, Entry 1220.

105 Robert Peters, *For You, Lili Marlene* (Madison: University of Wisconsin Press, 1995), 55. See also MHI, WWII Survey, Box 9th Infantry Division, Chester Jordan, "Bull Sessions: World War II, Company K, 47th Inf., 9th Infantry Division from Normandy to Remagen," 87–88.

106 In September 1945, the American provost marshal for Normandy uncovered a large-scale black market operation including rooms of American items to be traded for sexual services. See SHGN, 76E 200, Brigade territoriale de Cany-Barville, registres de correspondance courante au départ, report dated 25 September 1945. A similar operation was discovered in Reims, where gasoline sold by German prisoners was used to smuggle French prostitutes into POW camps. See Jacques Pernet and Michel Hubert, *Reims: chronique des années de guerre* (Saint-Cyr-sur-Loire: Éditions Alan Sutton, 2003), 73.

107 Aramais Hovsepian was the exception when he wrote his father that the French whores were "real nice. No gold-diggers. Just girls knowing what men like us need." See *Your Son and Mine* (New York: Duell, Sloan and Pearce, 1950), 80.

108 Peters, *For You, Lili Marlene*, 58.

109 MHI, WWII Survey, Box 71st Infantry Division, Ichelson, "I Was There," 198–99.

110 Saylor, *Remembering the Good War*, 246.

111 MHI, John McGinnis Papers, untitled memoir, 58–60.

112 *112 Gripes about the French*, 43.

113 Litoff et al., *Miss You*, 204

114 Plano, *Fishhooks, Apples and Outhouses*, 252

115 MHI, WWII Survey, Box 18th Infantry Division, Damsky, "Shipping Order," 38–39.

116 *112 Gripes about the French*, 43.

117 *Havre libre*, 13 August 2003. See also Aubéry, *Les américains en France*, 38.

118 Gimlette, *Panther Soup*, 159.

119 MHI, Chester Hansen Collection, diary entry dated 20 September 1944.

120 Frank Costigliola, "The Nuclear Family: Tropes of Gender and Pathology in the Western Alliance," *Diplomatic History* 21, no. 2 (Spring 1997): 170.

121 Quoted in Kenneth Rose, *Myth and the Greatest Generation: A Social History of Americans in World War II* (New York: Routledge, 2008), 36.

122 MHI, WWII Survey, Box 71st Infantry Division, Ichelson, "I Was There," 62.

123 Jacques-Pierre-Georges Pénaud, *La Prostitution (vers un contrôle humain)* (Bordeaux: Imprimerie Librairie Delmas, 1945), 117.

124 *Ouest-France*, 9 August 1944. See also *Havre-éclair*, 6 June 1945.

125 *Journal de la Marne*, 24 January 1945.

126 ADMar, 162 W 359, Rapports sur la prostitution, letter dated 5 October 1945, and letter dated 13 October 1945.

127 ADMar, 162 W 359, letter dated 21 September 1944.

128 Alfred Scheiber, *Un Fléau social: le problème médico-policier de la prostitution* (Paris: Librairie de Médicis, 1946), 195.

129 APP, DB409, Articles de presse, affaires diverses, imprimés, cartes de visites (hereafter DB409), *Qui? Police l'hebdomadaire des faits divers*, 9 September 1946.

130 APP, DB409, *Qui? Police l'hebdomadaire des faits divers*, 31 July 1947

131 Jean-Charles Bertier, *La Prostitution à Bordeaux de 1939 à 1945, son contrôle sanitaire* (Bordeaux: Imprimerie Librairie Delmas, 1945), 12. For the same fears in the Marne, see ADMar, 162 W 359, report dated 13 April 1945.

132 *France libre*, 5 September 1944; and see also *France libre*, 27 September 1944.

133 *Le populaire*, 9 September 1944.

134 *Marie-Claire*, 17 November 1944.

135 Lucie Aubrac, *Cette exigeante liberté* (Paris: Éditions de l'Archipel, 1997), 153.

136 APP, DB409, *Qui? Police l'hebdomadaire des faits divers*, 13 October 1946.

137 John Dower, *Embracing Defeat: Japan in the Wake of World War II* (New York: W. W. Norton, 1999), 135–36.

138 *Journal de la Marne*, 24 June, 25 June, and 2 July 1945.

139 Scheiber, *Fléau*, 130–31.

140 As the historian K. H. Adler has put it, prostitution "became a metaphor for the uncertain status of national identity." See K. H. Adler, "Reading National Identity: Gender and Prostitution during the Occupation," *Modern and Contemporary France* 7, no. 1 (1999): 50, 52. See also Adler, *Jews and Gender in Liberation France* (Cambridge: Cambridge University Press, 2003), 42–44.

141 Scheiber, *Fléau*, 125. On this issue, see also Sarah Fishman, *We Will Wait: Wives of French Prisoners of War* (New Haven, CT: Yale University Press, 1991), 47–50; Fabrice Virgili, *Naître ennemi: les enfants de couples franco-allemands nés pendant la Seconde Guerre mondiale* (Paris: Éditions Payot, 2009), 71–73.

142 Aubéry, *Les américains*, 56. *112 Gripes about the French*, 46, admonished soldiers: "Don't judge France by the Montmartre: the Montmartre *caters* to foreign tourists in search of the risqué."

143 *Le figaro*, 15 September 1944.

144 *Havre-éclair*, 6 June 1945. See also *Journal de la Marne*, 21 September 1944.

145 Vercors, "A Plea for France: A Nation Weak and Uncertain Needs Our Understanding," *Life*, 6 November 1944. The image is not in the text. Instead, *Life* editors chose to illustrate the article with a photograph of a woman praying in a church, her hand covering her eyes in contrition.

Chapter 5

1 On the sometimes violent treatment of prostitutes at the Liberation, see Louis Chevalier, *Les ruines de Subure: Montmartre de 1939 aux années 80* (Paris: Éditions Robert Laffont, 1985), 84. In *La prostitution en Touraine à l'époque des maisons closes (1920–1946)*, 2 vols. (Chambray-lès-Tours: C.L.D., 1999–2001), 1:271, Claude Croubois argues that the FFI did not go after the professional prostitutes.

2 Marie-Thérèse [Cointré], *Histoire d'une prostituée* (Paris: Éditions Gonthier, 1964), 70–73. For prostitutes at the Liberation, see also US Army Military History Institute, Carlisle Barracks (hereafter MHI), World War II Veterans Survey Collection (hereafter WWII Survey), Box 9th Infantry Division, Chester Jordan, "Bull Sessions: World War II, Company K, 47th Inf., 9th Infantry Division from Normandy to Remagen," 84–85.

3 For the characterization of Paris as the "brothel of Europe," see Alfred Scheiber, *Un fléau social: le problème médico-policier de la prostitution* (Paris: Librairie de Médicis, 1946), 115. For Paris as the favored destination of American GIs, see Judy Barrett Litoff, David C. Smith, Barbara Wooddall Taylor, and Charles E. Taylor, *Miss You: The World War II Letters of Barbara Wooddall Taylor and Charles E. Taylor* (Athens: University of Georgia Press, 1990), 147. The other major destination for GIs on leave was Nice. According to Harvey Levenstein, *We'll Always Have Paris: American Tourists in France since 1930* (Chicago: University of Chicago Press, 2004), 79, six thousand GIs a week spent leaves there by the end of the war.

4 MHI, WWII Survey, Box 99th Infantry Division, Roger Foehringer, untitled memoir, 34.

5 MHI, WWII Survey, Box 99th Infantry Division, Casmir Rompala, untitled memoir, 47. Leonard D. Heaton, *Communicable Diseases Transmitted through Contact or by Unknown Means*, vol. 5 of *Preventive Medicine in World War II*, 9 vols. (Washington, DC: Office of the Surgeon General, Department of the Army, 1960), 5:245.

6 *Stars and Stripes*, 27 October 1944; Walter Brown, *Up Front with U.S.* (Oakland, ME: Author, 1979), 558–59; Robert Peters, *For You, Lili Marlene* (Madison: University of Wisconsin Press, 1995), 58.

7 Litoff et al., *Miss You*, 240.

8 Brown, *Up Front with U.S.*, 561.

9 Peter Belpulsi, *A G.I.'s View of World War II* (Salem, MO: Globe Publishers. 1997), 173. See also MHI, Payne Templeton Papers, "A Complete Change of Life—into World War II," 32.

10 *Défense de la France*, 13 September 1944. MHI, WWII Survey, Box 28th Infantry Division, Shapiro, "Memoirs of Murray Shapiro," np, and Box 1st Infantry Division, Bert Damsky, "Shipping Order___APO___," 38.

11 *How to See Paris: For the Soldiers of the Allied Armies* (Paris: Commissariat Général au Tourisme, 1945?), 32. See Bibliothèque Historique de la Ville de Paris, Séries 30, Fonds actualités, Box 35, Guerre 39–45.

12 Belpulsi, *A G.I.'s View*, 174.

13 Wisconsin Veterans Museum, Oral History Collection, OH74, Transcript of an oral history interview with William C. Brunsell, 1994. See also Jack Capell, *Surviving the Odds* (Claremont, CA: Regina Books, 2007), 213.

14 Charles Whiting, *The Battle of Hurtgen Forest: The Untold Story of a Disastrous Campaign* (New York: Orion Books, 1989), 64.

15 The American Expeditionary Forces served in the First World War. Omar Bradley, *A Soldier's Story* (New York: Modern Library, 1995), 384.

16 Paul Fussell, *The Boy's Crusade: The American Infantry in Northwestern Europe, 1944–1945* (New York: Modern Library, 2005), 39.

17 Janice Holt Giles, *The G.I. Journal of Sergeant Giles* (Boston: Houghton-Mifflin Company, 1965), 85. See also Paul Boesch, *Road to Heurtgen: Forest in Hell* (Houston, TX: Gulf Publishing Company, 1962), 103.

18 William M. McConahey, MD, *Battalion Surgeon* (Rochester, MN: Author, 1966), 176.

19 See speech of M. Amiot in *Bulletin municipal officiel de la ville de Paris*, "Débats des assemblées de la ville de Paris et du département de la Seine, Conseil Municipal de Paris, séance du 17 déc., 1945."

20 *Stars and Stripes*, 6 March 1945.

21 Whiting, *Battle of Hurtgen Forest*, 66.

22 For the case of Reims, for example, see Archives Départmentales de la Marne (hereafter ADMar) 162 W 359, Rapports sur la prostitution (hereafter 162 W 359), letter dated 15 April 1945; 16 W 268, Affaires réservées: incidents avec les troupes alliées, report dated 26 June 1945; 16 W 266, Relations avec les autorités alliées, notes et correspondance, report dated 9 August 1945; and 16 W 323, Incidents franco-américain, rapports 1944–46 (hereafter 16 W 323), report dated 26 June 1945.

23 John Gimlette, *Panther Soup: Travels in Europe in War and Peace* (New York: A. A. Knopf, 2008), 158.

24 For a clear summary of the French system, see Jacques-Pierre-Georges Pénaud, *La prostitution (vers un contrôle humain)* (Bordeaux: Delmas, 1945), 13–14. The classic work on the history of French prostitution is Alain Corbin, *Women for Hire: Prostitution and Sexuality in France after 1850* (Cambridge, MA: Harvard University Press, 1990.) For this period, see also Insa Meinin, *Wehrmacht et prostitution sous l'Occupation* (Paris: Éditions Payot, 2006); K. H. Adler, "Reading National Identity: Gender and Prostitution during the Occupation," *Modern and Contemporary France* 7, no. 1 (1999): 47–57; Alphonse Boudard, *La fermeture: 13 avril 1946: la fin des maisons closes* (Paris: R. Laffont, 1986); Fabienne Jamet, *One two two* (Paris: Olivier Orban, 1975).

25 Archives de la Préfecture de la Police, Paris (hereafter APP), DB409, *Libération soir*, 27 September 1946; Speech of Amiot, *Bulletin municipal officiel*; Archives Municipales de la Ville du Havre (hereafter AMH)), FC I1, 49-2, "SOS à la santé publique, communication du Docteur Abel Lahille sur la prostitution." See also National Archives and Records Administration (hereafter NARA), Record Group 331, Records of Allied Operation and Occupation, Headquarters, World War II (SHAEF) (hereafter RG 331), General Staff Divisions, G-5 Division, Secretariat, Numeric File, August 1943–July 1945, Entry 47 (hereafter Entry 47), Box 31, memo dated 21 February 1945.

26 For the persistence of the French system in the twentieth century, see Molly McGregor Watson, "The Trade in Women: 'White Slavery' and the French Nation" (PhD thesis, Stanford University, 2000); and Michelle Rhodes, "'No Safe Women': Prostitution, Masculinity, and Disease in France during the Great War" (PhD thesis: University of Iowa, 2001).

27 On these three houses of prostitution, see APP, DB408, *Paris villages*, no. 9 (1985): 40–55.

28 Meinin, *Wehrmacht et prostitution*,112. On the Japanese system of prostitution, see Yoshiaki Yoshimi, *Comfort Women: Sexual Slavery in the Japanese Military during World War II* (New York: Columbia University Press, 2000).

29 Meinen, *Wehrmacht et prostitution*, 142–48, 151. We don't know how many women were actually prosecuted under this law. In *Le vice ou la vertu: Vichy et les politiques de la sexualité* (Toulouse: Presses Universitaires du Mirail, 2005), 232, Cyril Olivier argues that regulations were put in place after an explosion of clandestine prostitution at the beginning of the war.

30 Philippe Aziz, *Tu trahiras sans vergogne* (Paris: Éditions Fayard, 1970), 271.

31 For an example of how this custom prevented the French police from entering into a room, see APP, BA1822, *Libération*, undated report signed by policemen René Lhermite, and Pierre Bihan.

32 Roxanne Pitt, *The Courage of Fear* (New York: Duell, Sloan and Pearce, 1957), 75–76. See also John Costello, *Virtue under Fire: How World War Two Changed Our Social and Sexual Attitudes* (Boston: Little Brown, 1985), 218.

33 For women who did compulsory labor in Germany, see K. H. Adler, "Reading National Identity," 53.

34 For the bombing of Hamburg, see Jörg Friedrich, *The Fire: The Bombing of Germany, 1940–1945* (New York: Columbia University Press, 2006), 165–68.

35 Corbin, *Women for Hire*, 343, 347.
36 Speech of Marthe Richard, *Bulletin municipal officiel*. For the diminution of the legal system in the Marne, see ADMar, 161 W 323, report dated 31 August 1945; and 162 W 359, report dated 2 July 1945 and charts titled "Dénombrement des maisons de tolérance."
37 APP, DB409, *Libération soir*, 28 September 1946.
38 Boudard, *La fermeture*, 37–38; Speech of Marthe Richard in *Bulletin municipal officiel de la ville de Paris*; APP, DB409, *Libération soir*, 2 October 1946.
39 For this Marthe Richard earned the nickname "la veuve qui clôt" after the *maison de champagne* Veuve Cliquot. See http://fr.wikipedia.org/wiki/Marthe_Richard.
40 The story is told by Andy Rooney in *My War* (New York: Public Affairs, 1995), 215.
41 MHI, WWII Survey, Box 71st Infantry Division, David Ichelson, "I Was There," 65. See also MHI, WWII Survey, Box 1st Infantry Division, Damsky, "Shipping Order," 38–39.
42 Heaton, *Communicable Diseases*, 246; Costello, *Virtue under Fire*, 247. For the segregation of brothels in Cherbourg, see Archives Départmentales de la Manche (hereafter ADM), Rapports américains, 13 num 2521.
43 AMH, FC II 49-2, "Prostitution, conférence tenue à la mairie du Havre le 9 octobre 1945."
44 For some of the problems of the system in 1944–45, see Paul Reboux, *Le guide galant* (Paris: Éditions Raoul Solar, 1953), 67; Adolphe Pinard, "De la propagation des maladies vénériennes," in *Les scandales de la prostitution réglementée*, ed. Paul Gemähling et al. (Paris: Éditions de l'Union Temporaire, 1938), 37; Marie-Thérèse, *Histoire d'une prostituée*, 84–85; René Delpêche, *Les dessous de Paris: souvenirs vécus par l'ex-inspecteur principal de la brigade mondaine Louis Métra* (Paris: Les Éditions du Scorpion, 1955), 153.
45 See MHI, John J. Maginnis Papers, untitled memoir, 224.
46 NARA, RG 331, Entry 47, Box 31, report dated 21 February 1945. In the French sources, see ADMar, 130 W 11, Rapports mensuels sur la situation générale adressés par le Sous-Préfet, letter dated 28 August 1945.
47 On the *abattoirs*, see Boudard, *La fermeture*, 31, 127; Maxence van der Meersch, *Femmes à l'encan* (Paris: Éditions Albin Michel, 1945), 20–22; Reboux, *Le guide galant*, 68.
48 Pinard, "De la propagation des maladies vénériennes," 36. See also Marthe Richard's condemnation of the *abbattoirs* in *Bulletin municipal officiel*.
49 Van der Meersch, *Femmes à l'encan*, 20.
50 Pinard, "De la propagation des maladies vénériennes," 36.
51 Marie-Thérèse, *Histoire d'une prostituée*, 78–79. See also Scheiber, *Fléau*, 187. In the secondary literature, see Jane Mersky Leder, *Thanks for the Memories: Love, Sex and World War II* (Westport, CT: Praeger Publishers, 2006), 121.
52 Chevalier, *Les ruines de subure*, 81–82; Leder, *Thanks for the Memories*, 121.
53 Boudard, *La fermeture*, 139.
54 NARA, RG 331, Entry 100 Special Staff, Headquarters Command, Decimal File, 1944–45 (hereafter Entry 100), Boxes 40, 41.
55 Registres d'écrou at La Petite Roquette in 1945 denote several *souteneurs* who stated their profession as "gérante hôtel" or "hôtelière" or "employée d'hôtel." See Archives de Paris (hereafter AP), 1433 W 47 1945, 166, 252, 399. On the *hôtels*

de passe, see also APP, DB408, "La ruine des tauliers"; Delpêche, *Les dessous de Paris*, 159.

56 Scheiber, *Fléau*, 183.

57 For the use of hotel bars and cafés, see Scheiber, *Fléau*, 184; NARA, RG 331, Entry 100, Boxes 40, 41.

58 For a prostitute who lived in a hotel, see also APP, A 1949/1 (H.428.877). Out of 145 arrest reports on prostitutes recorded in APP, CB 39.98, 39ème commissariat de police du quartier de la porte Saint-Martin, 31 October 1944–22 October 1945 (hereafter CB 39.98) and APP, CB 10.43, 10ème commissariat de police des Enfants Rouges, June 1945–October 1945 (hereafter CB 10.43), 21.4 percent of the women were homeless and resorted to hotels for their domicile. Others said they lived with friends or relatives; still others gave a permanent address outside of Paris.

59 Corbin, *Women for Hire*, 343; Adler, "Reading National Identity," 51. In *We Will Wait: Wives of French Prisoners of War* (New Haven, CT: Yale University Press, 1991), 47–50, Sarah Fishman argues that French officials provided high numbers of married prostitutes as a ploy to get better allocations for wives of French POWs when they faced resistance from the minister of finances.

60 *Bulletin municipal officiel*. See also Archives Nationales, Séries AN F^{1}a 4023, report of 15 June 1945.

61 APP, BA 1822, Libération, report dated 1 July 1945.

62 To sketch a profile of the Parisian prostitute at this time, I examined *registres d'écrou* at La Petite Roquette, a common prison for prostitutes, as well as a sample of police arrest records. See AP, 1443 W 45, no. 1-603, 1945 (30 January–18 April); 1433 W 46, no. 1-903, 1945 (18 April–31 July); 1443 W 47, no. 1-603, 1945 (31 July–15 September); 1443 W 48, no. 10600, 1945 (15 September–3 November). For similar results in the police records, see APP, CB 39.98, 31 October 31 1944–22 October 1945; and APP, CB 10.43, June 1945–October 1945. Of course, women could have been married and not reported that fact to the police. At the same time, the figures roughly match Scheiber's profile of prostitutes before the war in 1936 (*Fléau*, 27). See also Croubois, *Prostitution en Touraine*, 1:125, where he also argues that single prostitutes outnumbered married ones roughly two to one.

63 See APP, CB 10.43, June 1945–October 1945; CB 39.98. For the case of Normandy, see Archives Départmentales du Calvados (hereafter ADC), 726 W 16 865 Prostitution, police report dated 22 December 1945. For the Marne, see ADMar, 162 W 359, letter dated 25 June 1945; report dated 2 July 1945.

64 NARA, RG 331, Entry 100, Boxes 40, 41.

65 AP, Registres d'écrou, La Petite Roquette, 1433 W 45, 1945 (30 January–18 April); 1433 W 46, no. 1-903, 1945 (18 April–31 July); 1433 W 47, 1945 (31 July–15 September); 1433 W 48, 1945 (5 September–3 November). In the provinces, the situation was much the same. For the Marne, for example, see ADMar, 8 U 197, Tribunal civil de Châlons-sur-Marne, 1945; 162 W 359, report dated 2 July 1945.

66 Paul Gemähling, "Le proxénétisme en France, son organisation, les moyens de le combattre," in Gemähling et al., *Les scandales de le prostitution réglementée*, 18. According to van der Meersch, *Femmes à l'encan*, 25, some of these women were as young as twelve.

67 Jack Plano, *Fishhooks, Apples and Outhouses* (Kalamazoo, MI: Personality Press, 1991), 252. Not all prostitutes were young. See MHI, WWII Survey, Box 9th Infantry Division, Jordan, "Bull Sessions," 127–28; Brown, *Up Front with U.S.*, 153. Nor were all prostitutes single. See APP, A-1945/3 (H.7.002); APP, BA1822, "Déclaration par soldat américain de suspicion d'entôler."

68 APP, CB, 39.98 and 10.43. See also *La marseillaise*, 21 November 1945.

69 APP, A-1946/8 (H95.707).

70 APP, DB409, *Libération soir*, 26 September 1946; Scheiber, *Fléau*, 26.

71 See APP, CB 39.98; AP, Registres d'écrou, La Petite Roquette, 1433 W 45, 1433 W 46, 1433 W 47, 1433 W 48, 1945. Croubois found that 206 prostitutes in Tours during the years 1940–44 had similar professions before going into prostitution. As in my sample, *couturière* came up frequently as a profession in Croubois's study, causing him to call it "l'anti-chambre de la prostitution." The profession of *couturière*, he argued, was both badly paid and very competitive. See Croubois, *Prostitution en Touraine*, 1:127–30.

72 NARA, RG 331, Entry 100, Box 40.

73 APP, CB 10.43, 1778; APP, A 1949/1 (H.428.877); APP, BA1822, Libération "Déclaration par soldat américain de suspicion d'entôler." An American GI identified a sexual contact as "Elaine, Polish, 24 Brunette." See NARA, RG 331, Entry 100, Box 40. For Polish prostitutes in the Marne, see ADMar, 161 W 323, report dated 26 June 1945; and 162 W 359, letter dated 6 September 1944.

74 *La marseillaise*, 21 November 1945.

75 ADMar, 162 W 359, undated letter to the prefect [April or May 1945].

76 Scheiber, *Fléau*, 9, 24, 29. See also Reboux, *Le guide galant*, 50; and Jean-Charles Bertier, *La prostitution à Bordeaux de 1939 à 1945, son contrôle sanitaire* (Bordeaux: Imprimerie Librairie Delmas, 1945), 11.

77 NARA, RG 331, Entry 100, Boxes 40, 41.

78 NARA, RG 331, Entry 100, Box 40.

79 MHI, WWII Survey, Box 9th Infantry Division, Jordan, "Bull Sessions," 84–85.

80 MHI, John J. Maginnis Papers, untitled memoir, 224.

81 MHI, Robert E. Seale Papers, "WW II as I Remember It," 58.

82 For the economy at the time of the liberation, see Antony Beevor and Artemis Cooper, *Paris after the Liberation, 1944–1949* (New York: Penguin Books, 1995), 103–5; Raymond Ruffin, *La vie des français au jour le jour, de la Libération à la victoire, 1944–1945* (Paris: Cheminements, 2004).

83 Andrew A. Thomson, "'Over There' 1944/45, Americans in the Liberation of France: Their Perceptions of, and Relations with, France and the French" (PhD thesis, University of Kent at Canterbury, 1996), 201.

84 APP, DB 409, *Qui? Police l'hebdomadaire des faits divers*, 31 July 1947. See also APP, A-1945/1 (F.477.872).

85 APP, CB 39.98, 636, 1008, 1066, 1067. See also APP, CB 10.43, 1508.

86 APP, CB 39.98, 36, 1945; ADM, Séries 3 U, Justice, Fonds du Tribunal de première instance de Cherbourg, procès-verbal (hereafter Séries 3 U), report dated 16 April 1945.

87 APP, A-1946/8 (H95.707).

88 Plano, *Fishhooks, Apples and Outhouses*, 254. For Cherbourg, see also ADM, Séries 3 U, reports dated 14 November 1944 and 1 March 1945.

89 *112 Gripes about the French* (Fontenay-aux-Roses: US Army, 1945), 43.

90 MHI, WWII Survey, Box 28th Infantry Division, "Memoirs of Murray Shapiro," np.

91 Dor Hesselgrave, "Paris Recollections, ca. 1944–1946," unpublished mss., 2008.

92 Marie-Thérèse, *Histoire d'une prostituée*, 115–16. For another case of a boyfriend-souteneur, see APP, A-1945/10 (F.459.164).

93 APP, DB409, *Libération soir*, 2 October 1946. For *souteneurs*, see Pénaud, *La Prostitution*, 24–25; van der Meersch, *Femmes à l'encan*, 18. For a fascinating look at a wartime pimp, see Cyril Olivier, "Un proxénète écrit à Suzy en 1941," *clio* 17 (2003): 115–36.

94 APP, DB409, *Qui? Police l'hebdomadaire des faits divers*, 31 July 1947.

95 Marie-Thérèse, *Histoire d'une prostituée*, 75–76.

96 Ibid., 80, 86–87; Chevalier, *Les ruines de Subure*, 82.

97 Chevalier, *Les ruines de subure*, 82.

98 Whiting, *Battle of Hurtgen Forest*, 65.

99 APP, A-1949/1 (H.428.877); A-1945/1 (F.477.872); A-1946/8 (H.95.707); A-1945/5 (F.491.058). All names have been changed. The four murders took place on 1) rue Rochechouart, ninth *quartier*; 2) rue Victor Massé, ninth; 3) rue Thorel near boulevard Bonnes Nouvelles, second; and 4) rue Mont-Doré, seventeenth. For the importance of the second and ninth *quartiers* to the prostitution trade, see René Delpêche, *L'hydre aux mille têtes: un document sur la prostitution à Paris et en France* (Paris: Éditions Karolus, 1961), 30. Two of the four murder cases resulted in the arrest of a suspect. One suspect confessed; the other's fate is unknown.

100 Henriette remained conscious for some time, so was able to tell this story to the police. It resembles another case recorded in APP, DB545, report dated 22 December 1944. This case concerned the attempted murder of a prostitute who had picked up an American soldier on the boulevard de la Madeleine. He initially offered her two thousand francs, then later three thousand more to go to Montmartre with him. When they arrived there, he shot her behind the ear and stole her money. The wound was not serious and the woman survived.

101 On this case, see also APP, BA1822, Libération, report dated 30 September 1945. Still another police case concerned a prostitute shot by a group of men at the café Le Campi on the rue de Picpus. See APP, A-1945/4 (F.480.001).

102 Orval Eugene Faubus, *In This Faraway Land* (Conway, AR: River Road Press, 1971), 450.

103 For prostitutes working together, see APP, CB39.98, 1836–37, 98–99, 100, 1008–9, 1211–12, 1254–55, 1259–60, 1305–6, 1408–9, 1456–57. In CB36.43, see 575–77, 1127, 1132, 791–92. For sisters, see CB 39.98, 1657–58, 1241–42, 1397–98, 1657–58; and also Peters, *For You, Lili Marlene*, 58–59. For outside of Paris, see the case recorded by the Cherbourg police in ADM, Séries 3 U, report dated 19 may 1945.

104 AMH, FC H4 15-6, Letter dated 17 November 1945.

105 APP, CB 39.98, 914.

106 Marie-Thérèse, *Histoire d'une prostituée*, 73.

107 See APP, CB 36.43, 1596–98, arrests made at L'Hôtel Crétet.

108 APP, BA1822, Libération, Undated report signed by policemen René Lhermite and Pierre Bihan.

109 Whiting, *Battle of Hurtgen Forest*, 65

110   Chevalier, *Les ruines de Subure*, 82. For the observation that the MPs only *looked* big to the French, I thank Dor Hesselgrave, who was an American MP in Paris during the war.

111   Meinin, *Wehrmacht et prostitution*, chap. 4.

112   APP, A-1946/8 (H.95.707).

113   APP, BA1822, Libération, "Declaration par soldat américain de suspicion d'entôler."

114   APP, CB 39.98, 1427; APP, CB 36.43, 1224.

115   MHI, Pleas B. Roberts Papers, 1917–45, letter dated 17 November 1944. See also NARA, RG 331, Entry 100, Box 40. Soldiers had an uncanny memory of the dates on which they were exposed, probably because they remembered the dates during which they had leave.

116   Brown, *Up Front with U.S.*, 561.

117   Peters, *For You, Lili Marlene*, 57. For the Parisian geography of prostitution, see also Louis Chevalier, *Histoires de la nuit parisienne* (Paris: Fayard, 1982), 65–83.

118   MHI, WWII Survey, Box 28th Infantry Division, "Memoirs of Murray Shapiro," np.

119   Whiting, *Battle of Hurtgen Forest*, 64.

120   Capell, *Surviving the Odds*, 214; MHI, WWII Survey, Box 71st Infantry Division, Lewington S. Ponder, "Recollections of World War II," 133.

121   For the boulevards, see APP, A-1949/1 (H.428.877); for Pigalle, see MHI, WWII Survey, Box 9th Infantry Division, Jordan, "Bull sessions," 161; for the avenue de l'Opéra, see APP, BA1822, Memo 4 juin 1945.

122   Peters, *For You, Lili Marlene*, 57–58.

123   APP, BA1822, Libération, unsigned letter dated 4 June 1945.

124   MHI, WWII Survey, Box 1st Infantry Division, Leroy Stewart, "Hurry Up and Wait," 75.

125   NARA, RG 331, Entry 100, Box 40. GIs filling out army VD surveys recorded that they had met their women "outside Red Cross Club" or had sex "in room above bar near American Red Cross." For the Red Cross in Paris and the services it provided to the GIs, see MHI, Payne Templeton Papers, "A Complete Change of Life," 63.

126   APP, DB409, *Libération soir*, 26 and 28 September 1946. For the prostitutes at Versailles, see NARA, RG 331, Entry 100, Boxes 40, 41. For the cigarette camps, see MHI, WWII Survey, Box 1st Infantry Division, Damsky, "Shipping Order," 98.

127   APP, A-1949/1 (H.428.877). See also *La marseillaise*, 21 November 1945. For a prostitute who specialized in black soldiers, see ADM, Séries 3 U, report dated 18 February 1946.

128   See, for example, the café on the rue Tour Carrée in Cherbourg, ADM, Séries 3 U, report dated 18 February 1946.

129   *Stars and Stripes*, 16 December 1944.

130   MHI, WWII Survey, Box 71st Infantry Division, Ichelson, "I Was There," 64.

131   For prostitutes that picked up GIs in bars and cafés, see APP, A-1949/1 (H.428.877) and A-1945/3 (H.7.002).

132   For a waitress who was propositioned in this way, see APP, A-1945/5 (F.486.741); Scheiber, *Fléau*, 178.

133   Delpêche, *Les dessous de Paris*, 159.

134 APP, A-1945/3 (H.7.002).

135 APP, A-1946/8 (H.95.707).

136 Whiting, *Battle of Hurtgen Forest*, 64; Boesch, *Road to Heurtgen*, 103.

137 Scheiber, *Fléau*, 185.

138 Marie-Thérèse, *Histoire d'une prostituée*, 77.

139 NARA, RG 331, Entry 100, Boxes 40, 41. For the name "Lili," see APP, A-1945/10 (F.459.164). German women were the most unknown to the GIs, not only because of language differences, but also because, in contrast to France, there was no infrastructure of prostitution in Germany by the spring of 1945. GIs had sex with women in parks, woods, wheat fields, bombed-out houses, and along the autobahn.

140 APP, DB 409, *Qui? Police l'hebdomadaire des faits divers*, 7 August 1947; Jean Bazal, *Marseille galante* (Marseille: Éditions Paul Tacussel, 1980), 205.

141 Marie-Thérèse, *Histoire d'une prostituée*, 74.

142 Faubus, *In This Faraway Land*, 450.

143 MHI, WWII Survey, Box 5th Infantry Division, Karl Clarkson, "The Story of G.I. Joe (Karl): A Combat Infantryman in World War II," 13. See also Leder, *Thanks for the Memories*, 121. Paul Fussell claimed that "Voulez vous coucher avec moi" was the French phrase most familiar to the GIs. See his *Boy's Crusade*, 239.

144 MHI, WWII Survey, Box 71st Infantry Division, Ichelson, "I Was There," 61.

145 Peters, *For You, Lili Marlene*, 57; Walter Brown, *Up Front with U.S.*, 46, 369.

146 Pierre Aubéry, *Les américains au Havre* (Paris: La Bibliothèque Française, 1948), 34–35.

147 *Oxford English Dictionary*, 2nd ed., 1989, vol. 20, sv "zigzag."

148 Usage of the word was not confined to France. In Salzburg, Austria, a lewd show put on by an American military unit featured signs saying "Beaucoup Zig-Zag." See NARA, RG 498, Records of Headquarters, ETO, US Army, 1942–46, Adjutant General's Section Administration Branch, Classified General Correspondance, 1945, 250–50.2, Box 363, "Report of Investigation with Regard to Allegedly Indecent Show Produced by the 798th AAA Automatic Weapons Battalion."

149 Plano, *Fishhooks, Apples and Outhouses*, 253.

150 Vernon McHugh, *From Hell to Heaven: Memoirs from Patton's Third Army* (Ardmore, PA: Dorrance and Company, 1980), 8.

151 See MHI, WWII Survey, Box 5th Infantry Division, Mark Goodman, "Unit History of Company A," 48.

152 On this problem, see APP, A1949/1 (H.428.877).

153 According to historical conversion charts, the 1945 franc was worth 0.11 Euro in 2008. Therefore, the equivalent to the price of sex in 1945 in 2008 terms would be twenty-two to thirty-three euros. Five dollars in 1945 would be worth $59.91 in 2010.

154 MHI, WWII Survey, Box 71st Infantry Division, Ichelson, "I Was There," 62.

155 MHI, WWII Survey, Box 28th Infantry Division, Shapiro, "Memoirs of Murray Shapiro," 87. When Marie-Thérèse started "doing" Americans, she charged about one hundred to two hundred francs a "pass." But when she and another women got to Rouen, they charged two hundred and fifty francs, with fifty francs going to their pimps. See *Histoire d'une prostituée*, 74.

156 *112 Gripes about the French*, 44.

157 APP, CB 39.98, entry 1976.

158 Marie-Thérèse, *Histoire d'une prostituée*, 89. For a similar kind of prostitution in Africa, see Luise White, *The Comforts of Home: Prostitution in Colonial Nairobi* (Chicago: University of Chicago Press, 1990).

159 APP, DB409, *Qui? Police l'hebdomadaire des faits divers*, 9 September 1946 and 7 August 1947. See also APP, CB 39.98, 702, 1259, 1699.

160 For a Cherbourg case in which the prostitutes tried to bribe the police, see ADM, Séries 3 U, report dated 19 May 1945.

161 Marie-Thérèse, *Histoire d'une prostituée*, 85; Scheiber, *Fléau*, 13. See also Delpêche, *L'hydre aux mille têtes*, 46.

162 APP, CB 39.98, 734, 1326. Marie-Thérèse, *Histoire d'une prostituée*, 83–84.

163 MHI, WWII Survey, Box 28th Infantry Division, Shapiro, "Memoirs of Murray Shapiro," 87.

164 APP, DB409, *Qui? Police l'hebdomadaire des faits divers*, 7 August 1947.

165 Service Historique de la Gendarmerie Nationale (hereafter SHGN), 76E173, Section Yvetot, registres de correspondance courante au départ, 16 juillet 1945 au 12 avril 1946, report of 29 November 1945. See also ADM, Séries 3 U, report dated 4 November 1944; ADC, 726 W 16 865, Prostitution, police reports dated 22 December 1945 and 9 October 1944.

166 *La marseillaise*, 21 November 1945.

167 APP, BA 1822, Libération, report dated 4 June 1945.

168 APP, BA 1822, Libération, report dated 1 July 1945.

169 See APP, BA 1822, Libération, reports dated 1 July and 1 November 1945.

170 SHGN, 76E173, Section Yvetot, registres, report dated 29 November 1945.

171 Heaton, *Communicable Diseases*, 248. For this situation in the Marne, see ADMar, 130 W 9, Rapports mensuels sur la situation générale adressés par le Sous-Préfet au Préfet septembre–décembre 1944 (hereafter 130 W 9), letter dated 7 December 1944, and 162 W 355, Rapports journaliers des relations avec les troupes, report dated 22 October 1945.

172 APP, DB409; *La marseillaise*, 21 November 1945.

173 Dor Hesselgrave, "Paris Recollections."

174 *La marseillaise*, 21 November 1945; ADMar, 130 W 9, letter dated 7 December 1944.

175 Brown, *Up Front with U.S.*, 366.

176 Raymond Gantter, *Roll Me Over: An Infantryman's World War II* (New York: Ivy Books, 1997), 11. See also Whiting, *The Battle of Hurtgen Forest*, 63.

177 Nat Frankel and Larry Smith, *Patton's Best: An Informal History of the Fourth Armored Division* (New York: Hawthorn Books, 1978), 75.

178 Aramais Hovsepian, *Your Son and Mine* (New York: Duell, Sloan and Pearce, 1950), 114.

179 Giles, *The G.I. Journal of Sergeant Giles*, 73.

180 Gimlette, *Panther Soup*, 169.

Chapter 6

1 Gen. Charles H. Gerhardt (1895–1976) was educated at West Point, graduating in 1917. He assumed command of the Twenty-Ninth Division in July 1943. On Ger-

hardt, see Geoffrey Perret, *There's a War to be Won: The United States Army in World War II* (New York: Random House, 1991), 311; Andy Rooney, *My War* (New York: Random House, 1995), 180; A. J. Liebling, *Normandy Revisited* (New York: Simon and Schuster, 1958), 72–73. The French praised Gerhardt for his liberation of Breton towns. See, for example, Bernard Festoc's memoir, *La vie à Airel et Saint-Fromont pendant la seconde guerre mondiale* (Périers: Imprimerie X. Garlan, 1994). Gerhardt's personal papers are in the US Army Military History Institute at Carlisle Barracks, Pennsylvania. On how quickly the house of prostitution was established, see also Joseph Balkoski, *Beyond the Beachhead: The 29th Infantry Division in Normandy* (Harrisburg, PA: Stackpole Books, 1989), 48.

2 National Archives and Records Administration (hereafter NARA), Record Group 331, Records of Allied Operation and Occupation, Headquarters, World War II (SHAEF) (hereafter RG 331), Headquarters Twelfth Army Group, Special Staff, Adjutant General Section, Administrative Branch, Decimal File, 1943–45, Entry 198 (hereafter Entry 198), Box 83: 250.1 to 250.2, Morals and Conduct (hereafter Box 83), Report of Investigation to Determine the Facts Surrounding the Establishment of a House of Prostitution for Members of the 29th Division, Conducted by Lt. Col Francis B. Lineman, IGD, 14–17 November 1944 (hereafter Lineman Report), 31.

3 NARA, RG331, Entry 198, Box 83, Lineman Report, 28. The Twenty-Ninth Infantry Division is nicknamed the "Blue and Gray" because it was composed of men from both northern and southern states who had fought each other in the American Civil War.

4 Ibid., 20. Word of the new "cathouse" had "got around like fire," according to one officer.

5 During those five hours, seventy-six men managed to avail themselves of the Corral's services, for an average of nineteen men per woman.

6 According to Perret, *There's a War to be Won*, 471, the Twelfth Army Group G-2 Section also started its own whorehouse. France was also not the only country in which the US military unofficially supervised prostitution. According to Yuki Tanaka, similar brothels were established in the Caribbean, Ecuador, Australia, North Africa, Liberia, Eritrea, and New Caledonia. See *Japanese Comfort Women: Sexual Slavery and Prostitution during World War II and the U.S. Occupation* (London: Routledge, 2002), 92, 99–100, 102, 106, 107.

7 Graham A. Cosmas and Albert E. Cowdry, *The Medical Department: Medical Service in the European Theater of Operations* (Washington, DC: Center of Military History, 1992), 540; Leonard D. Heaton, *Communicable Diseases Transmitted through Contact or by Unknown Means*, vol. 5 of *Preventive Medicine in World War II*, 9 vols. (Washington, DC: Office of the Surgeon General, Department of the Army, 1960), 5:243. Further evidence of so-called GI brothels can be found in the 1944 Preventive Medicine Report, where French health officials related their frustration at "the operation of brothels in Commercy and elsewhere by the United States Army." Quoted in Heaton, *Communicable Diseases*, 5:249. Paratrooper Robert E. Seale remembers how the medical staff of his infantry regiment set up a brothel in Soissons they called the "Idle Hours Athletic Club" with the full cooperation of the local female mayor, who helped recruit prostitutes from Paris. See US Military History Institute, Carlisle Barracks, (hereafter MHI), Robert E. Seale Papers, "WW II as

I Remember It," 62. Official denial of such whorehouses was common. See, for example, NARA, RG 331, Entry 65, Special Staff, Medical Division, Decimal File, January 1944–July 1945 (hereafter Entry 65), Box 7, memo dated 16 May 1945.

8 NARA, RG 331, Entry 198, Box 83, Lineman Report, 5.

9 Peter Schrijvers, *The Crash of Ruin: American Combat Soldiers in Europe during World War II* (New York: New York University Press, 1998), 181.

10 In the First World War, French authorities blamed women as dangerous carriers of disease and threats to men's health. See Michelle Rhodes, "'No Safe Women': Prostitution, Masculinity and Disease in France during the Great War" (PhD thesis, University of Iowa, 2001), 14, 138. For the same attitude among Vichy officials in the Second World War, see Fabrice Virgili, *Naître l'ennemi: les enfants de couples franco-allemands nés pendant la seconde guerre mondiale* (Paris: Éditions Payot, 2009), 77. For the similar Belgian example, see Peter Schrijvers, *Liberators: The Allies and Belgian Society, 1944–1945* (Cambridge: Cambridge University Press, 2009), 217.

11 This was de Gaulle's perspective as he relates a conversation with President Roosevelt's emissary Harry Hopkins in January 1945. See *The Complete War Memoirs of Charles de Gaulle* (New York: Collins, 1955), 761.

12 In referring to American political, military, and cultural dominance in Europe during the Cold War, I argue for the more nuanced notion of Americanization that has emerged in recent years, which sees American dominance as a two-way process of appropriation and cultural coproduction between the United States and Europe. See, among many other possibilities, Heidi Fehrenbach and Uta G. Poiger, eds., *Transactions, Transgressions, Transformations: American Culture in Western Europe and Japan* (New York: Berghahn Books, 2000), xiii–xl; Jonathan Zeitlin, "Introduction," in *Americanization and Its Limits: Reworking US Technology and Management in Post-War Europe and Japan*, ed. Jonathan Zeitlin and Gary Herrigel (Oxford: Oxford University Press, 2000); Richard Pells, *Not Like Us: How Europeans Have Loved, Hated, and Transformed American Culture since World War II* (New York: Basic Books, 1997), particularly 278–324; Oliver Schmidt, "No Innocents Abroad: The Salzburg Impetus and American Studies in Europe," in *"Here, There and Everywhere": The Foreign Politics of American Popular Culture*, ed. Reinhold Wagnleitner and Elaine Tyler May (Hanover, NH: University Press of New England, 2000), 64–79; Malachi Haim Hacohen, "The Congress for Cultural Freedom in Austria: *Forum*, the Rémigrés, and Postwar Culture," *Storiografia* 11 (2007): 135–45.

13 NARA, RG 331, Entry 56, General Staff Divisions, G-5 Division, Information Branch, Historical Section, Numeric-Subject Planning File, 1943–July 1945 (hereafter Entry 56), Box 121, memo dated 31 December 1943.

14 NARA, RG 331, Entry 65, Box 7, memo dated 22 April 1944.

15 Cosmas and Cowdrey, *The Medical Department*, 72–73, 137–38, 143.

16 Heaton, *Communicable Diseases*, 141.

17 Thomas Parran and R. A. Vonderlehr, *Plain Words about Venereal Disease* (New York: Reynal and Hitchock, 1941), 1.

18 For the May Act, see Allan M. Brandt, *No Magic Bullet: A Social History of Venereal Disease in the United States since 1880* (New York: Oxford University Press, 1985), 162–63; Sonya O. Rose, "The 'Sex Question' in Anglo-American Relations in the Second World War," *International History Review* 20, no. 4 (1998): 890. For a longer

history of commercial sex and the military, see Cynthia Enloe, *Bananas, Beaches and Bases: Making Feminist Sense of International Politics* (Berkeley: University of California Press, 1990).

19   Charles M. Wiltse, *The Medical Department: Medical Service in the Mediterranean and Minor Theaters* (Washington, DC: Center of Military History, 1987), 60.

20   Heaton, *Communicable Diseases*, 208, 213–16, 220.

21   NARA, RG 331, Entry 65, Box 7, memos dated 22 April and 13 December 1944; Wiltse, *The Medical Department*, 258–59; Cosmas and Cowdry, *The Medical Department*, 172.

22   Quoted in Wiltse, *The Medical Department*, 258.

23   NARA, RG 331, Entry 47, General Staff Divisions, G-5 Division, Secretariat, Numeric File, August 1943–July 1945 (hereafter Entry 47), Box 47, 2514/2 Public Health Branch: Venereal Disease (hereafter Box 47), Extract from the minutes of the Sixth Meeting of the Combined Civil Affairs Committee, 16 May 1944. For the language of "protection," see NARA, RG 331, Entry 47, Box 28, 850/6 Internal Affairs Branch: Weekly Report Civil Affairs Summary No. 6, 21 July 1944.

24   NARA, RG 331, Entry 65, Box 7, memo dated 22 April 1944.

25   For the Victorian emphasis on manly sexual self-control, see John D'Emilio and Estelle B. Freedman, *Intimate Matters: A History of Sexuality in America* (New York: Harper and Row, 1988), 69–72, 179–80; George L. Mosse, *Nationalism and Sexuality: Respectability and Abnormal Sexuality in Modern Europe* (New York: H. Fertig, 1985), 13.

26   On the connection between masculinity and military strength, see Christina S. Jarvis, *The Male Body at War: American Masculinity during World War II* (Dekalb: Northern Illinois University Press, 2004), 10–55; and Mosse, *Nationalism and Sexuality*.

27   For a similar case during and after the First World War, see Judith Surkis, "Enemies Within: Venereal Disease and the Defense of French Masculinity between the Wars," in *French Masculinities: History, Culture and Politics*, ed. Christopher E. Forth and Bertrand Taithe (New York: Palgrave Macmillan, 2007), 116.

28   NARA, RG 331, Entry 56, Box 121, memo dated 2 June 1944.

29   On the issue of stigmatizing African American GIs as overly sexual, see Sue Son Yom, "Sex and the American Soldier: Military Cinema and the War on Venereal Disease, 1918–1969," (PhD diss., University of Pennsylvania, 2003), 91–92.

30   NARA, RG 331, Entry 56, Box 121, memo dated 2 June 1944. Bonner argued that the high rate of disease among black soldiers was caused by "congested housing conditions, lack of medical facilities, poor educational opportunities, social segregation, general poverty and so forth." On the issue of VD among black troops, see also The Schomburg Center for Research in Black Culture, Layla Lane Papers, 1933–51, Sc MG 54, Correspondance, Box 1, Folder 1, letter from Norridge S. Maylan dated 17 August 1945.

31   For an example of this blame, see NARA, RG 331, Entry 65, Box 7, memo dated 28 April 1944. Even official army histories do not agree on VD statistics for black men. Cosmas and Cowdrey argue that black troops throughout the war had a venereal rate about four and a half times that of white troops; see Graham A. Cosmas and Albert E. Cowdry, *The Medical Department: Medical Service in the European Theater of Operations* (Washington, DC: Center of Military History, 1992),147. Heaton puts the rate at eight to twelve times higher; *Communicable Diseases*,

188–89. Heaton gives the following reasons for higher venereal rates among "Negro" soldiers: low educational level, inadequate repression of prostitution in black communities, and "lack of recognition of the seriousness of the problem, together with reluctance to face the facts." He also argues that "the failure to control venereal disease among Negroes in the Army was, at least in part, a reflection of the failure of society through individual and governmental efforts to develop a satisfactory race relationship between the white and Negro populations"; ibid., 196. In *The Employment of Negro Troops* (Washington, DC: Center of Military History, 1966), 277, Ulysses Lee maintains "the presence of venereal diseases bulwarked personal prejudices in the training and use of Negro troops." On the issue of a higher venereal disease rate among black soldiers, see also Samuel A. Stoffer et al., *The American Soldier: Adjustment during Army Life* (Princeton, NJ: Princeton University Press, 1949), 545–50; Sun Yom, "Sex and the American Soldier," 85–86. Sun Yom argues that white doctors stigmatized black men (but not whites) by officially registering their venereal disease. White men with VD were often not accepted into the military, whereas black men were, "based on the conviction that virtually all blacks were malingerers or carried disease." Sun Yom gives these statistics: among the first two million draftees in the late 1930s, forty-eight out of one thousand white men were found to carry syphilis, whereas 272 out of one thousand black men were registered with the disease.

32 NARA, RG 331, Entry 56, Box 121, memo dated 24 May 1944.

33 John Hinchman Stokes, "A Statement on Prostitution in Venereal Disease Control," in *Morals in Wartime*, ed. Victor Robinson (New York: Publishers Foundation, 1943), 155–56.

34 Rose, "The 'Sex Question,'" 901.

35 NARA, RG 331, Entry 65, Box 7, memo dated 22 April 1944.

36 Ibid., memo dated 4 May 1944. For samples of this literature, see Eliot Ness, *What about Girls?* (Washington, DC: Office of Community War Services, Federal Security Agency, 1943); *Important! Venereal Disease Information for Military Personnel* (Atlanta: Atlanta Army Air Base, Office of the Base Surgeon Army Airport, 1944); RG 331, Entry 100, Special Staff, Headquarters Command, Decimal File, 1944–45 (hereafter Entry 100), Box 40. In the secondary literature, see Elizabeth Alice Clement, *Love for Sale: Courting, Treating and Prostitution in New York City, 1900–1945* (Chapel Hill: University of North Carolina Press, 2006), 248–58; Brandt, *No Magic Bullet*, 163; George H. Roeder Jr., *The Censored War: American Visual Experience during World War II* (New Haven, CT: Yale University Press, 1993), 52–53.

37 Susan Gubar, "'This Is My Rifle, This Is My Gun': World War II and the Blitz on Women," in *Behind the Lines: Gender and the Two World Wars*, ed. Margaret Higonnet et al. (New Haven, CT: Yale University Press, 1987), 249–50.

38 MHI, WWII Survey, Box 1st Infantry Division, Bert Damsky, "Shipping Order___ APO___," 98.

39 Robert Peters, *For You, Lili Marlene* (Madison: University of Wisconsin Press, 1995), 60.

40 Thomas Saylor, *Remembering the Good War: Minnesota's Greatest Generation* (St. Paul, MN: Historical Society Press, 2005), 246.

41 Jack Plano, *Fishhooks, Apples and Outhouses: Memories of the 1920s, 1930s, 1940s* (Kalamazoo, MI: Personality Press, 1991), 255.

42 Paul Fussell, *Wartime: Understanding and Behavior in the Second World War* (New York: Oxford University Press, 1989), 256.

43 NARA, RG 331, Entry 56, Box 121, memo dated 24 May 1944.

44 Cosmas and Cowdrey, *The Medical Department,* 143; NARA, RG 331, Entry 56, Box 121, Circular 49 dated 2 May 1944

45 Raymond Gantter, *Roll Me Over: An Infantryman's World War II* (New York: Ivy Books, 1997), 5.

46 Michel Renouard and Manonmani Restif, eds., *Les malouins et la Libération: combats et vie quotidienne* (Saint-Malo: Éditions Cristel, 2006), 192; Claude Boisse, *Jeunesse ardente, 1943–1945* (Montségur-sur-Lauzon: C. Boisse, 1997), 28.

47 Fussell, *Wartime,* 256.

48 Cosmas and Cowdrey, *The Medical Department,* 144–45.

49 NARA, RG 331, Entry 65, Box 7, memo dated 2 May 1944.

50 Heaton, *Communicable Diseases,* 143. In January 1943, the War Department discovered that air force pilots had been doing missions while treating their unreported VD with sulfa drugs. Such drugs were known to impair a man's ability to navigate an airplane, and had already led to one pilot's death by anoxemia. In response to pressure from the air surgeon, the War Department repealed a law docking a soldier's pay if he contracted VD, and instead made *concealing* contraction the punishable offense.

51 NARA, RG 331, Entry 65, Box 7, memo dated 9 September 1944; NARA, RG 331, Entry 100, Box 41, memo dated 11 March 1945.

52 NARA, RG 331, Entry 65, Box 7, memo dated 20 September 1944 and memo dated 8 November 1944.

53 Ibid., memo dated 13 December 1944.

54 Quoted in Clement, *Love for Sale,* 248.

55 NARA, RG 331, Entry 56, Box 121, memo dated 13 September 1944.

56 NARA, RG 331, Entry 65, Box 7, memo dated 20 September 1944. Because antivenereal posters had to be locally made and mimeographed, they were crudely designed. The army held poster-design contests, but they seemed to generate excitement only for the leave passes awarded as prizes. Heaton, *Communicable Diseases,* 226. See also NARA, RG 331, Entry 65, Box 7, memo dated 17 November 1944; Cosmas and Cowdrey, *The Medical Department,* 143.

57 Heaton, *Communicable Diseases,* 227.

58 John Costello, *Virtue under Fire: How World War Two Changed Our Social and Sexual Attitudes* (Boston: Little Brown, 1985), 98–99.

59 Elizabeth Coquart and Philippe Huet, *Le jour le plus fou: 6 juin 1944, les civils dans la tourmente* (Paris: Albin Michel, 1994), 22.

60 Cosmas and Cowdrey, *The Medical Department,* 144–45.

61 MHI, WWII Survey, Box 28th Infantry Division, "Memoirs of Murray Shapiro," 87. See also MHI, Robert E. Seale Papers, "World War II as I Remember It," 62; and Peters, *For You, Lili Marlene,* 60.

62 See NARA, RG 331, Entry 56, Box 121, ETOUSA Circular 49 dated 2 May 1944. For copies of the reports, see NARA, RG 331, Entry 100, Boxes 40, 41. See also Cosmas and Cowdrey, *The Medical Department,* 173, 541.

63 For the German system, see Insa Meinin, *Wehrmacht et prostitution sous l'Occupation* (Paris: Éditions Payot, 2006), 112.

64 Heaton, *Communicable Diseases,* 249.

65   NARA, RG 331, Entry 100, Boxes 40, 41.

66   Heaton, *Communicable Diseases*, 246; Costello, *Virtue under Fire*, 247. Brothels were also segregated in Cherbourg and other minor cities. See Archives Départmentales de la Manche (hereafter ADM), Rapports américains, 13 num 2521.

67   NARA, RG 331, Entry 65, Box 7, letter dated 15 September 1944.

68   Costello, *Virtue under Fire*, 95.

69   Archives de la Préfecture de la Police (hereafter APP), DB409, *Qui? Police l'hebdomadaire des faits divers*, 7 August 1947.

70   It is not clear from Mauldin's cartoon whether this is a French bar or a brothel, both of which could have been off-limits to Americans. (Many bars also served as brothels.) Besides the American MP, Mauldin portrays several members of the French Resistance dressed in American uniforms.

71   ADM, Rapports américains, 13 num 2770–71, report dated 10 August 1944. See also the statement of Adj. Gen. T. J. Davis in NARA, RG 331, Entry 65, Box 7, memo dated 13 December 1944.

72   See, for example, NARA, RG 331, Entry 198, Box 83, Lineman Report. For the importance of the circular, see also Heaton, *Communicable Diseases*, 241.

73   NARA, RG 331, Entry 56, Box 121, Circular 49 dated 2 May 1944.

74   Sonya Rose also notes the mixed message given soldiers in the ETO, although her focus is on American soldiers in the UK. See "The 'Sex Question,'" 899–900.

75   NARA, RG 331, Entry 56, Box 121, memo dated 31 December 1943 and 5 June 1944.

76   "Clean, active, sound minds and bodies of the members of a command are of primary importance in the endeavor to control venereal disease," wrote one adjutant general. See NARA, RG 331, Entry 56, Box 121, memo dated 12 September 1944; and also NARA, RG 331, Entry 100, Box 40; NARA, RG 331, Entry 65, Box 7, memo dated 22 April 1944; and Cosmas and Cowdrey, *The Medical Department*, 143.

77   Heaton, *Communicable Diseases*, 224.

78   Wisconsin Veterans Museum, Oral History Collection, OH29, Transcript of an oral history interview with John W. Dunn, 1994.

79   Schrijvers, *The Crash of Ruin*, 181.

80   Wisconsin Veterans Museum, Oral History Collection, OH74, Transcript of an oral history interview with William C. Brunsell, 1994.

81   Cosmas and Cowdrey, *The Medical Department*, 540.

82   Quoted in Heaton, *Communicable Diseases*, 249. By December, headquarters so mistrusted commanders in the air force, where VD rates were very high, that it established nonmedical VD advisors whose role it was "to informally impress others," including "other officers, particularly junior officers" in the methods of VD prevention. See NARA, RG 331, Entry 65, Box 7, memos dated 17 November 1944 and 15 December 1944.

83   Harry Benjamin, "Morals versus Morale in Wartime," in Robinson, *Morals in Wartime*, 193.

84   NARA, RG 331, Entry 198, Box 83, Lineman Report, 1. The Corral was the object of an official investigation led by Lt. Col. Francis B. Lineman in November 1944.

85   Ibid., 2, 76; in fact, Louis Gosom was the acting chief of staff in the last week of August when Gerhardt gave his instructions about the brothel. McDaniel was not implicated in its creation, but he did testify in the investigation.

86   Ibid., 4, 6, 50, 90.

87   Ibid., 2.
88   Ibid., 1, 26, 60.
89   Ibid., 1.
90   See, for example, NARA, Record Group 338, Records of US Army Operational, Tactical and Support Organizations, XV Corps Subject Files, 1942–46, Box 75. Report of Investigation Concerning Alleged Cases of Rape Occurring at Closfontaine, France, 31 August and 2 September 1944. The belief that prostitution could prevent rape was widespread at the time. See, for example, Philip S. Broughton, *Prostitution and the War*, Public Affairs Pamphlet No. 65 (Washington, DC: Public Affairs Committee, 1942), 19.
91   ADM, Rapports américains, 13 num, 2766–68.
92   Balkoski, *Beyond the Beachhead*, 45–46, 48; Perret, *There's a War to be Won*, 471. Less than a week after the Corral had been shut down, Gerhardt tried once again to establish a brothel in Brest. This time, however, Civil Affairs officer Asa Gardiner made it clear that if the business could not be "handled in such a way as to prevent information about it being noised abroad, he would not be responsible for it." See NARA, RG 331, Entry 198, Box 83, Lineman Report, 39. Gerhardt received no penalty for the Blue and Gray Corral. Although he was downgraded to the rank of colonel after the war, army historians speculate that his demotion resulted from high casualty rates in his division rather than any moral lapse. See http://www.arlingtoncemetery.net/chgerhardt.htm.
93   NARA, RG 331, Entry 198, Box 83, Letter from Gerhardt to General Bradley. Gerhardt did repeat the same arguments to Bradley concerning hygiene and rape prevention. For example, he boasted that soldiers who frequented the Corral had reported no cases of venereal disease. (Considering the house was open five hours, this was no great accomplishment.)
94   Ibid.
95   Benjamin, "Morals versus Morale," 199. See also Brandt, *No Magic Bullet*, 166.
96   Allan Berube, *Coming Out under Fire: The History of Gay Men and Women in World War Two* (New York: Free Press, 1990), 192. See also John D'Emilio, *Sexual Politics, Sexual Communities: The Making of a Homosexual Minority in the United States, 1940–1970* (Chicago: University of Chicago Press, 1983), 31–32, 38. In *Wartime*, 109, Fussell argues that homosexuality was a common practice among men in POW camps.
97   Rose, *Myth and the Greatest Generation*, 150. Rose argues that some fifty thousand men a year were discharged from the military as a result of a homosexual charge. For the official army position on discharge of homosexuals, see NARA, RG 498, Records of Headquarters, ETO, US Army, 1942–46 (hereafter RG 498), Box 363, Adjutant General's Section Administration Branch, Classified General Correspondance, 1945, 250–50.2, memo dated 31 October 1945.
98   Peters, *For You, Lili Marlene*, 21–22.
99   NARA, RG 331, Entry 198, Box 83, Lineman Report, 7, 50, 81. Comments made by the Commanding General to Assembled Chaplains, 29th Infantry Division, October 1944.
100 Ibid., 2; Costello, *Virtue under Fire*, 97, 245. See also Ben Tumey, *G.I.'s View of World War II: The Diary of a Combat Private* (New York: Exposition Press, 1959), 24.
101 Edward M. Coffman, *The Regulars: The American Army, 1898–1941* (Cambridge, MA: Harvard University Press, 2004), particularly chap. 10.

102 NARA, RG 331, Entry 198, Box 83, Testimony of Edward H. McDaniel, np.

103 For another case of cooperation, see MHI, Robert E. Seale Papers, "WW II as I Remember It," 62.

104 Valérie Moulin, Daniel Baccara, and Jean-Michel Harel, *Le Havre 16th Port of Embarkation, Northern District Normandy Base Section* (Le Havre: Maison des Gens de Mer, 1997), 35.

105 Quoted in Rose, *Myth and the Greatest Generation*, 36.

106 See *Complete War Memoirs*, 669–77, 771–98. See also Antony Beevor and Artemis Cooper, *Paris after the Liberation, 1944–1949* (New York: Doubleday, 1995), 103–5; Raymond Ruffin, *La vie des Français au jour le jour, de la Libération à la victoire, 1944–1945* (Paris: Presses de la Cité, 2004); Andrew Knapp, "Introduction: France's 'Long' Liberation, 1944–47," in *The Uncertain Foundation: France at the Liberation, 1944–47* ed. Knapp (New York: Palgrave McMillan, 2007), 9.

107 NARA, RG 331, Entry 47, Box 31, 931 Public Safety: Control of Civil Population, Brothels, Prostitution and V.D., report dated 25 January 1945.

108 Paul Reboux, *Le guide galant* (Paris: Éditions Raoul Solar, 1953), 67; Pinard, "De la propagation des maladies," in Gemähling et al., *Les Scandales de le prostitution réglementée* (Paris: Éditions de l'Union Temporaraire, 1946), 37.

109 Marie-Thérèse, *Histoire d'une prostituée*, 84–85.

110 René Delpêche, *Les dessous de Paris: souvenirs vécus par l'ex-inspecteur principal de la brigade mondaine Louis Métra* (Paris: Les Éditions du Scorpion, 1955), 153. See also the testimony of Marthe Richard in *Bulletin municipal officiel de la ville de Paris,* "Débats des assemblées de la ville de Paris et du département de la Seine, Conseil Municipal de Paris, séance du 17 décembre 1945."

111 Parran and Vonderlehr, *Plain Words*, 90.

112 US Army Service Forces, Army Information Branch, *A Pocket Guide to France* (Washington, DC: War Department, 1944), 16.

113 See the report filed by Chef Defrene in Service Historique de la Gendarmerie Nationale, (hereafter SHGN), 76E6, 200 Brigade territoriale de Cany Barville, registres de correspondance courante au départ (hereafter 76E6, 200), report dated 5 September 1945.

114 NARA, RG 331, General Staff, G-5 Division, Information Branch, Historical Section, Numeric-Subject Operations File, Entry 54 (hereafter Entry 54), Box 193, "Minutes of Second Meeting on Public Health and Welfare."

115 Emphasis mine. NARA, RG 331, Entry 65, Box 7, memo dated 22 January 1945.

116 Ibid., memo dated 17 November 1944.

117 Clement, *Love for Sale*, 245–46.

118 See chapter 5.

119 For more on Le Havre as a port of the ETO, see Jean-Claude Marquis, *Les camps "cigarette"* (Rouen: Éditions Médianes, 1994); Moulin et al., *Le Havre 16th Port of Embarkation.*

120 See Gilles Morris, *Assasin, mon frère* (Paris: Éditions de Rocher, 1990), 22.

121 For a detailed account of the liberation of Le Havre, see Jean Legoy et al., *Le Havre, 1517–1986; du Havre d'autrefois à la métropole de la mer* (Rouen: Éditions du P'tit Normand, 1987), 43; Eddy Florentin, *Le Havre 44 à feu et à sang* (Paris: Presses de la Cité, 1985); Georges Godefroy, *Le Havre sous l'occupation, 1940–1944* (Le Havre: L'Imprimerie de la Presse, 1965).

122   Roger Gobled, *Voici Le Havre de 1944 à 1963: recueil de documents écrits et photo-graphiques* (Le Havre: Imprimerie M. Etaix, 1963), 12–17; Legoy et al., *Le Havre, 1517–1986*, 44–53. There were five thousand deaths, eighty thousand left homeless, and 12,500 buildings ruined.

123   See also Archives Municipales de la Ville du Havre (hereafter AMH), FC I1 49-2, Prostitution, letter dated 7 November 1944.

124   Ibid.

125   SHGN, 76E6, 200, report of 5 October 1945.

126   AMH, FC I1 49-2, Prostitution, letters dated 30 January 1945 and 2 February 1945.

127   Armand Frémont, *La mémoire d'un port, Le Havre* (Paris: Arléa, 1997), 115.

128   Archives Départmentales de la Marne (hereafter ADMar), 16 W 266, report dated 9 August 1945.

129   Because the camps constituted American military domain, the French police had no jurisdiction there. See SHGN, 76E6, 200, report of 5 September 1945.

130   AMH, FC I1 49-2, Prostitution, letter dated 24 January 1946.

131   AMH, FC H4 15-6, Prostitution, letter dated 14 March 1945.

132   AMH, FC H4 15-6, Agressions, déprédations, méfaits, letter dated 17 November 1945.

133   Ibid., letter dated 4 September 1945.

134   Ibid., letter dated 13 June 1945.

135   Ibid., letter dated 9 October 1945.

136   Ibid., letter dated 6 December 1944.

137   Ibid., letter dated 10 September 1945.

138   Ibid., letter dated 2 July 1945. Still another popular spot was the public baths on the rue Dr. Richard. Here, according to one citizen, the GIs brought women at night and stayed until the early hours of the morning. See ibid., letter dated 8 October 1945; AMH, 15-6, Prostitution, report dated 6 July 1945.

139   André Corvisier, *Histoire du Havre et de l'estuaire de la Seine* (Toulouse: Éditions Privat, 1983), 272.

140   AMH, FC H4 15-6, Agressions, déprédations, méfaits, letter dated 4 July 1945.

141   AMH, FC H4 15-5, Armée et autorités américains, letter dated 20 September 1945. Weed was born in Texas in 1892, and had served in the army twenty-nine years at the time of his stewardship of the Le Havre port.

142   AMH, FC H4 15-6, Prostitution, memo dated 29 August 1945.

143   Ibid., letter dated 30 August 1945.

144   SHGN, 76E6, 200, report dated 5 October 1945.

145   Rhodes, "No Safe Women," 10; Christelle Taraud, *La prostitution coloniale: Algérie, Tunisie, Maroc (1830–1962)* (Paris: Éditions Payot, 2003), 341–42. In the primary litera-ture, see Alfred Scheiber, *Un fléau social: le problème médico-policier de la prostitution* (Paris: Librairie de Médicis, 1946), 115.

146   NARA, RG 498, Box 27, Adjutant General's Section Administration Branch, Gen-eral Correspondence (1944–45), 250.1 Morale & Conduct, translation of letter from Central Commissaire de Police dated 18 [month unclear], 1944.

147   Once again in this case, fear of publicity lay at the heart of the American refusal to in-stitutionalize sex labor. See Jean Yves Le Naour, *Misères et tourments de la chair durant la Grande Guerre: les moeurs sexuelles des français, 1914–1918* (Paris: Aubier, 2002), 205–11.

148   AMH, FC H4 15-6, Prostitution, letter dated 30 August 1945.

149 Ibid., letter dated 1 September 1945.

150 Ibid., letter dated 10 September 1945

151 Ibid., letter dated 17 September 1945.

152 Ibid., letter dated 4 January 1945.

153 While there is no evidence that the Americans supplied hospitals in Le Havre with penicillin, SHAEF did this elsewhere in France beginning in early 1945. See Schrijvers, *The Crash of Ruin*, 182.

154 According to Costello, *Virtue under Fire*, 95, Eisenhower's staff also gave "very serious consideration that licensed houses should be provided under Army supervision" in Germany because the nonfraternization policy posed a "problem" to order and discipline.

155 For the Hawaiian brothels, see Beth Bailey and David Farber, *The First Strange Place: The Alchemy of Race and Sex in World War II Hawaii* (New York: Free Press, 1992); Bailey and Farber, "Hotel Street: Prostitution and the Politics of War," *Radical History Review* 52 (1992): 54–77. See also Maria Höhn and Seungsook Moon, eds., *Over There: Living with the U.S. Military Empire from World War Two to the Present* (Durham, NC: Duke University Press, 2010).

156 Bailey and Farber, "Hotel Street," 58–59. Not all of the women were white. Some were Hawaiian, Puerto Rican, and Japanese. Also, brothels were segregated.

157 Ibid., 63.

158 Stokes, "A Statement on Prostitution" in Robinson, *Morals in Wartime*, 157.

159 NARA, RG 331, Entry 65, Box 7, memo dated 16 May 1945.

160 See Sarah Kovner, "Prostitution in Postwar Japan: Sex Workers, Servicemen, and Social Activists, 1945–1956" (PhD diss., Columbia University, 2004), 24–25. See also "Base Cultures: Sex Workers and Servicemen in Occupied Japan," *Journal of Asian Studies* 68, no. 3 (August 2009): 777–804.

161 Roeder Jr., *The Censored War*, 114. When the chaplain of the Twenty-Ninth Division caught wind of the Blue Gray Corral, he was shrewd enough to fight it by urging his men to write their pastors and folks back home. See NARA, RG 331, Entry 198, Box 83, Lineman Report, 3.

162 MHI, Robert E. Seale Papers, "WWII as I Remember It," 62.

163 MHI, WWII Survey, 28th Infantry Division, Murray Shapiro, "Memoirs of Murray Shapiro," 87.

164 See D'Emilio and Freedman, *Intimate Matters*, 257, 260.

165 Clement, *Love for Sale*, 242.

166 For the myth of the manly GI, see chapter 2 and Mary Louise Roberts, "Le mythe du G.I. viril: genre et photojournalisme en France pendant la seconde guerre mondiale," *Le Mouvement social* 217 (2007): 35–56.

167 SHGN, 76E6, 200, report of 5 October 1945.

168 ADMar, 162 W 355, Rapports journaliers des relations avec les troupes, report dated 6 July 1945.

169 ADMar, 161 W 323, Incidents franco-américains, rapports, 1944–46, report dated 26 June 1945.

170 ADMar, 162 W 359, Rapports sur la prostitution (hereafter 162 W 359), report dated 2 July 1945.

171 Archives Départmentales du Calvados, 726 W 16 865 Prostitution, letter dated 25 April 1945.

172 ADMar, 162 W 359, report dated 13 October 1945; 16 W 268, report dated 26 June 1945.

173 ADMar, 162 W 359, reports dated 21 April 1945 and 20 July 1945; 161 W 323, Incidents franco-américains, rapports, 1944–46, report dated 26 June 1945; 16 W 266, Relations avec les autorités alliées, notes et correspondance, report dated 6 December 1944, letter dated 11 December 1944.

174 ADMar, 16 W 268, Affaires réservées; incidents avec les troupes alliées, report dated 26 June 1945.

175 AMH, FC I1 49-2, Prostitution, report dated 4 May 1946.

176 Ibid.

177 Ibid., letter dated 31 January 1946. There is some evidence that the regulatory apparatus in the garrison city of Reims was also intensified to satisfy the Americans. See ADMar, 16 W 266, "Exposition de bon voisinage pour les GIs." Prostitutes also tried to escape from venereal wards in Reims. See 162 W 355, letter dated 3 August 1945.

178 *Stars and Stripes*, 18 October 1944 and 20 October 1944; US Army, Twelfth Army Group, *Report of Operations, Final After-Action Report*, 14 vols. (np, 1945), 10:179–80.

179 Quoted in David Reynolds, *Rich Relations: The American Occupation of Britain, 1942–1945* (New York: Random House, 1995), 206.

180 Note the parallels between how the Americans managed sexual commerce in France and how Linda Bryder describes colonial sexual management by the European powers: "In the colonies, the systems designed to regulate sex between European men and indigenous women were imposed by the imperial powers. It was assumed that men needed an outlet for their sexual energies and prostitution was the preferred one. There was little concern for the rights or health of the women involved, who were blamed for the spread of venereal disease." Bryder, "Sex, Race and Colonialism: An Historiographical Review," *International History Review* 20, no. 4 (1998): 821.

181 AMH, FC I1 49-2, Prostitution, report dated 4 May 1946.

182 Ibid., letter dated 1 April 1946.

183 Ibid., letter dated 3 April 1946.

184 SHGN, 76E6, 200, report dated 5 October 1945.

185 Judith Surkis, "AHR Forum: Sex, Sovereignty and Transnational Intimacies," *American Historical Review* 115, no. 4 (October 2010): 1090.

186 For the anti-Americanism of the 1950s, see Harvey Levenstein, *We'll Always Have Paris: American Tourists in France since 1930* (Chicago: University of Chicago Press, 2004), chap. 8. Philippe Roger has argued that French anti-Americanism reached its peak in the interwar rather than the postwar years. See *L'ennemi américain: généalogie de l'antiaméricanisme français* (Paris: Éditions du Seuil, 2002).

Chapter 7

1 National Archives and Records Administration (hereafter NARA), Record Group 498, Records of Headquarters, ETO, US Army, 1942–46 (hereafter RG 498), Adjutant General's Section Administration Branch, General Correspondence (1944–45), Box 27, 250.1 (hereafter Box 27), report dated 10 October 1944. It is possible that some of these rapes were committed in Belgium. The theater provost marshal was in charge of the military police throughout the ETO. According to the judge advocate general's office, between July 1942 and November 1945, there were 904 rape accusations in the ETO; 526 of those accused were proclaimed guilty as charged. See *History Branch Office of the Judge Advocate General with the United States Forces, European Theater, July 18, 1942–November 1, 1945* (hereafter HBO-JAG), 2 vols. (St. Cloud, France: Branch Office of the Judge Advocate General, 1945), 1:13. In *Taken by Force: Rape and the American GIs in Europe during World War II* (New York: Palgrave McMillan, 2007), 12, 106–7, Robert Lilly argues that the JAG figures above grossly underrepresent the number of rapes that took place in the ETO because it is such an underreported crime. There are no composite statistics on how many rapes were reported by the French police. Therefore it is impossible to know to what extent the military police and the French police were reporting the same rape accusations. In my own research, I have found some overlap in the rape charges (identifiable by the accuser's name), but also many cases in which charges appearing in the French police records do not appear in the official case record of the military courts, *Holdings and Opinions, Board of Review, Branch Office of the Judge Advocate General, European Theater of Operations: Judge Advocate General Corps. Board of Review* (hereafter HOBR), 34 vols. (Washington, DC: Office of the Judge Advocate General, 1943–46). This means that such rape accusations were not legally prosecuted in the US military courts, either because they did not come to the attention of the military police, or because no one individual was charged with the alleged rape.

2   HBO-JAG, 10, 13. Of those men in the ETO sentenced to death, 86 percent were black and 14 percent were white. The judge advocate's general corps was responsible for military justice in the ETO. The JAG provided legal services to the army at all levels of organization; it was composed of officers who were also lawyers. The JAG conducted and reviewed court-martial trials and kept statistics on crime in the European theater. These kinds of executions also occurred in Italy, most famously to Louis Till, an American soldier who fought in Italy and was executed 2 July 1945 for the crime of rape and murder. Till was the father of Emmett Till, whose murder in 1955 for talking with a white woman became a cause célèbre for the civil rights movement.

3   Significantly, the prosecution and execution of African Americans for the crime of rape is not mentioned in the highly regarded, official military history of blacks in the army during World War II, Ulysses Lee, *The Employment of Negro Troops* (Washington, DC: Office of the Chief of Military History, US Army, 1966).

4   See Alice Kaplan, *The Interpretor* (New York: Free Press, 2005); and Lilly, *Taken by Force*.

5   While such accusations were most often aimed at African American soldiers, some targeted colonial West African or other nonwhite soldiers. For examples where the "problem" clearly concerns North African soldiers, see Archives Départmentales du Calvados (hereafter ADC), 9W 45, Rapports du préfet, rapports mensuels et bimensuels, 1945, reports dated 10 April, 30 April, 10 May, 24 May, 10 June, and 25 June.

6   Archives Municipales de la Ville du Havre (hereafter AMH), FC H4 15-6, letters

dated 18 November and 21 November 1944, 25 June 1945. See also the letters dated 14 June, 19 June, and 19 July 1945.

7 HBO-JAG, 1:13.

8 For such a case, see HOBR, Court Martial Case (hereafter CMC) 5017, 14:53-63.

9 To a great extent, of course, rape had already been racialized in the United States. See Martha Hodes, *White Women, Black Men: Illicit Sex in the Nineteenth-Century South* (New Haven, CT: Yale University Press, 1996), 2-3, 176-208; and Diane Miller Sommerville, *Rape and Race in the Nineteenth-Century South* (Chapel Hill: University of North Carolina Press, 2004).

10 For a treatment of rape on the eastern front, see Wendy Jo Gertjejannsen, "Victims, Heroes, Survivors: Sexual Violence on the Eastern Front during World War II" (PhD thesis, University of Minnesota, 2004); Birgit Beck, "The Military Trials of Sexual Crimes Committed by Soldiers in the Wehrmacht, 1939-1944," in *Homefront: The Military, War and Gender in Twentieth-Century Germany*, ed. Karen Hagemann and Stefanie Schüler-Springorum (New York: Berg, 2002), 255-74. For a comparative approach, see Raphaëlle Branche et al., eds., *Viols en temps de guerre* (Paris: Éditions Payot, 2011).

11 For more on rape and the Red Army, see Catherine Merridale, *Ivan's War: Life and Death in the Red Army, 1939-1945* (New York: Henry Holt and Company, 2006), chap. 9. For the rape of German women, see Atina Grossman, "A Question of Silence: The Rape of German Women by Occupation Soldiers," *October* 72 (1994): 43-63; and Grossman, *Jews, Germans, and Allies: Close Encounters in Occupied Germany* (Princeton, NJ: Princeton University Press, 2007), chap. 3. See also Norman Naimark, *The Russians in Germany: A History of the Soviet Zone of Occupation, 1945-1949* (Cambridge, MA: Harvard University Press, 1995), 69-140; and Anonymous, *A Woman in Berlin: Eight Weeks in the Conquered City* (New York: Metropolitan Books, 2005).

12 HBO-JAG, 1:10.

13 HBO-JAG, 1:249. There is no documentary evidence of mass rape in the Pacific Theater. However, Yuki Tanaka has used eyewitness testimonies and Japanese police intelligence reports to argue that there were gang rapes in Okinawa in March of 1945, and significant numbers of rapes in the Japanese homeland after it was occupied by the Americans in September 1945. See Yuki Tanaka, *Japan's Comfort Women: Sexual Slavery and Prostitution during World War II and the U.S. Occupation* (London: Routledge, 2002), 110-11, 116-17.

14 Lilly, *Taken by Force*, 16, 76-77, 91.

15 See HBO-JAG, 1:10-13, 237.

16 In its final report, the Twelfth Army Group noted that in August 1944, "by far the greatest number of known offenders and suspects" for the crime of rape were "colored service troops." See US Army, *Twelfth Army Group, Final After-Action Report*, 15 vols. ([Bad-Hamburg?]: Twelfth Army Group, 1945), 10:223.

17 HBO-JAG, "Introduction," 1: np. That percentage was up from 23 percent in June, and it dipped to 28 percent in August. Although these figures are for the European theater as a whole, they apply mostly to France, where the majority of American troops were fighting during the late summer months. The rape figures for Belgium were minimal.

18 Maggie M. Morehouse, *Fighting in the Jim Crow Army: Black Men and Women Remember World War II* (Lanham, MD: Rowman and Littlefield Publishers, 2000), 3.

19 Stephen E. Ambrose, "Blacks in the Army in Two World Wars," in *The Military and American Society: Essays and Readings*, ed. Stephen E. Ambrose and James A. Barber Jr. (New York: Free Press, 1972), 178, 182–83.

20 See Richard Dalfiume, *Desegregation of the US Armed Forces, Fighting on Two Fronts, 1939–1953* (Columbia: University of Missouri Press, 1969), 31–33, 64–81.

21 Phillip McGuire, ed., *Taps for a Jim Crow Army: Letters from Black Soldiers in World War II* (Santa Barbara, CA: ABC-Clio, 1983), xxx–xxxvi; McGuire, *He, Too, Spoke for Democracy: Judge Hastie, World War II and the Black Soldier* (New York: Greenwood Press, 1988), 31; Graham Smith, *When Jim Crow Met John Bull: Black American Soldiers in World War II Britain* (London: I. B. Tauris & Co., Ltd., 1987), 21–24. On the boycott and the role of the black press, see Neil Wynn, *The Afro-American and the Second World War* (New York: Holmes & Meier, 1975), 22–26; and Allan Brandt, *Harlem at War: The Black Experience in World War II* (Syracuse, NY: Syracuse University Press, 1996), 109.

22 On Hastie's appointment, see McGuire *Taps*, xxxi; McGuire, *Hastie*, xiv.

23 For the complaint letters that Hastie received at the War Department, see the William Henry Hastie Papers, Harvard Law School Library, Part IX, Segregation, Discrimination: Armed Services, Boxes 102-8 to 102-14. For the complaint letters that Hastie received through the NAACP, see Papers of the NAACP, Part 18, Special Subjects, 1940–55, Series B, General Office Files, William H. Hastie, and Part 9, Series A, Discrimination in the US Armed Forces, 1918–55, General Office Files on Armed Forces' Affairs. Most of these complaints date from the years 1940–41 and also concern discrimination in training and promotion. In the secondary literature, see Clayborne Carson et al., *African American Lives: The Struggle for Freedom* (New York: Pearson Longman, 2005), 406.

24 Wynn, *The Afro-American*, 27; Brandt, *Harlem at War*, 137.

25 A pamphlet given to white officers was meant to address the "special" issues of commanding black soldiers. See *Command of Negro Troops*, War Department Pamphlet No. 20-6, 29 February 1944.

26 The Schomburg Center for Research in Black Culture, New York Public Library (hereafter SCRBC), James Watson Papers, Sc MG 464. See also Ruth Wilson, *Jim Crow Joins Up* (New York: William J. Clark, 1944), 10; Brandt, *Harlem at War*, 101–2; McGuire, *Hastie*, 67.

27 SCRBC, Layle Lane Papers, Sc MG 54 (hereafter LLP) Box 1, Folder 1, Correspondence, Soldiers, 1942–46 (hereafter 1.1 Corr.), letter dated 26 February 1943.

28 Ibid., letter dated 9 May 1943.

29 Ibid., letter dated 27 April 1943.

30 Ibid., letter dated 9 May 1943.

31 SCRBC, Committee against Jim Crow in Military Service and Training, Sc MG98, Folder 2, Hearings before Commission of Inquiry into the Effects of Segregation and Discrimination on the Morale and Development of the Negro Soldier (hereafter Folder 2). This folder contains a written transcript of hearings before a Commission of Inquiry into the Effects of Segregation and Discrimination on the Morale and Development of the Negro Soldier, May 1948. It includes testimonies from black soldiers concerning their training and deployment in the Second World War.

32 Lee, *Employment of Negro Troops*, 300. See also Kenneth Rose, *Myth and the Greatest Generation: A Social History of Americans in World War II* (New York: Routledge, 2008), 135.

33 SCRBC, LLP, 1.1 Corr., letter dated 6 April 1944.

34 SCRBC, Committee against Jim Crow in Military Service and Training, Sc MG98, Folder 2.

35 SCRBC, LLP, 1.1 Corr., letter dated 10 March 1943.

36 Ibid., letter dated 14 August 1944.

37 Ibid., letter dated 24 December 1944. See also Walter White's exposé of racist practices in the military in England: *A Rising Wind* (Garden City, NY: Doubleday, Doran and Company, 1945), 16; and excerpts from *Militant*, 30 September 1944; "Britons Reject Racist Indoctrination," in *Fighting Racism in World War II*, ed. C. L. R. James et al. (New York: Monad Press, 1980), 311. In the secondary literature, see Smith, *When Jim Crow*, 133–34, 139–41; and Neil R. McMillen, "Fighting for What We Didn't Have," in *Remaking Dixie: The Impact of World War Two on the American South*, ed. McMillen (Jackson: University Press of Mississippi, 1997), 97.

38 SCRBC, LLP, 1.1 Corr., letter dated 24 December 1944.

39 On interracial hostilities of this type in England, see NARA, RG 338, Records of US Army Operational, Tactical and Support Organizations, V Corps Adjutant General Section, Central Decimal File, 1940–45 (hereafter RG 338), Box 14, reports dated 18 and 22 May 1944; Samuel Stouffer et al., *The American Soldier: Adjustment during Army Life*, 2 vols. (Princeton, NJ: Princeton University Press, 1949), 1:544–50; Lawrence Cane, *Fighting Fascism in Europe: The World War II Letters of an American Veteran of the Spanish Civil War* (New York: Fordham University Press, 2003), 64. In the secondary literature, see Smith, *When Jim Crow*, 150, 188–89; Lee, *Employment of Black Troops*, 440; Wynn, *The Afro-American*, 29; Christopher Paul Moore, *Fighting for America: Black Soldiers, the Unsung Heroes of World War II* (New York: Ballantine Books, 2005), 173.

40 SCRBC, LLP, 1.1 Corr., letter dated 24 December 1944.

41 William Weaver, *Yankee Doodle Dandy* (Ann Arbor, MI: Edwards Press, 1958), 216–19; and see also George H. Roeder Jr., *The Censored War: American Visual Experience during World War II* (New Haven, CT: Yale University Press, 1993), 56–57.

42 For African American soldiers in combat roles, see Alexander Bielakowski, *African American Troops in World War II* (Oxford: Osprey Publishing, 2007); Charles Sasser, *Patton's Panthers: The African American 761st Tank Battalion in World War II* (New York: Pocket, 2005); Kareem Abdul-Jabbar, *Brothers-in-Arms: The Epic Story of the 761st Tank Battalion* (New York: Broadway Books, 2005); Morehouse, *Fighting in the Jim Crow Army*, 160; Paul Goodman, *A Fragment of Victory in Italy: The 92nd Infantry Division in World War II* (Nashville, TN: Battery Press, 1993).

43 Wynn, *Afro-American*, 35–36; Mary Motley, *The Invisible Soldier: The Experience of the Black Soldier, World War II* (Detroit, MI: Wayne State University Press, 1975).

44 SCRBC, Alan Morrison Papers, "Negro Service Troops Overseas," unpublished ms., nd, 12–18. Morrison was the first black reporter for *Stars and Stripes* in the ETO.

45 Morehouse, *Jim Crow Army*, 4; Lee, *Employment of Negro Troops*, 348–79, 437.

46 *L'Occupation et la Libération de Saint-Clair-Sur-Elle: témoignages de ses habitants* (Saint-Lô: Ateliers Beuzelin/Esnouf, 1984), np.

47 For a clear explanation of how ComZ functioned, see Steven R. Waddell, "The Communications Zone (ComZ): American Logistics in France" (PhD thesis, Texas A&M, 1992).

48 For the liberation of Cherbourg and its function as a major supply port, see Robert Lerouvillois, *Et la liberté vint de Cherbourg: la bataille logistique de la Libération* (Cherbourg: Isoète, 1987); and André Picquenot, *Cherbourg sous l'Occupation* (Rennes: Éditions Ouest-France, 1983), 95–96.

49 For statistics, see NARA, RG 498, Box 27, "Offenses by Colored Soldiers." For the provost marshal's remarks, see ibid., "Recapitulation of Major Crimes."

50 Lee, *Employment of Negro Troops*, 631.

51 SCRBC, Alan Morrison Papers, "Negro Service Troops Overseas," 14.

52 Régine Torrent, *La France américaine: controverses de la Libération* (Brussels: Éditions Racine, 2004), 236.

53 Ernie Pyle, *Brave Men* (New York: Henry Holt, 1944), 318.

54 US Military History Institute, Carlisle Barracks (hereafter MHI), World War Two Veterans Survey (hereafter WWII Survey), Box 18th Infantry Division, Warren E. Eames survey.

55 These concerns are voiced in *Twelfth Army Group, Final After-Action Report*, 10:28.

56 NARA, RG 498, Box 27, "Offenses by Colored Soldiers" dated 22 August 1944.

57 Hodes, *White Women, Black Men*, 2. See also John D'Emilio and Estelle B. Freedman, *Intimate Matters: A History of Sexuality in America* (New York: Harper and Row, 1988), 297, where the authors remark that between 1930 and 1964, 90 percent of men executed for rape were African American.

58 SCRBC, Committee against Jim Crow in Military Service and Training, Sc MG98, Folder 2.

59 Ambrose, "Blacks in the Army," 183; NARA, RG 338, XV Corps Subject Files, 1942–46, Box 75 (hereafter Box 75), "Report of Investigation Concerning Alleged Cases of Rape Occurring at Closfontaine, France, on 31 August and 2 September 1944" (hereafter "Report"), 12–13.

60 Archives Départmentales de la Manche (hereafter ADM), Rapports américains, 13 num (hereafter 13 num), 3045. The "13 num" series is a collection of SHAEF Intelligence reports from Normandy that were photographed by ADM personnel at the NARA for their own archives.

61 NARA, RG 498, Box 27, memo dated 24 October 1944. In the French archives, see ADC, 21 W 15/2, Rapports mensuels du préfet: documents préparatoires de synthèse, 1944, reports dated 16 December 1944, 3 February and 1 March 1945.

62 US Army Judiciary, Arlington, Virginia, (hereafter USAJ), CMC 3740, James B. Sanders, Florine Wilson, and Roy W. Anderson, 5; and ibid., CMC 3933, George Ferguson and Henry Rorie, 3, 6.

63 NARA, RG 498, Box 27, "Recapitulation of Major Crimes."

64 HOBR, CMC 4172, 11:53–63.

65 HOBR, CMC 8270, 19:161–69.

66 In order to explore the rape accusations in France during the period 1944–45, I looked at seventy-six summaries of court cases described in HOBR by the reviewing judges of the JAG office. These were cases in which the accused was tried for rape, attempted rape, or rape and murder. From these cases, I requested, pursuant to the Freedom of Information Act, fifteen records of court-martial trials from the US Army. I chose cases that appeared to have unanswered questions concerning evidence, the identification of the accused, and/or the credibility of the accuser. Because the sample is biased toward "problem" cases, I don't claim it to be representative. The large majority of these cases fell into the period July–October 1944, when the first rape wave was said to occur. To learn how the rape accusations were handled by the French authorities, I read police and prefect reports in Le Havre (AMH, FC H4 15-6); in Saint-Lô (ADM, Séries 3 U, Justice, Fonds du Tribunal de première instance de Cherbourg, procès-verbal [hereafter Séries 3 U]); in Caen (ADC, Cabinet du préfet, 9 W 52–55 Police); and Reims (Archives Départmentales de la Marne [hereafter ADMar], 8 U 180, 196–97.)

67 See US War Department, *A Manual for Courts-Martial* (Washington, DC: Army, Judge Advocate General's Department, 1943).

68 Frederick Bernays Wiener, *Military Justice for the Field Soldier* (Washington, DC: Infantry Field Journal, 1943), 25. Wiener's book was meant as a more comprehensible field guide to accompany *A Manual for Courts-Martial*. See also John A. McComsey and Morris O. Edwards, *The Soldier and the Law* (Harrisburg, PA: Military Service Publishing Co., 1941).

69 USAJ, CMC 3858, Arthur E. Davis and Charles H. Jordan. The legal limit of time between formal charge and trial was five days, except in cases of military necessity. In the review of the case by the judge advocate general's office, the judges acknowledged the brief period between the formal charge and trial, but they argued "it appears that there has been substantial compliance in that ample opportunity was afforded for the preparation of their defense." The two men had for their defense counsel a field officer and a captain in the JAG Office. Neither counsel appeared to be a lawyer. The two soldiers were executed on 22 November 1944.

70 USAJ, CMC 4775, Wilford Teton and Arthur Farrell.

71 USAJ, CMC 3691, Eugene Houston; CMC 2740, Sanders, Wilson, Anderson; CMC 3750, Leonard Bell. See also CMC, 4589, Edward Powell, Andrew Clay, Ebbie Sweet, and J. B. Ketchum.

72 These issues are raised in Gail Williams O'Brien, *The Color of Law: Race, Violence, and Justice in the Post–World War II South* (Chapel Hill: University of North Carolina, 1999).

73 Wiener, *Military Justice*, xi–xii.

74 Hilary Kaiser, ed., *Veteran Recall: Americans in France Remember the War* (Paris: Graphics Group, 1994), 108.

75 NARA, RG 498, Box 27, carrier sheet dated 16 November 1944.

76 SCRBC, Alan Morrison Papers, "Armed Forces," unpublished mss., nd, 7–8. Morrison also states here that it "cannot be denied that many Negro soldiers were guilty of criminal offenses which warranted severe punishment."

77 MHI, WWII Survey, Box Quartermaster, Companies, Unprocessed, William R. Preston survey. See also the testimony of MP Alvin Bridges in Studs Terkel, ed., *The Good War: An Oral History of World War Two* (New York: Ballantine Books, 1985), 390.

78 To determine if the rape charges followed any geographical pattern, I mapped their locations in August and September 1944, as reported in HOBR, vols. 16–23.

Of seventy rape accusations during these months, only five were made in Cherbourg. There were no rape accusations at all in small cities such as Rennes, Brest, Saint-Lô, Saint-Malo, and Coutances, where the GIs had a presence during these months. There was one rape accusation in Le Mans, two in Morlaix, and one in Valognes. Otherwise, the accusations arose in small and often obscure rural villages. It is possible that the alleged rapes took place in locations where there was greater war damage, more fervent Catholicism, or more collaborationist activity. But such distinctions are difficult to analyze systematically given the paucity of information about the small villages and towns where most of the rapes occurred.

79 Marcel Leveel, *Rails et haies: la double bataille de l'Elle et de Lison* (Marigny: Éditions Eurocibles, 2004), 182.

80 Lilly, *Taken by Force*, 94.

81 ADM, Séries 3 U, reports dated 11 July, 17 August, 5 September, and 2 October 1944.

82 HOBR, CMC 5170, 14:227–39.

83 HOBR, CMC 5363, 15:357–65.

84 HOBR, CMC 7209, 18:7–13.

85 USAJ, CMC 3858, Davis and Jordan, 30. The accuser claimed that one of her attackers was short, the other tall. But Davis and Jordan were the same height. For other cases in which the crimes took place after dark, see HOBR, CMC 5362, 14:339–55; CMC 6585, 17:153–61; CMC 8166, 19:65–69; CMC 9246, 20:157–63.

86 HOBR, CMC 3859, 10:391–407. See also USAJ, CMC 3740, Sanders, Wilson, and Anderson.

87 HOBR, CMC 5362, 14:339–55.

88 HOBR, CMC 6193, 16:157–73.

89 HOBR, CMC 7209, 18:7–13.

90 HOBR, CMC 7867, 19:269–83.

91 USAJ, CMC 18599, Joseph E. Striggle.

92 HOBR, CMC 4292, 12:221–31.

93 NARA, RG 338, Box 75, "Report," 12.

94 Ibid., 23.

95 One of the accused left a raincoat at the crime scene with his name and unit written in it. But the owner of the raincoat had reported it lost several days before the alleged rape, so he did not become a suspect in the case.

96 Ibid., 22.

97 Lilly, *Taken by Force*, 38.

98 USAJ, CMC 4775, Teton and Farrell.

99 Three cases in which no medical evidence was presented are USAJ, CMC 3740, Sanders, Wilson, and Anderson; HOBR, CMC 3141, 8:351–61; HOBR, CMC 3749, 10:283–87. Two cases in which the medical exam occurred several days afterward are HOBR, CMC 5362, 14:339–55; HOBR, CMC 6545, 17:87–91. A case of medical examination by candlelight was HOBR, CMC 10103, 22:91–95.

100 See, for example, ADM, Séries 3 U, report dated 4 November 1944. Pregnancy was not an issue in any case I examined.

101 USAJ, CMC 3933, Ferguson and Rorie, 23–24.

102 See, for example, USAJ, CMC 8163, Tommie Davison; ADM, Séries 3 U, report dated 28 August 1944.

103 See USAJ, CMC 4194, Scott; USAJ, CMC 3750, Bell. See also HOBR, CMC 3141, 8:351–61; CMC 4072, 11:337–43; CMC 4253, 12:185–87; CMC 6224, 16:217–23; CMC 6545, 17:87–91; CMC 7869, 18: 291–301; CMC 11589, 24:219–25; CMC 11590, 24:227–33.

104 ADM, Séries 3 U, report dated 17 August 1944. Peronneau took possession of the soldiers' dog tags, which was how she was able to identify them.

105 Extortion could explain what happened in Le Havre some months later when a prostitute was allegedly assaulted in her home by a black soldier who wanted to have sexual relations with her. When a fight broke out between them, the soldier shot her and fled. See AMH, FC H4 15-6, letter dated 11 May 1945.

106 ADM, Série 3 U, report dated 12 June 1945.

107 USAJ, CMC 14986, John Robert Louis Phenix. A physical examination of Rouvrière "showed no evidence of external violence or trauma."

108 ADM, Séries 3 U, report dated 12 June 1945.

109 USAJ, CMC 14986, Phenix. The original sentence for Phenix was hard labor for life. But the reviewing judges claimed to find no strong evidence of lack of consent on the part of Rouvrière, so they changed the charge from "Rape" to "Intent to Rape," and reduced Phenix's sentence to ten years. Phenix requested and was denied clemency in 1947 and 1948.

110 Another case that came down to "the relative credibility of the witnesses," according to the JAG review was USAJ, CMC 8163, Davison. Davison was sentenced to death by hanging, and he proclaimed his innocence on the scaffold.

111 USAJ, CMC 3933, Ferguson and Rorie, 23–25. For another case in which a refugee was an accuser, and whose uncorroborated testimony was key to the conviction of the defendant, see USAJ, CMC 4309, Theron McCann.

112 USAJ, CMC 3933, Ferguson and Rorie.

113 USAJ, CMC 4589, Powell, Clay, Sweet, and Ketchum. Once a conflicting testimony had been resolved by court-martial in favor of the accuser, it could not be changed by the board of review. See USAJ, CMC 8163, Davison; HOBR, CMC 9246, 20:157–63. For two other cases in which black soldiers were prosecuted for rape and the word "orgy" was used, see USAJ, CMC 3740, Sanders, Wilson, and Anderson; and USAJ, CMC 3933, Ferguson and Rorie.

114 USAJ, CMC 4155, Ora Broadus.

115 Service Historique de la Gendarmerie Nationale, (hereafter SHGN), 76E 200, Brigade territoriale de Cany-Barville, registres de correspondance courante au départ, 7 September 1944 to 11 December 1946, report dated 8 August 1945. For other positive civilian assessments of black behavior, see SHGN, 76E 173, Section Yvetot, registres de correspondance courante au départ, 16 July 1945 to 12 April 1946, report dated 11 August 1945; NARA, RG 338, Box 14, Folder "Race; Walter White, *A Rising Wind.*"

116 Terkel, *The Good War*, 276.

117 Ibid., 369.

118 See HOBR, CMC 3749, 10:283–287; CMC 4775, 13:281–89; CMC 5170, 14:227–39; CMC 5363, 14:357–65.

119 Jack Sacco, *Where the Birds Never Sing: The True Story of the 92nd Signal Battalion and the Liberation of Dachau* (New York: Harper Collins Publisher, 2003), 193–96.

120 See Marie-Thérèse [Cointré], *Histoire d'une prostituée* (Paris: Éditions Gonthier, 1964), 75–77.

121 Lilly, *Taken by Force*, 90, 93.

122   Hodes, *White Women, Black Men*, 201–2.

123   USAJ, CMC 3750, Bell, 10, 14. Bell was sentenced to hard labor for twenty years. His requests for clemency were repeatedly denied.

124   See also USAJ, CMC 3740, Sanders, Wilson, and Anderson, 22.

125   See HOBR, CMC 3707, 10:195–99; CMC 4309, 12:277–83; CMC 4775, 13:281–89; CMC 5009, 14:53–65; CMC 10103, 22: 91–95. See also USAJ, CMC 4309, McCann.

126   See USAJ, CMC 3740, Sanders, Wilson, and Anderson; USAJ, CMC 8163, Davison. For still other cases, see also HOBR, CMC 3691, 9:183–87; CMC 3707, 10:195–99; CMC 3858, 10:385–89; CMC 4294, 12:239–59; CMC 4775, 13:281–89.

127   Walter Brown, *Up Front with U.S.* (np: Author, 1979), 46, 369.

128   See USAJ, CMC 3691, Houston, 32. Houston was sentenced to life in prison.

129   USAJ, CMC 8163, Davison.

130   HOBR, CMC 6227, 16: 233–38.

131   See USAJ, CMC 309176, Wilbur Starr. Starr was a Chippewa Indian from Fond du Lac, Wisconsin. See also USAJ, CMC 3740, Sanders, Wilson, and Anderson; HOBR, CMC 3691, 9:183–87; CMC 4072, 11:337–43; CMC 5009, 14: 53–65.

132   132 HOBR, CMC 10103, 22:91–95.

133   USAJ, CMC 3750, Bell; USAJ, CMC 4775, Teton and Farrell.

134   USAJ, CMC 4194, Scott.

135   Peter Schrijvers notes that the prosecution of African Americans for alleged rapes against Belgian women also resulted in harsher penalties than in the cases of white soldiers. See Peter Schrijvers, *Liberators: The Allies and Belgian Society, 1944–1945* (Cambridge: Cambridge University Press, 2009), 229–30.

136   Lilly, *Taken by Force*, 61–63. On this point, see also Barbeau and Henri, *The Unknown Soldiers*, 144.

137   HBO-JAG, 10.

138   Terkel, *The Good War*, 391–92; NARA, RG 338, Box 75. Correspondence in this box reveals attempts by the American military to find an experienced hangman.

139   Hodes, *White Women*, 2–3, 6, 147–48, 157, 175–208.

140   For the motive of deterrence, see NARA, RG 498, Box 27, memo dated 16 November 1944.

141   NARA, RG 498, Adjutant General's Section Administration Branch, General Correspondence (1944–45), Box 28, 250.1–250.4 (hereafter Box 28), memo dated 31 August 1944.

142   NARA, RG 498, Box 27, "Let's Look at Rape." The pamphlet is not dated but given its placement in the file, it was probably circulated to black chaplains in the fall of 1944. According to a letter in the file by Brig. Gen. Benjamin O. Davis, the pamphlet was written by Chaplain Beverly War, Sixty-Fourth Ordnance. Davis claims that the pamphlet received a positive response from black soldiers.

143   See ADM, 145 W 26, Relations avec les autorités alliés.

144   Ibid.

145   See Lilly, *Taken by Force*, 163. See also Frank Irgang, *Etched in Purple* (Caldwell, ID: Caxton Printers, 1949), 163.

146   ADM, 13 num 3133.

147   ADM, 13 num 3135.

148   I found very few cases concerning violence on the part of British and Canadian troops in all the archives I consulted, and certainly no evidence of any widespread problem.

149 ADM, 13 num 3172.

150 NARA, RG 331, Entry 6, Box 11, letter dated 3 November 1944. Maj. Gen. Alphonse Juin passed along the article to Eisenhower as well as a memo about it written by French Lieutenant General Legentilhomme, at that time commander of the French Third Military Region in Rouen. In the memo, Legentilhomme argued that "if the Americans cannot bring women for the needs of their men, at least let them respect French women." Eisenhower received a different translation of the "warning" than the one presented by Norman Intelligence. Both translations were bad, which is why I provide my own here.

151 ADM, 13 num 3172.

152 ADM, 13 num 3177. The British also began to use the Cherbourgeoise rhetoric of terror to describe African American troops. See, for example, ADC, 726 W 16 905, "Correspondance avec les autorités militaires alliées au sujet de sepultures alliées et enemies," undated memo titled "Violation of French Women by American Black Soldiers."

153 Institut d'Histoire du Temps Présent (hereafter IHTP), ARC 1074–62 Alliés (2), *Voici nos alliés, Les États-Unis*, no. 2; and ARC 074 Alliés (7), Saint-John de Crèvecoeur, *Qu'est-ce qu'un américain?* [reprint of 1774 text] (Washington, DC: OWI, 1943).

154 IHTP, *USA*, 1, 2, nd; ARC 1074-62 Alliés (2), *Voici nos alliés, Les États-Unis*, no. 2 (nd); *L'Amérique en guerre*, 12 April 1944.

155 *Voici nos alliés*, no. 2 (nd); *USA*, 1, 2. *Les combattants des États-Unis* (Washington, DC: OWI, 1944) contains a portrait of a "red-skinned American" as a "typical" American soldier "who is very proud that his ancestors were the first Americans."

156 In Rennes, for example, a "Gala Cinema Night" was held 11 August at the Royal, the Celtic, and the Select theaters downtown. Here civilians applauded films on the American jeep and an oil pipe built across Texas, as well as newsreels lauding Allied military victories. See *Ouest France*, 11 August 1944.

157 NARA RG 331, Entry 6, Box 11, memo dated 17 February 1945.

158 *Saturday Evening Post*, 21 October 1944.

159 Harvard Sitcoff, "African American Militancy in the World War Two South," in McMillen, *Remaking Dixie*, 72–74.

160 Roeder Jr., *The Censored War*, 44.

161 On this issue, see Nelson Peery, *Black Fire: The Making of an American Revolutionary* (New York: New Press, 1994), 52.

162 Roeder Jr., *The Censored War*, 4, 8, 44–47, 56–57.

163 Kim Munholland, "Donald Duck in the South Pacific, or the Americanization of New Caledonia, 1942–1945" (unpublished ms.). Munholland argues, 10, that between February and November 1943 there were twenty-five cases of rape, attempted rape, or assault with intention to commit rape. Of the twenty-five accused, eighteen were African American. On New Caledonia, see also Peery, *Black Fire*, 233. In New Guinea, six black soldiers were convicted and executed by rope for allegedly raping two white nurses in March 1944. On this case, see Ray Luszki, *A Rape of Justice: MacArthur and the New Guinea Hangings* (Lanham, MD: Madison Books, 1991); and Moore, *Fighting for America*, 214–16. For black soldiers in Australia, see *Chicago Defender*, 3 June 1944.

164 According to MacGuire, *Hastie*, 87–88, these problems included a forced confession and inadequate acknowledgment on the part of the court that the accuser

had a reputation for dishonesty and sexual promiscuity. A French colony, New Caledonia was occupied by American troops during the Second World War in order to use as an air base. It was the French governor of the colony who brought the original charges against the two black soldiers, and who also stated to the press that "the colored troops are the terror of the white women of Caledonia." See *Chicago Defender*, 8 January 1944.

165 For a full account of the case, see Moore, *Fighting for America*, 211–15.

166 For commentary in the black community on the role of the British press, see *New York Amsterdam News*, 24 June 1944; *Atlanta Daily World*, 14 June 1944; *Pittsburgh Courier*, 17 June and 1 July 1944; *Richmond African American* and *Baltimore African American*, 17 June 1944; *Chicago Defender*, 30 September 1944; *Crisis*, July 1944.

167 On the petition campaign, see *Pittsburgh Courier*, 24 June 1944, and *New York Amsterdam News*, 29 July 1944.

168 On the militant role of the black press during the war, see Lee Finkle, "The Conservative Aims of Militant Rhetoric: Black Protest during World War II," *Journal of American History* 60 (1973): 692–713, and Finkle, *Forum for Protest: The Black Press during World War II* (Rutherford, NJ: Fairleigh Dickinson University Press, 1975).

169 Christopher Waldre, *African Americans Confront Lynching: Strategies of Resistance from the Civil War to the Civil Rights Era* (Lanham, MD: Rowman and Littlefield Publishers, 2009), 86.

170 Glenda Gilmore, *Defying Dixie: The Radical Roots of Civil Rights, 1919–1950* (New York: W. W. Norton, 2008), 394, 397.

171 *The Crisis*, March 1944.

172 *The Crisis*, June 1944.

173 *The Crisis*, July 1944.

174 *New York Amsterdam News*, 8 July 1944 .

175 *Chicago Defender*, 14 October 1944.

176 *Pittsburgh Courier*, 1 July 1944.

177 NAACP'S *The Crisis* (March 1944) christened the Caledonia case the "Army Scottsboro Case," linking it to the overturned 1931 convictions of nine black men for allegedly raping two white women in Scottsboro, Alabama. Because one of the accusers in the Scottsboro case had admitted to lying about the alleged rapes, it produced what Glenda Gilmore calls a "tectonic shift" in the southern landscape, after which white women claiming rape could no longer count on racist stereotypes of black men to avoid court chauvinism (*Defying Dixie*, 125). The *Pittsburgh Courier* made the same comparison with the Scottsboro case on 22 July 1944.

178 NARA, RG 498, Entry 82, Special Staff, Public Relations Division, Executive Branch, Decimal File, 1943–45 (hereafter Entry 82), Box 6, Folder "Negroes."

179 Brandt, *Harlem at War*, 164.

180 Thomas Hachey, "Walter White and the American Negro Soldier in World War II: A Diplomatic Dilemma for Britain," in *Freedom's Odyssey: African American History Essays from Phylon*, ed. Alexa Benson and Janice Sumler-Edmond (Atlanta: Clark Atlantic University Press, 1999), 456–57.

181 Walter White, *A Man Named White, the Autobiography of Walter White* (New York: Viking Press, 1948), 246.

182 Hachey, "Walter White," 463.

183 White, *A Man Named White*, 244. White recalled that Eisenhower ordered the judge advocate general of the European theater to investigate specific cases and take corrective action both on them and on court-martial procedure more generally. According to White, "some of the more flagrant injustices were corrected."

184	White, *A Rising Wind*, 24, 48–49. See also SCRBC, Committee against Jim Crow in Military Service and Training, Sc MG98, Folder 2, 8 May 1948.

185	NARA, RG 498, Judge Advocate Section, Decimal File, 1942–45, 250–250.1, Letter dated 3 April 1944.

186	Ibid., memo dated 4 April 1945.

187	NARA, RG 498, Box 27, memo dated 21 November 1944.

188	An exhaustive search of the African American press during the period 1944–45 did not turn up any mention of the rape accusations and court-martial trials in France. Some black newspapers did report on charges of sexual assault made against black soldiers in Germany. See *Pittsburgh Courier*, 16 June 1945, and *Chicago Defender*, 28 March, 21 April, 26 May, and 21 July 1945.

189	Papers of the NAACP, 1940–55, General Office File, Part 16, Board of Directors, Correspondence; ibid., William Hastie, 1943–45. Hastie spent at least part of the summer in New York reorganizing the offices of the NAACP. In the Correspondence file, see a letter dated 25 August 1944 from White to Lewis Gannett, a reporter for the *Herald Tribune* posted in France. White expresses his pride with black accomplishments in France, and writes to Gannett "I envy you for being in the midst of the accomplishment of that which I saw being prepared."

190	USAJ, CMC 3858, Davis and Jordan. Neither was she given her son's personal effects, including "a valuable wrist watch and war bonds."

191	Col. Benjamin O. Davis was promoted to brigadier general as part of the same arrangement in 1940 between Roosevelt and black leaders that brought Judge William Hastie to the War Department. After refusing to end segregation in the army, Roosevelt sought to win back the black vote in the election of 1940. See McGuire, *Taps*, xxxi. Davis does not mention the trip to France in his memoir, *Benjamin O. Davis, Jr.: An Autobiography* (Washington, DC: Smithsonian Institution Press, 1991).

192	NARA RG 331, Entry 82, Box 6, memo dated 7 July 1944.

193	*Chicago Defender*, 19 August 1944. Toles was a black correspondent with the First Army in France. I was unable to find memoirs of African Americans who served in France. For black-authored novels about the ETO, see William Gardiner Smith, *The Last of the Conquerors* (New York: Farrar, Strauss, 1948); Avery Kolb, *Jigger Witchett's War* (New York: Simon and Schuster, 1959).

194	For Eastland's trip to Europe, see Chris Myers Asch, *The Senator and the Sharecropper: The Freedom Struggles of James O. Eastland and Fannie Lou Hamer* (New York: New Press, 2008), 105–6.

195	*Congressional Record*, 29 June 1945; Asch, *Senator and Sharecropper*, 114–18. For the NAACP's response to Eastland's filibuster, see Papers of the NAACP, 1940–55, General Office File, Part 18, Special Subjects, Series B, "James Eastland."

196	*Congressional Record*, 29 June 1945. Eastland's fantasy of the violent hypersexual black male extended beyond African Americans to the peoples of the French Empire. The senator went on to describe an alleged mass rape in Stuttgart where, he claimed, Senegalese soldiers in the French Army sexually assaulted "christian German girls from good families." The French were quick to dismiss Eastland's story. See *Chicago Defender*, 30 June, 7 July, 18 August 1945; *New York Amsterdam*

News, 7 July 1945; *Chicago Daily Tribune*, 8 July, 18 July, 25 July, 27 July 1945; *New York Amsterdam News*, 14 July 1945.

197 For the mainstream press response, see *Los Angeles Times*, 30 June 1945; and the *New York Times*, 30 June 1945.

198 *Atlantic Daily World*, 6 July 1945; *Chicago Daily Tribune*, 3 July and 6 July 1945; *Chicago Defender*, 14 July 1945, and *Pittsburgh Courier*, 14 July 1945.

199 *Atlantic Daily World*, 8 July 1945. The statement was at best disingenuous. Eastland had connected the alleged rapes in Normandy to the fact that black soldiers were given guns. There was a difference between saying that black troops did not engage in combat and saying that they were not armed. See also *The Crisis*, August 1945.

200 Eastland's remarks were reprinted extensively in southern newspapers. In places such as Charleston, South Carolina, and Columbia, Missouri, the papers were censored to leave out the most offensive of Eastland's statements. See *Atlanta Daily World*, 17 July and *Chicago Defender*, 21 July 1945. In August *The Crisis* reprinted Eastland's remarks, describing them as "vicious and shocking." In December 1945, *Negro Digest* again reprinted an edited version of Eastland's filibuster in the form of a roundtable addressing the question, "Are Negroes Good Soldiers?"

201 *Pittsburgh Courier*, 7 July 1945; *Atlanta Daily World*, 1 July, 5 July, and 8 July 1945; *New York Amsterdam News*, 7 July 1945. For the comparison to the Nazis, see also *New York Amsterdam News*, 14 July 1945.

202 Adriane Lentz-Smith, *Freedom Struggles: African Americans and World War I* (Cambridge, MA: Harvard University Press, 2009), 99. For a personal account of the French response to African Americans during the First World War, see SCRBC, William Holmes Dyer Memoirs, 1917–18.

203 The classic account of African Americans in France is Tyler Stovall, *Paris Noir: African Americans in the City of Light* (Boston: Houghton Mifflin, 1996). See also Marc Hillel, *Vie et moeurs des GI's en Europe, 1942–1947* (Paris: Balland, 1981), 136.

204 *New York Amsterdam News*, 2 September 1944. See also Ollie Stewart's account of the Liberation in the *Richmond African American*, 2 September 1944.

205 As Lentz-Smith argues for the First World War (*Freedom Struggles*, 99), "women became a means through which both black and white Americans expressed their thinking about manhood and civil rights."

206 *New York Amsterdam News*, 2 September 1944.

207 *Richmond African American*, 26 August and 14 October 1944.

208 *Chicago Defender*, 30 September 1944.

209 *Baltimore African American*, 7 July 1945.

210 *Chicago Defender*, 11 August 1945.

211 *Chicago Defender*, 11 August 1945.

212 *Chicago Defender*, 18 August 1945.

213 *Chicago Defender*, 21 July 1945.

Chapter 8

1 *La presse cherbourgeoise*, 17 October 1944.

2 In particular the paper was responding to an incident that occurred in La Pernelle, east of Cherbourg. Three African American soldiers, Milbert Bailey, John

Williams, and James L. Jones, were accused of raping a woman in La Pernelle, then murdering her father when he tried to protect his daughter. The three were condemned by court-martial on 14 December 1944 and executed in La Pernelle on 19 April 1945. See *Holdings and Opinions, Board of Review, Branch Office of the Judge Advocate General, European Theater of Operations: Judge Advocate General Corps. Board of Review* (Washington, DC: Office of the Judge Advocate General, 1943–46) (hereafter HOBR), Court Martial Case (hereafter CMC), 7518, 18:157–65; Archives Départmentales de la Manche (hereafter ADM), 145 W 26, Relations avec les autorités alliés, letter dated 16 October 1944; Hilary Footitt, *War and Liberation in France* (New York: Palgrave Macmillan, 2004), 85.

3   National Archives and Records Administration (hereafter NARA), Record Group 331, Records of Allied Operational and Occupation HQ, World War II (SHAEF) (hereafter RG 331), Entry 6, General Correspondence, 1944–45, Box 16, "Extracts of Censorship Submissions on Relations of Allied Personnel with Civilians" dated 24 November 1944.

4   Archives Municipales de la Ville du Havre (hereafter AMH), FC H4 15-6, letter of 18 November 1944.

5   Archives Départementales du Calvados (hereafter ADC), 726 W 16 905, letter dated 5 November 1944. In this same dossier, see also the letters of 15 September and 3 October 1944, which refer to "the atmosphere of fear and worry" in the region of La Cambe and Maisy.

6   Archives Nationales, (hereafter AN), Séries AJ 384, Gendarmerie, synthèse pour la période du 15 octobre au 15 novembre 1944.

7   ADC, 9 W 45, Rapports du préfet, rapports mensuels et bimensuels, 1945, report dated 23 December 1944.

8   US Army Judiciary, Arlington, Virginia (hereafter USAJ), CMC 4194, Richard Scott, 4.

9   AMH, FC H4 15-6, letters dated 10 September 1945 and 8 October 1945.

10   ADM, Rapports américains, 13 num (hereafter 13 num) 3051 and 13 num 3136.

11   ADM, 1366 W, Comité vérité historique, *Liberté 44, la Manche témoigne: de l'occupation à la libération; les Manchois se souviennent* (hereafter *MT*), témoignage de Madame Dold-Lomet, 285.

12   ADM, 1366 W, *MT*, Colette l'Hermitte, "La bataille de Carentan," 625. See also ADC, 13 T II / 44, *Liberator*, 30 June 1944.

13   NARA, RG 331, Entry 54, General Staff, G-5 Division, Information Branch, Historical Section, Numeric-Subject Operations File, 1943–July 1945 (hereafter Entry 54), Box 111, Relations with General and Special Staffs, Psychological Warfare Division (hereafter Box 111), report dated 25 June 1944. See also ADM, 13 num 3039 and 13 num 3105.

14   Footitt, *War and Liberation*, 76.

15   NARA, RG 331, Entry 54, Box 111, report dated 14 August 1944.

16   René Herval, *Bataille de Normandie: récits de témoins recueillis et présentés par René Herval*, 2 vols. (Paris: Éditions de "Notre Temps," 1947), 1:191, 195. See also 1:204.

17   Jacques Petit, *Au cœur de la bataille de Normandie: souvenirs d'un adolescent, de Saint-Lô à Avranches, été 1944* (Louviers: Ysec, DL, 2004), 20, 23, 98. See also Herval, *Bataille de Normandie*, 1:38.

18   Prashant Bordia and Nicholas DiFonzo, "Problem Solving in Social Interactions

on the Internet: Rumor as Social Cognition," *Social Psychology Quarterly* 67, no. 1 (March 2004): 34. See also Warren A. Peterson and Noel P. Gist, "Rumor and Public Opinion," *American Journal of Sociology* 57, no. 2 (September 1951): 160. Here the author argues that "sex deviation" is a frequent subject of rumor. In the French historical literature, see Marc Bloch, "Reflexions d'un historien sur les fausses nouvelles de la guerre," *Mélanges historiques*, 2 vols. (Paris: S.E.V.P.E.N., 1963), 1:41–57; Alain Corbin et al., eds., *De bouche à oreille: naissance et propagation des rumeurs dans la France du xixe siècle; collection historique* (Paris: Aubier, 2003).

19 NARA, RG 331, Entry 54, Box 111, report dated 25 June 1944. For a French acknowledgment that rumors were circulating, see Marcel Leveel, *Rails et haies: la double bataille de l'Elle et de Lison* (Marigny: Éditions Eurocibles, 2004), 126.

20 ADM, 13 num 3051.

21 ADM, 13 num 3046.

22 ADM, 13 num 3045.

23 ADM, 13 num 3084.

24 Timothy Tackett, "La grande peur et le complot aristocratique sous la Révolution française," *Annales historiques de la Révolution française* 333 (2004): 15–17.

25 Georges Lefebvre, *The Great Fear of 1789: Rural Panic in Revolutionary France* (Princeton, NJ: Princeton University Press, 1973), 159. For other instances in French history where rumor has played an important historical role, see Alain Corbin, *Le village de "cannibales"* (Paris: Flammarion, 1999), and Jean-Yves Le Naour, *Le corbeau: histoire vraie d'une rumeur* (Paris: Hachette Littératures, 2006).

26 Les Archives de la Préfecture de Police, Paris (hereafter APP), BA 1822 Libération. This thick file contains scores of police reports with charges against American soldiers for theft and fighting, but not a single rape case. The archive also holds (*sous dérogation*) dossiers concerning African American soldiers charged with homicide, but again there are no accusations of rape. See also AN, F1a 3350, report dated 12 December 1945; Louis Chevalier, *Les ruines de Subure: Montmartre de 1939 aux années 80* (Paris: Éditions Robert Laffont, 1985), 82, 91–92.

27 US Army, *Twelfth Army Group, Final After-Action Report*, 15 vols. ([Bad-Hamburg?]: Twelfth Army Group, 1945), 10:225.

28 Brett A. Berliner, *Ambivalent Desire: The Exotic Black Other in Jazz-Age France* (Amherst: University of Massachusetts Press, 2002), 237.

29 Antoinette Oriot, *La fille du boulanger* (Charenton-Le-Pont: Presses de Valmy, 1998), 351. See also Elizabeth Coquart, *La France des G.I.s: histoire d'un amour déçu* (Paris: Albin Michel, 2003), 77; André José Lambelet, "'Liaison Factice' and 'Schwarze Schande': Black Soldiers, French Officers, and the Ideology of Conscription," *Proceedings of the Annual Meeting of the Western Society for French History* 28 (2002): 271–81; Christian Koller, "Race and Gender Stereotypes in the Discussion on Colonial Troops: A Franco-German Comparison," in *Home/front: The Military War and Gender in Twentieth-Century Germany*, ed. Karen Hagemann and Stephanie Schaler-Springorum (New York: Berghahn, 2002), 141.

30 Tyler Stovall, "Love, Labor and Race: Colonial Men and White Women in France during the Great War," in *French Civilization and Its Discontents: Nationalism, Colonialism, Race*, ed. Tyler Stovall and Georges van den Abbeele (Lanham, MD: Lexington Books, 2003), 299–300. See also William H. Schneider, *An Empire for the Masses* (Westport, CT: Greenwood Press, 1982), chap. 7.

31 Arthur E. Barbeau and Flotette Henri, *The Unknown Soldiers: Black American Troops in World War I* (Philadelphia: Temple University Press, 1974), 143. During this war French women from Lorraine brought charges of rape against black soldiers. See Adriane Lentz-Smith, "Settling Mr. Negro: African Americans at War in the Terrestrial Heaven," unpublished ms., 2, and see also Lentz-Smith, *Freedom Struggles: African Americans and World War I* (Cambridge, MA: Harvard University Press, 2009); Régine Torrent, "L'image du soldat américain en France, de 1943 à 1945," in *Les américains et la France, 1917–1947: engagements et représentations*, ed. F. Cochet et al. (Paris: Maisonneuve et Larose, 1999), 237; Jean Bazal, *Marseille galante* (Marseille: Éditions Paul Tacussel, 1980), 63.

32 Claude Malon, *Le Havre colonial de 1880 à 1960* (Caen: Presses Universitaires de Caen, 2006), 516–17, 532, 545.

33 ADM, 1366 W, MT, Yves Bouder, "La rédaction imaginaire," 101.

34 Pierre Aubéry, "Le Camp Tareyton," *Le Havre-éclair*, 12 June 1945.

35 Danièle Philippe, *J'avais quinze ans . . . en juin 44, en Normandie* (Paris: Éditions France-Empire, 1994), 144. See also *Front National*, 12 September 1944.

36 NARA, RG 331, Entry 6, Box 11, report dated 16 March 1945.

37 The parallel to 1789 is again helpful. Fear was a pervasive emotion in the French countryside in 1789, not only because of political upheaval but also low grain supplies.

38 NARA, RG 331, Entry 6, Box 11, report dated 28 November 1944.

39 Quoted in Footitt, *War and Liberation*, 91.

40 Mémorial de Caen (hereafter MDC), TE 277, Marcelle Hamel-Hateau, "Des mémoires d'une petite maîtresse d'école de Normandie: souvenirs du Débarquement de juin 1944," 19.

41 HOBR, CMC 3859, 10:391–407.

42 MDC, Séries FN–France Normandie, Trevières, "Américains—Normands—Omaha—1944," 35. Marguerite Gidon was twenty-six in 1944. Bernesq is a small village at the base of the Cotentin Peninsula. In this document, see also the *témoignage* of Madame Marie Jeanne Leneveu, 43.

43 NARA, RG 331, Entry 6, Box 11, report dated 15 December 1944.

44 NARA, RG 331, Entry 6, Box 11, report dated 21 November 1944.

45 Service Historique de la Gendarmerie Nationale, (hereafter SHGN), 76E 200, Brigade territoriale de Cany-Barville, registres de correspondance courante au départ, 7 September 1944 to 11 December 1946, report dated 8 February 1945. Not all civilians had a negative view of black soldiers. See, for example, MDC, Séries FN–France Normandie, "Grancamp-Les-Bains-Maisy, 1939–1945, témoignages, ouvrage réalisé par l'association Grexpo," 1994, témoignage of Madame Claude Anquetil.

46 NARA, RG 331, Entry 6, Box 11, report dated 1 April 1945.

47 ADC, 9 W 45, Rapports du préfet, rapports mensuels et bimensuels, 1945, reports dated 30 April, 20 May, 24 May, 10 June, 25 June. See also ADC, 9 W 55/2 Police, rapports bimensuels de gendarmerie, report dated 3 May 1945; ADC, 21 W 17, Rapports mensuels de préfet, documents préparatoires de synthèse, 1945, reports dated 20 April, 19 June.

48 ADC, 9 W 45, Rapports du préfet, rapports mensuels et bimensuels, report dated 23 December 1944. See also ibid., reports dated 23 February, 28 February 1945; and ADC, 21 W 16, Rapports mensuel du préfet, documents préparatoires de synthèse, report dated 19 March 1945.

49 ADC, 21 W 16, Rapports mensuels du préfet: documents préparatoires de synthèse, report dated 19 February 1945.

50 AMH, FC H4 15-6, letter dated 19 September 1945. Voisin himself so disliked African American soldiers that on the first anniversary of the liberation of Le Havre, he ordered his assistant to call local American officials in order to let them know that "only white soldiers will be admitted" to the celebration. See AMH I1 46-7, letter dated 6 September 1945.

51 There were accusations of rape in the Marne. See Archives Départmentales de la Marne (hereafter ADMar), 16 W 268, Affaires réservees: Incidents avec les troupes alliées, report dated 20 September 1944. Overwhelmingly, however, the police reported thefts and minor assaults.

52 See chapter 7.

53 See chapter 1.

54 Herval, *Bataille de Normandie*, 1:70.

55 ADM, 13 num 3047.

56 For complaints about American requisitioning of property in Le Havre, see AMH, FC H4 14-15; FC I1 68-4; FC H4 15-5. For the Marne, see ADMar, 16 W 266, Relations avec les autorités alliées; ADMar, 132 W 276, Mission militaire française de liaison après de l'armée américaine. For Caen, see ADC, 21 W 16, Rapports mensuels du préfet: documents préparatoires de synthèse, report dated 19 February 1945; ADC, 726 W 16 905, Correspondance avec les autorités militaires alliées au sujet de sépultures alliées et enemies.

57 Roger Hilliquin, *Les années de guerre d'un adolescent havrais, 1939–1945* (Luneray: Éditions Bertout, 2002), 118.

58 *Le Havre-éclair*, 12 August 1945.

59 ADM, 1366 W, *MT*, memoir of Raymond Avignon, 30.

60 ADM, 1366 W, *MT*, diary of Henri Dabrin, 175.

61 Footitt, *War and Liberation*, 72, 86. She concludes that "the population felt swamped by the presence of the Liberators."

62 ADC, 726 W 16, 865 Prostitution, report dated 5 March 1945. In November 1944, Yvette Mesnil, accused by the police of prostitution in Cherbourg, knew to evade the charge by arguing she was too "disgusted" to have sex with the black soldiers at a nearby camp. See ADM, Séries 3 U, Justice, Fonds du Tribunal de première instance de Cherbourg, procès-verbal (hereafter Séries 3 U), report dated 14 November 1944.

63 ADM, Séries 3 U, reports dated 24 January 1945 and 26 July 1945.

64 Frantz Fanon, *Black Skin White Masks* (New York: Grove Press, 1967), 63. In the secondary literature, see Richard Fogarty, *Race and War in France: Colonial Subjects in the French Army, 1914–1918* (Baltimore, MD: Johns Hopkins University Press, 2008), chap. 6.

65 Pamela Scully, "Rape, Race, and Colonial Culture: The Sexual Politics of Identity in Nineteenth-Century Cape Colony, South Africa," *American Historical Review* 100, no. 2 (April 1995): 338. The Indian mutiny of 1857 is perhaps the most famous example of the links between political rebellion and sexual transgression. See Jennie Sharpe, *Allegories of Empire: The Figure of Woman in the Colonial Text* (Minneapolis: University of Minnesota, 1993), 57–84. Historian Ann Stoler has observed the coincidence of political tensions in interwar Algeria with the widespread diffusion of images defining Algerian men as sexually hyperaggressive. See Stoler, *Carnal*

Knowledge and Imperial Power: Race and the Intimate in Colonial Rule (Berkeley: University of California Press, 2002), 58–59.

66 See Pap Ndiaye, *La Condition noire: Essai sur une minorité française* (Paris: Calmann-Lévy, 2008), 130–33. According to Ndiaye, 134,000 Senegalese soldiers fought in France during the First World War. See also Marc Michel, *Les Africains et la Grande Guerre: l'appel à l'Afrique (1914–1918)* (Paris: Éditions Karthala, 2003).

67 See Raffael Scheck, *Hitler's African Victims: The German Army Massacres of Black French Soldiers in 1940* (Cambridge: Cambridge University Press, 2006); Gregory Mann, *Native Sons: West African Veterans and France in the Twentieth Century* (Durham, NC: Duke University Press, 2006), 111–16; Myron Echenberg, *Colonial Conscripts: The Tirailleurs Sénégalais in French West Africa, 1857–1960* (Portsmouth, NH: Heinemann, 1991), chap 6; Ndiaye, *La Condition noire*, 148–61.

68 Jean Yves Le Naour, *Misères et tourments de la chair durant la Grande Guerre: Les moeurs sexuelles des Français, 1914–1918* (Paris: Aubier, 2002), 204–5; Christelle Taraud, *La prostitution coloniale: Algérie, Tunisie, Maroc (1830–1962)* (Paris: Éditions Payot, 2003), 341–42, 346–47; Fogarty, *Race and War in France*, chap. 6. Some GIs remembered the brothels trailing behind North African units. See Robert Adleman and George Walton, *The Champagne Campaign* (Boston: Little, Brown and Company), 219.

69 Vincent Joly, "Sexe, guerres et désir colonial," in François Rouquet et al., eds. *Amours, guerres et sexualité, 1914–1945*, ed. François Rouquet et al. (Paris: Gallimard, 2007), 67.

70 Taraud, *La Prostitution coloniale*, 351–52.

71 Tony Judt, *Postwar: A History of Europe since 1945* (New York: Penguin Press, 2005), 112–13; Maurice Larkin, *France since the Popular Front, Government and People, 1936–1986* (Oxford: Clarendon Press, 1988), 119–21.

72 See chapter 3.

73 Alice Kaplan, *The Interpreter* (New York: Free Press, 2005), 151.

74 ADM, 13 num 3054, 13 num 3068. See also ADMa, 132 W 276, Mission militaire française de liaison après de l'Armée américaine.

75 ADC, 9 W 53, Police, rapports journaliers, reports dated 21 April and 26 April 1945.

76 ADM, 13 num 3128.

77 ADM, 13 num 3039; NARA, RG 331, Entry 54, Box 111, reports dated 1 August and 14 August 1944.

78 See ADMar, 130 W 9, Rapports mensuels sur la situation générale adressés, report dated 28 December 1944.

79 ADC, 21 W 16, Rapports mensuels du préfet: documents préparatoires de synthèse, report dated 3 March 1945.

80 Suzanne Bigeon née Arnault, "Journal tenu pendant les jours précédant la Libération de Cherbourg: Le Débarquement. Les Allemands. Les Américains." MDC, TE 207. Bigeon's journal was recorded in 1944, then revised and edited by Colette Arnault in 1979–80.

81 Keith Nelson, "The Black Horror on the Rhine: Race as a Factor in Post–World War I Diplomacy," *Journal of Modern History* 42 (December 1970): 613. See also Jean-Yves Le Naour, *La honte noir: l'Allemagne et les troupes coloniales françaises, 1914–1945* (Paris: Hachette Littératures, 2003).

82 Nelson, "Black Horror." See also Julia Roos, "Women's Rights, Nationalist Anxiety, and the 'Moral' Agenda in the Early Weimar Republic: Revisiting the 'Black Horror' Campaign against France's African Occupation Troops," *Central European History* 42, no. 3 (2009): 473–508; Ruth Simms Hamilton, "Orchestrating Race, Nation, and Gender: African Peacekeepers in Germany, 1919–1920," and Dana S. Hale, "Brothers in Arms? African Soldiers in Interwar France," in *Routes of Passage: Rethinking the African Diaspora*, ed. Ruth Simms Hamilton, 2 vols. (East Lansing: Michigan State Press, 2007), 1:337, 361.

83 Nelson, "Black Horror," 613, 619.

84 Two other sets of rape accusations point to the links between sexual violence and national humiliation during these years. First, in the Italian campaign of 1943–44, rumors circulated of Moroccan soldiers committing rape after the population was liberated by the French Army. See Olivier Wieviorka, *La mémoire désunie: le souvenir politique des années sombres, de la Libération à nos jours* (Paris: Éditions du Seuil, 2010), 262. Second, there were widespread rumors that Senegalese troops had supposedly raped German women in Stuttgart. American senator James Eastland referred to these rapes in his filibuster against the Fair Employment Practices Committee. See chapter 7.

85 ADC, 13 T II/44, *Liberator*, 24 June 1944. See HOBR, CMC 7518, 8:351–61 for the case in question.

86 SHAEF Intelligence report dated 21 October 1944, quoted in Andrew A. Thomson, "'Over There' 1944/45, Americans in the Liberation of France: Their Perceptions of, and Relations with, France and the French" (PhD thesis, University of Kent at Canterbury, 1996), 206–7.

87 Jean Galtier-Boissière, *Mon journal depuis la Libération* (Paris: La Jeune Parque, 1945), 35.

88 Lucien Lepoittevin, *Mémoire de guerres (1692–1993)* (Cherbourg: Isoète, 1994), 107–8.

89 G. Morris, *Assassin, mon frère* (Monaco [Paris]: Éditions de Rocher, 1990), 22, 59.

90 Louis Guilloux, *Ok, Joe* (Chicago: University of Chicago Press, 2003), 7–9.

91 Ibid., 67–70.

92 Ibid., 41.

93 Ibid., 78.

94 For wartime propaganda about the United States as the "greatest democracy in the world," see Institut d'Histoire du Temps Présent, ARC 074-61 Alliés (1) and (2); ARC 074-62 Alliés (2); and ARC 074-67 Alliés (7)—États Unis.

Conclusion

1 Archives de la Préfecture de Police, Paris, F.446.559. In accordance with French law, I have changed the names of those involved in the accident.

2 André Siegfried, "Les États-Unis à la croisée des chemins," *Le figaro*, 26 March 1945.

3 For an analysis of the photograph as a form of public culture, see John Louis Lucaites and Robert Hariman, "'The Time Square Kiss: Iconic Photography and

Civic Renewal in U.S. Public Culture," *Journal of American History* 94, no. 1 (June 2007): 122–31. Another photograph that appears evocative in relationship to "Time Square Kiss," is Robert Doisneau's "Le Baiser de l'Hôtel de ville." This equally famous photo shows a French man kissing a French woman in front of the Parisian City Hall. Taken in 1950, five years after the war, the photo can be read as an iconographic response to both Robert Morris's 1944 photograph of a GI kissing a French woman and Eisenstadt's "Time Square Kiss." Doisneau posed the picture on an assignment for *Life* magazine, where the other two photographs initially appeared.

4 Carol Gluck, "Operations of Memory: Comfort Women and the World," in *Ruptured Histories: War, Memory and the Post–Cold War in Asia*, ed. Sheila Myoshi Jager and Rana Mitter (Cambridge, MA: Harvard University Press, 2007), 48.

Index

Page numbers followed by the letter *f* indicate illustrations.

abattoirs (whorehouses), 140
AEF (American Expeditionary Forces), 135
African American soldiers: assignment of black
    soldiers to service units, 202; behavioral
    assumptions by both black soldiers and
    French women, 220–21; belief in a "special"
    relationship with the French people, 236–38,
    333n205; French prejudices against (*see* black
    terror on the *Bocage*); military's denial and
    hiding of any racial discrimination, 233–35,
    332nn188–90; postliberation designation of
    segregated brothels, 169, 315n66; racial ten-
    sions surrounding interracial socializing,
    201; rape accusations against (*see* racializa-
    tion of rape); segregationist policies and
    practices in the military, 199, 200–201,
    323n23, 323n25, 323n31; white soldiers lever-
    aging prejudices against blacks, 219–20
Allied Military Government for Occupied Ter-
    ritories (AMGOT), 5, 263n6
Allied Signal Engineer Corps, 49
Ambrose, Stephen, 11, 16, 17, 98–99, 116,
    264n20
America Comes of Age (Siegfried), 9
American Expeditionary Forces (AEF), 135
American GIs and French civilians: black
    market system, 116–20, 295n37; contrast be-
    tween the robust GIs and the small French,
    103–4; deterioration of GI-to-civilian
    relations, 123–24, 297n80; French disgust at
    the sexual behavior of the women, 129–31,
    300n140; French view of prostitutes, 115–16;

GI attitude that the French owed them
    a debt, 124; GIs profiting from chocolate
    and cigarettes, 122; GIs' belief that they de-
    served the sexual prerogatives of conquest,
    108–9; humiliating effect of US generosity,
    120–22; impact of sex as a commodity on
    the American liberators, 115; prostitu-
    tion's availability, 125–29; sexual behavior
    of French women connected to French
    national identity, 131–32; shift in meaning
    of American surplus as a token of friend-
    ship, 124–25; surplus products' use as tools
    of corruption, 122–23, 297n76; US global
    power shaped by its wealth, 113–14, 132
American Mercury, 108, 110
American Red Cross, 150–51, 307n125
American Soldier, The (Stouffer), 264n17
American women: *Life* magazine's depiction of,
    70–71f; military's use of pinups as a motiva-
    tional tool for the GIs, 61–62, 63f; public's
    awareness of GI bad behavior, 75; reaction
    to the GI photos, 68–72
Amerilots, 103, 104, 108. *See also* American GIs
    and French civilians
AMGOT (Allied Military Government for Oc-
    cupied Territories), 5, 263n6
Anderson, Roy, 207
Anne, Antoine, 24–25, 32, 33
Armagnac, Cécile, 48
Aubéry, Pierre, 109, 113, 125, 131, 152
Aubrac, Lucie, 25
Avignon, Raymond, 26

Bailey, Milbert, 333–34n2

Barbès, Violette de, 148

Battle of Normandy: civilian casualties due to the campaign, 17, 265n8; damage done to lives and towns, 24–27; D-day military casualties, 15; disrespect for civilians by the GIs, 30–31; errors in Ambrose's portrayals of French civilians, 17–18; French civilians' reactions to D-day, 20–22; GI prejudices about the French, 19–20, 258, 260; GIs and the Norman children, 37–39, 42–43; GIs' difficulty with the French language, 43–47; GIs' dismay at the results of the bombings, 27–30; GIs' reaction to cultural differences and brought stereotypes, 19–20; GIs' sense of alienation in France, 18–19; growing anti-Americanism due to the imprecision of the bombing campaign, 22–24, 266n29, 267n35; historians' marginalization of the French, 16; impression the US military complex made on the Normans, 48–49; legacy of the Normandy landings, 15–16, 265n2; means of communication between civilian and soldier, 47–48; mutual mistrust between the GIs and civilians, 35–36; negative impression made by Norman quality of life on the Americans, 49–54; Norman anguish due to uncertainty of the outcome, 27; Norman memories of the Americans, 33, 39; Normans' difficulty with the English language, 47; Normans' exposure to the fighting, 32–34; Normans' provision of aid to the Americans, 34–35; Normans' reactions to first seeing Americans, 17; Norman stoicism during, 29, 36–37; Norman treatment of the bodies of German versus American soldiers, 40–42; "perfume of cigarettes," 42, 227n216; price paid by the population for liberation, 27, 255–56, 268nn73–77; reality of Norman women's attitude toward sex, 53; remembrances of the smell of death, 39–40; resurfacing of historical racial prejudices of the French, 257–58; sounds of war, 31–32; tastes associated with the liberation, 42–43; violence against the civilian population in Le Havre, 74–75

Baxter, John, 18

Bazin, Charles-Henri-Guy, 103–4, 105, 106

Béchot, Michel, 120

Bell, Leonard, 207, 221, 329n123

Belpulsi, Peter, 46, 61, 117, 118, 122, 134

Bertier, Jean-Charles, 130

Bertreux, Chanoine, 33

Berube, Alan, 174

Bigeon, Suzanne, 250

Bistrica, John, 96

Black, Timuel, 219

black market: civilian awe at American food supplies, 117; interactions based on cigarettes' popularity, 118–20, 296n52; kinship with prostitution, 125–26; levels of operation during the war, 116; mutually beneficial trading, 117–18

black soldiers. See African American soldiers

black terror on the Bocage: absence of rape cases in Paris, 242, 335n26; American "invasion" symbolized by black soldiers, 247; French critiques of the military court system, 252–53; French equating of sexual violence to national humiliation, 249–51, 339n84, 339n94; French history of power dynamics based on sex and white supremacy, 247–49, 337n65, 338n68; French reaction to the swiftness of rape convictions, 252–54; prevalence of rumors in rural France, 241–42; racial prejudice of the French, 240, 243; rape hysteria in the provinces, 243, 245–47, 336n31; resurfacing of historical racial prejudices of the French, 257–58; spread of fear of African American soldiers in Normandy, 244–45, 336n37, 336nn50–51; widespread reports and fear of rapes in France, 239–40, 333n2

Blaise, Louis, 35, 40

blond cigarettes, 118–19

Blue and Gray Corral, 159, 310n3, 319n161

Blum, Léon, 106, 292n144

Boesch, Paul, 29, 53, 119

Boislambert, Claude Hettier de, 31

boîtes aux soldats (factories of love), 140

boniches, 130–31, 132

Bonifas, Aimé, 102, 104

Bonner, Walter, 165

Boudier, Norman Yves, 243

Bourdon, Claude, 24

Bourret, Victor, 284n7

Bowen, Sidney, 28

Bradley, Omar, 174

Braley, Michel, 32, 34, 48

Bré, Gilles, 38

Bridges, Tommy, 224

Brinton, Crane, 90–91

Broadus, Ora B., 218

Broeckz, Fernand, 32

brothels. *See* military's view of prostitution
Brown, Walter, 122, 126, 134, 157, 221
Bruller, Jean (Vercors), 284n6
Brunet, Abbé, 268n74
Brunsell, William, 134, 172
Bryder, Linda, 320n180
Bureau, Jacques, 102, 103
Burgett, Donald, 35

CA (Civil Affairs), 6, 24, 124
Cagny, Bernard and Solange de, 31
Camp Philip Morris, 293n170
Cane, Lawrence, 49, 97–98, 117
Capa, Robert, 79
Capell, Jack, 122, 150
Cardot, Robert, 104–5
Castex, André, 102
Caussé, Georges, 103, 105
Cazaux, Yves, 98
Ce soir, 67, 123
CFLN (French Committee of National Liberation), 5, 23, 263n7
Champs Elysées, 150
Chamson, André, 86
Chauffier, Louis Martin, 91
chef de famille role of French men, 86–87, 92, 284nn3–7
Chevalier, Louis, 296n93
Chevance-Bertin, Maurice, 76
chewing gum, 42–43, 274n216
Chicago Defender, 232, 238
children: French civilians' outcries against public prostitution, 188; GI photos ignoring GIs bonding with children, 62–63; GIs' relationships with the Norman children, 37–39, 42–43, 47
chocolate, 35, 42, 47, 122
Churchill, Winston, 5
cigarettes: GIs profiting from, 122; interactions based on cigarettes' popularity, 118–20, 296n52; shift in meaning as a token of friendship, 125; use as tools of corruption, 122
Civil Affairs (CA), 6, 24, 124
Clarkson, Karl, 51, 52, 152
Clausse, Robert, 33
Cointré, Marie-Thèrèse, 133, 137–38, 142, 145–46, 147, 150, 152, 154
Coletti, James, 124
Communications Zone (ComZ), 202–4
condoms distribution by the army, 168, 171
Conversy, Marcel, 102

Cooper, John David, 210
Copans, Sim, 25
Costigliola, Frank, 128
Couillard, Auguste, 33
Coulet, François, 6, 264n11
Crayton, Corporal, 28
Crisis, The, 232, 331n177
Curtis, Jean-Louis, 100

Dabrin, Henri, 246
Daladier, Edouard, 103
Damsky, Bert, 126, 128, 166
Dargols, Sergeant, 53
Davis, Arthur E., 207, 326n69
Davis, Benjamin O., 234–35, 329n142, 332n191
Davis, John, 207, 209, 327n85
Davison, Tommie, 222
"Dear John" letters, 68
Debû-Bridel, Jacques, 87
de Gaulle, Charles, 5, 6, 90, 91, 130, 162, 177, 263n7, 311n11
Delpierre, Christiane, 38, 47, 117
Denis, Christianne, 119
Dépériers, Madame, 35
Dernier Village, Le (Chamson), 86
Déroute (Debû-Bridel), 87
Des Moines Register, 68
Desprairies, Pierre, 32
Destors, Madame, 39
Devers, Jacob, 162
displaced person (DP) girls, 105, 292n140
Dold-Lomet, Madame, 25
Dower, John, 131
Downes, William, 210
Duckett, Alfred, 219
Dufaut, Victor, 105
Dufour, Abbé, 119
Duhamel, George, 24, 131
Dumbarton Oaks, 90, 91
Dunn, John, 172
Dutourd, Jean, 87, 284n5

Eames, Warren, 108
Earle, John, 122, 124
Eastland, James O., 235–36, 333nn196–200
Easton, Robert, 28, 89, 92
Edinger, Joseph, 37, 44
eggs market, 118
Eighty-Second Airborne Division, 15, 34
Eisenhower, Dwight, 60, 227
Eisenstaedt, Alfred, 258
Enderton, Herbert, 30

Eudes, Odette, 34
Eudier, Louis, 107
European Theater of Operations (ETO), 18, 162, 195, 196, 198, 199, 201, 209, 213, 225, 233, 235, 240
Eustis, Morton, 28, 29

Fabre-Luce, Alfred, 23
factories of love (*boîtes aux soldats*), 140
Fanon, Frantz, 248
Farrell, Arthur, 207
Faubus, Orval, 19, 29, 61, 147, 152
Ferguson, George, 207, 216–17
Ferrary, Pierre and Yvonne, 34
FFI. *See* French Forces of the Interior (FFI)
figaro, Le, 9
filles soumises, 136, 137–38. *See also* Parisian prostitutes
Finance, Paul, 103, 107, 120
Flavian, C. L., 99
Fleeson, Doris, 61
Foehringer, Roger, 43, 134
Folies Bergère, 150
Foncine, Jean-Louis, 103
forêts de la nuit, Les (Curtis), 100
franc-tireur, Le, 67, 121
Frank, Anne, 20
Frankel, Nat, 157
Freese, Frank, 25, 29, 117
Frémont, Armand, 49
French Committee of National Liberation (CFLN), 5, 23, 263n7
French Forces of the Interior (FFI), 5, 77, 78f; American dismay at FFI's role in *épuration* of collaborators, 97, 289n83; American view of, 95–97, 288n76; GIs' divided view of, 98–99; GIs' view of female members, 287n58; treatment of female German collaborators, 133; view of Americans and of their own manhood, 99–101
French national identity: American view of the French Army, 94–95; centrality of gender norms to how Americans treated France, 83–84; consistent denigration of French masculinity by *Stars and Stripes*, 77–78, 81–83; damage done to French male authority by the war, 110, 172n172; damage to the French male ego done by the war (*see* wartime male gender damage); ex-prisoners' marginalization upon return home, 107–10; France's dismay at its geopolitical decline, 90–92; French equating of sexual violence

to national humiliation, 249–51, 339n84, 339n94; the French man's shame and rage at not being able to fulfill his task as *chef de famille*, 86–87, 92, 284nn3–7; French men's attempt to ignore the Americans' attitude, 105, 292n137; French men's response to American "rescue" of their country, 85; French view of America as a wealthy nation (*see* American GIs and French civilians); GI condescension of French men, 88–89, 92–95; impact of uncontrolled GI behavior on Franco-American relations, 76–77; influence of perception of French sexual attitudes on the military's imperialistic view of France, 54–55; parallels between sexual relations and the struggle over people and territory, 192; prostitution's contribution to American disrespect for the French, 128–29; sexual behavior of French women connected to, 131–32; symbolism of the *tonte* for, 87–88, 98, 108, 133
French women: connection between their sexual behavior and French national identity, 131–32; deep-seated beliefs in the hypersexuality and debauchery of black men, 204–5; French men's disgust at the sexual behavior of the women, 129–31, 300n140; GI discomfort with the *tonte* rituals, 97–98, 288n80; GIs' view of French women as transferred property, 89; "kissing" photos compared to *tonte* photos, 80–81; military propagandists leveraging myths about French women to motivate the GIs, 7–9; officers shifting responsibility for infection onto the French, 160, 163–64, 176–77, 178–79, 311n10; presentation of American men and French women in photos, 60–62; prostitution and (*see* Parisian prostitutes; prostitution); rape accusers' motivations for claiming rape, 214–15, 328nn104–10; *tonte* ritual's symbolism, 87–88, 98, 108, 133; US Army ignoring the male role in transmission of disease, 178; US rise to power reflected in sexual exploitation of French women, 257
Friang, Brigitte, 104
Frohman, Charles E., 19
Fussell, Paul, 264n20

Galtier-Boissière, Jean, 253
Gantter, Raymond, 29, 157, 166
Gardiner, Asa, 159
Gatti, Coradino, 117

gender damage. *See* wartime male gender damage

Gerhardt, Charles, 159, 160, 173–75, 310–11n1, 316nn92–93

German women and prostitution, 308n139

Gidon, Marguerite, 244

Giles, Jan, 19, 28, 29, 30, 37, 45, 158

Gilmore, Glenda, 331n177

GI photos: American public's awareness of the GIs' bad behavior, 75; American women's reaction to the photos, 68–72; centrality of gender norms to how Americans treated France, 83–84; consistent denigration of French masculinity by *Stars and Stripes*, 77–78, 81–83; depiction of a protector role of the United States, 83; eroticization of the liberation by Americans, 64–66, 73; French view of the liberation of Paris, 66–67, 279n29, 280n33; ignoring GIs bonding with children, 62–63; impact of uncontrolled GI behavior on Franco-American relations, 76–77; "kissing" photos compared to *tonte* photos, 80–81; mapping of sexual relations onto American war aims, 62, 63f, 64; military's use of pinups as a motivational tool, 61–62, 63f; myth created by the photos, 58–59, 67–68; position as an icon of the liberation of Europe, 57–58, 278nn2–3; post-liberation troubles with the Americans' behavior, 73–76, 280n42, 280n44, 281nn48–50, 282–83nn60–66; presentation of American men and French women, 60–62; reassurance for the GIs of their manhood, 67–68; *Stars and Stripes'* use of, as an instrument of propaganda, 60, 77–78; technological advances contributing to wartime photojournalism, 59–60; *tonte* ritual coverage, 78–83, 283n74; unintended consequences of the myth of the manly GI, 9–10

Girard, Lt. Col., 286n29

Gluck, Carol, 260

Goodman, Mark, 118

Gosom, Louis, 315n85

Gourbin, Bernard, 37, 49

Gray, Peyton, 238

Griswold, Alvin, 43

Gubar, Susan, 68, 280n37

Guernier, Georges, 246

Guilloux, Louis, 125, 253–54

Hamel-Hateau, Marcelle, 53, 244

Hansen, Chester, 25, 29, 51, 52, 95, 96, 97, 128, 288n76

Harlinski, Anthony, 51, 92, 119, 122

harlots. *See* prostitution

Hastie, Henry, 199, 233, 234, 323n23

Haug, Charles, 29

Hauteclocque, François, 30, 39

Havre-éclair, Le, 121, 132, 243

Hawaii, 184–86, 319n156

Hawley, Paul, 190

Health Is Victory, 166

Helm, Dale, 30

Hendricks, James, 211

Henry, Leroy, 231, 232

"Hershey bars," 126

Hill, Abe, 237

Hilliquin, Roger, 246

Hodes, Martha, 204, 224

Hodges, Joe, 44

Hodulik, Henry, 28

homosexuality in the army, 174–75, 316n97

Hope, Bob, 44

Hopkins, Harry, 311n11

Houston, Eugene, 207, 222, 329n128

Hovsepian, Aramais, 19, 45, 158, 299n107

How to See Paris, 134

Hualla, Lucie, 213

Huntoon, Raymond, 100

Hurkala, John, 27

Ichelson, David, 51, 52, 117, 124, 126, 127, 129, 139, 151, 152, 154

Idle Hours Athletic Club, 186, 310n7

Irgang, Frank, 29, 35

Italy, 163–64

Iwo Jima flag raising (photo), 57, 58, 278n2

Jacqueline, Marie-Madeleine, 117

JAG (Judge Advocate General), 198, 205, 231, 242, 253

Japan, 131, 186, 258, 294n9, 310n6

jeep, 33, 73, 270n120

Jones, James L., 333–34n2

Jordan, Charles H., 207, 209, 326n69, 327n85

Jordan, Chester, 45, 143

Jourdain, Marcel, 40

journal de la Marne, Le, 121, 129, 131

Joyon, Charles, 106

Judge Advocate General (JAG), 198, 205, 231, 242, 253

Juin, Alphonse, 330n150

Kayser, Jacques, 6, 27, 40, 109

Kennedy, Renwick, 128

Kenner, A. W., 167
Knapp, Andrew, 90
Koopman, Norbert, 38
Kovner, Sarah, 186
K rations, 117

Lagarde, Geneviève, 137
Lane, Layle, 200
Larisisien, Clementine, 222
Launay, Marcel, 42
Launey, Jean-Pierre, 27, 49
Leblond, Francine, 38
Le Bourg, Monsieur, 41
Lecadet, Guillaume, 27
Leclerc, General, 64
Lee, John, 233
Lee, Ulysses, 203
Le Havre, France: destruction done to, by
   bombing campaign, 24, 246; mayor's
   complaints about the soldiers, 1–2; mayor's
   proposal of a military-regulated sex trade,
   181–84, 318n147; military ignoring the public
   sex problem, 2; popularity of the town for
   prostitutes, 179–80; problem of dealing
   with infected women, 191; problem of
   sexual tensions between French and American men, 109–10; prostitution regulation
   difficulties, 180–81, 318n122; residents' complaints about the situation, 181, 318n138; use
   of GI camps for prostitution, 180, 318n129;
   violence against the civilian population by
   the GIs, 74–75; Weed's response to Voisin's
   proposal, 183–84, 319n153
Lelouey, Jules, 216–17
Lemeland, Charles, 26, 32, 38
Lentz-Smith, Adriane, 236, 333n205
Lepage, Jacques, 31, 33
Lepottevin, Marie, 210
Lessafre, Robert, 105
Letellier, Roger, 218
Letourneur, Christian, 40
"Let's Look at Rape" pamphlet, 224–26,
   329n142
Levasseur, Simone, 255
Levoy, Fernand, 119
Levrault, Angèle, 15
Libération soir, 138
Life magazine, 2, 28, 60, 68, 70–71f, 75, 132,
   300n145
Lilly, Robert, 220, 321n1
Logrippo, Gerald A., 173
Loisel, René, 128

Look magazine, 60
looting by GIs, 73, 280n44
Lovett, R. B., 186
Lovry, Zozet, 211–12
Lyddon, Donald, 98
Lyon, Allan, 51

Maginnis, John J., 95, 120, 127, 143
Maginot Line, 94
maisons closes, 135–36
maisons de massage, 151
maisons de tolérance, 135–36
Malaparte, Curzio, 293n171
Malraux, André, 284n5
marché noir, le. *See* black market
Maresquier, Augustin, 24
Marie, Alfred, 49
Marie-Claire, 130
Marthe Richard Law, 138
Martin, Germaine, 35
Mauldin, Bill, 2, 3f, 46, 81, 82f, 93, 170, 286n42,
   315n70
May Act, 163
McCloy, John J., 263n7
McConahey, Bill, 122, 126, 135
McDaniel, Edward H., 173, 176
Meissner, William, 126
Mesnil, Yvette, 337n62
Messore, Joseph, 44, 45
Michel, André, 103, 106
military court system for rape trials: black lead-
   ers exposing racially motivated convictions,
   230–33, 331n177, 331n183; black soldiers' vul-
   nerability in the court system, 208, 326n76;
   French critiques of, 252–53; military's
   construction of rape as a fact of racial
   depravity, 227–29; mind-set contributing to
   black convictions, 223; process used, 206–8,
   325–26nn66–69; prosecutors' assumptions
   of guilt and failure to verify credibility,
   215–18, 222–23, 238n113; punishments for
   rape, 223–27; standard of proof for rape in a
   military court, 213–14; time between formal
   charges and trial, 207, 326n69
Military Justice for the Field Soldier (Wiener),
   326n68
military's view of prostitution: army efforts
   to reduce exposure to VD, 166–69, 314n50,
   314n56; army leaders' support for military
   brothels, 159–60, 310nn6–7; army officers
   blaming French women for infecting US
   soldiers, 160, 163–64, 176–79, 311n10; army

officers ignoring the "off-limits" order regarding prostitution, 172–73, 315n82; army officers' motivation to conceal VD cases, 172; army's failure to trace sexual contacts, 169; army's fear of homosexuality, 174–75, 316n97; army's fear of scandal over the management of prostitution, 186–87, 319n161; asymmetries in attitudes toward France versus other countries, 189–90; basis of the soaring rates of VD infection, 167; belief that prostitution could prevent rape, 174, 316n90; brothels in Honolulu, 184–85, 319n156; concern over venereal disease's impact on war readiness, 162–63; conflicting messages sent by the War Department to personnel, 171, 175–76, 315n74, 315n76; Corral establishment, 159, 310nn1–5; differences between the French and Hawaiian situations, 185–86; failings of French medical care for prostitutes, 177–78; French anti-Americanism and, 192, 230n186; French civilians' outcries against public prostitution, 187–88; Gerhardt's rationale for and defense of the Corral brothel, 173–75, 316nn92–93; ignoring of the male role in transmission of disease, 178; in Le Havre (see Le Havre, France); parallels between sexual relations and the struggle over people and territory, 192; policy of secrecy regarding indiscrete overseas activities, 187; postliberation initial designation of segregated brothels, 169, 315n66; postwithdrawal continuation of prostitution, 189; problem of dealing with infected women, 191; racist basis of attitude toward African American soldiers, 164–65, 312nn30–31; soldiers' complaints about condoms and pro stations, 168–69; successful avoidance of MPs by the GIs, 169–71, 315n70; symbolic connection between VD and Allied anxieties, 165–66; symbolism of prostitution regarding American virility, 164; US military's insistence on a right to manage sexual commerce, 160–62, 311nn11–12

Miller, Arthur, 128
Monod, Claude, 101
Moorehead, Alan, 36, 116
Morin, Monsieur, 40, 41, 48
Morot, 159
Morris, Gilles, 109, 114, 125, 253
Morris-Dumoulin, Gilles, 293n170
Morrison, Alan, 203, 208

Morse, Ralph, 68, 69f, 258
MPs, 155–56
Munholland, Kim, 330n163
Murphy, Robert M., 15

National Association for the Advancement of Colored People (NAACP), 199, 231, 233
Nelson, Keith, 251
New York Amsterdam News, 232, 237
Nicolle, Jacques, 119, 296n52
Nidub, André, 102
Normandy landings. See Battle of Normandy

Office of Censorship, 230
Office of War Information (OWI), 228
Ok, Joe (Guilloux), 253–54
101st Airborne, 34
112 Gripes about the French, 127, 128, 144
On Photography (Sontag), 278n3
Otts, Lee, 47
Ouest-France, 121
OWI (Office of War Information), 228

Pacary, Arthur and Berthe, 34
Pacific Theater, 322n13
Page, Getty, 124
panpans, 131
Panther Tracks, 115
Parisian prostitutes: acceptance of a new culture of prostitution, 156–57; accounts of GI violence against prostitutes, 146–47, 306nn99–101; attempts to look rich in appearance, 142–43; attempts to maintain the integrity of the brothels, 139; bypassing of legal brothels by GIs, 139–40; communication challenges, 152–53, 308n139; corruption among the police, 154–55; cost of a prostitute, 153–54, 308n153, 308n155; dependence on police and MPs for safety, 148, 307n110; economic factors forcing women into prostitution, 143–44; failings of the French medical care for prostitutes, 177–78; GIs' collusion with the prostitutes, 155–56; GI's ease in finding women, 149–51, 307n115; legality of prostitution in France, 135–36; measures taken to protect themselves, 147–48, 307n110; misconduct by, 149; Nazi brothel system, 136–37, 302n29; Paris's reputation as a place for sex, 133–35, 300n3; pickup process, 151–52; political reasons for the end of legal prostitution, 138; postliberation growth in number of illegal

Parisian prostitutes (*continued*)
  prostitutes, 137–38; prevalence of venereal
  disease, 135, 140; profile of, 141–42, 304n62,
  305n71; prostitutes aiding the Allies, 137;
  prostitutes' willingness to work outside the
  regulations, 140, 304n58; psychology of the
  GI craving for sex, 157–58; switch from Ger-
  man to American soldiers, 133–34; system of
  money and barter, 153; vulnerability of the
  freelance prostitute, 145–46
parisien libéré, Le, 66, 67
Parrott, James, 210
Patton, George, 160, 172
Peronneau, Madeleine, 214
Perret, Jacques, 17, 31
Peters, Robert, 94, 127, 150, 166, 175
Petesch, Angela, 50
Petit, Jacques, 25, 32, 39, 42, 47, 241
Phenix, John, 215
Philippe, Danièle, 36, 39, 47, 49, 243, 274n203
Pinard, Marcel, 140
Pitt, Roxanne, 137
Pittsburgh Courier, 233, 331n177
Plano, Jack, 45, 115, 128, 141, 144, 153
Pocket Guide to France, 53
Popineau, Jacques, 48
populaire, Le, 130
Pottier, Marguerite, 33, 34
presse cherbourgeoise, La, 239, 241
propaganda by the military: alleged German
  rapes used to create a moral imperative for
  war, 87, 285n12; army's fear of scandal over
  the management of prostitution, 186–87,
  319n161; censorship used to hide the rape
  problem from the American public, 229–30;
  military propagandists leveraging myths
  about French women to motivate the GIs,
  7–9; military's use of pinups as a motivational tool for the GIs, 61–62, 63f; photos of
  GIs used to create an image (*see* GI photos);
  policy of secrecy regarding indiscrete
  overseas activities, 187; rape's threatening
  of America's carefully presented image,
  228–29, 330nn155–56; as supported by newspapers (see *Stars and Stripes*)
pro stations, 168–69, 171
prostitution: army's response to (*see* military's
  view of prostitution); connection between
  the sexual behavior of the women and
  French national identity, 131–32; contribution to American disrespect for the
  French, 128–29; French disgust at the sexual

behavior of the women, 129–31, 300n140;
  French view of prostitutes, 115–16; GIs'
  contemptuous view of the women, 127–28,
  299n107; kinship with the black market,
  125–26; money measured in terms of sex,
  126, 296n93; in Paris (*see* Parisian prostitutes); robustness of the market for, 122–23;
  willingness of the women, 126–27
Pyle, Ernie, 37, 50, 64, 118, 138

Quillen, Bill, 44
Quillien, Maurice, 31
Quonian, Denise, 216–17

racialization of rape: accusers' motivations
  for claiming rape, 214–15, 328nn104–10;
  advantages of due process for white accused, 218–19; African Americans' belief
  in a "special" relationship with the French
  people, 236–38, 333n205; American investigators' readiness to assume a black assailant,
  212–13; assignment of black soldiers to
  service units, 202; black leaders exposing
  racially motivated convictions, 230–33,
  331n177, 331n183; black soldiers' vulnerability
  in the court system, 208, 326n76; censorship
  used to hide the rape problem from the
  American public, 229–30; circumstances
  behind the ComZ statistics about rape,
  202–4; common failure to conduct an
  adequate medical exam, 214, 327n99; courts'
  deference to white women accusing black
  soldiers, 211–12; deep-seated beliefs in the
  hypersexuality and debauchery of black
  men, 204–5; disproportionate number of
  black soldiers convicted of sexual assault,
  195–96, 320–21nn1–5; explanation for the
  harsher sentences given to black men,
  223–24, 329n135; geographic distribution of
  rapes, 208, 326–27n78; military court system
  for rape trials, 206–8, 325–26nn66–69;
  military's construction of rape as a fact of
  racial depravity, 227–29; military's denial
  and hiding of any racial discrimination,
  233–35, 332nn188–90; military's use of public
  hangings as a demonstration of its power,
  226; mind-set contributing to black convictions, 223; miscommunication problem,
  220–23; problem of accurate identification
  of the accused, 208–13; problem of witness
  credibility, 213–20; prosecutors' assumptions of guilt and failure to verify credibil-

ity, 215–18, 222–23, 238n113; punishments for rape, 223–27; questions about, 196–97; racial tensions surrounding interracial socializing, 201; rape's threatening of America's carefully presented image, 228–29, 330nn155–56; reactions to Eastland's reports of rapes by blacks, 235–36, 333nn196–200; results of behavioral assumptions by both black soldiers and French women, 220–21; segregationist policies and practices in the military, 200–201, 323n25, 323n31; standard of proof for rape in a military court, 213–14; time between formal charges and trial, 207, 326n69; uniquely American problem of GI promiscuity, 227, 329n148; War Department's discriminatory treatment of black soldiers, 199, 323n23; white soldiers leveraging prejudices against blacks, 219–20

rape: French prejudices against blacks reflected in accusations of (see black terror on the Bocage); in the Pacific Theater, 322n13; rape waves in the ETO, 197–98, 322n10, 322n13, 322nn16–17; statistics in France, 195, 321n1. See also military court system for rape trials; racialization of rape

Rasmus, Robert, 29
RECCE, 285n18
Red Ball Express, 202
Reeves, Maurice, 213
Resistance, the. See French Forces of the Interior (FFI)
Richards, Marthe, 138, 141
Richmond African American, 237
Rising Wind, A (White), 233, 234
Rist, E., 142
Roeder, George, 230
Roger, Philippe, 320n186
Rogers, Edward, 36
Rooney, Andy, 26, 27, 45, 60
Roosevelt, Franklin D., 5, 90, 199
Rorie, Henry, 207, 216–17
Rose, Sonya, 315n76, 316n97
Rouvrière, Marie, 215
Rudesal, James P., 209
Ryan, Robert, 119

Sacco, Jack, 94, 220
Saint-Lô, France, 25
Sampson, Francis, 37
Sanders, James, 207
Sartre, Jean-Paul, 284n5
Saylor, Thomas, 127

Scheiber, Alfred, 129, 131
Schrijvers, Peter, 329n135
Scott, Richard, 222
"Scottsboro" cases, 233, 331n177
Scully, Pamela, 337n65
Seale, Robert, 143, 186, 310n7
Second French Armed Division, 95
Sédouy, Jacques-Alain de, 17, 103, 120
Seligman, Françoise, 20
Service du travail obligatoire (STO), 104
SHAEF. See Supreme Headquarters Allied Expeditionary Forces
Shapiro, Murray, 144, 150, 154, 168–69, 186
Siegfried, André, 9, 256, 264n18
Signoret, Simone, 117
silence de la mer, Le (Vercors), 86, 268n77
silver foxhole, the. See Parisian prostitutes
Simon, Robert, 25
Skin, The (Malaparte), 293n171
Skinner, Robert, 209
Smith, Grant, 210
Smith, Jean Edward, 263n7
"Soldier and Girl" (photo), 69f
Sontag, Susan, 278n3
Stanislawa, Hus, 211, 212, 327n95
Starr, Wilbur, 329n131
Stars and Stripes: consistent denigration of French masculinity, 77, 81–83; depiction of a protector role of the United States, 83; equating of territorial conquest with sexual conquest, 67; eroticization of French women thanking the GIs, 73; eroticization of the liberation of Paris by Americans, 65–66; mapping of sexual relations onto American war aims, 62, 64; negative impression of Norman quality of life reported in, 50; portrayal of the FFI as buffoons, 77, 78f; publishing of the GI photo, 57, 60; reports on prostitution in Paris, 151; symbolic effect of the prevalence of women in liberation photos, 61–62, 279n15; tonte ritual coverage, 78–83, 283n74; use as an instrument of propaganda, 60
Stewart, Leroy, 50, 94, 119, 124, 150
STO (Service du travail obligatoire), 104
Stoler, Ann, 337n65
Stouffer, Samuel A., 264n17
Striggle, Joseph, 210–11
Supreme Headquarters Allied Expeditionary Forces (SHAEF), 95, 96, 163, 165–67, 171, 172, 177, 186, 224, 226, 229, 231, 234–36, 242, 252, 254, 285n18

Tanaka, Yuki, 310n6
taxis de la Marne, Les (Dutourd), 87
Taylor, Charles, 50, 51, 54, 134
Teton, Wilford, 207, 213
"Times Square Kiss" (photo), 258, 259f,
    339n3
Tocqueville, Comtesse de, 39
Toles, Edward, 235, 237, 332n193
Tomas, Salvador, 201
tonte ritual: coverage of, in the press, 78–83,
    283n74; GI discomfort with, 97–98, 288n80;
    reflection on the French men, 98; symbol-
    ism of, for French men, 87–88, 108, 133
Toole, John, 95
Traynel, le Marquis de, 239–40

United States military in France: American ste-
    reotyping of French social norms, 2, 263n3;
    authorities' reaction to rape accusations,
    10–11; *commissaires'* reports on Franco-
    Allied relations, 5–6, 264n11; French view of
    America as a wealthy nation (*see* American
    GIs and French civilians); historians mar-
    ginalizing sexual contact between GIs and
    women, 11; historical significance of sex to
    the US military presence in France, 260–61;
    impact of uncontrolled GI behavior on
    Franco-American relations, 76–77; impact
    on the French male (*see* wartime male
    gender damage); influence of perception
    of French sexual attitudes on the military's
    imperialistic view of France, 54–55; in-
    stances of good Franco-American relations,
    106, 292n144; leaders' efforts to manage the
    military's image (*see* GI photos; military's
    view of prostitution; propaganda by the
    military); military propagandists leveraging
    myths about French women to motivate
    the GIs, 7–9; political issues facing France
    regarding US-Franco relations, 4–5; political
    meanings behind sexual relations, 7; price
    paid by the population for liberation, 27,
    255–56, 268nn73–77; prostitution and (*see*
    Parisian prostitutes; prostitution); rape
    prosecutions (*see* military court system for
    rape trials; rape); situation for black sol-
    diers (*see* African American soldiers); spread
    of venereal disease, 10; theater of war
    (*see* Battle of Normandy); "Times Square
    Kiss" symbolism, 258, 259f; unintended
    consequences of the myth of the manly GI,
    9–10; US military's condescending attitude

toward postwar France, 2–4; US policy
    toward France's leadership, 5–6, 263n7; US
    rise to power reflected in sexual exploita-
    tion of French women, 257; view that com-
    mand of geographical territory signaled
    command of sexual territory, 87
USO shows, 44

Vanier, Jean, 132
Vautier, Jean-Jacques, 47
venereal disease (VD): army efforts to reduce
    exposure to, 166–67, 314n50; army's failed
    initiatives to reduce instances of, 167–69,
    314n56; basis of the soaring rates of infec-
    tion, 167; concern over its impact on war
    readiness, 162–63; in Italy, 163–64; military's
    view of black soldiers' exposure to, 164–65,
    312nn30–31; officers' motivation to conceal
    cases, 172; prevalence among Parisian pros-
    titutes, 135, 140; spread of, by the soldiers, 2,
    10; symbolic connection between VD and
    Allied anxieties, 165–66
Vercors, 86, 132, 268n77, 284n6, 300n145
Virgili, Fabrice, 79, 87
Voisin, Pierre, 1, 74–75, 181–84, 239

WAC (Women's Army Corps), 165–66
War, Beverly, 329n142
Wardlaw, Fred, 44
Wartime (Fussell), 264n20
wartime male gender damage: alleged German
    rapes used to create a moral imperative
    for war, 87, 285n112; American dismay at
    the FFI's role in *épuration* of collabora-
    tors, 97; American power illustrated by
    GIs' ability to command favors of women,
    105–6, 292n140; Americans' lack of respect
    for the French Army, 94–95; damage done
    to French male authority by the war, 110,
    172n172; ex-prisoners' marginalization upon
    return home, 107–10; FFI view of Ameri-
    cans and of their own manhood, 99–101;
    France's dismay at its geopolitical decline,
    90–92; French man's shame and rage at not
    being able to fulfill his task as *chef de famille*,
    86–87, 92, 284nn3–7; French men's attempt
    to ignore the Americans' attitude, 105,
    292n137; French men's response to Ameri-
    can "rescue" of their country, 85; French
    peoples' ignorance of the war due to poor
    news access, 89–90; frustration over repa-
    triation progress, 106–7, 292n148; GI con-

descension of French men, 88–89, 92–95; GI discomfort with the *tonte* rituals, 97–98, 288n80; GI reviews of the Resistance, 95–97, 98–99, 287n58, 288n76; GIs' belief that they deserved the sexual prerogatives of conquest, 108–9; GIs' condescending attitude toward liberated detainees, 103–4; GIs' need to assert their own manliness, 93–94; GIs' view of French women as transferred property, 89; instances of good Franco-American relations, 106, 292n144; liberated French prisoners' dismay at GI treatment of them, 101–3, 290n103, 290n108; problem of sexual tensions between French and American men, 108–10; *Stars and Stripes'* consistent denigration of French masculinity, 77, 81–83; *tonte* ritual's symbolism, 87–88, 98, 108, 133; US Army's reasons for not being friendly toward the liberated, 104–5; US view that command of geographical territory signaled command of sexual territory, 87; war's impact on French global status related to, 90, 92, 286n29
Washington, Forrest, 222

Watson, James, 200
Weaver, William, 201
Weed, T. J., 1, 2, 75, 182, 318n141
Westfield, Fred, 210
Weston, Joe, 2, 75
White, John, 222
White, Walter, 199, 233, 234, 331n183
Whiting, Charles, 135, 146, 150
whorehouses (*abattoirs*), 140
Wicker, Paul, 104
Wiener, Frederick Bernays, 326n68
Wilkins, Roy, 199, 232
Williams, John, 333–34n2
Williams, L. C., 209, 210
Wilson, Florine, 207
Wilson, J. P., 210
Winston, Keith, 54, 121, 122
Women's Army Corps (WAC), 165–66
Worton, Samuel D., 218

Yalta, 90
Yom, Sun, 313n31

Zig Zag phrase, 125, 153, 308n148